CW00820472

FOREWORD

FROM the end of World War Two in 1945 until 1947 men were conscripted into the services under wartime legislation for as long as they were needed, which could often be up to three years. Then a fixed period of two years was set before the 1947 National Service Act was implemented and 18-year-olds were called up to serve 18 months. It was not long however, before the two-year commitment was re-established.

Before the last National Serviceman was demobbed in 1963 well over two-million young men had served their country all over the world. They were teenagers who suddenly found themselves thrown into a very unfamiliar environment. Old-Etonians, grammar school swots, shop assistants, office boys and farm labourers were all in the mix. Most of them didn't want to be there, and prayed for demob from the very beginning when they drew their first demob chart and began filling it with crosses. Day one, 729 to go.

Some found themselves with "cushy" numbers in places like Paris, Jamaica and Gibraltar. Others were sent into battle against the Mau Mau in Kenya, the Communists in Korea and terrorists in Malaya. Some were part of the occupation force in Germany. Some were sent to Egypt.

But wherever they served, as I spoke to the now elderly men who have contributed to this book it became obvious that whatever their experiences, what most remember is the comradeship they found in the services. "We were disparate groups of teenagers who would never have met one another in normal circumstances," said one, "but we all mucked in and helped one another. We bonded together in friendship."

Brian Davis
May 2010

ISBN 978-0-9529151-1-9

Published by Brian Davis
Wayletts, Brentwood Road, Dunton Wayletts, Brentwood CM13 3SH
Printed by Black Square Litho
Radford Way, Billericay, Essex CM12 0DE

INDEX

Everything in Trinidad cost one dollar, including a local girl

UNLIKE many of my contemporaries I was fortunate to be able to complete my BSc course in electrical engineering at Edinburgh before being called up. During the final year I took part in the activities of the university OTC in preparation for call-up, and I opted for the signals group, as my interests were in the area of communications.

So there was an introduction to some of the radio equipment then in service, WS No189 for one. And the everlasting lead-acid batteries which had to be carried in a backpack on map and compass treks over the Scottish moors so that we could check in at regular intervals.

I graduated in1947 and began my six weeks of training at Glencourse, near Edinburgh, in July.

I had recently sold my first Morgan three-wheeler — an early non-reversing tricycle — and acquired a quite respectable AJS 350 motorbike which I was allowed to have at camp. This enabled me to go home to Dalkeith at weekends.

All I can remember about the training was the continual changes of clothing from battledress to gym shorts and back, plus boot-shining and Blanco application *ad nauseum.*

Then there was a WOSB which I flunked, but I was given a choice of trade, and chose Signals. The reward for that was, at the end of six weeks, to be sent to Catterick to train as a radio mechanic.

This took an inordinately long time, I felt. In fact, it was not until the April of 1948 that I came up for a posting.

In addition to the many trades catered for at Catterick, Royal Signals had an orchestra. Some evenings two trainees who were in the orchestra would play on the two old pianos in the NAAFI.

They were brilliant pianists. One we knew as Don, and the other was Alec Gibson. Together they would perform a piano concerto, one playing the soloist's part and the other reading the orchestral part from a pocket score.

I am very fond of classical music, and befriended Alec. After demob I met him again in London where I was studying at Imperial College and he was at the Royal College of Music. Later he became conductor of the Scottish Na-

tional Orchestra and was knighted. Sadly, he died a few years ago.

Most of my fellow conscripts at Catterick were being sent to West Germany, so I was surprised to be called before the CO and told I was going to Jamaica. I had no idea what the Army could be doing in Jamaica, but decided it was safer not to ask questions.

There followed a lengthy train journey to Southampton where three of us in Signals boarded the troopship Empire Windrush, along with a host of servicemen from the Gloucestershire Regiment.

The transatlantic crossing was uneventful. We all had jobs on board, and I worked on a nocturnal assignment in the bakery producing bread for the morning.

After about a week we sighted land, Trinidad. I remember that each of us had one Trinidad dollar to go ashore. Of course all the locals in Port of Spain knew this, and had various wares that cost exactly that — including a local girl if we felt so inclined!

The next day we were off again, and in a couple of days docked at Kingston harbour, Jamaica.

Most land transport was accomplished with the ubiquitous three-ton truck, and one of these took us to Up Park Camp, home of a battalion

Aboard the Windrush with Jack Paton (centre) and Pete Wickens (right)

1

of Glosters. Not for me to reason why, but these troops were presumably there to keep the peace in the British Caribbean islands and territories, notably Jamaica, Trinidad and British Honduras. Even Bermuda was included in our communications roster.

A picture taken in 2003

Royal Signals had decreed that two radio mechanics were required to maintain the equipment needed to keep in communication with the areas under British jurisdiction.

And so I soon met John Murray, and we became firm friends. He, like me, had an interest in all radio equipment. He came from a very good family, and was expecting his Norton 500 motorcycle to be shipped out from Scotland. So we were all envious.

Signals were waiting for the delivery of three new WS53 transmitters from Britain, but in the meantime we had a couple of old American transmitters to keep the service going. These were limited to CW operation, meaning that all communication was via Morse code.

I soon made friends with other auxiliary service personnel, principally REME and RE lads, also doing their National Service.

Rae Gooch in REME had access to a variety of vehicles, mostly 15cwt trucks and Army Norton 500 bikes, plus the occasional three-tonner which he had to maintain.

Eventually the WS53s arrived and were set up in a newly created workshop

Undoubtedly my best experiences in Jamaica were the trips we were able to do in the 15cwt trucks from Rae's workshop. We drove all around Jamaica, swimming and picnicking at many beautiful beaches.

In June 1949 several of us were scheduled to return to Britain for demob and we embarked on the MV Georgic which had arrived in Kingston on her way home from a round-world cruise.

This was no troopship, and we were in comparative comfort, able to enjoy the company of civilians who had some interesting travel tales to tell.

When the Georgic docked in Liverpool I was able to make my way home by train. Waiting for me was a Government communication to the effect that I was eligible for a Further Education and Training Grant to cover a year's rehabilitation study and brush up on my qualifications.

And then...

After demob in August I did a post-grad Diploma course in electronics at Imperial College. This was very helpful, and I was given a fairly abstruse thesis topic which took me until May 1952 to submit.

I took a job at Ferranti and worked on my thesis in the evenings. The work consisted of the design and construction of circuits related to the gyro gun-sight used in most fighter aircraft during WW2.

I joined the field test department which was concerned with flight evaluation of the sight. With me as observer in the back seat of a Gloster Meteor, we would dive on the target recording information. A very interesting project, if a little scary at times.

Then I went to Canada, eventually joining Boeing and being assigned to the flight-test facility at Cape Canaveral.

Then, joining Canadian Aviation Electronics, I worked on a weather radar data processing development that came to the attention of a research group at McGill University. And I was offered a job there on a new radar installation to be used for precipitation research.

I remained at McGill for 25 years during which I did radar installation work in every Canadian province, as well as Hong Kong, Spain and Brazil.

I retired in 1993 and have been engrossed in hobbies since then, one of them being building and sailing a 16ft sailboat.

— Ernest Ballantyne©

23046219 Cpl Tony Barber

I got Cyprus buzzing with my Christmas dance plans

I HAD hoped to join the Pay Corps when I was called up in 1954, but when my papers arrived I was told to report to the RASC barracks at Farnborough. After two weeks we were dispersed to our appropriate training camps, and I was directed to a clerical trade and posted to Willems Barracks in the centre of Aldershot, where apart from soldiering we had our clerical training.

This finished in October 1954 and after 17 days' leave I was posted to the Canal Zone. Prior to embarkation I spent a week in a transit camp in Bordon, Hampshire which was merely to keep us occupied — numerous kit inspections and drilling — awaiting the next troopship.

The day finally arrived when we were transferred to Southampton and embarked on the Empire Ken, which was thrown all over the place in the Bay of Biscay.

Some months earlier a troopship also making its way to Egypt caught fire off Algiers, so it was necessary to take extra fire precautions. Those chosen for night fire duty were shown where all the extinguishers were located. However when carrying out firewatching duties at night it was difficult to find where these were because the troops had used them for clothes hangers. So much for fire precautions!

We stopped at Algiers for refuelling and food and water. Those wanting to go ashore were allowed to do so in uniform.

We eventually arrived at Port Said, and the pungent smell in the dock area as we approached the port in the very early morning is something that will always stay with me. Some of the locals clambered aboard trying to sell leather goods.

Once ashore we boarded the train that took us down the Canal Zone to a place called Fayid on the Great Bitter Lakes.

I was headed for the headquarters of Middle East Land Forces at Namur Camp. I had to find a tent, which I eventually did, and the other occupants ere two Scotsmen and an Englishman from Hereford who thought he was more Welsh than English. November soon went and Christmas was approaching. My job was located a few miles away where I dealt with officers'

records. Guard duties were numerous because we not only had to do these to cover our working area but also our separate dormitory area.

Christmas 1954 was my first in the Army. It is tradition that on Christmas morning officers bring round a cup of "Gunfire" (rum and coffee) which they serve to the other ranks in bed.

Our camp was based along the Sweet Water Canal where there was a large filtration plant. This was necessary because our water supply came from the canal in which the locals did everything. And I mean everything! I can't think why it was called *Sweet Water*.

Happy now my training is over

Having been posted to this unit I expected to be doing just my clerical duties, because once initial training was completed there was usually very little more drill.

No such luck. Just before I got there a couple of squads had attended a Queen's Birthday Parade and made a pig's ear of the whole thing. So a new OC was brought in, along with an ex-Guards drill instructor, and we were drilled for a whole year, getting up at 5.30am before the sun rose. When the day arrived for the following year's parade our uniforms were specially dhobied so they could stand up on their own. When the vehicles arrived to take us to the parade we stood all the way to avoid creasing them.

Having spent a year in preparation, it was probably hardly surprising that we won the "best on parade" award — and no more drill.

Colonel Nasser now insisted that the British forces vacate the Canal Zone, and it was announced that those with six months' service still to do would be posted back to the UK. But shortly before we were due to leave we were told that instead, we would be transferred to

3

Cyprus. The Greek Cypriots were not happy that large numbers of troops were arriving on their island, because they were fighting for independence from Britain.

We embarked at Port Said on an LST (Landing Ship Tank) for the two-day voyage to Limassol. On arrival I was directed to be a guard in a Standard Vanguard staff car because so many vehicles were being shipped over, and the threat of terrorism was in the air.

Once settled in our new camp at Episkopi I was promoted to lance-corporal because of the sensitivity of the work I was doing. A few months later I took over from a sergeant who was returning to the UK and received further promotion to full corporal.

Back to insurance after demob

As well as my clerical work I still had to do guard duties escorting vehicles around the island.

The RASC band was due to tour Cyprus at Christmas 1955 and the New Year. As the corporal in charge of GHQ office I had a visit from a sergeant-major in the Seaforth Highlanders, based nearby, to discuss the possibility of a couple of dances over the holiday period while the band was with us.

We had a suitable venue in Episkopi, and I agreed to make contact with units all over the island to inform them of the dances. So phones were soon buzzing with details of this grand event which would help relieve the constant security duties carried out by all our forces to try to combat the EOKA terrorists.

I was constantly getting phone calls asking for tickets, and became so popular as "the arranger" that vehicles were pulling up outside the office with troops asking "can I see Tony about dance tickets."

It was great to see them going away delighted that they had something good to look forward to over the holiday period.

The turnout on the first dance night was fantastic. We were all in uniform because we were never really off duty, and the array of Army regiments and members of the women's services was something to remember.

The RASC band was all we expected, and any soldiers who had any idea of dance steps were in their element. The Seaforth Highlanders CSM, who had the idea in the first place, was a sight to behold dancing around in full Highland regalia.

The New Year event was as good as the first dance, and there were a few tears when Auld Lang Syne struck up.

My return home was fast approaching when I was told that if I signed on as a regular I would be made up to sergeant. But I had a job to return to, so did not take up the offer.

I returned to the UK on the troopship Empire Fowey. A tender took us out to board her because Limassol is not a deep water port. We had to clamber up the rope steps with full kit, and it was surprising that nobody fell into the water.

As well as Cyprus the ship called at all ports where British servicemen were serving, Japan, Korea, Singapore Malaya, Aden and Malta before arriving in Southampton.

And then...

Once I was demobbed I returned to my clerical job in a City insurance brokers. It was important for me to take my insurance exams, and as I had no GCEs — having attended a secondary modern school — I first had to sit a preliminary exam consisting of maths, English history and geography,

Passing this exam meant that I could now study insurance at night school where I found myself with mainly ex-grammar school boys who felt it was a doddle. I knew that I needed to study hard for the whole six months before sitting the exam.

I passed my Part 1 and then continued to pass each year for the next two years and became an Associate of the Chartered Insurance Institute.

I married before my exams, but my studies went on for another few years until I attained my Fellowship of the Chartered Insurance Institute.

During this period my wife and I had two children and I also moved from a broker's to an insurance company. I became a new-business inspector, calling on brokers for business, and also carried out insurance surveys. I worked for various companies, eventually becoming an insurance manager.

My last post was with the Cornhill Insurance Company who at that time sponsored Test cricket, so I had the opportunity to take guests to Lords and the Oval. I retired in 1995 and my wife and I have been able to have some memorable holidays, including Antarctica, cruising the Amazon and South Africa.

— Tony Barber©

22014674 LCpl John Bathurst

I chose the Tanks because they wore smart black berets

AT TAUNTON'S School, Southampton, I had ambitions to go on to university and then teach history. In those days it was necessary to have Latin in order to go to university — and I was absolutely useless at the subject. I failed at School Certificate level and was put back a year to retake it. I found myself in a form of the most brilliant scholars the school had had for many years, the further ignominy being that they were all at least a year younger than I, yet streets ahead academically. But the headmaster had promised to send a young lad to a local insurance company, and I suddenly left school and drifted into the world of insurance.

I was 15, and the Union Assurance Society, Southampton branch, welcomed me with reasonably open arms. For the princely salary of £60 a year I filed papers and found papers, and gathered lists of their "elevenses" requirements from the old men in the office (the young ones had not yet been demobbed) and a room full of glamorous young ladies. I collected their pennies and sixpences and proceeded each morning to the local bakery, there to buy sausage rolls and cakes.

After a lunch break of one hour it was back to the paper-chasing routine until 2.30pm, when it was my task to make tea for the whole office of around 30 people.

At 4.30pm it was time to start collecting the post. Scores of memos and letters to be enveloped and weighed on ancient scales. Stamps to be licked, and then a mad dash to the post-office to be sure to catch the 6pm collection. Then I could go home.

And so it went on, year by year. I left the post department and became an accident insurance clerk, helping to produce motor and home insurance policies, all of which were drafted individually, typed individually, checked individually and ledger-entered individually.

In November 1947 National Service beckoned. The Royal Navy was my first choice, and after an initial medical and very brief interview in a Southampton Church Hall I was instructed to attend a suitability testing session.

At the time the Navy wanted technicians. If

A real soldier now, and so well turned out. But my pal with his hand in his pocket doesn't look quite so smart!

ever there was a non-technician it was me. End of seagoing service ambitions.

There was no second choice and it was the Army to which I was called up. Fortunately there WAS a sort of choice as to which arm one might go. The only thing I knew about the Army was that I hated the look of the awful floppy khaki caps that most soldiers then wore. The ones who wore the smartest looking hat were the Royal Tank Regiment, and they had black berets.

"That's for me" I thought, and asked for the Tank Regiment, giving no thought whatever to the fact I was non-technical.

I got my wish and was told to report to Waitwith Lines, Catterick Camp on March 18 1948. It was a long train journey from Southampton to Waterloo and then to York, where there were many more young men from various parts of the country, all experiencing their first day in the services.

We were taken on to Richmond and met by a small fleet of three-ton Army lorries. On arrival at the 8th Royal Tank Regiment lines we were divided into squads. Basic Training took place over the next 12 weeks, during which time proper battledress uniforms replaced the denims that were issued initially. Some fitted their owners well. Mine fitted where it touched.

We were trained how to march at 120 paces to the minute and salute to the front. We mastered ceremonial pistol drill. We did fire picquets and peeled thousands of potatoes for the next day's meals.

We learned how to bull virgin-leather pimply Army boots by ironing them, spitting on them, ceaselessly putting layer upon layer of boot polish on them with circular motions until eventually they gleamed like patent leather. We Blancoed webbing and polished brass.

Verbal abuse from lance-corporals upwards was a daily routine. Shocking to many at the start, we got used to being told and then having to repeat, that we were "Lousy sodding bastards" or "F---g festering pimples." But gradually we became a team, developed thicker skins than those with which we arrived, became fitter and healthier and learned to realise that the only thing that was free was the air we breathed.

There was always one lad who was picked on by the squad sergeant as the example of how NOT to do certain things. Sadly and wrongly he was not only pilloried by those in charge but also by the squad for letting us down. One particular memory is watching this poor unfortunate being brought out in front of the squad to demonstrate how to salute on the march. He couldn't march to save his life and would somehow get into a position of trying to march swinging both arms forward at the same time.

To a cruel set of soldiers this was high entertainment with an accompanying inner prayer of thanks that it wasn't them who were being made to look an idiot.

After square-bashing came selection tests for various jobs. Drivers, gunners, wireless operators, mechanics, cooks, clerks – all were needed for the smooth running of a regiment. And this is where the non-technical element and my lack of forethought came back to kick me in the rear.

My technical tests were a disaster and I was marked down to become what I had been in Civvy Street, a humble clerk. Images of proudly sticking my head out of a tank turret with earphones on and pointing the way forward,

suddenly vanished. While others went to train on the tanks, I and several other technically incapables were sent to clerks school. This was presided over by an ill-tempered, fiery Scots corporal.

He didn't want to do the job and obviously felt that he could relieve his feelings by making us wish that we had never met him. This took all of 10 minutes, and the rest of the four-week course was misery and best forgotten. We learned little and remembered less of form-filling, absentee procedures and the like.

In July we were ready to be posted to regiments, and forms were issued with three choices. I opted for The Queen's Bays at Chester, the 2nd Tanks in Germany and the 4th Tanks in Egypt. The 4th Tanks won, and a week later I was on two weeks' embarkation leave.

On a very hot day in July 1948 those of us who were going to Egypt were mustered and driven to Richmond. From there the slow train journey to London and transport with full kit to an underground barracks near Tottenham Court Road.

No-one was allowed out. We sweltered for some hours at this cavern of a place before

being taken to Waterloo. By then the news had filtered through that we were to embark on a troopship from, of all places, Southampton. It was a bittersweet journey from then on, passing through my home town and yards away from the back garden of my girl-friend's house.

On the Empire Ken to Egypt

The Army obviously feared that some men would try to "escape," and we were closely guarded by Military Police all the way to the dockside. The vessel concerned was the Empire Ken, and we were soon down below – still sweltering – stowing our kit as best we could on racks of triple bunks.

Suddenly I was told by one of my pals that I

should go on deck immediately. My mother, father and girlfriend were on the dock!

My father was a clerk in the port health office and had found the details of the Empire Ken's movements. My mother and girlfriend had somehow done the rest. They obtained permission to go into the docks, and there the three of them were — the only civilian relatives of anyone on board to be there — waving up to where I was.

I went to the officer at the gangplank and stammeringly explained the situation. Unbelievably, he said I could have five minutes, under Military Police escort, to go back on shore to say goodbye. Very few words were said, but it was a poignant moment. And, as it happened, the very last time I would see my father.

It took 11 days to reach Port Said, during which there was little to do but write letters, avoid fatigues and join in bingo and other limited games. I am a good sailor and, while others were rather unwell and incapacitated, enjoyed two or three helpings of some meals at their expense.

At Port Said we spent two weeks under canvas at 156 Transit Camp. We swam (always under escort) and once or twice visited a rather well appointed NAAFI club.

Then came an uncomfortable journey in a packed troop train in open carriages to Fayid, and from there by lorry to an ex-RAF airfield called Shandur where were based the 4th Tanks.

I was drafted into the motor transport section as an MT Clerk. The MT section was a mile and a half away from the tents where we were accommodated and the mess tent.

It was difficult to get to either place without a lift in a truck or jeep, particularly because of the always-urgent time constraints placed on eating meals or other "free time" activities.

I didn't drive so had to beg lifts from anyone who happened to be going in the desired direction. Being the sole duty clerk on a weekend was purgatory. Stuck in what seemed miles from anywhere, completely alone apart from the MT and tank park, it was often difficult to get anyone to answer the phone back at base in order to get a ride to the cookhouse.

One spot of enjoyment in this unhappy period was the visit of an Ensa Party, the highlight being the Beverley Sisters.

Relief came in a bizarre way. I had started to feel unwell, with headaches and spells of diffi-

Back in Blighty

culty in focusing and a feeling of great tiredness. Eventually I reported sick and received a chitty permitting me to draw a supply of aspirin and the common "medicine and duty" label.

Next day I began to shiver uncontrollably at the same time perspiring heavily. It was obvious something was wrong, and within an hour I was being taken by road to British Military Hospital, Fayid.

No-one at that time was contracting malaria, but I had managed to do so! I don't remember much of the first two days except the sheer heaven of being in a proper bed with clean, cool sheets. Sadly I also had a mild dose of dysentery. However, I was in the right place, and at least (if I could eat any of it) the cookhouse came to me.

There then occurred something I have never been able to explain but which will remain with me for the rest of my life.

Early one morning, in the quiet and as yet sleeping ward, I heard my father's voice. It said just one word, "John." But it was so obviously unexpected that I said "Yes dad," and was suddenly wide-awake. Clearly it had been a dream, and I a felt a fool for calling out.

In the early afternoon of that day I was called by a nurse and told to report to the medical officer. He told me that my father had been taken very seriously ill, and arrangements were being made to fly me back to the UK.

I was given an advance of pay and told to buy myself a civilian shirt, light slacks and a suitcase and be ready to move out the next day.

The following morning I was taken with another soldier to the railway station and from there to Cairo. We were met by a BOAC representative and taken to a hotel for the night. Next morning we went to the flying boat departure point on the River Nile, and took off a short time later.

Flying boats did not fly at night, so we put down in Augusta Harbour in Sicily and from there to the BOAC hotel. Dinner was served by waiters, after which a room was provided. After breakfast the next day the launch took us to the plane and by 2.30pm we arrived on Southampton Water.

I had no Army kit other than a battledress top and trousers and a beret. No boots, no gaiters. When I reached my parents' house my mother's face told me all I needed to know. My father had died on his 64th birthday. His funeral had already taken place.

Within a few days I was told to report to the transport camp on Southampton Common, where I was given four weeks' compassionate leave.

Further instructions came later telling me to report to the Royal Armoured Corps depot at Bovington in Dorset in early November. There I was roundly upbraided by the SQMS for arriving in such a disgraceful and inadequate a state, although he did tone it down when I explained my absence of kit.

Then it was then a question of awaiting orders for return to the regiment. Because of my clerical status I was temporarily employed in the Orderly Room documents section. My job was to ensure that all transient soldiers either had a full set of documents on arrival or, if not, to ensure they had such when they left.

It was a routine, clearly defined, administrative job that my predecessor had managed to leave in a chaotic mess. He was probably an "enforced" clerk, whereas I was used to the work. In any event, what I did seemed to satisfy my employers.

Further, the unit had a hockey team, a game that I had played both at and after school.

Anyone who has been in the forces knows that if you can play a game and your face fits the chances of being retained in the particular unit are greatly enhanced.

By the time the order for Return to Unit had arrived it had been suggested that I might wish to stay on in the Orderly Room and continue the work I had started. I duly applied for a home posting and this, supported by the adjutant, was granted.

Bovington was the turning point in my short services experience. I played hockey and cricket for the depot team, ran the home documents section for the rest of my time, was given a stripe and placed on the permanent staff.

Of course, there were guard duties, parades and special duties (such as guards of honour at military funerals or general inspections) but, all in all, it was a very happy posting.

In January 1950 I received my release instructions — and an invitation to stay on at Bovington and "take my turn" for promotion. But I decided to return to Civvy Street, and travelled to Aldershot for the final procedure.

I had spent just short of two years in the Tank Regiment, and had still not got on to, let alone into, a tank. But I did see one once!

And then...

I continued in insurance after the Army, then left to teach at a training college. I left that to go into training and personnel work and then had my own very small admin consultancy — a grand phrase for doing clerical work for anyone who would employ me.

— John Bathurst©

You will have an interview with the Personnel Selection Officer, who has already had a report from the officer you saw at the Ministry of Labour before you joined up. The object is to find out, right at the beginning of your Army career, what work you want to do and for what work you are best suited. The Army tries very hard to put the right man in the right job. Don't be disappointed if you don't get the job you want. You can be certain that the Army has examined the matter thoroughly before assigning you to a particular type of employment. You must realise that perhaps the jobs you want to do are already filled. There is, however, always the possibility you will later be transferred to the work that appeals to you. Remember that you are now a member of a fighting service, and as such a basic knowledge of your weapons is vital, even if you become a highly technical tradesman, for this knowledge may save your life and those of your comrades one day.

—From You and the Army, a booklet issued to every NS army conscript

Do I stand to attention, or offer my girl's cousin a cigarette?

WHEN I was told to report to Exeter for my National Service and then secured a job on the permanent staff there I felt my luck was in. I lived only 14 miles away at Sidmouth, which meant that I could still enjoy home comforts at every available opportunity, often by scrounging a lift from a Sidmouth friend who commuted daily by car.

At that time Diana, who later became my wife after a romance that had begun at school, worked at a hotel in Torquay, so the plan was to spend one evening each week with her.

The return fare and a couple of seats at the cinema left me without the cost of a taxi back to the barracks, so it was usually the long, and sometimes wet, hitch-hike at around 1.30am.

At Topsham the officer in charge of basic training was Lieut Douglas Lovejoy, which produced a somewhat awkward situation. He was Diana's cousin, and we would meet from time to time when he visited her parents in Exeter.

I could never decide whether to stand to attention, offer him a cigarette or just wait quietly until one of us left. And I am sure he was as embarrassed as I was with this unusual off-duty officer and private soldier relationship.

Douglas went on to become a lieutenant-colonel, while I remained a lowly private in Depot Company, sharing the office and the post of documents clerk with George Burgess from North Devon.

I remember being sent on a clerical course at Chichester when some of us decided to hitch-hike home one weekend. But the journey took so long that by the time we reached Tiverton Junction we had only a few hours of home comforts before it was time to return.

Before I was called up my father ran two cinemas in Sidmouth, which meant that I spent much of my youth watching films for free. Particularly useful when attempting to impress girlfriends.

I also became part of the local musical-show scene, a wonderful vehicle for showing off.

And I have no doubt that this early insight into showbusiness was a major influence in my later life.

At Topsham Barracks a group of us, which

I'm made up to go on stage at Topsham (left), and (right) at a reunion there 54 years later

included regular soldiers and National Servicemen, persuaded Bandmaster Boulding that with the assistance of the regimental band it would be a good idea to provide some entertainment

This we did by putting on two shows, Wessex Whimsies and More Whimsies. I still have some of the scripts, now rather faded. Much of it is buttock-clenchingly dreadful, but that was at a time when variety was still flourishing. Shades of ENSA, and light years away from Big Brother and The X Factor.

And then...

Following National Service I worked in sales management for a short time at Cadbury's Bourneville and then with Kraft Foods in Cheltenham. Then I became south-west area manager with Unilever, obtaining a convenient transfer back to Devon where Diana and I were married.

Diana served as an Exeter city councillor and became mayor in 1989 with Yours Truly as her escort. A wonderful role, rather like Dennis Thatcher, two steps behind the boss with a gin and tonic in hand.

At 50 Unilever decided that I was past my sell-by date and enabled me to take early retirement.

Having established some very useful contacts over the years, Diana and I immediately began running an entertainment agency as well as taking on the management of a 17-piece big band in the Glen Miller vein, which continues to play at venues across the West Country.

— Gordon Bess©

9

I was chosen to help put Civil Defence on the map

I REPORTED to RAF Cardington on August 6 1953 to begin two years' National Service. After six days kitting out we were posted to RAF Hednesford for basic training. Eight weeks later, and very much fitter, we assembled to receive our postings. One of the lads thought he was going to Germany until it was explained to him that Weston Zoyland was actually in Somerset.

Six of us were posted to 216 Maintenance Unit at Sutton Coldfield. And five of us disliked it. You could say that 216 unit kept the RAF on the move because it supplied bicycles and bicycle parts to all the other RAF stations.

There were huge sheds there with hundreds of upright cycles hanging, greased ready for action.

After a few weeks I saw a queue at the notice board reading a request for volunteers for an experimental Civil Defence mobile column. One hundred National Servicemen were to be selected from the RAF and 50 from the Army. The odds seemed rather long, but I decided to apply.

This was the early Fifties when it was realised that a threat posed by atomic and hydrogen bombs was very real. Up to this time civil defence had been handled by local government, and was staffed by volunteers. Many councils appointed the town clerk or chief constable to take charge in the event of an attack. Now the idea was to set up a group which could be rushed to the scene of action to deal with serious incidents anywhere in the country.

And a few weeks after I had read the notice I heard that two of us had been chosen. The general opinion was that we were both expendable!

Arriving at the Civil Defence depot at Epsom I found what appeared to be a bomb site. Further inspection revealed that it WAS a bomb site, purpose-built and featuring half a hotel called The Spreadeagle.

After redundancy I ran a taxi business

Now, for three months, but with every weekend off, we had classroom and practical work taught by some of the top Civil Defence instructors. Exercises followed until we were ready to tour. The column consisted of three units, each with a jeep and six rescue vehicles carrying eight men and equipment. There were also two cars and four motor-cyclists.

In the RAF, but soon I changed into Civil Defence uniform

The lessons learned from the Epsom experiment signalled the foundation of Civil Defence and Britain's potential to survive nuclear war. The plans were to establish some 100 mobile columns to serve near likely target areas in time of war. From Epsom we took part in demonstrations all over the country. We wore Civil Defence uniform and had our own civilian catering staff with a top-class chef. On smaller exercises catering would be carried out by the local WVS, who did a great job.

We were very well received by most local authorities, and drinks, cinema tickets and other goodies were often provided.

One exception was Coventry, where the local council regarded Civil Defence as a waste of time and money.

The argument for and against was featured in the Picture Post in October 1954 in which the reporter wrote that anyone who witnessed our exercise at Swansea could not fail to have been impressed by the expertise of the mobile column.

Many local authorities wrote in support of the column, but the Home Office decision was to disband it at the end of December in 1954.

The site where we trained at Epsom has now been sold and developed to include a Sainsburys supermarket. But the mobile column lives on through an association, for which I am the researcher.

I have many memories of my time with the mobile column, and particularly remember an occasion when an exercise was cancelled and a group of us decided to have a hand of cards in the meeting room.

After about 20 minutes the senior NCO, Harry

Stubley, could be heard shouting: "Outside on parade — maintenance day." Our reaction was to open the window and leg it.

The next day Harry stopped me and wanted to know if I had been in the meeting room the previous morning. "Why, what was going on there sergeant?" I asked, with what I hoped was innocence written on my face.

He said: "I found five poker hands on the table, the windows were open and the curtains were swinging gently in the breeze. I thought it was the blooming Marie Celeste."

When the column was closed I was posted to RAF St Eval for the remaining eight months of service. I had been there for only two weeks when I was given a weekend duty in charge of the petrol compound.

I was told that all I had to do was refuel the petrol bowsers and move them ready for collection to refuel the aircraft. But on the Sunday a huge tanker arrived with supplies.

I looked at my chart, which showed that tank two was a quarter full. So I instructed the driver to fill it. After he had discharged about 5,000 gallons I noticed fuel rising above the grass. There was six feet of earth between the top of the tank and the grass, so you can imagine my concern. But the driver said I shouldn't worry because the fuel would evaporate very quickly. Later that afternoon fuel could still be seen, but by evening it was below the level of the grass.

I had got away with it. But if the orderly officer had come on the scene I would probably have been in the RAF for another 10 years to pay for it.

And then...

After demob I joined the police force, but following a serious motorcycle accident had to quit and I worked then for International Paints. When the company moved to Southampton I took redundancy and ran a taxi and minibus business until retirement.

— ***Malcolm Bidder©***

My rifle-shooting was not quite in the Annie Oakley league

SOON AFTER I finished my electrical engineering apprenticeship at the Crompton Parkinson company in Chelmsford in 1951, the dreaded long brown OHMS envelope dropped through the letter-box. Inside were my call-up papers to serve as a National Serviceman for the next two years.

One had the choice of which branch of the armed forces one could join. Although the human body is composed of 60per cent water, I felt you could have too much of a good thing, so that ruled out the Navy straight away.

In the air force, however gently one might climb into the sky, the prospect of a possible sudden and unwanted return to earth was not appealing. The final option was the Army, and I felt that if it had been good enough for my father, who had been in the RAMC and served aboard a hospital ship in the First World War, then it was good enough for me.

Being a peace-loving individual, the prospect of being turned into an efficient, ruthless, fighting and killing machine, was not something that I could look forward to.

Once in service however, things turned out rather for the better, though like most National Servicemen, I felt the time for final discharge couldn't come soon enough!

On June 21 1951, a date never to be forgotten, I set off with some trepidation to begin my six weeks' basic training. This was to be at the Army camp at Blandford Forum in Dorset, situated a short distance away at the top of a hill on Salisbury Plain.

After being collected with the other conscripts from the railway station, I clambered into the back of a three-ton Bedford truck and we were transported to the camp.

First impressions were not good as we surveyed the rows of dismal barracks huts, the parade ground, the guardroom, cookhouse and a few run-down administrative buildings. My only positive thought was that at least after six weeks we would be moving on, though where to at that time was not known.

Our first job was to get kitted out in the quartermaster's stores. This was achieved by moving in single file along a counter that stretched the length of the building, behind which were stationed at intervals the quartermaster-sergeant's men.

I was not exactly the Army's big-shot

They rapidly issued greatcoat, beret, battledress, blouse and trousers, boots, thick underwear, socks, denims, mess-cans, eating implements, boot-brushes, blankets, gaiters, etc, and we staggered out of the end of the building with all this gear like something out of a silent film comedy. Sizes of clothing and boots were all "guesstimated" as the items were issued, and these could be changed later, if it was felt to be really necessary, though this practice was rather frowned upon.

From here we moved on to our allotted wooden hut, the interior of which had a worn wooden floor upon which were iron bedsteads with well-used mattresses. Around the room were individual wooden clothes lockers for each inmate. We all had, as instructed, brought our own flannel, soap, toothbrush and razor.

Most of us had decided to have a final short civilian hair-cut before coming to the camp. Despite this, everyone went to the camp barber and we all ended up with a uniform "minimalistic" haircut which made the possession of a comb totally unnecessary.

The six weeks' basic training was an immense shock to the system. We were woken at 6am every morning by the platoon corporal crashing into the barrack-room and shouting at the top of his voice. Beds had to be stripped and partly remade, blankets and sheets arranged in a specific order in a block at the head of the bed. All kit had to be laid out for inspection on the bed — mess-tins, clothing, cutlery, the lot.

At the same time the 30 lads in your troop had to wash and shave and be spotlessly dressed, ready for inspection by the platoon sergeant, who was sometimes accompanied by an officer. Any fault found, real or imaginary, on one's equipment — for example a speck of Blanco on the polished brasses — usually brought cookhouse fatigues or extra guard duties as a punishment.

After an indifferent breakfast our working day included what seemed like endless foot and weapons drill, until we would respond automatically to the orders given.

As a diversion we were given extremely mundane tasks to perform, such as cutting the grass round the huts on our hands and knees using pocket knives. Other less pleasant challenges, such as scraping away the crystalline deposits in the urinals with a razor blade, I was fortunate enough to be able to avoid.

It was only much later that I realised the aim of these totally pointless tasks was to instil in us blind obedience to any instruction given by an NCO or officer.

Recruits were issued with a .303 Lee-Enfield bolt-action rifle and a pull-through, which was drawn repeatedly through the barrel until its rifled interior gleamed like a mirror.

We went to the ranges for live firing at bulls-eye targets which seemed very small. I found that despite keeping the rifle steady, holding my breath and gently squeezing the trigger as instructed, my aim was certainly nowhere near Annie Oakley standard.

Despite firing the entire magazine of rounds I found that my target usually remained in pristine condition. And my comrades either side of me were mystified to find additional holes in their targets. It was abundantly clear that I did not have a future at Bisley.

One took one's turn in the butts, where the targets were hauled up and down by ropes from the safety of a deep trench immediately in front of the line of targets.

As the targets were pulled down after each series of shots, any bullet holes were covered with sticky paper and hauled up again. For extra excitement an occasional bullet would hit the wooden posts supporting the targets, showering one with splinters.

Back in the barracks we were instructed in the art of dismantling and reassembling bren-guns. Firing these was far more comfortable than the .303s as they had a recoilless action which didn't bruise the shoulder. Sten guns were simple firearms that sprayed bullets rather indiscriminately at short range only. If your fingers were not carefully positioned, they could suffer from the high-speed stream of ejecting empty cartridge cases.

We went over the inevitable assault course, scaling and jumping down with rifle and full kit from the top of a 10-foot wall. I don't know how we didn't all end up with broken ankles.

I must grudgingly admit, however, that at the end of basic training, I felt in the best physical condition that I have ever been, either before or since.

After the official platoon photograph had been taken, there was one final and important event to take place. A selection process had to be gone through to find out where we were to go next. After an interview where simple questions were asked, it was decided I should undertake an electrical trade test, using some basic clapped-out items of equipment.

Following this test, and much to my amazement, the Army actually managed to fit a round peg into a round hole and I was destined to join the ranks of the Royal Electrical and Mechanical Engineers.

In August 1951 I was posted to the REME training camp at Arborfield in Berkshire. Though we still had daily morning parades under the beady eye of a remarkably fierce, moustachioed RSM, there was a perceptible slackening of the very severe discipline we had encountered during basic training.

The camp, situated in the Thames valley, was often wreathed in thick morning mists coming off the surrounding low-lying fields.

One morning as we assembled for parade, the fog was so thick that visibility was reduced to about six feet. You could see the men in the row in front of you, but the sergeant taking the parade could see virtually nothing. We followed the orders in a relaxed fashion, as our actions could not be observed.

I was able to get a 48-hour pass most weekends, enabling me to go home on the Royal Enfield for a brief break from Army routine. Returning to camp late on one warm summer evening, with little traffic on the roads, I was speeding along with the throttle wide open. Suddenly I awoke with a start to find that with a gentle bend ahead of me, the bike had drifted on to the opposite oncoming traffic lane and was heading for the verge.

Slamming the throttle shut, I just managed to steer round the bend and eased the bike back to the left-hand side of the road. My progress back to camp after that was at a much more leisurely pace.

Lectures in the classrooms, together with practical experiments in the laboratories, were similar to my earlier college experiences. While some recruits worked on control equipment for anti-aircraft guns, the remainder, including myself, were being trained to become ECEs, that is Electricians, Control Equipment.

We were employed after the six-week intensive training period to maintain, service and repair the turret and gun controls on armoured fighting vehicles. These turned out to be 52-ton Centurion tanks, one of which was held at the camp for us to practise on.

The brick-built two-storey barracks housed our rooms. These had hardwood floors which had to be buffed daily to a mirror-like shine. After preparation each evening for the following morning's inspection, we wore only socks to avoid scratching the floor. Just prior to inspection pieces of blanket would be tied to our boots, only to be removed as the inspecting officer approached.

One rather amusing event still sticks in my memory. At that age and right through to the present time, I have always been a loud snorer. One morning I awoke to find that I was no longer in the barrack room, but in a side alcove some way down the main corridor.

My colleagues, fed up with my snoring, had during the night picked up my bed and transported it, with me still sleeping soundly, though noisily, to its new location.

Time moved on, and having passed the final trade tests I was posted with two fellow electricians to Germany.

Here I became a member of a Light Aid Detachment, LAD for short, a small section of REME attached to the VIIIth Kings Royal Irish Hussars.

The Hussars, formerly a cavalry regiment, had been converted to an armoured regiment based in the German town of Luneberg, close to where at the end of the Second World War,

Montgomery had accepted the German surrender.

We were housed in old German cavalry barracks consisting of two large three-storey blocks facing one another across a vast central parade ground. An administration block, containing the canteen and NAAFI shop were situated at one end of the square, while at the other end were the officers' quarters.

The buildings were very old and built of stone blocks, with an early form of double glazing. The walls were more than 18 inches thick, and fitted with two sets of hinged windows, one on the inner side of the wall and one on the outside. I felt that the intervening air space between the two sets of windows might have helped to keep out the intense winter cold, but in spite of this I was always feeling frozen.

The regiment formed part of the 7th Armoured Brigade, known more famously as the Desert Rats. The chances of my getting anywhere near a nice hot desert were unfortunately nil.

Two squadrons made up the regiment, each being sub-divided into platoons. We were responsible for servicing the control equipment on about 30 Centurion tanks.

The camp itself lay on gently rising ground to the north of Luneberg. A long, cobbled road led down to the town, where one of the main attractions was a large NAAFI club serving the surrounding area. Here excellent evening meals could be obtained at reasonable prices.

Even more important was the chance to relax in a steaming hot bath, a luxury sadly not provided in the barracks complex.

In the NAAFI was also a small dance floor, with music provided by records. As most of us could only tell with difficulty the difference between a quickstep and a foxtrot, we could only watch in admiration when one soldier nightly went through an elaborate dance routine with a local German girl. I still get flashbacks to those days whenever I hear the Blue Tango tune played.

Back in camp I had the good fortune to be selected to go on an explosives and demolition course. This rather appealed to the obviously latent destructive urge lurking within me!

The course started off in grand style, when on the first lesson the somewhat eccentric demolitions officer, rather aptly named I thought, Major Clutterbuck, strolled into the room. He

At Luneburg in 1952, with Bob (centre) and Stan (right)

pulled a fuse detonator out of his pocket, lit the fuse and casually tossed it out of the window. The loud explosion a few seconds afterwards certainly helped to focus everyone's minds as to what might be coming next!

We learned all about plastic explosive, a type in existence long before Semtex had been invented, together with time-delay fuses, and Cordtex, which allows separate charges to be connected together for simultaneous firing. This is often used when old tower blocks are demolished.

The most useful application of plastic explosive for our purposes was when it became necessary to remove bent and damaged links from the tank tracks.

Being made from very high-grade hardened steel, once distorted in situ they were impossible to release in any other way.

The method used was simple but remarkably effective. We made two shallow U-shaped rectangular troughs cut from a sheet of tinplate, just like a baked bean can is formed from. One trough was filled with plastic explosive, then the other trough was inverted over it. The two halves were then taped together.

A detonator was inserted in the explosive charge, together with a length of slow-burning fuse. The package was placed across the top of the offending tank track and completely covered with sand bags. These would then direct the force of the explosion downwards, cutting cleanly through the track.

On one occasion Major Clutterbuck took us to a location where there were several rows of raised earthworks. These all pointed towards a huge shallow concrete cavern set into a hillside. This was where the German army used to test their heavy armaments, firing directly into the now crater-impacted walls of the cavern.

The major decided we could benefit with a practical test of our new-found skills by blow-ing up a narrow bridge linking two of the parallel earthworks.

Carefully we calculated the amount of explosive that would be needed, unaware whether or not the bridge contained any steel reinforcing rods.

Major Clutterbuck checked our calculations and pronounced himself satisfied, but then said: "Well, I always double the amount used, just to make sure."

Having set up the charges, we adopted the age-old method of selecting who was going to light the fuse. And I was the one to draw the short straw!

While everyone else rapidly retired to a safe position behind the earthworks, I lit the 10-second fuse.

I had been given strict instructions to walk to cover, and not run, just in case I tripped. None of us had any helmets or protective gear, so the whole situation struck me as really rather dodgy. I had just got into the shelter of the earthworks when mud and lumps of shattered concrete rained down on us from above.

After the smoke had cleared we went back to survey the results of our handiwork. There was not a sign of the bridge, just a huge pile of rubble. As it turned out, there had been no reinforcing rods in the bridge.

Back in the workshops we continued our maintenance and repairs on the Centurions. Once a repair had been completed to our satisfaction in the barracks, we then had to find a driver to take the tank out on a proving test-run on Luneberg Heath.

During one of these tests, I had a very narrow escape from serious injury. Off we went on to the heath, just the driver and myself. I was in the seat normally occupied by the gunner, so I had easy access to the turret controls.

As we went on our way, the equipment started to malfunction, and as the gun was positioned at right angles to the direction of travel, I decided the only course of action to take was to wind the turret round so the gun faced forward, and return to the workshops.

The handle to turn the turret was in a very restricted space, as it was very seldom used. It was fitted with a clutch mechanism, so that in the event of the turret being inadvertently rotated by hitting an external obstruction, the handle would not be rotated at a dangerous speed.

We were travelling at about 30 mph when the

gun barrel hit a solitary tree, the only one around for miles. I was just preparing to grab hold of the handle when the impact occurred. The turret spun round, and the clutch mechanism failed to work. The handle therefore rotated at an incredibly high speed!

A few seconds later and my right hand would have been smashed to pulp. I was very lucky indeed to have escaped serious injury.

I remember another incident with one of our tanks when late one evening a drunk Centurion driver broke into the vehicle hangar and drove out at speed between the brick pillars leading from the camp.

He disappeared into the night over Luneberg Heath with the Military Police in hot pursuit. As it would have been more than a little imprudent for the MPs to put their vehicle anywhere near 52 tons of speeding tank, they bided their time until it ran out of petrol. With the Rolls-Royce Merlin engine using four gallons of fuel to the mile, they did not have long to wait. The driver was then arrested to be charged the following day.

Life went on in the camp, and following successful upgrading trade tests, my two fellow ECEs and I gained promotion, first to lance-corporal and then full corporal. The increase in pay, though modest, was very welcome.

The only downside of promotion was the additional non-technical responsibility that fell on our shoulders. Our new duties included guard commander, being in charge of fire pic-

quets, canteen corporal and the duty I only undertook once, that of prophylactic ablution corporal.

This was a rather lonely job, being stationed in a small room near the main entrance to the barracks. As it is a chargeable offence for any soldier to catch a venereal disease, the Army would issue free condoms, via the prophylactic ablution corporal, to any soldiers leaving camp in the evening. Each issue would be entered into a record book, together with the name and number of the recipient.

On returning to barracks, the squaddies were supposed to report back and utilise some special cream to kill off any infection that might have been caught. But nobody seemed to bother.

When it came to guard duties the guard commander, such as myself on occasions, would be issued with a .38 service revolver and four live rounds.

At the start of the four-hour patrol around the camp and its perimeter, we would have carefully loaded the four rounds into the six-chamber barrel. This was done in such a manner that the first two pulls on the trigger impacted the two empty chambers, and consequently no shot was fired.

The strategy behind this was that on first challenging an intruder with the standard "Halt! Who goes there?" failure to stop would be responded with a pull on the trigger. The intruder, hearing the click, would assume that although the trigger had been pulled, he had been lucky in that a misfire had occurred.

This would normally stop most people dead in their tracks. Then the next challenge would be made: "Friend or foe?" Assuming the answer to be "Friend" then the instruction would be given: "Advance friend, and be recognised." If necessary, one more warning click could be made before a live round would be fired.

Fortunately I never had to use the last option, although at night one

Seated cross-legged, left, with my pals on a Centurion at Arborfield training camp

16

At our inspection. I am second left

always had to be prepared to challenge the commissioned guard officer as he sneaked round in the darkness trying to catch one off guard.

The daily work routine often involved walking between different areas of the compound where the workshops and vehicles were located.

After a while I became increasingly irritated by regular challenges from senior NCOs and officers who appeared to have nothing better to do than ask what you were doing.

This niggle was soon overcome when I decided to adopt the simple expedient of always carrying a clipboard and pencil during my travels, while wearing a look of extreme concentration on my face.

It then immediately became apparent to any anyone that I must be engaged in some sort of official survey. And from then on I walked around unhindered by interruptions.

One day I was talking to the driver of a huge Scammell recovery vehicle. Always keen to broaden my driving experiences, I managed to persuade him to let me have a go at the wheel.

This was somewhat risky, because if we had been challenged he would have been immediately charged with allowing an unqualified person to drive. And I also would be in trouble, not being an official driver.

We clambered up into the high cab, and I viewed the 16-speed gearbox with some apprehension. Starting in the fourth gear, I progressed up through the gears feeling rather pleased with myself.

This initial confidence instantly evaporated when I realised with some alarm that we were heading at speed towards the end wall of the compound.

Desperately trying to change down with maximum revs proved futile, as the diesel engine speed limiter kept cutting out the engine. As a

last resort I stood on the brakes and we managed to stop just short of the concrete wall.

We both climbed down from the cab rather weak at the knees, having had a lucky escape from near disaster.

One day all the squadron's tanks were driven down to the local railway station, and one by one shackled down securely on a train of flat trucks. A couple of standard passenger carriages were attached to the end of the train to carry the troops, and we set off on a slow journey to the tank firing ranges at Hohne.

Once there, the tanks were lined up in a long row on a level concrete platform. In the distance was an arrangement similar to the moving ducks targets found in a fairground. The only difference was that instead of ducks, and on a much larger scale, were cutouts of "enemy" tanks and lorries.

We were working away on repairs in a 15cwt canvas sided truck, about 30 yards behind the firing line. With no such luxury as modern-day ear-protectors, the noise of the 25 pounders firing, together with the associated shock waves was overwhelming. The air blast from each explosion flapped the canvas sides of the truck in an alarming manner.

All this was going on in the middle of winter and it was seasonable weather, bitingly cold. After completing a day's firing, it was unfortunately my turn to be guard commander in charge of security at the ranges. We broke up empty ammunition boxes and with a generous helping of the aviation fuel used on the Centurions, soon had a roaring fire going.

This heat was essential, as there was no shelter whatsoever and we all sat round the fire trying to keep warm in a howling blizzard.

A single narrow road led to the firing site. Because of the atrocious conditions I recalled the two sentries, who would normally be guarding the road, so they could keep warm.

Sleep was impossible and I told everyone to keep a sharp watch out for the approaching headlights of the officer's jeep, as we knew he would carry out an inspection sometime during the night. Immediately the lights were spotted, I sent the two sentries back down the road to stop and challenge him.

This worked out fine. The officer was only too keen to get back to the nice warm barracks, and I withdrew the sentries once more as his vehicle's tail lights receded into the distance.

During this time on the ranges it again fell to

my lot to be on duty in the evening, this time as canteen corporal. As usual, as time progressed, everyone was getting well tanked up on the local brew. It was my unenviable task to keep an eye on things, to try to break up any parties causing trouble and hopefully get through the evening without too many major disturbances.

I decided to go and patrol a first-floor corridor with one other soldier during the evening, just to check that all was well. We were following a severely drunk soldier who had just staggered up the stairs ahead of us and turned into a long corridor. I

Playing at being a band in recreation time at Arborfield. I am on the left at the back

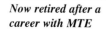

Now retired after a career with MTE

noticed at the far end of the corridor was a wide-open window.

Then the drunk took it into his head to run erratically at speed down the corridor. I yelled to my mate: "Get him," and we both raced after him. We just caught up and managed to grab his legs between us as he shouted "Geronimo" and attempted to dive head-first through the open first-floor window.

One shudders to contemplate what might have happened if we had not arrived in the nick of time.

Eventually we arrived back in barracks and when the weather had warmed up, we approached the annual celebration of Balaclava Day.

Quite why the VIIIth Kings Royal Irish Hussars, who were almost completely massacred in the infamous Charge of the Light Brigade, should wish to celebrate this event on an annual basis was beyond my comprehension. However this was an event to break the usual routine, and consequently quite a lot of effort went in to making sure that everybody had a good time.

A large rotary spit was set up at the side of the square, and on this a whole calf was slowly roasted through the day ready for consumption in the evening.

For one of the entertainments a high-tensile steel wire was stretched right across the parade ground. At one end it was about 40 feet above the ground and on the opposite side about another 10 feet higher. A motorcyclist, presumably recruited from a local circus, mounted a motorcycle which was positioned at the lower end of the wire.

The bike had no tyres, but ran on the grooves on the wheel hubs. In order for the rider to keep his balance on the wire, a counter-balance weight was slung underneath the machine.

Then the rider would drive up the wire at speed, the noise from an open exhaust contributing to the sense of danger. Pausing briefly at the top of the wire, he then freewheeled backwards to the bottom of the wire. This would be repeated several times at intervals until the novelty wore off.

In the evening came the highlight of the day, namely the officers' ball, to which everyone was invited. Unlike what one might imagine, this was no romantic evening spent dancing, but rather a great opportunity for all the squaddies to consume as much liquid refreshment as possible.

By the end of the evening my two pals and I were feeling very much under the weather. Unbeknown to us, all our drinks had been spiked. The resulting effects we all suffered were horrendous and took the form of blinding headaches which continued for the next three days. I must say I have never felt so ill.

Fortunately the staff-sergeant in charge of our section was a very understanding chap, and realising what had happened kept our duties to an absolute minimum until we got back to normal.

Yet another ordeal was set to face us, and this occurred when we were sent on manoeuvres on the north German plains in the middle of February. The plains are, as their name suggests, flat, featureless and with no shelter from the biting cold winter winds.

At night we had to sleep out in the open. On top of my battledress I wore my working dungarees and greatcoat, with one blanket on top. Two other blankets were underneath me in an attempt to stop the cold penetrating from the frozen ground.

I lay on my back all night, looking up at the cloudfree sky, where a myriad of stars twinkled to provide an unforgettable scene. It was too cold to sleep, and in the morning I really knew what an ice-lolly felt like!

On the previous day the Centurion tanks had been out on manoeuvres over a slightly undulating section of the plain. During their travels they had driven through some quite deep water, and not being totally waterproof, a certain amount of water had penetrated the interior.

The water had drained down and collected in a shallow trough running under the floor of the tank. In this trough lay the heavy control rods that ran from the forward driver's compartment to the engine, gearbox and brake mechanisms at the rear.

The following morning after the bitterly cold night, all the control rods in the trough were entombed in solid ice.

It took most of the morning, lying on the freezing metal floor and taking it in turns with club-hammer and chisel, to break away the ice and free the control rods.

Back at camp I forgot the cardinal rule in the Army, namely never volunteer for anything. One day the sergeant casually enquired whether any of us knew anything about motorcycles. In our naive enthusiasm to be as helpful as possible, a few of us raised our hands. The instant reaction to this was promotion to the post of Don-R. We were now to be the squadron's despatch riders.

We were issued with cumbersome 500cc side-valve BSA machines, which we duly had to sign for. Even tank drivers had to sign and take responsibility for their tanks, which cost many hundreds of thousands of pounds.

The bikes, with old-style front girder forks, had to be kept in pristine condition. This was not too difficult, as the German workers employed in the workshops had to be kept busy, and frequent paint re-sprays were the order of the day.

When out on schemes we went round delivering despatches from field commanders, often finding that by the time we had reached our destination, the troop of soldiers had upped sticks and moved to a new unknown location.

Other duties consisted of shepherding convoys across unknown country routes. One would take up a position at a road junction, ensuring all the convoy went the right way, and then chase along behind, overtake and proceed on ahead to the next junction.

The officer commanding our Light Aid Detachment was a heavily-built man with a bushy ginger moustache who was absolutely passionate about motorcycles. He encouraged us in off-duty moments at weekends to accompany him with our bikes to some nearby sand-dunes.

Here we would take a run at a steep hill, with the bike in second gear and the throttle wound right open, seeing who could get farthest up the hill. Then the bike ground to a halt and one slid back down again.

These bikes, very heavy and certainly not designed for hill-climbing, proved to be quite a handful to control, but nevertheless a good time was had by one and all.

During my two years' service I was only on two charges, a remarkably low average by any standards. Once, as a corporal in charge of ensuring the barrack-room corridors were washed out in the morning before parade, I was unable to galvanise the troops into action in time.

Being the Monday morning after a heavy night before, there was little response to my entreaties, and the floor went unwashed. Despite a vain hope, this omission did not go unnoticed by the platoon sergeant, so it was an extra guard duty for me.

On another occasion I completely overlooked the fact that I was the duty corporal responsible for unlocking the gates leading into the tank hangars and workshops area.

This did not go down at all well and I was

quickly marched in at high speed to face the OC. This was a more serious charge, and I was racking my brains as I stood in front of him to think of how I could talk my way out of the situation. The chances of doing this were virtually nil.

After the charge had been read out, I was invited to give my side of the story. Then I had a brainwave. I pointed out to the officer that he already knew that standing orders relating to conduct within the workshop area had been in existence for a good while. He listened, curious as to what I would say next. I then explained that the workshops had been moved to a new location only that weekend. And as this was the first morning in the new location, I felt that new standing orders should have been issued to supersede those orders relating specifically to the old location.

Not exactly being a Perry Mason, I waited with some trepidation to see what his reaction might be.

The officer considered the situation, and after a while looked up ready to make his pronouncement. It seemed to me there was a twinkle in his eyes as he declared: "Charge dismissed."

I saluted, turned and left at high speed under the barked commands of the sergeant: "Left right, left right, left right left." I went back to my daily duties, amazed that I had actually beaten the system.

Time went by, and we started to make preparations for the celebration of the Queen's Coronation in 1953. A huge military parade was to be held in Hamburg and so everyone was busy ensuring all was ready for the great day.

Yet again every tank, truck, motorcycle and other piece of mobile equipment was resprayed and polished until everything gleamed. I must admit that everything looked in far better condition than was actually the case. Hurrah for a coat of paint!

Again the Centurions were driven to the railway station and loaded on to trucks for the relatively short journey north to Hamburg. Driving tanks on civilian roads is not recommended, as every time direction is changed, the road surface — mostly cobbled in those days — is likely to be churned up.

This did not go down well with the local authorities, though there was little they could do about it except have a good moan.

On Coronation Day, June 2 1953, the Centurion tanks would form part of the procession, driving through the main thoroughfare past the saluting base.

The tanks would approach the saluting base, the turrets would be turned to face the base as they passed and the main gun barrel would be dipped in salute. On passing the base the turret would continue to rotate until the gun barrel faced the rear of the tank.

All the tank commanders, either young 2nd lieutenants, or in some cases sergeants, would be standing on their commander's seats, head and shoulders sticking out of the hatch on top of the gun turret.

They were all extremely jittery before the parade, afraid that an electrical or mechanical fault might develop in the equipment at a crucial moment, thus letting the side down.

One sergeant agitatedly asked me to sort out a problem just before the display started. Guessing where the fault lay, I gave a swift kick on the equipment with my Army boot and cured it!

My two colleagues and I were tucked away out of sight in a back street, in a converted Centurion tank being used as a standby heavy recovery vehicle.

Fortunately all went well at the parade and no recovery was necessary.

During Christmas in Germany, I obtained a 72 -hour pass which, though not long enough for a trip home, enabled me to visit the Haurand family, friends of my grandmother.

I travelled by train to the town of Halve in Westphalia, and met the father, mother and three daughters. Father, who had been a strong anti-Nazi, and the rest of the family all spoke reasonably good English, which was a great help, as my German was sketchy to say the least.

They had the traditional tannenbaum (Christmas tree), and I enjoyed good meals complete with wine. I recollect there was some snow, to give my short stay a suitably festive air.

Back at camp, we were able to get extra cash from the German civilians by selling our cigarette allowance which, being a non-smoker, was of no interest to me.

Coffee was a rarity, virtually unobtainable in Germany so soon after the war. Anyone coming back from leave in the UK would always bring a few jars of coffee with them to sell to the Germans working on the camp. This was a strictly illegal, but extremely useful way of boosting ones meagre service pay, and was widely practised by the troops.

For the majority of National Servicemen the months dragged on seemingly endlessly. Every squaddie had a self-designed demob chart pinned up in his locker. Mine was a rotary one, being moved on one division on a daily basis as I slowly approached the longed-for demob day. And on June 17 1953, a never-to-be-forgotten date, I and my colleagues at last boarded the train leaving Germany for the Hook of Holland, where we would catch the ferry to Harwich, and demob

At last my Army connections were due to be severed, or so I thought when I left the demobilisation barracks on top of the cliffs at Shorncliffe, near Folkestone.

But the following year I was recalled as a reservist for six weeks, on a completely time-wasting, so-called refresher course. After that it really was all over, so I could breathe a sigh of relief and get back to being a civilian again.

And then...

I now had to consider my future in Civvy Street. The opportunity came up to be a draughtsman in a small electrical firm called MTE, which specialised in the manufacture of electrical controls for industrial machinery.

This company, with 100 employees, steadily expanded and re-located to larger premises, and the workforce increased to more than 500. I progressed into the research and development department, and eventually became chief development engineer, retiring in 1994.

—_John Bird©_

Pay is a matter which is naturally of great interest to you! To begin with you will be paid as a recruit at 28 shillings a week and this rate will generally be increased to 35 shillings after six months' service.That is the basic pay for the lower Army ranks. It might be of interest to you that it can rise to approximately £9 a week for a regimental sergeant major, though, of course you can't expect to reach that rank in two years! After 18 months however you will receive the Regular Army rates of pay, an increase of approximately £1 1s a week. In addition to your basic pay, if you are married you will receive an additional marriage allowance of 35s a week. To qualify for this allowance, you will be required to make an allotment from your basic pay of 10s 6d per week to your wife, so that she receives a total of 45s 6d (marriage allowance plus qualifying allotment). Don't forget that you also receive food, clothing and accommodation free.

—From You and the Army, a booklet issued to all NS army conscripts

They broke our spirit — until we had no more left to break

I WORKED at the Bournemouth Daily Echo after leaving school at 15, first as office boy and later moving into the advertisement department. Then in 1956, shortly after I had become engaged to a very pretty girl I had known since she was 14 and I only 15, I received my call-up papers.

On January 2 1957 we had a very tearful farewell, and on the following, bitterly cold day, I caught the train from Christchurch to Farnborough where I was collected and delivered to Blenheim Barracks, Aldershot with a number of other recruits.

The first order was to strip naked and undergo medical examination in a wooden billet. I can't remember if there was any heating, but I don't think so. Passing through that I was issued with various items of clothing and my own was taken away — including a navy blue beret and a monkey suit with webbing plus a pair of black boots.

We were deposited at our billets and given instructions to the effect that parade would be at 6am and we had to be ready. Breakfast would be from 5am and it was up to you if you wanted it. Parade meant that what you had been provided with had to be smart. Boots had to have the toecap pimples burnished off with hot spoons and candlewax. Gaiters had to be treated just so. Because of all the work that had to be carried out before parade none of us got any sleep at all.

I had just had a haircut and was ordered to attend the regimental barber and have it done again at my own expense. I looked like an escaped convict, practically no hair at all.

I did not enjoy my two weeks at Blenheim. It was absolutely awful, and I missed my fiancee and all she meant to me.

Having survived Blenheim I think most of us were transferred to Willems, also in Aldershot. I understood this was a former women's prison converted to Army barracks. I am sure that the two weeks at Blenheim were to break any spirit you had. The two months' training at Willems ensured that we had no spirit left at all.

I remember the drill corporal shouting: "If you don't swing those arms I will tear them off and beat you about your heads with the soggy stumps."

We had jabs for cholera and other diseases. Perhaps they knew something we didn't. After the first one I felt I was dying, and cried for my mother.

Another memory was that my football team, Bournemouth, were FA Cup giant-killers having beaten Wolves 1-0 and were due to meet Tottenham Hotspur. My next-door bedmate was a Spurs supporter and bet me 6d they would win. I took him on, and when Bournemouth won he was so upset he refused to pay me.

The next match was the sixth round against Manchester United at home and Bournemouth lost 2-1 with a disputed penalty.

At Willems guard duty was compulsory, but the smartest man on parade was excused. My first turn came, and looking as smart as ninepence I descended the wrought-iron Victorian outside staircase. But some bright spark decided to wash it at the same time and I got showered with dirty water. But I still achieved smartest man on parade.

In the spring, and after my trade exams I achieved 82per cent. Anyone with 100per cent was likely to get a much-sought posting to New York, Paris or the Bahamas. Those with 84per cent were off to Cyprus. My 82per cent earmarked me for Singapore.

First we were moved to Bordon just south of Aldershot and I managed to see my fiancee several times in the three months prior to sailing, which led to more tearful farewells.

We left Southampton on the Dunera, a 12,000-ton captured German troopship with about 500 on board for the five-week trip taking in Dakar (Senegal), Cape Town, Mauritius, Colombo and finally Singapore.

At ease, Blenheim Barracks, Aldershot

Senegal was dreamlike. Cape Town was drizzly but pleasant because a lady we met invited three of us to lunch in her home. Mauritius was also a marvellous experience and in Colombo we could exchange a one-pound note and get 22s 6d — not a bad deal.

When we arrived in Singapore we were told we were going to Kuala Lumpur, an active service station in Malaya, so off the boat and on a train to travel 350 miles into the jungle. The following morning at Kuala Lumpur — the most fantastic railway station I have ever seen in my life — we were met by a truly remarkable Army Catering Corps sergeant who provided us with cooked breakfast on aluminium trays on the pavement. I will always remember his good humour and banter. I could feel the sun on my face and felt better. I was to be here for 18 months.

We were stationed at Batu cantonment about seven miles outside the capital, with 27 Coy RASC charged with supplying the SAS, the South Wales Borderers, the Black Watch, Royal Hampshires, Special Boat Service and Air Despatch among others with whatever they needed to combat the remnants of the Communist guerrilla forces still hiding out in the jungle.

My job was to pay everybody below the rank of sergeant. But on my very first attempt at completing the imprest account I got it wrong, which resulted in the Pay Corps' sergeant and an officer spending hours correcting my work. Very embarrassing, but I never got it wrong again.

I did have other duties, mainly ceremonial because I was the right height. But I did go on manoeuvres in the jungle and roughed it with

At home today in the New Forest

the rest of them. I remember drawing a pistol and ammunition every week in case we were ambushed and the payroll taken. Very exciting. Our accommodation was in atap (grass) bashas (huts) and when away, under enormous canvas tents.

I was promoted to lance-corporal then corporal, which meant more money each time. I learned the ropes and rarely went on parade except a ceremonial duty for the visiting general, General Roe the head of Far East Land Forces.

I served under two OCs, Major Voller and Major Stephens. Major Voller was a bit like Capt Mainwaring of Dads' Army. I liked him a lot, and got away with murder because of my job. I was only a corporal, but many sought my advice. I used to pay chaps up front even though it was against regulations.

I never fell foul of anyone in Malaya. Everyone trusted me and I often used to be asked to stand alongside soldiers guilty of misdemeanour. I remember one driver being arrested for being drunk in charge of his vehicle. He pleaded not guilty, with the defence that a rubber tree suddenly jumped out in front of him which caused him to swerve. He got a deduction of seven days' pay.

Everyone had to do guard duty, which was usually four hours on and two off, and which was not very pleasant with dead mosquitoes dropping down your collar from the overhead lights. When the Malays were on religious holidays this could be a 96-hour stretch.

Most of the time the sky was white, with the sun a pale yellow orb and high humidity. Everyone was a rather pale peach colour. All those due for demob were called Peachy as they tried to get some colour on their bodies before returning home.

While I was in Malaya I wrote to the home address of an old school friend who had worked with me at the Bournemouth Echo after I got him a job there. Eventually I received a

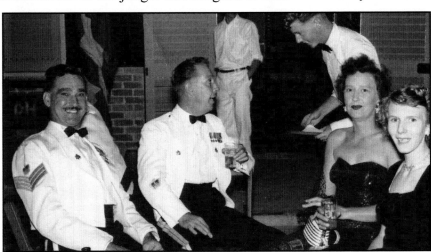

This is New Year's Eve 1957 when I acted as a steward at the warrant-officers' ball. I am serving CSM Nixon, who reprimanded me on demob day for turning up in "a most god-awful outfit."

reply from Singapore where he was serving with the Royal Army Veterinary Corps. I was due to go to Singapore on an education course, so we managed to meet there.

Some time into my service I received a letter from my fiancee telling me she had met a young man and had basically removed me from her affections. It was someone I knew who was employed on the Weymouth to Guernsey ferry and making money from running duty-free cigarettes.

When demob day came I was instructed to appear before CSM Nixon who said to me: "To the very last, Cpl Blythe, you have managed to turn up in the most god-awful outfit."

My uniform was an old jungle green shirt and shorts that had faded to almost white, flipflops and a beret lifted from a REME workshop. I suffered the humiliation of his dressing-down knowing that he couldn't do anything about it.

For the journey home I was put in charge of a party of 12 soldiers who, like me, were to be demobbed. We travelled to Singapore and boarded the 22,000-ton Nevasa. When we arrived at Southampton, one of my party immediately absconded, but luckily I was not charged with allowing him to escape.

And then...

On my return to civilian life a job was waiting for me with my employers, the Bournemouth Daily Echo as a space salesman. To support my income and to cheer myself up after the loss of my fiancee I bought a nine-year-old Sunbeam Talbot coupe, and to keep it maintained I took two evening jobs, putting greyhounds in their traps at Poole stadium and working on the turnstiles.

I was also a barman in a Bournemouth wine bar, and one evening there I swapped National Service stories with a man who had been stationed in Malaya in the Royal Signals.

I thought was a bit odd when he suggested that we should "get-together" and invited me to a milk bar he ran with his business partner. However, one day I popped in only to discover that they were gay. I hadn't realised it, but the wine bar where I was working was for gays.

I left the Echo around 1961 to sell Rolls-Royce and Bentley cars, and later joined an advertising agency in Bournemouth.

Leaving them after 10 years I formed with others a company which I sold in 1990 and joined the purchaser, an American ad agency group. I left within the year because of the stress and started up on my own again but computers were taking over and I suffered several setbacks and now I work just part-time

National Service and the loss of my childhood sweetheart taught me to be a man and put me on the path to success even though I was sometimes foolish enough to be involved in losses caused by the actions of other people. But I have survived. I have a wonderful wife, three grown up children — one working for the sultan in Qatar — and nine grandchildren. And I live in a beautiful New Forest village in a large house with its own grounds. How lucky can you get?

— Deryck Blythe©

March-past by 27 Coy RASC for the visiting general at Kuala Lumpur

Shirtsleeves and shorts were the order of the day

It was just a training exercise, but I was a real casualty

I WAS BORN in November 1937. My mother was hospitalised immediately after my birth, and my father was working as a builder's labourer away from home. So I was adopted into my Uncle Bill's family (my mother's brother) and I became Uncle Bill and Auntie Elsie's fifth child. I was lucky to have my four cousins Bill, Dot, Charlie and Joyce Hayter as my "brothers and sisters." We lived at Longham in Dorset and I attended Ferndown School until, at the age of 13, I went to Bournemouth Technical College to complete a three-year course in building trades. After leaving college, I started a five-year apprenticeship with a large local firm as a plumber.

In 1958 I had just completed my apprenticeship and was about to earn a "proper wage." So I was peeved to learn that I had to serve in Her Majesty's armed forces on £1.50 a week.

I was enlisted into the Devon and Dorset Regiment, with instructions to report to Topsham Barracks in Exeter. On the train journey I met a schoolfriend, Brian Cameron. When we arrived at Exeter station, it was pouring with rain. Brian and I were so keen to start our military training we decided that, rather than wait for the Army lorry to take us to the barracks, we would avail ourselves of the comfort of a taxi. It was still teeming down when we strolled through the gates.

We spoke to a chap in Army uniform and very casually asked him where we had to report for the National Service intake. He obviously did not approve of our laidback manner, and proceeded to give us the first of many severe reprimands in how to address a soldier of higher rank.

This first experience of service life was a bit of a rude awakening for a couple of timid country boys. But we were pointed in the right direction by this soldier, whose uniform was covered by a heavy watercape. For all we knew he could have been a general.

Weeks later, I discovered that he had more stripes going down his sleeve for his many years' service than upwards for authority.

We were kitted out, and finally I hit the pillow at about two in the morning, only to have my dreamworld shattered at 5.30am by our training NCOs.

On duty, but looking pretty relaxed about it

After the new experience of washing and shaving with cold water in an outside toilet block, I went in my new Army uniform to the cookhouse for breakfast.

My first day was spent learning general discipline rules and the correct way to march.

After the first three weeks of training, we were allowed to go home for the weekend. The number of times we were told we had lost this privilege during training was not recorded, but we dreaded the threats being carried out, wanting some respite from the intense discipline and to see our families.

We did get our leave, although we still had to get past the guardhouse. Several of us were sent back for having a top button undone, or some similar offence.

However, the training officers, who were most feared, came to our rescue and ordered the guards to let us through the gates. Outside, hitching a lift home was no a problem because motorists always helped boys in uniform.

But I never completed my 10 weeks' basic training. During a night manoeuvre near Honiton, where we were playing soldiers in the dark, one ran into me. The hot sights of his rifle, which had been firing blanks, were accidentally thrust into my face.

I don't know to this day who caused the accident, but I ended the night in Exeter General Hospital with eight stitches in my cheek. Fortunately, the scar I still carry resembles an attractive dimple!

Next morning I returned to the barracks where, despite my "war wound" I was still expected to clean my own rifle ready for inspection. And the cooking pans we had used on the exercise. After the night manoeuvres, we were entitled to another weekend's leave, and I was given per-

25

mission to travel home so long as it was not by public transport.

This may have had something to do with the fact that I now looked like the Invisible Man with my head covered in bandages — a sight which horrified my Auntie Elsie when I arrived.

While I was on leave the wound began to pour saliva down the outside of my face, and my own doctor referred me to Poole Hospital. There, a small repair was carried out on the saliva gland.

I was quite enjoying the attentions of the nurses when I received a command ordering me to return to barracks as I was AWOL. By this time my cheek had healed, and arriving back at Exeter station I was greeted by two regimental policemen who escorted me back to camp.

As I had now missed the draft to Cyprus, I did not join my Devon and Dorset friends on active service.

Instead I was sent to join the regimental police at the School of Infantry, Warminster where I did guardhouse duty and traffic control and escorted prisoners to-and-from meals and work.

On one occasion during my duty on the control gate, I encountered Idi Amin, who was making his way to the health centre. He had just completed an exercise as an officer on Salisbury Plain.

After a year as a regimental policeman I heard there was a vacancy for a plumber in the Pioneer Shop. As this was my trade, I applied for the position, and was able to continue my plumbing, working at various locations and on the officers' private houses in the Salisbury Plain area.

Our nights out were usually spent at the Bell Inn in Warminster, where fights often broke out between the various units stationed in the town.

One particular night I remember the jukebox was playing Connie Francis singing Lipstick on Your Collar. A beer bottle flew straight through

the glass of the jukebox and on to the record-player. The record slurred to a stop but the fight continued. Military Police arrived and peace was restored, but hearing that song always brings back the memory.

I joined the School of Infantry's football team, which involved matches against teams *My injury is now* across the Salisbury Plain area, *just a dimple* and I played for Warminster Town when time permitted.

There was no objection to this from the officers as most of the town team consisted of Army personnel. Unfortunately, we did not win any medals. The opposing Army teams had more-experienced players, some internationals, on their sides.

My National Service continued in this pleasant vein and I was able to pick up my plumbing career again when I completed my two years. I can honestly say that I do not regret having to do National Service, nor the time I spent making new friends and learning new disciplines.

And then...

I see Brian Cameron — who also suffered an injury during our training period — at the Ferndown School reunions and I am still in contact with my Army pal Geoff who came from Bolton and now lives in Cornwall.

The plumbing trade has served me and my family very well. I ran my own one-man business for 40 years, gaining work on the recommendation of clients and never having to advertise.

I have been married to Barbara since 1961. We have three sons and a daughter, eight grandchildren and five step-grandchildren.

— Brian Bowey©

23389717 Pte Mike Bowyer

Look, said the sergeant-major, can't you see you're on fire?

MOST PEOPLE visit the Tower of London to see the Crown Jewels, gape at Traitors Gate or photograph the Yeoman Warders in their colourful uniforms. But on April 25 1957 I showed a letter to the policeman on the gate and strode into history wearing a scruffy old blue raincoat. It was the beginning of a journey which took me half way round the world and back.

HM Tower of London is the depot of the Royal Fusiliers (City of London Regiment) — and that was where I was to undertake my National Service basic training. And when you live in something as old as the Tower, you soon discover that history of a very sobering nature is around every corner.

This usually takes the form of a very loud gentleman in khaki with stripes all up his arm. Bumbling recruits are let on to the drill square for public humiliation only a few days into their 24-month government-sponsored holiday. Large crowds swarm forward to the chain barrier in front of the White Tower gleefully telling offspring: "Look, soldiers." Not really, madam.

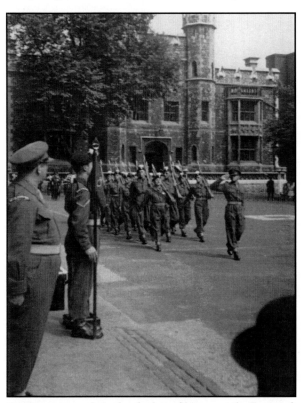

Passing out parade in the shadow of history at the Tower of London. I am, as usual, right marker

They watch in anticipation as some poor wretch is verbally abused and humiliated. It was just the same in the days of public hanging.

On one drill parade a spectator, type: female, model: ferocious, was so incensed by the sight of a poor boy being shouted at that she broke from the normally amused crowd and physically attacked the offending sergeant-major with her umbrella.

But the greatest horror to befall recruits on the awe-inspiring drill square — an open box formed by the Wellington Barracks, officers mess and White Tower — was to receive drill instruction from the depot RSM. He was a 6ft 6ins, ex-Guards warrant officer first class, nicknamed Tiny.

Even the ravens hopped smartly around the corner and hid when the cobblestones creaked at the arrival of this colossus. He marched effortlessly, just like a metronome. Tick-tock, tick-tock. Pick-up-the-step. Tick-tock.

He would arrive just before the Big Clock struck the hour. Turning smartly to face his trembling squad he waited motionless as the clock laboriously struck 10 times, staring at all the assembled mincemeat. Sheer theatre. When the last strike faded away he hit vocal mode with a straight-from-the-gut showman's performance.

As a 6ft 2¼in beanpole, I was always right-marker. This meant that I was the most conspicuous in the squad and guaranteed to attract verbal entertainment fairly often.

On one hot, sunny day the RSM was operating at full blast, watched by a particularly animated crowd of American visitors.

Suddenly he paused in mid-command, sniffed and marched straight at me. I was in an advanced stage of shock by the time he reached about a fag-paper width from my nose. "Can't you smell it, laddie?" No sir. "Well, for god's sake boy, you're on fire!" Yes sir. "Look at your right foot."

He was, of course, correct. A cigar butt had been flicked from the crowd and settled in the fold of my battledress trousers, just above the gaiter, from whence a smouldering was in process.

27

Deftly the RSM flicked the butt away with his pace-stick and extinguished it with his boot. A policeman was instructed to move the visitors on. "Nobody messes with the British Army. Now let's get on with it."

After one rare weekend leave I returned on Sunday night and made my way upstairs to bed in a building as modern as the Napoleonic Wars.

There would not be many lads back yet because they lived much nearer to the barracks than I.

But in the early hours I woke to the noise of incessant coughing and general moaning and groaning. Someone was fiddling about with kit in the darkness, and then spat on the floor.

Unusual, I thought, and eventually went back to sleep. Once more I was woken by unrest among the uneasy soldiery, but finally nodded off.

At dawn, a bright and breezy recruit from Gravesend kicked the end of my bed and asked why I was back so early. "There's no-one here yet," he said. And there wasn't. Not a crease in any of the perfectly boxed beds. No-one in the ablutions. The place was devoid of any living soul. "You look as if you've seen ghosts," he observed.

I said I hadn't seen them, but I sure had heard them. To this day, I know what I heard, and I could certainly feel the presence of people. A night alone in the Tower is not for the imaginative.

Months later, many thousands of miles away in the cold of an Arabian desert night, I had another noise experience of the unexpected.

Two sentries were posted at a water tower reached only by a long fenced causeway which stretched a couple of hundred yards out into the desert.

Reaching the tower quietly was impossible because the floor was steel planking laid loosely on a steel framework. Guards just peered out into the desert and hoped not to see anything during the two-hour stag.

One night I was on duty there with my mate Bert. All was quiet on the desert front until suddenly there was a crashing and banging on the causeway as someone or some thing started to gather momentum towards us.

The noise grew louder and the pace quickened as IT got closer. "I'm putting one up the spout," said Bert. I agreed that was perhaps a good precaution, and we flicked off safety catches and eased back the bolts ready for action.

Proud Fusilier

By now the noise was terrific, and getting very close. "Give me a shove up," said Bert, ascending the water tower with some speed. I joined him and waited with trepidation as THE THING crashed to a halt below. There was an eerie scream followed by much braying as a donkey disentangled itself from the pipework.

"I expect he only wants a carrot," remarked Bert, who then suggested that perhaps we could hide him in a tent and sell him off at market. But then, suddenly knowing all about donkeys as he had once ridden one on Brighton beach, Bert led our visitor back down the causeway. He woke up the guard commander and presented him with recruit Eeyore, which did not go down terribly well. Because we then spent night after night guarding that blooming tower in retaliation.

I recall another night-time incident when the battalion was preparing for overseas service on the Arabian peninsula by being marched, in the rain, across Salisbury Plain, presumably because we couldn't see it wasn't desert. This really stretched the imagination.

When we climbed a hill and shook off our kit a corporal arrived. As I just happened to be nearest, he ordered me to dig in, and led me to a spot half under a bush.

"Six foot long and four foot deep. Dig." But I can't see the ground, corporal. "Dig."

Well, I have to say I did not feel like something as tiring as digging. I tried a few tentative prods and struck concrete, or something equally resistant.

Nothing much else appeared to be happening, so I wandered around the back of the bushes and did a few exploratory thrusts with my spade and found soft earth. Brilliant. This was the site of a previous trench, and it didn't take me long to excavate it to an impressive size.

Come daybreak, and the corporal arrived to observe the night's work. I could now see that he was wearing the medal ribbons of the recent Korean war.

"What are you doing there? That's the wrong place." I quickly explained that this was, in fact, the correct position to withstand an enemy assault. It provided an arc of fire over the most likely route of attack because there was cover on this side, whereas there was no cover on the other side. Corporal.

"You f---g educated Archie, you do just as you're f---g told in future. What's your name?"

I thought it best not to reveal too much about my identity. So I replied: "Cooper, corp."

"Well Cooper, just you keep your f---g ideas to yourself."

The name of that corporal was Harry Wain, and it cropped up again some 35 years later when I was reading a copy of What's It All About, Alfie? the autobiography of film star Michael Caine.

Born Maurice Joseph Micklewright, I read, he was called up to join the Queen's Royal Regiment for his National Service. Subsequently, however, he volunteered with a group of his Queen's pals to transfer to the Royal Fusiliers to go to Korea. Among that group was one, Harry Wain. So that's what that was all about.

I hate water. Even sitting in the bath gives me aquaphobia. At school I was tall enough to walk along the bottom of the pool and make out I was swimming. So I only just about survived five weeks on the troopship to India and then Kenya. But within a month or so we were flown Transport Command Comet 4 to somewhere hot with plenty of sand.

This was a bit of an urgent operation, and the few regulars among us, being married men, were getting very jumpy about active service. However, we then went back to sea again for several months, courtesy of the Royal Navy.

All at sea. Our cramped accommodation on the quarterdeck of HMS Newfoundland

Packed like sardines on the quarterdeck — a holy place to matelots — and sleeping among enormous boltheads on steel decking we enjoyed the comforts of cruisers and destroyers, daily leaping over the side and slithering down rope nets into heaving landing craft.

We took part in a series of beach landing "operations," waving the flag around smelly oilfields in the Gulf. They were intended to ward off some never-to-be-seen enemy.

It was exhausting work, and once the temperature reached 140 degrees F.

After one tiring island beach assault some kind soul in the Navy nosh-house dished out ice-cream. Yes, real ice-cream!

I made a pig of myself and finished up in the bowels of this ship being treated for rather excessive runs and puking.

I was parked on a bench among rows of inhabited coffins. Then this bloke in the coffin next to me began to move and groan.

God, I thought, suddenly feeling much better. What the hell's going on?

A passing orderly informed me that the coffin-wallahs were in fact all alive and just having their temperature reduced by the ice packed around the said un-stiffs.

On another very hot day there was great activity. We guessed we were involved in something important when we saw the matelots gearing up guns and live ammo.

We soldiers were isssued with the usual clips of five — "don't waste any" — and lined up under this enormous great gun with twin barrels the size of telegraph poles.

Now no-one who is both knowledgeable and sane ever stands beneath six-inch naval guns when they fire! I have been discernibly deaf ever since.

Being tallish I was always ordered to the sharp end of the landing craft on exercises. They whizzed up the beach and dropped the front end and we were supposed to run out shouting. In reality I got pushed out first as a sort of human depth gauge. If I didn't disappear the others ran out using my steel helmet as a launchpad.

They later gave us a medal for all this aqua-lunacy, but it didn't improve my dislike of water.

We then did a spell of enemy-spotting from a three-seater buzzbox operated by the RAF, taking off and landing from the centre of a crater of a defunct volcano.

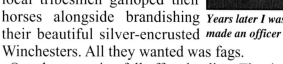
Years later I was made an officer

Landing was great fun because local tribesmen galloped their horses alongside brandishing their beautiful silver-encrusted Winchesters. All they wanted was fags.

One day our wing fell off on landing. The tiny RAF stores just happened to have a new one, which was bolted on, and away we went again.

All these adventures are now over. The whitewash on the back of my WD boot-brushes has almost faded away, along with the number I so carefully stamped on each one all those years ago. But still in daily use, they are virtually all that physically remains from a way of life that has since proved more useful to me than any academic university. The only regret I have of being an NS man is the morning I finally got home. Here I was, in deep mid-winter, a sun-tanned hero from the desert complete with medal to prove it, and I had survived.

My mum and gran looked up when I slung my kit on the floor, and said: "Oh, where have you been?"

And then...

I became a newspaper reporter, so satisfying the search for excitement, and then worked for a blue-chip company in public relations for 30 years.

In my spare time I joined the Territorial Army and then served in the Army Cadet Force, becoming — don't tell the boys — an officer, finally retiring with the honorary rank of major.

— Mike Bowyer©

Taking centre stage "on some foreign field..."

23276420 Cpl Mike Bracey

I quit shorthand course and landed a 'foreign holiday'

AS AN 18-year-old just leaving school in 1955 the thought of National Service was somewhat awesome and unknown. First, where to go? Army, RAF or Navy? As my father had been in the Army I decided this would be the avenue to go. I lived in Ealing and the Royal Army Education Corps carried out training not far away in Beaconsfield, after which you left as a sergeant. So I plumped for this.

I was successful in my application, but what I didn't know at the time was that all RAEC personnel first had to undergo eight weeks' training with the infantry.

So on January 19 1956 a Southerner stepped on the train to York to join the West Yorkshire Infantry for induction training.

To say this was quite an experience is putting it mildly. From the drill corporal threatening to get on the roof of the barracks and vomit all over us, to a morning on Strensall range in denims firing rifles and brenguns in four inches of snow.

The most harrowing experience however, was throwing the hand-grenade. Stand behind a wall, pull out the pin, count to three and lob it over the wall. There is always one chap who leaves a lot to be desired, and our group had him.

I had a dreadful feeling our friend might either not count correctly or worse still drop the grenade in our area. But I am pleased to say we survived.

After the invigorating experience in Yorkshire we moved to Beaconsfield for the eight weeks' teacher training. This was interesting, but a little boring. Many more-learned fellows were failing as the course progressed, while my pal Maurice and I were spending evenings in Ealing and even going to watch Brentford play football at Griffiin Park!

The course ended on the Friday of Whitsun weekend. That night

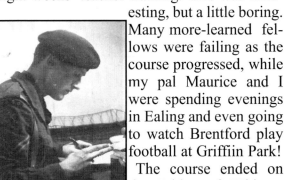
Hard at work in Germany

Maurice and I were on picquet duty strolling around the grounds with our pickaxe handles when our officer came up and said: "I have looking for you two to say that unfortunately you have failed, report back on Tuesday to decide where to go."

This gave us plenty to think about over the weekend, and as we hadn't really a clue what to

I quit the shorthand course

do, I suggested that as my father had been in the Engineers we might as well go for that. Maurice got into the RE, with a ultimate posting to Cyprus, but the powers-that-be decided I should join the Royal Army Service Corps as a clerk.

So off I went to Aldershot for the next session of training. On completion I applied for a nine-month shorthand course and was accepted. But after a couple of weeks of complete boredom I suddenly realised that I had been in the Army for some eight months and would now be a trainee for another eight, with daily bull and locker inspections.

Enough was enough, so I visited the office and said I wanted to get off the course. "No way," I was told. "You applied, and you're in." I then pleaded with someone I had got to know in the office and said I would go anywhere so long as I could leave the course.

And that led to a posting to Germany. Bearing in mind that foreign holidays hadn't been heard of in 1956, this sounded great.

After a week in the transit camp at Bordon we sailed from Harwich to the Hook of Holland to start the German experience.

It was interesting to note that all of us were potential clerks who had passed out from Aldershot, and as soon as we landed we were told there would be a week's refresher course. However, I missed this experience because I was sent on a special posting to help close the offices in Sennelager.

I was there for only a few weeks, but anyone who went there for their full time had a doddle. The living accommodation was in private

31

houses with Army furniture. The offices were a new block up the road, and the canteen had items like tablecloths and jugs of water. And to crown it all, the weekly inspection was on Saturday morning when the captain would give us the once over and even adjust the — officially legal but very smart — weights in our trousers above the gaiters.

National Service days now over

I didn't find the guardroom while I was there, so could come and go as I liked. A great pity I wasn't there longer!

From this sublime existence came the ridiculous. I received another "special" posting, this time to HQ 2nd Infantry Division at Hilden, 16 kilometres from Dusseldorf.

Though this meant back to the parade environment with an RSM from the Guards, I was promoted to corporal and found it to be a very pleasant period of my Army career.

We had several exercises in the country and one night we were sleeping in the roof of a hay barn with our Army vehicle parked inside below us. The staff sergeant used the vehicle to sleep in, and next morning we found him still sound asleep, slightly the worst for drink, and with most of his sleeping bag burnt from his last cigarette. It might also have been our last!

On another occasion I was guard commander, and on visiting the cells found all the prisoners in one cell playing cards. But they were causing no problem, so I turned a blind eye. At approximately 2200hrs the whole area was plunged into darkness and I was told that the fuse box was in the loft above the cells.

Fully armed and ready for action

I had visions of opening the main cell door and being run over in the rush for the prisoners to escape. But I plucked up courage, and opened the door only to find all the prisoners back in their cells and one in the loft repairing the fuse. Which shows that if you treat people with a little respect they return it.

While I was in Germany I managed to travel the country including a trip to the motor-racing Grand Prix at Nuremburg, and also visited Holland and Luxembourg. I was demobbed in January 1958 and my last memory of note was that on the train journey from Harwich to London it was amazing how many road workers were standing about doing nothing. Something never seen on the German sites.

In summary, my two years' service was memorable. In the Army one found true friendship. There would be no hesitation in giving a mate the last two coppers in one's pocket.

And then...

After National Service I worked in the planning department of the T Wall and Sons meat company before joining Lyons bakery where I held various senior roles in distribution. I was then a distribution operations director with Watney Combe Reid for six years before being involved with the company's takeover by Courage, and took early retirement in 1992.

— *Mike Bracey*©

2726790 SAC Mike Bromley

It was my first-ever flight, and the pilot managed to get us lost

NATIONAL Service caused problems for a lot of people because you had to decide whether to leave school at 16 and get a job for 18 months or so, or stay on and take A-levels, hope to go on to university and then be called up at 21 or older. That meant finding yourself at about 24 leaving the services with no work experience and competing for jobs with people who had been at work for some years.

I was lucky enough to pass the 11-plus exam and then GCE in 1952, but I had no idea what job I wanted. For no obvious reason I decided I'd like to be an auctioneer. This seems the silliest possible choice of job, because I was very reserved. But it actually turned out amazingly well.

I began as office boy in a small firm of auctioneers in Nottingham. They let me take the Chartered Auctioneers Institute exam which I passed in 1954, and then I was called up into the RAF at Cardington.

In the first week there was the AOC's inspection, complete with water glasses in the mess lined up with string. Then off to basic training on Cannock Chase at RAF Hednesford, said to have been a PoW camp in WW2.

It certainly looked the part in the worst summer of the twentieth century. Even the assault course was cancelled due to flooding. It was so cold and wet we were allowed a fire in the hut's iron stove, and when we said there was no coal, we were told we had spent two nights guarding the f---g fuel store!

Next there was the choice of trades. I had heard that the cushiest number in the RAF was operations clerk in Air Traffic Control so I put in for that. I was sent to Wittering near Stamford, about 50 miles from my home and reported to ATC.

The new boys were given the job of recording the radio messages. We had a small phone switchboard and records of aircraft movements to keep so I had no real problems except the ATC jargon. You could hold a conversation full of numbers and abbreviations which meant nothing at all as there was no trade course.

One poor chap had been a plumber and he really struggled, so they sent him off to the Intelligence Section!

One of the controllers was a Polish Spitfire pilot who asked if I would like a trip in the station twin-engine Oxford. This was my first-ever flight, and it was hair-raising. We got lost about three miles from the airfield and had to ask ATC for a course to find the airfield with 3,000 yards of runway.

ATC was issued with a new gizmo, a sort of mortar to fire rockets to help pilots locate the aerodrome in low cloud. This seemed to me to be something which might have been fine in WW1, but jet V-bombers ought to have had more modern kit.

Some nitwit put it on the tower balcony, next to the huge new double glazed windows, and fired the beast. Only later did we read the instructions to find it had to be 50 yards from any building. So it got moved, and I was sent to load it with a rocket.

Buttons were pressed to fire the gadget, without result. More reading of instructions and we waited for 30 minutes in case it was about to explode, then very carefully took the rocket out, only to find it was a practice round. Red faces everywhere.

There was still a flarepath party to provide emergency runway lights with glimlamps (a sort of battery lamp) and "goosenecks" which looked like a metal watering can filled with paraffin with a wick in the spout.

As these things were never used I'm not sure what else the chaps did all day, except smell strongly of paraffin.

The tower ran on three watches, supposed to cover 24 hours, seven days a week, and once or twice we tried this on exercises, but we couldn't have kept it up for more than a week or two as one watch was about 20 hours long.

Despite National Service providing lots of "erks," there never seemed to be enough to fully man the tower, and watches almost never had an NCO in charge.

One night the senior airman decided he wanted to drive the Land-Rover used to get out to ATC, and pulled rank on the MT driver, even

I tried to stop Canberra flight

though he couldn't drive properly. All went well until he got to the guardroom to hand in the tower keys. He misjudged the space. knocked a large chip off one of the white-painted plaster pillars and bent the chassis of the vehicle which had to be written off.

This resulted in his arrest, and for some days he was to be seen marching everywhere very closely followed by an RAF Police corporal. We all thought it would be jankers for ever, or even the glasshouse, but he was only fined two days' pay.

Perhaps my most worrying experience was one morning when one of the Canberra squadrons must have decided to see if ATC were on the ball. The tower opened at 0800 and when I arrived with the watch, there was already an aircraft on the runway waiting to take off.

There was no controller, only muggins, so when the pilot asked for take-off clearance, I told him that no qualified staff were on duty, the runway hadn't been inspected, there was no fire crew or runway controller and so on. This got me nowhere, and off they went, fortunately without mishap. Heaven alone knows what would have happened if they had crashed on take-off.

But as well as scary experiences, there were lots of amusing occasions, like when the Mess served blackcurrant tart, with fresh blackcurrants still on their stalks. And once one of the corporals decided that shooting rabbits at night from the Land-Rover with a shotgun would be fun — until the gun exploded.

I also remember that one of my mates got keen on the station warrant officer's pretty daughter, and was told to lay off or he would be posted to the worst place the SWO could think of.

Right at the end of my service I was sent to the Lancashire Fire Service training centre to learn firefighting for use in the Reserve. The instructor asked if any airman could drive, and as I was the only one in my team who had driven anything (1939 Austin 10) I got to drive a Green

Goddess fire appliance for two weeks. A lot better than rushing about with wet, heavy hoses. I didn't take up the opportunity to go to the top of the turntable ladder. Not me!

I'm not sure that my National Service did me any real good. I was able to go home most weekends, and I think most lads did the same from Wittering. I can't remember that there was anything to do if you stayed on camp.

And then...

In June 1956 I was demobbed and returned to auctioneering, but with a larger firm in Nottingham, and found it took six months to get used to civilian life. I passed the final exam in 1958 and by 1963 was in charge of the agricultural section of the firm under the senior partner.

But it was very much a family firm, and when I was offered a job by the Inland Revenue valuation office I thought it as well to move on.

Inevitably the VO posted me to an office that dealt only with property rating assessment, about which I knew nothing as farms are not rated, but I was surprised to find it interesting. After a couple of years I transferred to an office which did the full range of government valuation work.

In 1967 I went on a sailing holiday and met my wife, Shirley. We were married in April 1968 and in 1971 I got a job as estates surveyor to Basildon Council.

This, unfortunately, was not a good career move, and I was very lucky to find a job with the Civil Aviation Authority estates department in London in 1977. I think my RAF service helped me to get it. I stayed there for 18 years until retiring in 1996.

Much of the work was very specialised, involving the rating assessment of radio and radar stations, control towers and radio navaids, as well as London offices. I certainly got to some outlandish places in the UK and was amused on one occasion to meet a group-captain who addressed me as "Mike" as I had equivalent rank in the Civil Service. I managed not to stand to attention and call him Sir.

I still get some flak from Mrs B for asking her to "say again" and leaving her messages including "wef" and "tfn" and 24 hr. clock times. But the Air Traffic Control phonetic alphabet is handy to confuse call centre operators.

— Mike Bromley©

34

23160283 Cpl Frank Brown

If 30 minutes was needed to do a job, we would be given 20

WHEN I presented myself for my medical I was walking and breathing so was passed A1. Knowing how the Army mind worked I assumed that as I had been employed by a firm of chartered accountants in London I would be placed in the infantry or the Catering Corps. So it was with some surprise that I received an invitation to join the Royal Army Pay Corps at their training camp in Waller Barracks, Devizes.

On Thursday July 21 1955 I boarded a train along with other unfortunates who like me did not realise that this was the last day of freedom for two years. We were met by a lad not much older than ourselves, in a uniform with two white chevrons and full of his own importance shouting for us to get on to a three-ton truck. We would have boarded it even if he had asked nicely.

Most of us had never been away from home before, and what was to come was quite a blow to the system. We were divided into two squads, A Company and B Company. Those of us in A were given a label with CPC on. No-one bothered to tell us what this meant until later in the day I asked a chap and he said that we had been selected as company pay clerks. Still none the wiser.

The next introduction to Army life was to be taken to the "spider" which was to be our home for the next 10 weeks. It consisted of six wooden huts linked together with a common corridor containing a washroom, toilets and Blanco room to be shared by about 180 men. There were 30 in our hut, and we claimed our iron bed and metal locker with a space of some three to four feet between each bed.

From now on everything we did when not marching was at the double. At

the QM stores we were issued with our uniform and equipment. Battledress 2; berets 2; underpants, green, cellular 2; tin hat; mug china; KFS (eating irons); shirts and boots; blanket; pillow. You struggled to hold everything while doubling back to the spider. Many a mug was dropped on the way and had to be paid for. A new mug was 6d.

We then changed into our Army clothes and went around the hut swapping anything that didn't fit with our mates, who by now we were getting to know. A mixed bunch. Scots, Welsh, Brummies, West Country, Geordies and of course us Londoners.

We soon realised that if say 30 minutes was needed to do something, the Army would give you 20. We would be shouted at to get outside (nobody in authority seemed to call, it was always shouting), and then doubled to the mess hall for our evening meal. There was very little time to queue and then eat it before we were lined up outside again. The NCOs ate in a separate room with no queuing and very few of them so they could relax and finish their meal well before us.

Back in the spider we were shown how to bull our kit for the rest of the evening. Lights out at 10.30pm completed the first day for 23160283 Private Brown F T. The next day it was up at 6am and fighting for a sink in the washroom to wash and shave. Then double to the mess for breakfast — queuing and bolting your food. Back to the spider and on to the parade ground at eight to be shown how to become soldiers with marching, turning, saluting and standing to attention. This lasted until 4.30, with a morning NAAFI break and a break for lunch.

The weather was very hot and some

I am in the back row, right, in this picture of the Dorset Regiment pay staff in Germany, 1957

35

Demob day, 1957

lads fainted. But they were just put to one side until they came round and then had to get back in line. In the evenings it was back to the barrack-room for more bulling sessions, and we often continued by candle-light well after lights out because apart from our kit we had to keep the barrack room spotless for company commander's inspections.

Pay parade was held on Thursday when we were lined up before an officer and pay clerk plus two witnesses. Approach the table, salute with your right hand and at the same time give your paybook to the officer with your left hand. The pay clerk would read out the amount due (three shillings and six-pence a day, or 17 pence in today's money). Receive the paybook and cash in left hand, salute, about turn and march off smartly.

We all needed to be inoculated against any nasty diseases we might pick-up. This was done on the first Saturday because we had half-day off and all Sunday was free, consequently we could recover in our own time and not the Army's. Some lads were quite ill with the reaction but I was OK. The following weekend was a Bank Holiday and we were allowed a leave pass. My mother had died just 10 days before I was called up, but I spent a great time with my dad at Manor Road, Leyton.

Back at camp the training became more intense, with PE every morning, forced marches in full kit and long-distance runs. We learned how to shoot with rifle, bren and sten guns and raced around the assault course. We also had to go into the gas chamber, fortunately with gas-masks which had to be removed just before you came out to understand what it was like without protection.

After six weeks we started four weeks' technical training, which was a little easier, but we still had to rush for the washroom and double for meals, and there was still plenty of drill, kit inspections and guard duties.

Pay clerk days over

We were shown the various forms (the Army couldn't exist without its forms!) we would come across as pay clerks and the queries we would encounter. Then training came to an end with the passing-out parade — followed by an evening tour of the Devizes public houses before returning to camp and forcing our NCOs fully-clothed into the showers. Next day our postings were displayed on the noticeboard. Our intake was dispersed all over the world, and I was to be attached to 1st battalion, Dorset Regiment at Bulford Camp on Salisbury Plain. We collected our railway warrants and posting orders and went off on 10 days' leave, promising to keep in touch, but...

Life with the battalion was easy. No parades and no guard duties. I was promoted to lance-corporal, then corporal and passed a couple of trade tests which all gave me a pay increase.

I was enjoying life in the Army and was pleased when I was posted to Germany, where I was based at Minden. We had all weekends free and I managed to see quite a lot of the country.

If I been based in England I would have spent most weekends at home, whereas in Minden I joined in with battalion events, played football, helped with the local Scout group — I had joined the Scouts at the age of 11 and was connected with scouting until I was 65 — and made many friends.

And then...

Returning to Civvy Street I worked for Scottish and Newcastle Breweries as a sales ledger clerk. Then I became a retail accountant with the House of Fraser, and retired in 1992 after 18 years as regional administration manager for the Binns Group, part of the House of Fraser, which ran 16 stores in the North of England..

I am now parish treasurer for the Roman Catholic Church in South Shields, treasurer of the Credit Union and a member of the Royal Army Pay Corps Association in the North-east.

— ***Frank Brown©***

23348881 Sgt Terry Buchanan

On the Troodos patrol my bed was just an old cricket bag

MY NATIONAL Service basic training was not much different from any other conscripted soldier. At the passing-out parade the CO told us we were a shambles, that most of us would get foreign postings and that some of us would die. I was glad my mum didn't hear that one.

Then and now. As a photographer in Cyprus, and a fun photograph taken much more recently

A couple of days earlier I had had my service trade interview. The young subaltern, public-school and as much a sprog as myself peered at me tortoise-like from his ill-fitting uniform, a size 14 neck emerging from a size 17 collar.

"I have looked at your education and background, and we can offer you instant promotion in bomb disposal," he declared.

Bloody hell, I thought. I don't think my mum would like me messing about with bombs.

"Is that compulsory or voluntary, sir?" I asked.

"It's voluntary, and the alternative is to be a photographer."

"Yes please sir," I replied. "That's the one."

Four of us were duly despatched to a secret establishment in London for six weeks' training which consisted of processing covert photographs and being sent on missions to take unobserved photographs of people wandering in the streets of London.

Oh no, I thought. Out of the bomb disposal frying pan into the spy photographer fire!

Once trained, I was sent as an Army public relations photographer to Cyprus. This was just as the EOKA campaign to remove British troops from the island was getting into its stride.

When I boarded the aircraft at Southend to fly to Nicosia I had never been farther than Bournemouth from my East London home. The flight to Cyprus took 13 hours because the aircraft had problems,

and as we landed sparks and flames shot out of one of the engines. An indication, I thought, of the dangers that were to come.

My first test came within a matter of weeks. Cpl Ken Burtt and I were in a shop in Old Nicosia. "Don't turn round," he said. "There is a lad just outside showing a pistol to some other boys." Of course, I turned and saw the group concentrating on an ivory-handled gun.

"When I say run," said Ken, "follow me and run like mad."

And we did, pausing for breath in a photographer's studio shop reception area. Fortunately for us, this was deserted, because around the walls were hung hundreds of photographs of young EOKA men holding machine-guns.

We fled again to the Nicosia police station. And as we reported our experience pandemonium broke out. Two young military men had been shot in the back and killed in the area we had just left.

It was an untimely first step into the savage ways of men who use violence when seeking

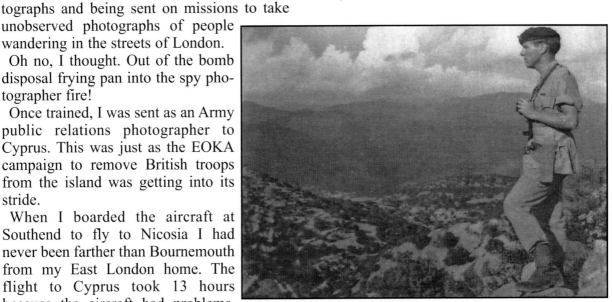

On the lookout in the Troodos, Cyprus

37

to right what they see as a wrong. The incident set the stage for the rest of my time in Cyprus.

One of my roles there was to photograph funerals for the families of the deceased and for the Imperial War Graves Commission. Young men, many of them the same age as me, were being interred in a foreign soil. Some of them I had met, spoken to and even photographed as they had gone about their work.

I was in a small group of photographers and journalists in Army public relations. We were under the command of a dyed-in-the-wool veteran, Major Stubbs.

I once followed him as he ran up the steps of the Ledra Palace Hotel with his Luger pistol on its lanyard bouncing along behind him. One day I gave him a ticking-off when he tore up some photographic prints that our printer had spent all day producing in the corrugated oven of a darkroom under a blazing sun. He was stunned into silence, then apologised.

But he got his own back when, at five minutes' notice, I was ordered to go into the Troodos mountains to join the search for the EOKA leader, Gen Grivas. For much of the time there I slept in an old cricket bag on bare earth, which didn't do much for my uniform.

Then I got back to base 10 days later and found I had another clothing problem. The trouble was that when I had to leave hurriedly for the mountains I had just put my cotton uniform into a bowl of water with half a packet of soap suds. I returned to be met by a furious staff-sergeant. "What do you call that?" he demanded. My bowl of dhobi had grown into a beautiful and enormous fungus. Impressive — but unhygienic.

Because I dealt on a daily basis with the most senior of Army ranks, there was no fear when I encountered authority. Usually I was called by my first name. But on one assignment I was despatched under a cloak of secrecy and met by a very friendly chap who was full of natural conversation. "Will you get some good photographs? he asked. "Yes sir," I replied, not knowing if there was some protocol on how one addresses the Prime Minister.

Harold Macmillan was visiting his old regiment, and we stood alongside his helicopter awaiting his departure. As I was preparing to take my final photograph, I was in line with a general, a brigadier and a colonel.

Macmillan surveyed the line, pondered, and then strode directly towards me and shook my hand. The roar that went up from the surrounding troops was deafening. The look that came down from the officers was intimidating. The three officers had failed to notice the instant raising of morale this simple gesture had made to the surrounding squaddies.

My period as a National Service soldier gave me many experiences. Sometimes I felt like a character in an Evelyn Waugh novel, particularly on the day that his son Auberon managed to get himself accidentally wounded while climbing out of a scout car.

But one terrible event is burned into my memory. One Saturday morning I was called into the photographic compound to photograph two Military Policemen who had arrived on gleaming motorcycles. The pictures were for "local boy stories" which we produced by the hundreds with captions to circulate to the men's local newspapers back home.

It was a great day, with lots of jokes, fun and laughter, and together we produced a great set of happy photographs. Each of the soldiers had a request to me — "a set of prints for mum."

I processed the films and printed the pictures the next day. On the Monday I was sorting them ready to be sent off for distribution when another soldier appeared and told me to destroy them. "Those two men are dead," he said. I was shocked to the point of despair.

But I did not destroy the photographs because I was determined to keep my promise to them and deliver them to their mothers. So I secreted the prints in my kit. But on my final departure from Cyprus they were confiscated by the duty officer at the airport. My promise was broken, and I despised that man.

The photographs' rightful place was with the families of those young men as a reminder that their final full day of life was a joyful one filled with smiles and laughter. And that their final words to me were "my mum."

And then...

Though I returned to my job training to be an architect, I was restless because my life in the Army which had shown me a possible new career path. So I obtained photographic qualifications, and finally when I retired I was chief photographer for Her Majesty's Royal Commission on the Historical Monuments of England. My stint as a National Serviceman had provided me with a fulfilling objective.
— ***Terry Buchanan***©

I failed the clerk's course and landed a great job in Jamaica

IN THE summer of 1947, just as I had completed the second year of evening class studies for the National Certificate in Building at Twickenham Technical College, my education was interrupted by National Service. But after completing a Royal Engineers' clerks course at Chatham I was given what must have been one of the best National Service postings in the world — Jamaica. Even the journey to the island was sheer luxury, as I travelled as a first-class passenger on the 7,000-ton SS Jamaica Producer.

This plum posting came about really because I was "a failure." At the end of the clerks' course most of the 70 candidates were sent to Barton Stacey for overseas postings. But two of us failed to obtain the necessary typing speed of 25 words a minute. So we had to stay for an extra week and sit the exam again. This time we passed and were promoted to lance-corporal.

But when we arrived at Barton Stacey we found that the others had been posted, mainly to Germany. And we filled in our time carrying out camp and barrack room chores.

Then in January 1948 came the news that I was to go to CRE, Up Park Camp in Kingston, Jamaica. I had reaped the benefits of being a slow typist, and at the end of the month I boarded the Jamaica Producer.

She was carrying a cargo of the new Mini Minor car for export to the West Indies. And the cabins accommodated just 50 first-class passengers who were served with seven-course dinners.

I was among a company of soldiers from various corps and regiments who were joining the Gloucesters, also based at Up Park Camp where a small army had been formed to guard a small part of our empire.

The number of Sappers at Up Park was 23, of which only Alick Hooper and I were National Servicemen. Our job was to employ direct labour to carry out the maintenance of the camp buildings, the married quarters, the NAAFI, the hospital and the Newcastle Camp nearby. My duty was to deal with the paperwork for all the maintenance carried out.

No more square-bashing, no pressure of office work. Life was just one big holiday.

My working day was mainly filling in forms, recording details of maintenance work that was being carried out, the number of miles travelled by our small van to

In my NS days

carry personnel around the island and the amount of petrol used.

Office hours were 9.30 to 4pm, and Wednesday afternoons were free. Most Sundays I was able to visit the coastal resorts of the island, often passing Noel Coward's Caribbean home. And I remember that one day in November 1948 I took a day trip with three Jamaican WRAC girls who worked in the office to Port Antonio where Errol Flynn's yacht was moored off Navy Island.

Often we would ride on a RASC ferryboat across the mouth of Kingston harbour to Port Royal, a small historic town at the end of the Palisadoes.

Now retired

Occasionally I walked out of camp in civilian clothes with my pal Alick Hooper to a parade of shops and bars called Crossroads. We would look around the shops, mainly owned by Chinese, and have a drink in a bar.

While at Up Park I started a correspondence course to keep in touch with the building world. But a barrack room is too noisy for studying, and I managed to arrange for one of our office rooms to be left open for me two nights a week. Then I found that was too quiet and lonely. So I wrote to the college back in England and cancelled the course.

Sometimes I played cards with a group in the barrack room. And I also went to whist drives with members of the Married Families Association which were held in the back garden of one of the Army bungalows.

Most other evenings I was writing letters home. One of those letters which has survived the years shows that I was having a good time. I wrote: *The other Sunday six of us borrowed* an Army lorry and went 20 miles along the coast to a little bathing place where all the high class people get to. They had all turned up in their posh cars, and in the middle of them was our big khaki Army lorry. I had a couple of games of football with the Army last week against the Navy but we lost both matches. The other Saturday I watched a wedding at our camp church, then afterwards I watched for the first time a game of polo.

Then and now. In Jamaica (I am on the right) with my pal Alick Hooper, and still together in 2005

"I think I told you that nothing out here is rationed and there is plenty of everything if you can afford to buy it, so when I can manage it I'll send home a small food parcel providing that you don't tell everybody. The only thing I'm allowed to send is sugar and local tinned fruit, but I suppose it will help."

In another letter I mentioned that I had taken part in an all-ranks Christmas party. The afternoon was devoted to the children of the married families, and the event was recorded in The Sapper magazine which referred to "Corporals Butler and Hooper tripping lightly to the tune of Nuts and May accompanied by the children."

The report added: "The said Cpl Butler also

Pictured, second left, on the high seas

proved a top-notch, if unconventional Santa Claus and aided and abetted by the CRE, Lt-col R Clayton, he dished out the eagerly awaited goods from the fairy-lit Christmas tree."

Occasionally I would go to the NAAFI, but I was teetotal so it was not very often. Besides, it was mainly occupied by the Glosters and we did not mix with them very well.

The swimming pool was also always full of the infantry men, and we corps chaps felt out of place there. So we would either walk or catch a bus to St Catherine's Monastery baths where we were charged only 6d for a swim. At

the Bournemouth baths next to the harbour we had to pay 9d, and I went there on a couple of occasions with the three WRAC girls from our office. But the best place was the open-air baths at the attractively-designed Myrtle Bank Hotel, a Victorian building in the middle of Kingston.

Soldiers were charged 2s, but it was a good atmosphere and popular with tourists. One day when I went there with John Murray, a REME pal from my billet, it was occupied by just three tourists. One of them was an attractive lady and we swam close to her, then, to attract her attention, John pushed me under the water. She smiled — and he was smitten.

Soon he began dating her. He found that she was not a tourist after all, but a short-stay resident connected to the Lascelles, part of the family tree of the Royal Family. When he was demobbed they married and John found work in Jamaica running a sugar cane business.

I came home to be demobbed on the MV Georgic, a wartime troopship converted to take £10 Pommies from Britain to Australia. On its return journey it picked up West Indians travelling to Britain answering the advertisements: "Train and bus drivers wanted."

And then...

Back in the UK I returned to college for three years and obtained the Higher National Diploma in Building. Later, after attending evening classes, I attained the Higher National Certificate in Civil Engineering.

I worked for various construction companies as a design draughtsman, and from 1966 to 1972 was an engineering assistant in drainage design with the Department of the Environment. After that, for eight years I was assistant engineer in main drainage at the London Borough of Hammersmith before returning to the Department of the Environment as a public health technical officer.

I am still in touch with Vera Hull, one of the Jamaican WRACs who worked with us as a typist. She trained later as a nurse in England, worked in Kingston then emigrated to Canada.

— Peter Butler©

23414718 Pte Mike Cairns

I hit the rifle range target, but it belonged to another bloke!

RECENTLY I took a trip to Cyprus to enjoy a relaxing break, and reawaken some memories. As the plane landed at Larnaca airport, many of those memories came flooding back. I had been on this exact spot before, but then it had not been an airport but the place where I had slept in a tent surrounded by barbed wire. Larnaca airport was the site of my National Service "home."

I was called up in August, 1957 after being deferred for a year to complete my college studies. My medical and aptitude tests pronounced me "A1, underweight, but service should rectify." Given the choice of which service to enter, in order of preference I picked the Navy, the RAF and then the Army. Needless to say, the Army became the unfortunate recipient of my body (and soul).

A one-way rail ticket and 5s advance pay arrived one morning in a very official-looking brown envelope. My posting was to Hilsea Barracks in Portsmouth.

I had to make my own travel arrangements from Teesside and arrive no later than 1600 hours on the allotted Thursday. This meant an overnight train to London, a trek across the city and a connecting train to Portsmouth. A quite-daunting 300-mile rail trip for a Fifties' teenager whose only previous journey had been to the nearby seaside!

I had been quite excited at the prospect of National Service. In my naivety, I envisaged it to be one big adventure, with Boy Scout-style gatherings around a campfire, outdoor pursuits, camaraderie, the opportunity to dress up and perhaps travel the world. How wrong I was!

The very first morning shattered the dream. We were hauled out of bed at an unearthly hour by a corporal bellowing obscenities, and given five minutes to complete ablutions and tidy our

Not looking too happy with life, I am on the left, middle row with some of the RAOC intake at Hilsea Barracks

bed spaces. After a breakfast of beans and something resembling sausages we were marched to the kitting out stores. Uniforms were issued, not by size, but by an "it looks your size, so it's yours" method of allocation.

Next we were given brown paper and string to parcel up our civilian clothes and return them home. The Army kindly paid the postage.

From day one we marched, quick marched or double quick-marched everywhere. Fear became the force that propelled us through those unreal weeks. After a lifetime of maternal pampering, the daily routine of being responsible for cleaning, ironing, polishing and all those domestic chores that I had happily left to others, was a shock to the system.

Morning muster parade became a daily terror. A minute speck of dust, gaiters not aligned, brasses and boots not super-gleaming, back not rigidly straight, thumbs not pointing south and a dozen other infringements attracted the most vitriolic tirade from the inspecting CSM or officer.

At first I was confused as to whom to address as sir. I found it difficult to identify officers, and was regularly cautioned for failing to salute. I ended up saluting everybody just in case they warranted it!

Though fairly short-sighted I had always been reluctant, through vanity, to wear glasses. Thus my first experience on the rifle range was a bit of a disaster.

I adopted the correct position, lying on my front, legs apart, rifle barrel tight against my shoulder. I could just about see the target, so took sight and pressed the trigger, and though the recoil almost lifted me from the ground I felt quite confident after discharging the full magazine.

But to my horror, there was not one hole on

my target. The corporal was not amused, and his blue vocabulary included something about disgrace and "God help Britain."

He then checked the target of the soldier next to me and discovered that this had 12 holes instead of six!

The well-oiled Army machine eventually tranformed me into something resembling a soldier.

Our first six-hour pass into Portsmouth generated the same feeling that escapees from Devil's Island must have experienced. As a major naval port Portsmouth boasts a large population of sailors.

And in the town centre an Army figure in an ill-fitting khaki battledress, with a ridiculously perched beret and comic gaiters, was no competition for the starched, eye-catching blue and white uniform of the sailors. Consequently, female attention was almost non-existent.

The time for passing-out finally arrived. In 1957, Asian flu was at its height and just before the big day, I fell victim. Missing the parade would have incurred the horror of being put back two weeks to pass out with the following intake. This was something I was determined would not happen.

In the true tradition of "all for one and one for all," the other squaddies rallied round and gave up their greatcoats and blankets, smothering me from head to toe to sweat out the virus overnight. It worked.

Postings followed. The one destination each soldier dreaded was Cyprus. It was an active service posting, as the Greek Cypriots were attempting to oust Britain from their island. It was the destination no-one wanted. We were informed that two of us were heading for Germany, three for Cyprus and the rest — lucky blighters — were to stay in Blighty.

Instinctively, I knew my fate. And there it was on the postings board: 23414718 Cairns to Cyprus. If it hadn't been for bad luck I'd have had no luck at all.

During the voyage to Limassol the implication of what lay ahead started to sink in. I was to spend 22 months away from home — in 1957 you only left home to get married, have a week at Butlin's or go to jail — and we were going to live on an island where most locals hated us and some would try to kill us. There were no tours of duty then. You were there for the duration of service. I was about to spend the best part of two years in a foreign land where the majority of the population didn't want me and would probably try to get rid of me by

whatever means possible. The voyage, with a stop at Algiers, took 10 days. On board we were shown films that warned rookie soldiers about the pitfalls of sneaky locals, bad hygiene and loose women.

After nine years as a clerk I became a teacher

We disembarked eventually at Limassol, and the following day my final destination was revealed. Two of us were to report to Larnaca and the RAOC sub-depot supplying the Army throughout the island.

I had never heard of Larnaca. Trucks transported us the 40 miles to the seaside town, and I got the first view of what was to be my home for almost two years. Surely those primitive tents were not the living quarters? Yes they were!

Sleeping four, the tents had one lightbulb, a paraffin stove, a bedside locker and a mosquito net.

A row of large open-air buckets with a seat on top served as the toilets. No partitions, so no privacy. They were emptied weekly by civilian contractors accompanied by dogs which chased the rats scampering all over the area during the operation. There were no showers, so as we were on the beach we used the sea to bathe, and were given soap that would create foam in salt water.

The whole place was surrounded by a barbed-wire fence patrolled by sentries with guard dogs.

Because of the political situation we were not allowed out of camp for six months unless on escort duty. Flies, heat, boredom, homesickness, periods of disappointment and sometimes fear were the main ingredients of life in camp.

There were hordes of flies, and ants appeared in their thousands if one crumb was dropped on the ground.

Our existence was punctuated by drinking sessions, watching old films and eagerly-awaited demob parties for the lucky blokes due to go home.

These parties were particularly welcome events. The whole camp, apart from those on duty, would assemble in the canteen and much cheap booze would be consumed.

On one occasion, in my naivety and inexperience I drank spirit after spirit. Slowly I became semi-comatose, and remembered nothing until next morning when I awoke feeling very, very ill and covered in blood from cuts all over my body.

It appears that in the middle of the night, desperate to relieve myself, I had staggered out of the tent in the blackness and run straight into the barbed wire fence. My shorts were ripped off and I sustained many cuts to my body — including my "three-piece suite." I was so far gone I hadn't felt any pain.

But I certainly did feel it when, covered in strips of Elastoplast, I forced myself to appear on morning muster parade. Missing a parade through drink was a court-martial offence, so I just had to bite the bullet and turn out.

Needless to say, future parties were treated with more restraint.

There was however, one morning parade that did cause me a problem. One button on my shirt had become undone and I was given seven days confined to barracks. Which, considering that we were confined to camp anyway, was laughable. But of course, I also had extra duties for those seven days and had to report to the guard commander for inspection in full battledress every night. All for having one button loose.

One other parade is firmly etched in my memory. A girl who had been raped in Larnaca complained that her attacker was a soldier who had an RAOC shoulder-flash. As our camp was the only RAOC base on the island we were ordered to attend an identification parade.

The girl walked slowly along the line staring a each face, and I began to sweat. What if I resembled the rapist? What if she wrongly accused me? Was it my imagination, or was she pausing too long in front of me? After an eternity, she moved on. My sigh of relief could be heard for miles. And I don't think the attacker was ever caught.

And then...

Eventually, my time was up and I returned to England and was greeted by a welcoming party of friends and family. But I realised how time had changed people. While I had been away I had received a Dear John letter, and those of my friends who had evaded National Service were well-established in careers and had made new friends in new social circles.

First I worked as a clerk with Dorman Long Steel. But after nine years of boredom I changed direction and attended teacher training college and became a primary school teacher.

When I returned to the now holiday island of Cyprus I discovered that Larnaca RAOC sub-depot had become Larnaca airport. And I was aware that the aircraft wheels were touching down on the very spot my tent had occupied for all those months back in 1957.

I looked out of the window and saw a skyline dominated by high-rise hotels and apartments covering the ground almost up to the airport. In 1957, Larnaca town was two miles away, and tourism non-existent. There was only one small hotel, which was usually empty, and one main bar situated on the front.

The town was divided into two areas, one occupied by the minority Turks and the other, larger area, by the majority Greek Cypriots.

Modern Larnaca is unrecognisable from its 1957 counterpart. The Turks have left and occupied the north of the island.

The biggest difference is that instead of driving them away with guns the Greek Cypriots now welcome the British to their shores.

I tried very hard, but could find no trace of Larnaca sub-depot. Now I have only memories and a few photographs to remind me of those eventful months.

National Service was an unpopular exercise, but it did provide lifelong memories, both good and bad. Did I enjoy it? No. Would I volunteer to do it again? No. Am I glad I did it? Yes. It was an experience that taught me the value of self-discipline.

— *Mike Cairns©*

23587211 Cpl Brian Cameron

I learned how to ride a horse, sail a dinghy and drink Keo!

I SERVED in Cyprus for a large part of my National Service but my only "war wound" was inflicted at Topsham Barracks, Exeter just a few days into basic training. While marching to a meal with my china mug held — as instructed — behind my back I slipped, fell backwards, smashed the mug and severed a tendon in one of my fingers. After a visit to Exeter General Hospital I was given a few days on light duties. And far from receiving compensation, I was made to pay for a new mug!

At least I now have a scar to impress old soldiers who had cushy numbers and not much to show for their two years in uniform.

I had been called up at the age of 21 in 1958 after completing my apprenticeship as a shopfitter's estimator. At the time I was living in Dorset where my family had been evacuated from North London. My father, by trade a carpenter and joiner, spent the war in boatyards in Poole harbour helping to build motor torpedo boats and harbour defence launches.

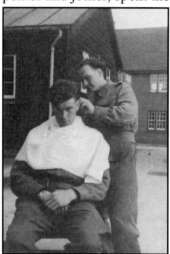
Alfresco haircut at Topsham

At the age of 13 I won a scholarship to the South Dorset Technical College in Weymouth where I completed a three-year course in building construction.

Then, after my apprenticeship, came the National Service medical and interview at which I expressed my choices to serve, in order of preference, in the Royal Navy, the RAF or in the Army with the Royal Engineers.

Shortly afterwards I received a letter from the War Office saying that my preferences had been "duly considered." But the letter concluded: "I am sorry to have to tell you that it has not been possible to meet your wishes because of the shortage of vacancies in these arms.

"Instead you are to go to the Gloucestershire Regiment where I hope you will enjoy your service."

Action man

Similar letters, I am sure, went to many, many conscripts.

Thus, in September 1958 a railway warrant arrived providing me with free travel to the headquarters of the Wessex Brigade at Exeter — and the beginning of two years in uniform.

Though the War Office said I would join the Glosters, at Exeter I was rebadged — with my old school pal, Brian Bowey — in the Devon and Dorset Regiment ready for posting to Cyprus.

But at the end of basic training I committed the Army's cardinal sin and volunteered for something — to join the Intelligence Corps.

That meant more training, this time on a course at the Intelligence Corps Centre at Maresfield Park Camp in Sussex.

From there I went to an offshoot of GCHQ Cheltenham at Woodhouse Eaves near Loughborough to learn decoding. Then, after a total of eight months training in the UK I was finally posted to a GCHQ wireless station at Ayios Nikolaos near Famagusta. So, flying out on one of the last Comet jet airliners, I went to Cyprus — which had just become quite peaceful — after all.

The unit, known as the 2nd Wireless Regiment and later renamed the 9th Signal Regiment, was involved in high-security work.

Our tin hut and tented base camp with its "long-drop" latrines, was guarded by local Turkish (Muslim) auxiliaries who protected us from the less-than-friendly Christian Greeks. But I spent an interesting and enjoyable time on the island.

I learned to ride a horse. I learned how to sail small racing dinghies. And I learned how to drink Keo beer, the local gut-rot that led to the "Grotch Shield" for the last man to be sick after drinking too much on an evening out, being hung over my bed on more than one occasion.

Still travelling in retirement

I am in the centre row, third from right in this photograph taken at Exeter

Gradually the days on my peechi (demob) chart were crossed off, and eventually I flew back to the UK all nice and bronzed ready for demob.

And that was the end of my military career except for an alarming Army Reserve stand-by some 12 months later due to one of the Middle East flare-ups. But Cpl Cameron was never needed.

And then...

After National Service I continued in shopfitting work, first as an estimator, then chief estimator and technical sales representative before becoming a sales manager. I ended up as services director for a national departmental store group. In 1963 I married Annabel, the girl I had been courting before my call-up, and since my retirement we now enjoy foreign travel — having visited, among many other locations, the Arctic Circle, Antarctica as far south as tourists can go, the Himalayas and the Galapagos Islands — walking and gardening. We have also gained gold medals for ballroom and Latin-American dancing.

— Brian Cameron©

Sadly Keo led to the death of one of the lads on Christmas Eve 1959. In a group that had been out and had a great deal to drink, he was unable to get out of the tent when it caught fire in the night.

The CO was returned to the UK over this incident because apparently there was some problem with the fire-fighting equipment in the camp.

Standing at ease in the Cyprus sunshine

The guardroom at Maresfield

45

23090359 Gnr Roy Chave

Our introduction to Army life was nothing to smile about

THE TRAIN on which I arrived with several others to begin basic National Service at Tonfanau in North Wales was met by a second-lieutenant who greeted us with the words: "Smile now, because you won't smile again for a long time!"

As part of the 41st Field Regiment, Royal Artillery, we trained on 3.7 anti-aircraft guns, and the drill was that if there was a miss-fire we should wait for a couple of minutes before the gun was unloaded and the shell carried away to a safe distance — about 100 yards.

One day when there was a miss-fire I discovered how fast one can run with a very heavy shell.

I actually missed quite a lot of the early training because I suffered from a chest infection and had to report to the MO.

Eventually I was posted to Egypt, sailing on the Dilwara. We stopped for a few hours at Malta where I got into trouble for saluting a warrant officer. Well, I was just a sprog!

In Egypt the regiment was stationed near Ismailia and I became a motor transport clerk at BHQ 88.

I had my own tent to work and sleep in, and when I was settling in I found a tin containing about 300 photos of naked girls, presumably left there by the previous occupant. They were quite tame by today's standards, but as it was a chargeable offence to have pornographic pictures I quickly buried them in the sand. They are probably still there today.

On one occasion a show was organised. It included several highly-attractive belly-dancers who put on a very erotic performance.

Once several of us were sent out to a place called Abul Sultan, which was in the middle of nowhere.

Two of us were ordered out on night patrol. I had a loaded rifle and the other chap had a sten. We were a couple of 18-year-olds just out of (very) basic training and there we were with weapons we had probably fired only a couple of times in our life.

But off we went into the desert, making our way in the bright moonlight. After a while we could see a man standing still in the desert ahead. My mate with the sten eased closer

while I covered him with the rifle.

The fellow did not move. Then, as we got about 12 feet away we realised we had been stalking a small unlit searchlight about the height of a man with the light at the top just the size of a head.

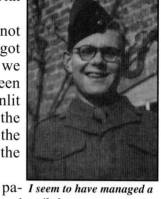

I seem to have managed a smile here

We continued patrolling, and then heard whispering in the darkness. We were terrified, thinking we were about to get our throats cut. So we legged it as fast as we could.

The regimental headquarters building was made of wood, and when the time came to pull out of Egypt we were issued with sledge-hammers and axes and told us to smash the

Those Army days are over now

place down so there would be nothing left for the Egyptians.

I'm afraid that some of the chaps got a bit carried away with the chance to destroy a building they had come to hate, and had to be calmed down.

I was in the advance party which went on ahead by rail to organise things at Port Said. In charge was 2nd Lieut Robinson, a National Service officer who was a train buff. He arranged rides for us, two at a time, on the footplate of a steam train. I still remember my ride at around midnight with the train driver in his long "nightshirt."

We sailed for England on the Empire Ken, and on the first day out had to parade in the gangway for inspection. But because we were in the gangway there was no room for the officers to inspect us. So we were ordered to lie at attention on our bunks for inspection.

When we docked at Southampton Customs were easy on us squaddies, but I heard that one sergeant had to pay duty on his suitcase.

Though I was due for leave, and lived at Salisbury, only 20 miles from Southampton, I first had to report to way up north to my new posting at Barnard Castle, and next day travel all the way back to Salisbury.

We were stationed at Barnard Castle for three months, during which time there was an IRA scare and we did patrols armed with pickaxe handles. We certainly meant business!

I was still an MT clerk, which was now a very quiet job, so on sunny days I would put some documents under my arm and go walkabout. Those documents never let me down. I was never asked where I was going.

But one night I was put on both battery guard duty and regimental guard duty at the same time.

As I thought the regimental guard was the more important I went on that. I was promptly charged for not doing battery guard. But commonsense prevailed and I was let off.

Before I completed my National Service I did some time in Germany, stationed in an old German army barracks near Essen. My MT office was a cellar, with another lock-up cellar for stores. More than once when it was quiet I slipped in there and had a kip on some old lorry seats.

I remember that though we were not allowed to wear jeans the CO used to go about in plus-fours with chukka boots and pale yellow knee-length socks.

My own dress style sometimes earned me a reprimand because I used to let the badge on my beret slip round to the front of my forehead — which is where the Tank Corps wore it — instead of being over the left eye.

So when I reported each day to Major Drake the dialogue frequently went: "Chave!" Yessir. "You are not in the bloody Tank Corps, are you?" No sir. "Then get that beret on straight." Yessir.

In addition to the camp NAAFI there was a YMCA where it was possible to buy a roll for a penny. Or for an extra halfpenny you would get peanut butter on it. Many a time I spent my last penny there.

We were expected to take annual tests that included marches and climbing walls and things like that, which I found difficult, especially — as I was only five foot four — trying to climb a six-foot wall. But a friendly clerk put on my records that I had done these tests.

Once a year the regiment was subject to an admin inspection. I remember one gunner who had a knack of getting into trouble was put in a truck during the admin, and the driver was told to drive him around to keep him out of the way until the inspection was over.

At about the time of my demob the Suez crisis raised fears that I might have to do another six months, but this didn't happen and soon I was on my way to Woolwich Barracks to return to Civvy Street.

The day I was demobbed I had to report to a TA Centre in Exeter. And once again, just like my Barnard Castle travel experience, I passed my home town of Salisbury, got to Exeter and then travelled all the way back to Salisbury.

And then...

I returned to my old job as a clerk with a bus company, but then went to work for the Wellworthy Piston Ring Co where I finished up as a C grade setter. I did 39 years there before ill-health forced my retirement.

When I was 24 I began dating a girl of 15. We were engaged when she became 17, married two years later and have now been together for 46 years.

— **Roy Chave**©

47

23938116 Gnr Len Chesham

The Army set me on the right road to a career as a driver

AFTER I completed my training in the Royal Artillery I was told I was to be trained as a driver. I had never even been behind the wheel of a car, but the Army said I was to become a driver, and set me on a road that led, via bulldozers, coaches, taxis, artics and lorries to the position of mayor's chauffeur.

My first two weeks of National Service in 1953 had been spent at Oswestry before I was sent to Rhyl in North Wales for more square-bashing. It was there, for no reason that I could fathom, they put me on a driving course and I passed my test on a Bedford three-tonner.

Then I was given a posting to Hong Kong, but while on embarkation leave I had a telegram telling me to report to Woolwich, which I thought would be for a boat. But when I got there I was put on a train to join the Royal Artillery HQ at Bunde in Germany.

Within two weeks I was driving staff cars, VW Beetles with crash gear boxes. Then I got a really cushy job.

The CO's driver left, and though this was a job that usually went to a regular soldier, I was chosen to take his place.

So I spent my time driving the brigadier around in an Opel Kapitan, which meant I was excused all duties. If anyone tried to get me to do something I only had to say I was the CO's driver and they would say OK.

I did once take part in an exercise on the Hohne ranges, and was involved in a frightening incident.

A gunner who was filling a Fordson vehicle spilled quite a lot of petrol, and some of it soaked into his denims. Then he decided to have a cigarette, and whoosh, his clothes caught fire. Instead of trying to put out the flames the chap ran off. Three of us chased him, and when we caught him jumped on top of him and rolled him on the ground. He was lucky to escape with just minor burns. After that we called him The Flaming Man Act.

Another incident I remember was very funny at the time, but could have got my pal and me into quite serious trouble.

We asked the batmen who were pressing a couple of officers' uniforms to lend them to us. We dressed up in the uniforms and called a group of recruits who had just arrived in the barracks to get on parade.

We then ordered them to do daft things like run around the parade ground with their rifles over their heads It was a real giggle. Well, it was for us, but the recruits were as scared as hell.

Of course, impersonating an officer is a serious offence, and next day the sergeant tried to find out who was responsible but never caught us.

And then...

Though my interest in motor vehicles which began in the Army continued after demob, my first driving experience in Civvy Street was on a bulldozer building bridges for the Lea Conservancy Board. But I was keen to get back into lorries, so took a job as a driver with a waste paper company.

In 1960 I passed the Advanced Driving Test, and two years later bought an Anglia 5cwt van to commute to work. I entered it in a Ford Anglia competition, and was delighted to become British champion in the van section. My prize was £250 and a camera.

In 1977 I obtained a PSV licence and had an 18-month spell as a coach driver. Then I

How times have changed. From an Army truck, polishing the CO's Opel to a wedding car

At your service. I swapped my Army beret for a peaked cap and ran a taxi business

One of the perks of the job — a close encounter with Barbara Windsor

But my choice of vehicle changed again in 1981 when I passed the Hackney Carriage test and ran a taxi service in Southend before becoming a chauffeur with Southend Council. Then I was appointed as the mayor's chauffeur and deputy civic mace-bearer.

So after being told in the Army that I was going to be a driver whether I liked it or not I have now driven just about every type of vehicle on the road.

However, I gave it all up in 1996 when I retired after meeting my partner Ros. A year later we had a son, my first child.

— Len Chesham©

changed jobs again, driving 32-ton artics, working mainly with container transport out of Tilbury Docks.

One of my proudest moments. British champion in the Ford Anglia van competition

49

23024521 Pte Cliff Chudley

Escaped prisoner came at us armed with a floorboard

SHORTLY after my eighteenth birthday, I received a letter from Her Majesty asking (I think that was the word, maybe instructing) me to attend a government building in Exeter. After a written examination and a medical I was asked what Army branch I wanted to join. I asked for the Royal Engineers — and got the Devonshire Regiment.

I was informed that my presence was required at Topsham Barracks, Exeter on May 6, 1954 and they sent me a railway warrant for travel purposes.

On arrival at Exeter I was dumped in an Army truck and taken to the barracks. I went through the indoctrination process, and was given another haircut, as it was deemed that the one I had the previous day was not short enough.

Then I was given my uniform, blankets and everything and taken to a barrack block where I stayed for 10 weeks.

We weren't allowed out for four weeks, and then they gave us a double dose of TAB and TT. Sent us home saying "don't go drinking, and get plenty of rest." I hit the sack and don't remember much of that weekend at all.

We did not know what hit us on the Monday morning as we had rifle drill with sore arms and muscles.

Anyway, on a nice wet day, we had our passing out parade. Presiding officer was the CIGS, Sir John Harding, a rather short man. Being six-feet tall I had to look down on him.

I was then sent to Chichester for a four-week clerical course. When I returned I was too late for the last draft to Kenya and was posted to the Topsham Barracks Orderly Room as the orders clerk.

I learned the hard way, as there was no-one to show me how. I made many mistakes, including saying that a sergeant had been married before I had issued details of his divorce. For my sins I was sent to Infantry Records for a day to be appraised of what went on.

I also remember being sent as relief clerk to the 130 Inf. Brigade TA. But I still had to do my own job in the evening on my return. As a result I forgot to issue orders for a chap to be posted to the Engineers at Chatham for some training.

From Orders Clerk to bowls

Three days as duty clerk was the punishment.

Speaking of punishments, I also had five days' duty clerk for not cleaning the adjutant's desk. We had the builders in at the time and my instructions were quite clear in my mind, "don't clean the office with all the work and dust going on."

However, being somewhat naive I literally interpreted that as "don't go in." I should have understood the military mind, because what they really meant was that I should clean and tidy the adjutant's desk but not bother about the rest of the room.

We had to do a lot of guard duties, particularly in the period when the IRA had attacked the REME at Arborfield. During this time, on one freezing winter's night, one of the regimental policemen had to go across the road to check that everything was in order at the TA Centre.

But he came back all bloodied and said he had been attacked. Whoops, the guard was doubled. But when the Special Investigations Branch came down he owned up to slipping on the icy stairs. I never saw anyone get posted to Malaya so quickly.

On another occasion a prisoner arrived to spend 28 days in our detention cells. He broke up two cells, got out of one and almost escaped before the CSM got him.

Then one evening when I was on duty eight of us plus duty officer and a regimental policeman faced him down the corridor of the cells. He had broken up the wooden floor, burrowed his way out, and came at us with a piece of flooring with nails sticking out.

A decision was made to place double guard on him at nights, and I was one of two who were put in the corridor to stop him breaking out.

Towards the end of my Army life I had jankers for dirty gaiters. I had just finished cleaning the Orderly Room and officers' rooms and had to go on parade at 0800 hours.

The officer did not like the colour and I was

duly charged. Another five days. But I telephoned the guardroom and said that I was duty clerk for that period. That way I avoided defaulters' bugle call and only had to turn up at 2200 hours for the last defaulters' call.

And then...

On return to civvy life in 1956, I went back to Torquay station where I had worked before call-up and spent the summer there. Then I went to a small station up the hill called Torre as a booking clerk.

Later that winter I moved to Newton Abbot Goods to learn all about accounts. With the opportunity to go to Paddington on secondment for about four months with a temporary raise in pay and grade I worked in the Commercial Department.

Life was enjoyable, and I earned a lot of overtime working in the Paddington Enquiry Bureau in the evenings. I was asked to stay on (must have done a good job), but would have had to lose the grade. I said that I could not live up there on a lower graded pay.

So I returned to the Exeter area and was put on the relief. Quite interesting, if you like getting up at four in the morning and cycling from Torquay to Teignmouth in pouring rain. Still, I saw plenty of life.

The year 1957 saw a big change in my life. One evening in Torquay I met a girl from Manchester, and suffice to say that we stayed together and have been married for some 48 years.

At this time I also moved back to Paddington and changed departments from Commercial to Operating and joined a research group. Spent three years travelling the Western Region working in marshalling yards also working on stations doing passenger surveys.

This was the time when cuts were being made, and I became redundant in 1960 and went to Bristol District Freight Train Office, quite a busy place. Dealt with everything, special train movements, timekeeping etc.

In the November of that year I went to Cardiff Division to the Freight Train Planning department, really enjoyable but hard work. This was especially so when the NCB decided to change their coal movements, usually telling us on the

Thursday before the changes operated on the following Monday. We then had to work until finish that day to revise the train service, issue train crew diagrams and the various notices.

Dieselisation came along, more changes when the powers-that-be thought that one diesel locomotive could do the work of four steam engines. Revised services and closure of marshalling yards were the order of the day. Then I ended up by being in charge of the planning of all passenger and freight train services for West Wales.

In 1970 I moved to Bristol in the freight planning office and became embroiled in more rationalisation (cuts, I called it), then moved across to a new section dealing exclusively with the movement of stone from the Mendips and South Gloucestershire to various locations, this being the time of the building of the motorways.

While in Bristol I moved to the Rolling Stock Section, and became involved in a computer system called TOPS (Total Operations Processing System) usually referred to as Tyneside's Own Promotion Scheme simply because of the number of people from the North East in it.

Had the opportunity to go back to Paddington on TOPS and I took it with both hands. I stayed with this group until it was broken up at Swindon. Then became head of the Freight Train Section, although somehow I think it was because of my knowledge of the workings of TOPS and the need for it to be introduced in the section.

Still, I became involved as a trainer in new TOPS schemes and attended meetings on freight train performance. My life of working permanently for BR came to an end in March 1993. The previous October, when the Freight Railways wanted to get rid of 18,000 people I volunteered and was accepted.

However, that was not the end of my railway career. Two months later I was headhunted by Regional Railways to do training for their passenger scheme and spent a further 18 months doing this work.

I now live in relative peace, having been treasurer, captain, president and secretary of a bowls club which I joined in July 1993.

—Cliff Chudley ©

2553647 SAC Mike Clift

RAF gave us all a 'housewife.' What a great joke that was!

NATIONAL Service for most 18-year-olds meant being peremptorily removed from the family home for the first time. For me it also meant a long train journey from Bournemouth to the RAF camp at Padgate. I soon met others making for the same destination, and we left the train at Warrington, which marked our introduction to being shouted and sworn at.

Then there was a visit to the stores to be provided with all the items of kit which comprised our new uniform. One item was called a housewife. I think this was a joke. It was just a collection of needles and threads. But it was much used, due to boots which seemed, certainly in the early days, to wear holes in your socks very quickly. One then just stitched the edges together. On leave later, I was shown just how to darn a sock. That's one thing that I have never forgotten.

We were also given our service number, which had to be memorised. Seven digits, but only the last three were normally used.

Health checks and frequent lectures followed, and during one I recall an officer informing us that we were being trained for war. Not what I wanted to hear!

After a few days we were despatched to Hednesford for a two-month period of square-bashing. The camp was high on windswept Cannock Chase, and about 20 of us occupied a hut where the only heat was from a coke stove. The conditions were primitive, having to wash and shave in cold water then get ready for parade at 8am.

One health problem arose, for which the control measure was to keep all windows permanently open, including the very cold nights.

Fortunately we were provided with another blanket.

One regular evening occupation was working on the toecaps of our boots to make them shine. This quite literally was spit and polish. Blanco was used to colour our belt and gaiters. Cap badges and brass buttons also had to be polished.

We were supervised, drilled and inspected by corporals who were not much older than us, but who wore these two stripes. So they were gods.

They had the task of turning a diverse group into a unified section that would respond immediately to orders.

We had injections, and on one occasion a booster, against what I don't recall. But the following morning we were on rifle drill with very stiff arms, which was far from fun.

One regular event was the kit inspection. All clothing had to be set out in a traditional manner. Blankets and sheets had to be in a regular block. Your clothing as well as knife, fork and spoon had to be placed on the bed in a predetermined order. This was then checked and demolished if our superiors perceived any slight imperfection. On occasional Saturday mornings we were detailed off to pick up dogends, matches and any other stray items from the parade ground.

Here I met up with another who, like me, had been employed in horticulture. Talking plants was a good way to relieve the boredom. We both met up again after National Service when students at the Royal Botanic Gardens, Kew.

After passing-out parade I was sent to RAF Celle, West Germany, to become an air traffic control clerk.

Hut 53 at Hednesford, where I am second from the right, front row

52

What a contrast. Here accommodation was in brick barrack blocks, originally built for the Luftwaffe, where just five or six people occupied a centrally-heated room.

Three squadrons were kept very active, flying De Havilland Vampire fighters during what was then the Cold War. We were just four minutes' flying time from the Russian Zone in East Germany.

The weather in Germany was more severe than in the UK. Very low temperatures and snow were regular in winter. Frequently when snow had fallen we were employed scattering sand over the runways from the back of lorry to keep the station open.

I remember once being asked by an air traffic controller to phone the met officer and ask why it was raining, as this had not been forecast. "This is not rain, it's just a little precipitation" was the reply.

During periods of night flying when the control tower was illuminated it became the attraction of many maybugs or cockchafers. They are quite sizeable insects and the noise they made colliding with the tower windows was constant.

It was decreed from on high that all flying stations in Germany must be mobile. One result of this order was that we had to vacate the control tower and work from caravans concealed among trees, apart from the one situated right at the end of the runway.

The other aspect of this directive suddenly became a reality when the entire camp was ordered to move. We travelled in long convoys for two days before arriving at a temporary flying station deep in Belgium.

We travelled along the autobahns and crossed the Rhine through war-torn Cologne, where rebuilding was then about to begin.

The exercise was against the American Air Force, which was flying Sabres. We lived under canvas, but those of us who were ex-Scouts managed to construct a framework to lift the bedding above the groundsheet.

The following year, on yet another mobility exercise, we moved to a temporary flying station just a few miles west of Cologne. This provided us with very different memories, particularly of the fine cathedral, the railway bridge which was then still operating on just one track and the 4711 Eau de Cologne factory.

To cross the North Sea between Harwich and the Hook of Holland troopships were employed. These had to accommodate a good number of forces' personnel on each journey, but stability was not their strongpoint. There was one particularly rough voyage when I returned from leave in January 1953 and we docked at the Hook several hours late.

Then we heard that Canvey Island and parts of East Anglia and had been seriously affected by this exceptional storm. Large areas were under water and there were many deaths. Over the next few days servicemen returning from leave were retained in Holland to provide flood assistance there.

I recall Coronation Day in 1953 when practically everyone on the station was on parade. It was, unlike in Britain, a very fine warm sunny day.

One day a carload of us went to the Belsen concentration camp. It was, perhaps appropriately, a dull, very cold December afternoon and the experience still today leaves me with horrific memories.

Cigarettes were rationed, costing one shilling (now 5 pence) a packet. I had never smoked, and many section colleagues happily took my allocation.

At this time I began to take an interest in music and attended the camp music group to widen my knowledge. Later the Combined Services Entertainment Organisation gave us the opportunity to see a real opera, Madame Butterfly, performed by a touring Italian opera group with the Hamburg Theatre Orchestra at the Union Theatre in Celle.

During my time in Germany I bought my first camera, a pre-war Ihagee using size 127 films, which I later updated to a new Zeiss Icon Nettar. This sparked my interest in photography, and the two are now part of my camera collection. Much later I bought an Olympus OM1 camera, but now I have joined the increasing numbers of people who use digital cameras.

And then...

Prior to National Service I began horticulture work at Stewart's Nurseries in Ferndown, Dorset and was involved with seed collection, cutting-making, potting and helping prepare display stands at flower shows.

One problem was how to learn all those Latin names. Common names were never mentioned. The manager had a different plant in his buttonhole each day. You were told the name once and then reminded when he next caught up with you. Afterwards you were expected to know it.

After National Service I continued to work in nurseries, spending a period at Hilliers Nurseries at Winchester until I was accepted as a student at Royal Botanic Gardens, Kew in October 1956.

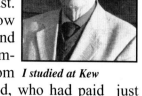

I studied at Kew

That was a total contrast. Here, in the show glasshouses, one met and was questioned by members of the public from many parts of the world, who had paid just one old penny to get in.

I was employed in the glasshouses or nursery by day. Lectures and studying took up most evenings. The gardens were open to the public at 10am. One morning at about 10.15 an American lady asked directions for the nearest exit. She wanted to "do" Hampton Court as well and get back to Heathrow to catch her plane at 4.30pm!

After Kew I worked for Waterers Nurseries at Bagshot, who were hybridising and raising a new race of compact hardy rhododendrons, now known as the Yakushimanum group. Today many of our introductions can be found around the world.

When we began looking at the idea of growing plants in containers I was involved in this development, formulating the compost ingredients after experimentation, watching for pest and disease attacks and controlling the nasties involved. All this was a continual challenge.

Horticulture, particularly the role of nurseries, has changed dramatically over the years with today only some specialist nurseries concentrating on the interesting aspects of plant production.

— Mike Clift©

The National Service Commemorative Medal, which is sponsored on behalf of the Royal British Legion, has already raised more than £440,000 for the Poppy Appeal. It is available only to those who performed national service, both military and civilian, between January 1939 and December 1960, their next of kin or direct descendants. Worn separately from campaign or gallantry decorations, it is available from Award Productions, PO Box 300, Shrewsbury SY5 6WP.

My job in the Orderly Room became a nice little earner

I WAS working in the advertisement department of the Western Morning News when I was called up and ordered to report to the Exeter headquarters of the Devonshire Regiment, who at the time were serving in Kenya.

At the end of basic training a notice went up saying "pay clerk required." I thought that if I could land this job I would miss the draft to Kenya and a confrontation with the very aggressive Mau Mau.So I put my

At Exeter in 1955

name down, in company I think with about 70 others. At the interview when asked what I did in civilian life I decided to say that I had been an accountant. At that they couldn't get me into the pay office quickly enough. And some six months later they couldn't get me out quickly enough. The damage I had done in my six months probably took them six years to put right.

But the period I spent there did help me to set up a little business. The pay office was at the end of the barracks next to the wall, and adjacent to a large pile of firewood chopped by chaps on jankers.

I would put these sticks into sacks and swing them over the wall into a field where I would collect them, haul them on to a bicycle and ride round the houses selling them.

But this useful source of income did not last long because I was put down for another draft, this time to Germany. Then it was decided that I should remain at Exeter as a clerk in the Orderly Room.

This was absolutely heaven-sent because I was put in charge of camp stationery and supplies. So I was able to take notebooks, boxes of typewriter ribbons and various other sundries to the council offices where the father of one of my friends would accept them for small amounts of cash. I would also sell big balls of string to the local allotments association.

One Christmas I was detailed to guard the camp armoury, which I did — but at a distance. I put on the radio to give the impression I was in the building in case anyone checked, and went out dancing.

Another Christmas incident I remember probably went down in the annals of the officers mess as The Strange Case of the Missing Turkey Legs. The cooked turkey had been left near a barred window to cool. So I put my arm through and tried to pull it out, but succeeded only in ripping the legs off. Next day when the officers arrived, the bird was found on the floor — minus its legs.

Demob eventually came but I actually served two years and one day because I got demobbed, returned to my bed that night, and next morning went to breakfast and then took my driving test and went home.

And then...

I had to think about work, and decided to start a catering company. I bought an Austin A35 van and had it painted with the words Southern Catering and my name and address. I obtained

I'm working today as a taxi driver

large plastic circles numbered one to 12 which I would stick on the passenger door and driver's door each day. Later I would peel them off and put on another number. So in the morning I would be driving, say van number three, and in the evening probably number seven. This made people think we had 12 vans and were a very big company.

Business blossomed, but I was doing this from home and it was really driving us all crackers. So I sold it and went to FW Woolworths where I worked as deputy manager or manager in 21 stores over 23 years.

One of my stores was at Dalston where the mother of ticket tout Stan Flashman worked on the groceries section. So I got invited to everything, international football, cricket Test matches and superb London shows. I had a great time.I then went home to Brighton and started a taxi business with three cars and six drivers. And that is what I am doing to the present day.

— *Dick Copp©*

2511099 Cpl Roy Damsell

How I managed to conjure up some extra time off duty

WHEN I was called to go for a medical prior to National Service my brother gave me some advice. He recalled that at his Navy medical during the war two men had difficulty producing a urine sample. So he told me to drink a pint of water before leaving home, which I did. But it was a 45-minute bus ride to the medical centre, and then we had a written examination.

So I was bursting when eventually I was given a glass jar and asked to provide a specimen. As I was approaching the top of the jar the examiner shouted out "stop" — which proved to be impossible. Luckily a galvanised bucket had been provided for just such a contingency.

On March 15, 1951 I caught the train to Warrington and from there a very large group of 18-year-old lads were transferred by coach to the RAF's kitting-out establishment at Padgate.

We were there for a week and during that time every recruit was issued with one best blue, one working blue, three shirts with separate collars, four pairs of socks, two black ties, one pair each of boots and shoes, a large ceramic mug, a knife, fork and spoon and a canvas kitbag to hold it all.

Spirits were raised when we heard we would each receive a housewife, only to be dashed again when we discovered that this was a small cloth bag containing a ball of sock-mending wool, some button cotton and a few needles.

To collect your uniform you had to walk slowly along a corridor in a large warehouse where stores personnel judged your size at a glance. A team of civilian women altered the garments to fit.

The rule was that any part of your uniform in your possession had to be worn, and for those items not yet received or being altered, you wore civilian clothing. You have never seen such a mixture of styles as those that appeared at the daily parades. By the end of the week however it had all come together, and everyone was then sent to recruit training schools around the country for six weeks' square-bashing. I went to Innsworth, near Gloucester.

We were placed in the charge of drill instructors who were all corporals. Some of these were career airmen but others were just doing their National Service. We were billeted in wooden huts, each holding about 30 beds in two rows of 15 with wooden lockers between. Heat was provided by two coke-burning iron stoves. Our drill instructor informed us that we had to keep our uniforms smartly pressed at all times, and since we were not allowed out of camp and therefore could not buy an iron, he could provide us with one at a cost of sixpence each. Of course, at the end of our training the DI retained the iron ready for the next intake.

So the six weeks went by, during which time we practised marching and drilled with rifles for five-and-a-half days a week, and were moulded from a bunch of untidy recruits into a smart group of proud airmen whose marching, though perhaps not Brigade of Guards standard, was nevertheless a sight to behold.

All this led up to the passing-out parade when a visiting air-marshal took the salute and we marched behind an RAF band and demonstrated every manoeuvre we had been taught. We were as proud as could be.

During the square-bashing period we were asked to choose the RAF trade we would prefer to follow for the next two years. Though shown a long list of trades there was no explanation of what they entailed. Both my father and brother had been in the services during the war and both told me I would not go far wrong if I could get into the stores. So I applied for the job of Clerk Provisioning.

However this turned out to have nothing to do with the stores, but was a system of stock control for every part of every RAF aeroplane, vehicle and piece of equipment. My first posting was to a maintenance unit at Sutton Coldfield.

I quickly realised that this massive intake of 18-year-olds doing National Service was putting a strain on finding sufficient jobs to keep them occupied, but the RAF welcomed anyone with a talent. This could often be used as a means of cutting down on the number of parades you had to attend. The station warrant officer at Sutton Coldfield loved parades and insisted that we had one every day.

I was not good enough at football to make the station team and so instead I joined the fencing club and quite soon found myself representing

Some of the occupants of Hut 145 at Innsworth in April 1951. I am in the middle wearing a vest

our station as part of the team which regularly travelled to other units for matches.

I also joined the station's concert party because I had been a magician for many years and was a member of two magical societies.

The entertainments officer arranged for me to have two days' leave and for a van and driver to be at my disposal to go to my home to pick up my equipment. It was surprising how frequently the concert party found it necessary to rehearse its shows!

We mainly worked a five-and-half day week except once a month when we were given both Saturday and Sunday off. From Sutton Coldfield I used to hitch-hike home to Ilford where I lived and then catch the train back from Euston to Birmingham late Sunday night. The train arrived in Birmingham at 3.15am. There was an elderly Post Office driver named Percy whose job was to meet the London train and transport the sacks of mail to Sutton Coldfield railway station.

He allowed servicemen to sit on the mail sacks, and at the railway station we would unload the sacks for him and he would then take us to the camp gates and we would all give him sixpence.

There was no other way of travelling from Birmingham to the camp at that time of the morning without this unofficial service.

Sutton Coldfield was a small maintenance unit, and with new National Servicemen arriving every week there was simply not enough accommodation or jobs for all of them and so I was posted to a very much larger unit at Stafford.

At this unit there was a large cinema which easily converted into a theatre with lots of facilities. The concert party here included three professional entertainers who were doing their National Service. The entertainments officer not only had all my equipment brought over from Sutton Coldfield by lorry, but also arranged for the two WAAFs who had been my assistants in my act to be posted to my new unit.

We had a large entertainments budget which allowed us to hire many lovely costumes and we started to produce shows of quite a high standard. This attracted the attention of the local RAF Association who asked if we would put on a fund-raising show for them. From this we received requests from other RAF stations and organisations.

But between concerts I still had to work at my job of stock control, and by taking examinations gradually I rose in rank from AC2 to AC1 to LAC to SAC to corporal.

We ate in large messes, and the food, although probably of a reasonable standard when it entered the cookhouse, was not very appetising when the cooks had finished with it. I have never been able to eat liver since those days because the liver served in the mess would have been better nailed to the sole of your shoe.

The evening meal was tea, and as you walked along the mess queue two thick slices of bread were placed on your tray. Then a spoonful of jam was put on one of the slices and finally a knob of butter was put on the jam. You sat at the table and tried to spread the butter under the jam.

The menus were designed to be filling rather than a gourmet's delight, but of course it must be remembered that many food items were still rationed from the war years.

Out of uniform, I went into advertising

And then...

Though some National Servicemen learned a trade during their period of service which they could use in civilian life very many of us considered it to be a waste of two years of our lives.

When I left the service I joined a large London advertising agency and stayed in advertising for the whole of my career. My wife and I have been married for 52 years and we have three children and four grandchildren. When I retired we moved from Amersham in Buckinghamshire to delightful Dorset, and I am still a member of the Magic Circle.

— Roy Damsell©

23010891 Pte Brian Davis

All go from morning to night — and that meant at the double

REVEILLE at the Devonshire Regiment barracks at Exeter was at 6.30. An unearthly hour, we thought. Until we were told that because there was so much to do on our first day training to be soldiers we would be getting out of our beds at 4am. At that point we would have readily accepted the luxury of lying in until 6.30.

The good news was that as soon as we could show we were fast enough to get everything done in time for inspection at eight we would be allowed to remain in bed for an extra half-hour, or even as late as 5am!

And there was certainly plenty to be done. As well as preparing ourselves and our personal kit, and laying out beds and bedding in regulation order we had to ensure the room was spotless.

Every surface had to be dusted and every crevice cleaned. And the floor in the recruits' block had to be polished and shone until the room corporal was content that his beautiful face was beautifully reflected in it.

This was achieved by buffing the floor with the heavy "bumper." This padded weight with a long handle was pushed and pulled across the floor, often with someone sitting on the end to give added weight and ensure the surface really gleamed.

By the time morning inspection arrived we felt we had done a day's work. But the day was only just beginning.

Now there was the real soldier training. Most of us were homesick, but we didn't have time for it. Every minute of the day was accounted for, and every minute belonged to the Army.

Drill, weapon training, lectures, Blanco-ing equipment, map-reading, field-exercises, gymnastics, the assault course. Change into denims, back into battledress and webbing. Two minutes to get into your vest and shorts and up to the gym. Now back into denims. We didn't stop.

And no chance of walking to the next location to get one's breath back. It was all at the double until an instructor — who probably himself wanted a break anyway — might say: "Okay, you can take five for a smoke."

There was usually some time to take things a little easy during meals, but even then one was always conscious that a great deal had to be done as soon as breakfast, lunch or tea was over.

What I remember most about meals were the ubiquitous baked beans, the tea-chests of sliced bread which had usually been in position long before mealtime and washing-up.

A sink of water was provided into which we had to rinse our plates, mug and cutlery. The water began hot and clear. But after scores of soldiers had made use of it, this very quickly became cold, greasy and decidedly murky.

Slowly, as we grew to be more adept at our work the daily programme became more interesting — like piling into trucks and riding to the rifle ranges to learn how to kill people.

Or there might be fieldcraft instruction on Woodbury Common. That was a mere six or seven miles away so obviously within walking distance!

Actually, we were often taken there by truck, but made to march back, along the roads where "normal" people could be seen in normal houses doing normal things. Another world. But we strode along singing the hit of the day I Long to go a'Wandering.

On return to our barrack room there was feet inspection, and blisters had to be burst with a needle sterilised in a lighted match.

On the common we hacked trenches into the ground and then attempted to sleep in these cold holes. Next morning before dawn we would attack or be attacked. Again we were finding out how to kill people. But my own chances of learning one of the methods of despatching an enemy were jeopardised on my first visit to Woodbury Common when I lost my bayonet.

This was a court-martial offence, but somehow my training instructor managed to "acquire" another for me.

I am in the back row, right, with some of my basic training pals

58

How he did it I never knew, but it gave me a lesson in the way a squad became a team with everyone helping everyone else.

Army days

Half a century on

This was the time of the Mau Mau troubles in Kenya and the war against the Communists in Korea. So anyone who appeared not to be learning the basics of survival, or finding that using a rifle or brengun was not the easiest task to accomplish, was told he had better learn quickly because "in a few weeks you could be doing this for real."

Eventually, after six weeks we were deemed to be sufficiently prepared as soldiers for our passing-out ceremony. The traumas of training were forgotten as we paraded in our immaculate uniforms in front of the inspecting officer and our proud parents.

In a "welcome" lecture on our first day a training sergeant had told us: "You scruffy, long-haired, unfit heap of misfits are going to be turned into soldiers. There's the easy way and the hard way. The easy way isn't easy, and the hard way is bloody hard."

Well, we had made it. We had become soldiers, and just as importantly, we had become a team. A group of teenagers from all backgrounds had been thrown together and learned how to work with one another. We mixed and made friends from all sections of society. Something that would never have happened without National Service.

Among my contemporaries at Exeter were grammar school boys, an old-Etonian and several farm labourers. But we learned to muck in and help each another, the slower or less-adept being helped by the others.

A "posh" education meant nothing when it came to ironing knife-edge creases into trousers or getting mirror-bright barrack room floors. We were all in it together, so we worked together.

After a week's leave many of the intake found themselves on the boat to Kenya or Korea. But I was among several selected to remain in Exeter where it was felt we would be better employed helping the wheels of the depot to run smoothly. "Davis, you are to be a clerk in the Orderly Room."

This meant working directly under Dick Shorland, a regular soldier who had served in Burma during the war. He was now a warrant officer with the grand title of Orderly Room Quartermaster Sergeant, and referred to simply as Q. A friendly man who would always try to get his staff off parades or inspections if he was able.

My job was mainly to type out the day's Company Orders and take dictation from the adjutant when he wanted to write letters.

Before National Service I had been a trainee newspaper reporter, and may perhaps have slightly exaggerated in my claim to be able to write shorthand. So every time Q said: "The adjutant wants you in his office with your notebook," I would wonder if this was the day I would be rumbled, and find myself on the next draft for a meeting with the Mau Mau.

But with the combination of some very basic shorthand, some very rapid longhand and a bit of guesswork, I managed to get by and retained my desk in the Orderly Room.

It was certainly not an arduous job, and work usually finished at 4pm unless one was duty clerk. This meant cleaning and tidying all the offices, and then next morning laying and lighting the CO's and adjutant's fires.

This could be a little unnerving because both officers expected their day to begin with a cheerful, warming blaze in their grates. And fires don't always perform as required. So there was always a nail-biting time after the application of the match.

More than one duty clerk found himself in trouble because the grate was full of newspaper ashes, charred sticks and cold lumps of coal when the officer arrived.

Often soldiers who were confined to barracks on jankers would be allocated to help the duty clerk. Sometimes this presented a bizarre situation, because many of them were in the potential officer cadre and might shortly be commissioned as second-lieutenants. Which meant that the chap I had just told to get on his knees and polish the floor would soon have to be saluted and called sir.

I once had my own saluting dilemma when I decided to hitch-hike home for the weekend. A coach pulled up beside me. "Jump in," said the driver, and I saw that all the passengers were in the uniform of the Parachute Regiment. No problem. Except that half-way along the aisle I recognised the officer in charge of them. It was Ken, a friend from my Wimborne Grammar

School days when we were both in the school cricket team. But now 2nd Lieut Ken.

What should I do? Army regulations demand that a private soldier salute an officer. But this was Ken, my old team-mate. I'd feel a bit silly snapping a smart salute to someone who had been a cricket pitch pal. On the other hand, I couldn't just say "Hi Ken, how's things?" Private soldiers don't talk to officers. They take instructions from them. And call them sir.

So I took the cowardly way out and strode quickly towards a seat at the back pretending that I had not noticed there was an officer on board. And when the driver reached the point where I had been asked to be let off I moved with equal speed in the opposite direction, not daring even to glance at that uniform with its single pip.

By now any other officer would probably have put me on a charge. But then, if it had been any other officer I would have known what to do. Salute.

A few years after this incident I did actually become an officer myself — just for a week. As a reporter on a weekly newspaper I was invited to join a Press trip and write about local men serving in Cyprus. And to give us some authority and the right to dine in the officers mess all the Press team were assumed to hold the rank of captain.

But at Exeter I was a mere Orderly Room "nignog" and as well as duty clerk duties I also had to take my turn on fire picquet. Six soldiers would draw lots for the pleasure of patrolling the barracks for two hours between 6pm and 6am.

Get the first or second "stag" and you were lucky. But to be woken by the midnight-to-two chap and told it was your turn to take the pick-axe handle and guard the sleeping barracks until 4am was, to say the least, not fun.

So instead of wandering around looking for trouble, the only thing to do then was to find a hut with an unoccupied bed or seat and hope that either the duty officer didn't come prowling or one hadn't fallen asleep when the time came to return to the guardroom and rouse the next man on duty.

But apart from the minor inconvenience of guards and duty clerk obligations, life was basically easy and enjoyable. Particularly after I managed to get myself a bunk in the postroom.

I cannot remember how I fiddled this, but it meant that instead of being in a Depot Company hut where beds had to be laid out in regulation style and where inspections and checks could be made, I had hidden myself away from authority where bed-making was simply a matter of hauling the blanket up over the pillow.

So this, combined with a one-week "excused boots" chitty that I managed to make last for most of my NS career, ensured that Exeter life was pretty good.

Also, as well as avoiding inspections by sleeping in the postroom, I was not subjected to the sort of pranks others had to suffer, like returning to the hut after an evening out to find one's bed hanging from the ceiling beams.

Sometimes, in the middle of the night, a bed with sleeping occupant would be quietly carried through the door and left outside. Such a laugh!

These tricks, though annoying at the time, were always without malice, and paradoxically usually strengthened friendships.

This comradeship is what I remember most of all about National Service. Always it was possible to find a pal for a game of football or a cuppa in the NAAFI or simply a natter on a barrack room bed.

Also among my pleasant memories are the two variety concerts I helped to produce for the barracks. National Servicemen and regulars, private soldiers and officers worked together to put on the two shows.

I also played in the depot snooker and cricket teams, and was once chosen for the rugby team. But after a 60-odd points defeat by the REME at Honiton I wasn't selected again.

One of my mates was Dick Copp, and often we would spend an evening in Exeter together. Dick was an inveterate practical joker, and on one occasion as we passed the guardroom in our civvy clothes Dick looked at the young recruit on duty, and in his poshest voice demanded: "Don't you usually salute when you see an officer, soldier?" The poor squaddie replied "sorry sir" and gave Pte Copp his best Army salute.

Another of my friends was Eric Watts, who worked in the Training Company office. We used to go cycling together, and in the summer of 1955 rode to Paris.

But most weeks it was a shorter journey when Eric and I cycled down to the youth club at Budleigh Salterton where we both found girlfriends. Q used to say: "Suppose you and Watts were out with those maids from Budleigh again last night, Davis. You're just a couple of old rams."

But Eric married his girl, and they have just

celebrated their golden wedding anniversary.

Though all these memories have survived 50 years, it is the music of the day that stirs the strongest emotions. I remember so well the singers and the songs that would blare from Radio Luxembourg on wireless sets that could be found in almost every barrack room — Edmund Hockridge, Doris Day, Tony Bennett, Lita Rosa. And the music from Kismet, the hit-show of the decade, which was based on the Polovtsian Dances.

I never hear those Borodin tunes without being transported back into the days of khaki and Blanco and marching feet.

And I remember the barrack dances in the gymnasium to which nurses from the local hospital were invited.

I can't recall the names or faces of any of the girls I danced with there. But I can still see the notices on the walls which ordered: No jitter-bugging!

And then...

When barrack dances, visits to the maids of Budleigh and Orderly Room duties came to an end, I returned to my interrupted career.

Reporting jobs on the Hertfordshire Mercury and Romford Recorder were followed by a sub-editing post on The Guardian. Then I became deputy editor of the Ilford Pictorial.

After this, I had 12 years as editor of the Brentwood Argus newspaper in Essex, where one of my trainee reporters was the later-to-be TV personality Richard Madeley.

This was followed by 10 years editing The Yellow Advertiser, one of the country's first free newspapers, before I retired in 1991.

— Brian Davis©

Now fully-fledged soldiers. No more 4am roll-calls, no more floor-polishing, no more screaming NCOs. Nive squad photographed before their passing-out parade. Back row, left to right: Govier, Hoare, Davis, Parkinson, Caine, Brown, Turner, ?. Front row, left to right: Herring, Traynier, Hancock, McGowan, Cpl Bradfield, (who helped turn these scruffy layabouts into soldiers), Osborne, Bradbeer, Pavey, Shaddick

My 'return to barracks' order was given on the cinema screen

I WAS CALLED to serve the King on September 12 1947, a day that had little in common with me for it was bright and cheerful and there wasn't a cloud in the sky. I was, however, somewhat dispirited about the prospect of giving up my liberty for the next two years.

I reached the station in comfortable time to board the Padgate train. Other recruits were meandering across the platform trying desperately to enjoy the last remaining moments of freedom. I approached the bookstall and picked up a little light reading to keep me amused during the journey.

The train pulled in but I was reluctant to be the first person aboard and I had a fleeting urge to stay put, but there was no turning back. My fate was sealed, and I sought a comfortable compartment far from the madding crowd. The thought of a pre-joining chat with other recruits didn't appeal to me.

At Warrington our new hosts were awaiting us. An RAF charabanc took us from the station to the camp which on first impressions, with its high fences and innumerable prefabs, looked much like a PoW camp. The picture of my brief stay at Padgate is very blurred, but without doubt it was perhaps the most miserable week of my life. The first night was almost an eternity, and all the new recruits were kept awake until dawn listening to an endless recital of dirty and obscene stories delivered in style by one of the more loquacious Brummies.

Preparing for service life was a painful process, for I was particularly sensitive and not in any way able to surmount easily the challenges which were increasingly more demanding.

A whole morning was set aside for issuing kit. Some of my fellow recruits were overjoyed because never before in their lives had they been issued with such a fine wardrobe. One of the Brummies told me he had never worn new socks before.

I was given the three standard airman's shirts, but received officers's collars in addition. This anomaly caused me much embarrassment, for on every inspection I was closely questioned about why I was wearing an officer's collar.

My underpants still loom large in my memory too, for they were incredibly voluminous and had to be supported by my braces. So they had to be worn inside my shirt, which was a practice I had studiously avoided in my previous life.

The boots were perhaps our most precious possession and had to be treated with great respect. I had to spit on them every night, set fire to the Cherry Blossom polish and rub it into them. I used almost the whole of a large tin of polish on the first night.

Receiving vaccinations and inoculations was another feature of the induction timetable. Most of us queued, rolled up our sleeves and faced the needle like good boys. But certain characters were really terrified by the whole thing and fainted even at the thought of a needle going into their arms.

Our photographs were taken and appended to our 1250s. The 1250 (the RAF identity card), we were told, was to be guarded with our lives, and anyone foolish enough to lose it would probably face a firing squad.

The only shining light in the entire week was my brief visit to the padre. It wasn't because I couldn't face life at Padgate, difficult as this was, but merely as part of the optional programme open to us. Just being welcomed and treated to refreshments was worth the visit and more than made up for the verbal battering we had come to accept as normal service life.

Then we were moved on to RAF Bridgnorth, which we reached in the twilight of a September evening. The journey from Padgate had seemed endless, for the train had stopped at almost every wayside halt.

The refreshments served by courtesy of His Majesty had little to commend them and included a giant doorstep sandwich of potted-meat, a cardboard-covered pork pie and a few dog biscuits. Our appetites were therefore inadequately satisfied.

The train finally drew into Bridgnorth station where the RAF gestapo were waiting on the platform. We were herded from the carriages like so many cattle awaiting slaughter and then packed sardine-fashion into a fleet of pre-war charabancs. Heads were counted but no words of welcome were uttered, for we were merely another batch of raw recruits ready for military indoctrination. The charabancs made hard work of the trek through the few miles of countryside and I almost hoped they would break down so our arrival at the camp would be delayed.

Eventually the lights of the camp came into view and I thought of my future captivity with a degree of foreboding.

We were rounded up and escorted to our billets and I found myself in Hut 7. Corporal Parley, a diminutive Cockney, appeared on the scene and his first utterances left us in no doubt that he was not full of the milk of human kindness.

At West Drayton with David Bates (left) and Bill Lock (right)

Standing in his immaculately tailored uniform he did his utmost to give us the shock treatment and compared us to all the more unfortunate members of the human race.

As the foul expletives fell from his lips the atmosphere was alive with vibrations. He enumerated strings of King's Regulations, the disobeying of which would be punishable by the RAF equivalent of fire and brimstone.

We were lectured on bed spaces, kit inspections, lights out, parades, boots, rifles and many other subjects. I was convinced that I would meet none of the requirements and would spend my entire service career in a detention camp.

After this volcanic initiation, we were dismissed and allowed to spend our few remaining minutes in the NAAFI.

Our first impressions of Cpl Parley proved to be well-founded. He was a bully of the worst kind and picked on the less-confident and the least-able and did his utmost to ridicule them.

He delighted in crudities and frequently burst into the billet in the late evening and asked if anyone had any obscene literature to quench his depraved appetite. Innocent sycophants used to strive to satisfy his cravings.

His language, even in ordinary conversation, was quite revolting. Every morning he likened the layout of the billet to a latrine. When mail arrived from girlfriends or parents, he hurled it almost contemptuously at the recipients, and often letters landed on the mud.

Bayonet drill was yet another occasion when he was in his element as a bully. The less earthy young men who did not pick up the Anglo Saxon vocabulary without difficulty, suffered frequent onslaughts from his biting tongue as they charged at the sandbags with their bayonets and failed to scream out the required flow of obscenities.

But some worshipped the ground the corporal walked on and showed him a deference reserved only for kings. They bowed and scraped before him, cleaned out his billet, Blancoed his belt and almost tucked him up in bed.

Kit inspections were the highlights of the week and shining photographs of the ideal kit layout were displayed in the billet for all to see. I stared at it in bewilderment and shuddered at the thought. To some it was a work of art and one could marvel at its symmetry and form.

The sycophants of the billet strained their limited mental resources to create the beautiful patterns and shapes the photograph demanded. Some would spend hours adjusting the position of their best boots under their beds, ironing their boot laces and flicking microscopic crumbs of cotton from their best blues.

Eventually all would be ready for the kit inspection rehearsal. The corporal strode in like a warder from Alcatraz eager to strike down all those who trembled before him.

He ranted and raved like someone possessed, and some of the less stable kitbags literally wobbled. The storm began. Kitbags were hurled in all directions and the neat sheet and blanket sandwiches were ripped apart and demolished. Within seconds the billet resembled a dormitory the morning after the night before. Hell was let loose.

The recruits whose creations had been so brutally destroyed stood still as though they were awaiting execution themselves. No-one breathed and tears were ready to flow, but the stiff upper lip prevailed. The corporal screamed abuse at everyone and threatened the entire flight with eternal detention, and then stormed out of the billet.

Despite the rigours of life at Bridgnorth, some of my fellow recruits took pleasure in the divers chores which made up their day. One inoffensive character, who revelled in the delights of bull, devoted almost an entire Sunday morning to arranging all the pebbles he could find under and around the hut in the shape of a huge figure seven. He sweated blood to create his masterpiece and could hardly await the corporal's congratulations the next day. When the squad assembled for morning parade the corporal kicked the neatly arranged pebbles in all directions. Our poor fellow airman looked as though his life had come to an end.

I made no friends at Bridgnorth. Individuality had to be suppressed, and one had to think like all the other members of the herd.

Evenings in the hut were dreary and monotonous and the less one thought, the easier it became. The only topics of conversation were sex and sport. To attempt to talk of other things meant that one was almost ostracised.

Activity was confined to pressing trousers, boning, burning and shining boots and polishing buttons

My next move was to RAF Spitalgate, one of the bleakest places in England. It lay at the summit of a long, winding hill above Grantham in Lincolnshire, exposed to the vicious biting winds from the North Sea. I remember being most conscious of it when I patrolled the camp on guard duty.

My sojourn there was not a great success. The reason for my going was ostensibly to learn something of the science of pay accounts, but the intricacies involved in the subject never ceased to be anything but a deep mystery to me.

I showed no yearning for a knowledge of balances, credits and debits. As I didn't seek work, I was rarely introduced to any.

Occasionally my leisure time was punctuated with addressing and licking envelopes, which widened my geographical knowledge of the whereabouts of RAF stations but played havoc with my saliva.

I was able to pursue my own interests with impunity and spent most of my time reading, writing letters and thinking about life in general. The months rolled by and my presence in the office became something of a liability and I began to feel that I was not really serving my country.

Eventually I had an interview with the big chief of the Pay Accounts em-

pire who said that arrangements had been made for me to take my trade test in accountancy at RAF Chigwell.

He had mistakenly assumed that I was now au fait with the accidence and syntax of ledger work. And I hadn't the confidence to enlighten him. He was a pompous ass with no sense of imagination or sensitivity — like so many of his breed. I was despatched together with railway warrant to Chigwell.

My knowledge of pay accounts was comparable to a dustman's knowledge of the classics. Notwithstanding, I attempted the paper set before me though I felt like an illiterate facing the 11-plus.

I used my imagination a little and put pen to paper, for I had to pass the time somehow and not just stare into space.

I left the examination room certain of my fate. My marks, I was convinced, would not reach double figures. And the outcome was as I had predicted. I had failed.

Mercy was however shown to me, and to my immense surprise, I was drafted to the Pay Accounts Training School at Credenhill, Hereford to follow a special course of instruction. So there was still a chance that I might one day become a fully-fledged accounts clerk.

If Credenhill had nothing else to recommend it, it was situated in a particularly beautiful part of the country. I paid many visits to Hereford, wandered round the cathedral and walked along the River Wye and sometimes I went to the cinema.

The course itself was not difficult, but it did not interest me very much. I realised however, that I had to take it seriously for if I failed I would be relegated to the lowest grade in the RAF and be known as an ACHGD and have to spend my time cleaning the toilets, working as a dustman and doing what would be regarded by others as fatigues.

Luckily for me, though I did not distinguish myself in the exam, I passed and became a fully-fledged pay clerk. The results were announced in the classroom and beforehand everyone was a little nerv-

Hut No 7 at Bridgnorth. I am fifth from left in the middle row

ous. One Lancastrian, who went by the name of Barber, was talking after the WO had begun to talk to us. He was given a dreadful dressing down for this misdemeanor, and at the end of his tirade the WO asked his name. "Barber sir."

The WO hurled yet more invective at him and rounded it off with "I expect you have failed the course." Looking down the results list he gleefully announced that poor old Barber had indeed failed. I was hoping that I was not going to suffer the same fate, but luckily I had passed, as had most of the candidates.

One of my principal roles while at Credenhill was to organise a charabanc service from the camp to Birmingham every weekend, from 12 on Saturday, until midnight on Sunday. My services were widely appreciated and little did I realise that organising coach trips was going to be an important role in my life many years later.

My stay at Credenhill was unfortunately extended because I went down with a bug at the end of July and found myself in the sick quarters for three weeks.

I recovered from my bout of sickness quite quickly, but I had apparently picked up an infection so had to be held in splendid isolation. Much of the time it was dreadful, and at times I believed I would never get to see the outside world again.

I passed the time writing to mother and my girlfriend, Joan Freeman, and reading novels by PG Wodehouse and Jack London, in addition listening to the Olympic Games, the first since 1936. Accommodation for the competitors was provided by RAF station West Drayton.

I listened to the cricket too, and followed the progress of the second and third Test matches. We were playing the Australians, and I was an avid listener to cricket commentaries. Boredom was kept at bay, for we all talked to one another a good deal.

Perhaps the most enduring memory I have of my stay at Credenhill occurred when I was a patient in the sick quarters.

One evening I was persuaded by my colleagues to go to the window and observe the senior medical officer, who was in an advanced state of inebriation, being helped on his drunken way back to his quarters.

I was quite shocked that a wing commander could behave in such a manner. Gradually I came to terms with it and realised that even doctors were human.

My captivity came to an end in the first week in August. As I was leaving the camp I was barked at quite savagely by one of the NCOs on the gate and he told me quite brutally to get my hair cut. I mumbled that I had spent three weeks in the sick bay, but this did not produce any sympathy.

The last part of my stay at Credenhill was passed just killing time awaiting my posting. All my contemporaries on the course had long since gone, so I was rather a spare part.

I went home on leave to fill in the time and after only one day was called back to take up my posting to Air Ministry Unit in West London. The news actually reached me on the screen at the Robin Hood cinema in Hall Green. I was a bit shaken, but couldn't be absent without leave — the most heinous of crimes a serviceman could commit — so I returned to the camp almost within minutes of receiving the message.

So finally I escaped from Credenhill and made my way to the Air Ministry unit in London. It was an unusual posting, for apart from wearing uniforms, one was not conscious of being in the RAF at all.

During the day we worked in office buildings in Great Portland Street and in the evenings we returned to Viceroy Court, formerly made up of luxury flats, which had been taken over by the RAF.

Quite naturally the place had lost much of its former glory, but it was more agreeable than the majority of service billets. It was located in Prince Albert Road opposite Regents Park, an ideal spot for visiting the West End.

Every morning I walked down to Baker Street and caught the Tube to Great Portland Street. I felt almost like a civilian again, travelling to work with the rest of mankind. Apart from sleeping, I spent little time in Viceroy Court and took advantage of exploring the haunts of London

I hitch-hiked home every weekend along the A5 and came back by train to Paddington and then walked back to the billet in the early hours of Monday morning.

The only drawback to my stay in London was cleaning up my room every Monday night and periodically preparing my kit for inspection, but life in general was not uncomfortable.

In November 1948 I was sent to RAF West Drayton. As an RAF camp it compared very favourably with the majority. There were few parades, billets were only occasionally inspected and we were subjected to few restrictions Much of the time there I enjoyed, for I made several friends and had an interesting social life. The work in the pay accounts office did nothing for me at all and I found it intensely boring, but it caused me few worries. Some of my contemporaries took the work very seriously and derived much satisfaction from

Teacher, then tour guide

messing about with ledgers, and talked with enthusiasm about credit balances, income and expenditure.

Life in our leisure time was much more rewarding. We had endless discussions about all manner of subjects over cups of coffee. We made weekly visits to the cinema in Uxbridge and played frequent practical jokes on one another.

One of the highlights of life at West Drayton was my spell on fire picquet duty. It was an absolute disaster and resulted in my being put on a charge for negligence.

I was rather foolish, for I took issue with Cpl Willbroughams, the character in charge of the fire picquet and told him that our time spent playing firemen was unlikely to prevent a fire, and that to spend our time in the fire hut instead of in our billets in the evenings was an infringement of our liberty. He didn't take too kindly to this and so I quickly found myself on the wrong side of him.

On one very wet morning I was called out to act as traffic warden at the entrance to the camp where a fire-fighting operation was taking place. One of the hoses was attached to a fire hydrant and was stretched across the road, and I was told to ensure that no traffic ran over it, and to redirect the traffic entering the camp.

This I completely failed to do. Within seconds of taking up my post, an approaching lorry ignored the hose and just ran over it. Willbroughams saw it all happen and immediately went berserk, screaming at me to double to the

guardroom. For "gross negligence" I was confined to camp for three days and had to report to the guardroom in full kit every hour. I think it taught me some sort of lesson.

One morning I was having coffee in the NAAFI when I was pounced on by this evil-faced Scottish corporal and told that I would do for his Guard of Honour. The parade was taking place because a scrambled-egg officer of some distinction was visiting the camp.

This was a wretched nuisance for I had to give up many evenings to parading, drilling and polishing my belt to rehearse for the big event. It also meant I had to spend my clothing allowance on a new blue, which seemed an incredible waste of money.

The event passed off all right and I suppose I did have the pleasure of walking round in a new blue uniform for my last few days in the RAF.

One of the practices which I regarded as particularly foolish was sleeping next to the safe in the pay accounts office.

I had to do this on two or three occasions but it was particularly irksome if it occurred at the weekend for it meant the surrender of one's 36-hour pass.

Words failed me when I discovered that there was nothing in the safe at all. The incident, if nothing else, introduced me to the world of the absurd.

During my stay at West Drayton I was promoted from AC2 to AC1. This did nothing to enhance my authority, but did result in a little more money in my pocket. We were given the questions before we took the trade test by our warrant officer, so we all passed with flying colours.

And then...

After NS I attended Saltley College, Birmingham to train as a teacher. I taught history at a school in Romford for 10 years before moving to Greensward School, Hockley, Essex where I was head of the history department. After that I was a tour guide in East Anglia for 20 years.

*— **Derek Davis**©*

Guards didn't want my flat feet, so I was put in the infantry

PRIOR to my call-up, which I knew was imminent, my workmates "persuaded" me to volunteer for the Guards. I went to Caterham and had a medical, a meal and a haircut, and then was told I had flat feet. Go back home! Six months later I was called up, and flat feet or not, had eight weeks' training with the Royal Norfolk Regiment. Next it was a posting to Colchester to join a holding battalion, the Royal Berkshires, where I had some leave but caught an infection and spent time in hospital. After I was discharged I went for convalescence to Arborfield where I recall making fire-bricks out of mashed paper and coal dust!

Then it was back to Colchester, and eventually I found myself on a train travelling through Germany and ending up in Hildesheim with the 5th Battalion of the Royal Berkshire Regiment, in what was formerly the quarters of the Luftwaffe.

Our time was spent mostly on guard duties at the displaced persons camp, as well as plenty of exercises. The battalion was warned not to fraternise, but going to the beer garden for dances this was quite hard to maintain! And children, as everywhere, enjoy chocolate and sweets.

This is me on Gibraltar with the sort of weapon I never came across during National service

When the 5th disbanded we returned to the UK to Dover Castle to prepare to join the 2nd battalion in Burma. We shipped out on the Empress of Scotland, and after weeks at sea arrived in Rangoon, then to Minghladon to join the battle-hardened men who had been fighting the Japanese during the war and hadn't seen home for a number of years.

The time we were there was spent controlling the Dacoits (Burmese renegades), and then we were moved again. I was in the advance party to return to the UK, and boarded the troopship Dilwara for the voyage first to Singapore and then a transit camp at Neesoon. After the delights of the camp and the city, we were shipped again to Egypt through the Suez Canal to Ismailia. I joined 286 Coy RASC under canvas at Tahag, where we spent Christmas.

On the move once more, we stopped at Malta and eventually made it to Bulford to prepare for demob.

I missed both the German and Japanese conflicts so I was able to enjoy my Army time and the travelling I did.

Looking back I am glad I failed the medical for the Guards, because I was in the infantry and I settled into Army life and was proud to have been in the Royal Berkshire Regiment.

It is sad that the Royal Berks has now disappeared for good and, as with many other fine regiments, is just relegated to museums.

Flat feet, but soldiering on

And then...

Before call-up I had worked for a firm that made caravans, and I returned to them after demob for a short while. Then I moved to the upholstery department of the Co-op before joining the Vickers aircraft plant at Hurn, now Bournemouth, airport. Work was just beginning on the Vickers Viscount, and I became an aircraft trimmer working on anything to do with furnishing on the plane. Eventually I was senior foreman there and then I spent 10 years before retirement with a small factory producing items of furnishing and sound-proofing.

— Raymond Dean©

22903249 Cfn Peter Elderfield

Your mattresses are fit for the Queen, so don't stain them!

BORN in Slough in 1935, I began work at the main dealers in Buckinghamshire for Jaguar cars. Unfortunately, when my father died I had to earn more money, so entered engineering where I stayed until the day the buff envelope came, inviting me to High Wycombe for X-ray and later to Reading for my medical.

On the fateful call-up day I made my way to

Lucky me. A posting to Stirling!

the train station where I and one other boarded the train bound for REME in Blandford, Dorset — miles away! We were met by a sergeant who told us we were very lucky boys and would we like a ride to camp, in which case "get those bloody fags out and get on the truck."

On arrival we were sorted into platoons and issued with our uniforms. No measuring, merely "take it and see the tailor later." Just as well, as my trousers were at least four inches too long.

They kept the best bit till last, with the hat issue. "Your 'at size, sir? Don't know? Then try these," and two dark blue pancakes were slapped on the counter. The things we did to make them take some sort of shape you could write a book about.

Next came the worst salad meal I have ever eaten followed by getting all the kit sorted and the famous bed-block demo.

Came the first day in the gym and we met the psychos called PTIs. Even today I break into a cold sweat thinking of what they put us through. Needless to say six weeks' later on pass-out day you felt you could take on Freddie Mills.

Then to Taunton, Zummerset, for trade training. What a lovely billet that was. An ex-Canadian hospital. It was there we met the infamous Black Tarantula, six foot six of pure hatred of National Servicemen. Skinny as a rake, immaculately dressed. C Company's sergeant-major.

He issued us with our mattresses with the commentary: "These mattresses are fit for the f---g Queen to sleep on. In the morning I inspect said mattresses, and if I see a stain I sniff that stain and if I smell piss you'll be in the shit, right up to here." He touched his chin.

Needless to say the bloke in the next bed to me obliged on the very first night.

He also warned us not to touch the local scrumpy, and that was a challenge willingly accepted. You could get three pints for two shillings and be transported to another world.

After six months qualifying as a "mechanic, vehicle for the use of" I was, in the words of my CSM, one of the luckiest people in the camp. I was being posted to his home town of Stirling, Scotland.

What a shock that was. On arrival at the camp gate at Back-of-Hill I was ordered up the zig-zag path to the castle to give a pint of blood. "And if you don't keep quiet we'll take a bloody quart."

Next day I was given the good news that as the

Now I sell at craft fairs

workshops were about 100 yards short of three miles away we had to march each way whatever the weather.

Then I had a stroke of luck. The guy who worked in the postings office asked me to do him a favour. Apparently he had fallen in love with a local girl, but was due to be posted to Edinburgh. So would I go instead?

After about a minute's consideration I agreed and finished up at Edinburgh EUOTC where the students at the university joined the TA to help pay their expenses.

I was under a very laid back sergeant and in

charge of 10 assorted vehicles and three motor-bikes which were used for all manner of winter camps at Aviemore and Findhorn, as well as summer camp at Otterburn.

The students were a great bunch who accepted me on equal terms and I had some great times, though I was often the victim of their pranks.

And then...

On demob in 1955 I returned to my old employer, a stationery equipment manufacturer. But I couldn't settle, so did a refresher course in metal turning, and worked for various firms making parts for Aston-Martin racing cars, jet engines and ships' propeller shafts.

Then I joined the Civil Service and taught centre-lathe turning as an instructor at Slough Skillcentre.

This was followed by a short spell training apprentices in High Wycombe, but when I saw a big DIY chain was advertising for skilled people to join the firm as "experts" in various trades I applied and was taken on. Put in charge of the power tool section I was given a free hand to build displays and demonstrate the latest tools.

This was work that I loved, and it lasted until I retired in 2000. But I am still active making and selling turned items at craft fairs.

— Peter Elderfield©

A fact seemingly lost to much of the present-day population, and almost certainly will be by all future generations, is the contribution made by the 2.2million National Servicemen who were conscripted to serve in one of the armed services between 1945 and 1963. But the part they played is recognised by the National Service Veterans Alliance, which was formed to work for the recognition of NS men of all arms. It is open to anyone who was conscripted by the British Government and the commonwealth and colonies from the end of the second world war through to the cessation of National Service. It is also available to those conscripted before the end of WW2 whose service extended into the period covered by the 1947 National Service Act. Membership costs £8.50, and application forms are available from Alan Tizzard, Robin Cottage, 220 Kingsground, London SE9 5EW. Phone 0208 859 8378.

I was sent to the haunted gallery to find the sergeant's nose

THE FAT sergeant-major got off the saddle of his bicycle. "Why are you shovelling coke, laddie?" "Because I'm educated sir and I don't have to go to education classes" I replied. His next question. "How long have you been in the Army?" "One week, sir." "Well, you're making a mess. Next time don't shovel the coke all over the road. Carry on laddie." And the fat sergeant-major mounted his bike and pedalled off.

That was one of my introductions to life in the Royal Army Medical Corps when in 1955 I signed up to do three years' National Service because I was told if I did the extra year I could guarantee to get my choice of trade, and extra pay.

I wanted something similar to what I had studied at school, like zoology, and got A-level GCEs. So they said I could do pathology. But first was the dreaded square-bashing at Crookham in Hampshire. I quite enjoyed it and learned how to drill, kill and salute on the march. I learned the corps' motto: In Arduis Fidelis and the stories of how the medics won so many VCs — a lot of them posthumously!

The others in my barrack room came from many backgrounds. I had never heard Scouse or Glasgow Scottish before, and some needed subtitles when they spoke, usually including a lot of words beginning with F.

Skiving was another word I had never known. But discovered it meant that after running up and down the football pitch carrying a squaddie on a stretcher the corporal said we could "skive off" for a smoke behind the air raid shelters while he went missing for an hour!

After basic training I was sent to the RAMC college at Millbank,

Off duty in Germany

London, where I learned how to do blood tests and recognise all sorts of tropical worms which could lodge in the bowels of unsuspecting soldiers in places like Malaya.

The Royal Herbert Hospital at Shooters Hill, Woolwich followed, where I was let loose on the wards to stab the heels of new-born babies for their blood tests and scrape squaddies' scrotums to investigate "crutch rot." Fungal growths stained with methylene blue were very interesting seen under the microscope.

Our captain and the sergeant were a pair of real characters. The sergeant gave an air-rifle to the officer who would shoot pigeons off the ward window ledges.

The sergeant organised "laboratory parties" where QARANC nurses were invited and plied with Coca-Cola laced with absolute alcohol (Ethanol). This resulted in many waking-up on a camp-bed in the Haematology Department next morning!

While at the Royal Herbert I nearly got sent to war when the Suez Canal invasion took place. Many of my colleagues went off to paint the ambulances sand colour, draw tropical kit and get ready to be dropped in by parachute. I didn't particularly fancy dangling on a line while a load of Egyptians were shooting at me from below, but luckily the invasion was soon over, and the ambulances were re-painted and the tropical kit handed back. And I was told it was Germany for me.

I was posted to the Munster Military Hospital where I started to teach myself German and ogle all the wonderful camera shops near the cathedral.

Here I saw my first dead bodies because we had to attend post-mortems on soldiers and their families. Some blokes fainted. But I had dissected earthworms and rabbits at school!

The British Military Hospital at Spandau was my next posting, where I saw the ruins of the Russian sector on an official coach visit, and real Russians marching up and down on their war memorial just inside the British sector by the Brandenburg Gate. In Spandau I got to do the blood tests on Rudolph Hess who was imprisoned there.

The hospital was a former Gestapo headquarters, and on the wall of the maternity wing one could dig out the remains of bullets where the Gestapo had shot prisoners. There was a "haunted gallery" above the wards, containing a large number of coffins. And one night when I was on duty I received a call to "go to the haunted gallery, find Sgt Steel's nose and bring it back for emergency surgery!"

Ready for action now as a photographer

There were no lights, and I had only a torch as I clambered among the coffins, trying to find the broken window through which a drunken sergeant had shoved his head and cut off his nose!

I found it on the ledge and picked it up in cotton wool and took it to the operating theatre.

Later I had to escort this sergeant by train through the Russian Zone and drop him off at Hanover from where he was to be returned to the UK. I continued to my next posting at Iserlohn. The British Military Hospital at Iserlohn was close to Lake Seilersee and had been a Panzer headquarters. The wards were where the German soldiers had been based but we Brits were given the old tank sheds for our accommodation.

It was here that I experienced the worse bullying of my Army service. A sergeant and corporal were in charge of the Path Lab, and the corporal really had it in for me. Once he came into my room drunk and in a rage and hit me with an iron before the sergeant pulled him off. Then there was a corporal in the Company Office who also was always on my back, watching every move I made and finding any small fault.

But by this time I was up for promotion myself and was made lance-corporal when the Path Lab sergeant and corporal were demobbed. Then I got made up to full corporal, the same rank as the Company Office bully, and he didn't like it one bit.

I ended specialising in post-mortem work, and did 65, including two children who had been murdered by their mother in woods near Dortmund, and a gunner who was drowned in the Mohnesee and didn't float to surface for three weeks. I heard that when his body was returned to England the bottom fell out of his coffin.

Being the original virgin soldier I had never seen a nude woman, but often had to undress soldiers' dead wives. One who suffered a heart attack was still warm.

Knowing I was so young and innocent, the reception staff would make fun of me as they ordered me to carry out another post mortem on a woman.

When I was interviewed by the colonel as my demob date came up I declined his invitation to stay on, even though he said I was an excellent technician and would be made up to sergeant.

And then...

I joined a photographic society and always hoped to get work in photography, but my first job after National Service was as a microbiological research technician at the May and Baker chemical research company. My boss there was always catching me looking at photographic magazines when I should have been looking for a cure for diseases by injecting his mice.

On his suggestion I did evening classes in photography to get some qualifications and passed the intermediate grade of the Institute of British Photographers.

Then I became a photographer at the Ministry of Aviation where I went round to aircraft factories taking pictures of the inside of aircraft. Another of my jobs was to make prints showing airmen how to use an ejector seat.

In the early days pilots had to pull two handles. But often they would pull just the handle that shot them out of the seat and forget to pull the other one that blew the cover off. So they were crashing their skulls against the canopy, and had to have a diagram in front of them showing what to do if they were about to crash.

After I had been at the Ministry for some time I got a job in school photography.

Then got work at University College, London in photomicrography, something I had tried in the Army by holding a camera in front of a microscope. One of my most interesting jobs there was photographing one of the first samples of dust scooped up from the moon.

It was just a few granules that NASA sent to the university on a slide. But my picture was published as a half-page in the Sunday Times.

In 1970 I decided to become a freelance photographer and did a lot of work for newspapers.
—Peter Elgar©

When swimming in the nude proved to be a bit expensive

WHILE I was serving in Tripoli as the commanding officer's driver I managed to retrieve a piece of the Army's stolen property — a wheel from a heavy ack-ack gun. It had disappeared despite the fact that it weighed about two-hundredweight and there was a 24-hour guard on the camp, which was surrounded by a seven-foot high wall.

At the time we had a pretty good regimental football team who played the local Arab teams. And a couple of days after the wheel went missing the CO asked me to take him to one of the matches. As he was watching the game I saw a lorry that seemed to be a bit lopsided, and looking closer discovered our stolen wheel on it.

At the finish of the match and I pointed out the lorry to the CO, who contacted the guardhouse. And quickly the Arab driver had a visit from two Military Policemen.

I had been called up for Army service in February 1946 and was sent to a camp in a small Yorkshire town called Snaith.

I had never been away from home before, and mixing with lads from all over the UK was very strange. I couldn't understand some of them because of their accents, and in the beginning it was the most miserable time of my life, but I soon got over it.

Born in Edmonton I was brought up in London until the age of six when the family moved to Slough. I was the fourth child of a family of eight, and times were very hard. I left school at 14 and was working for ICI Chemicals in Slough as a garage hand when my call-up papers arrived.

After two weeks at the training camp I was deemed to be underweight and height so I (along with about 20 others) was sent to a physical development centre in Oswestry, Shropshire for four weeks of intense physical training.

I put on two stones in weight and grew two inches in four weeks. Those who didn't reach the required standard of fitness had to do it all again, and because the training was so intense nobody had any desire to have to repeat it. We were then sent back to do our basic training, but because I had been in the Army Cadet Force, I

didn't have to do it.

I was sent on a driving course at a Royal Artillery camp at Kinmel Park camp in Rhyl, North Wales. Then I was put into a civilian garage in Bolton to do a four-week mechanics course, after which I was officially called a driver mechanic.

After serving in three different camps in the UK I was posted to Egypt. sailing from Tilbury on the 14,000-ton SS Chitral. From Port Said we took a boat down the Suez Canal to a transit camp called Port Tewfik, while they sorted us into different units.

Serving in Tripoli

I was posted to 74 Ack Ack Regiment, Royal Artillery in Tripoli, which had been used for Italian troops during the Second World War.

The battery CO used me as his personal driver, and as well as the stolen wheel incident I also remember another theft, and this one was a bit more embarrassing.

During the afternoons I often took several of the lads down to the beach in Tripoli, about four miles from our camp. Though it was for the use of the military, the Arabs used to take their camels into the sea to wash them. But we would drive them away and go for a swim.

Sticking out of the sea were a number of metal anti-invasion poles that had been put in during the war. And we would take off our swimming shorts, hang them over the posts and swim in the nude. One day when we got out to dress, we found that some Arabs had got into the back of our truck and stolen our clothes and shoes. So we had to go back to camp undressed. The guards were not amused, and we never lived it down. And we had to pay for new clothes.

On another occasion the CO and some other officers went out into the desert in my vehicle on a duck shoot. They had been gone for over three hours and I was getting panicky. The light was fading fast and in those circumstances the desert is a very big place. However, they eventually turned up with

From Army days to Airways

three ducks which I guess were on the menu in the officers mess the next day!

Eventually, in May 1948, I was demobbed and returned to Civvy Street. I had been kept in for two or three months over my two years, and there was a rumour that for every day we had to stay on we would be paid £50. Obviously that was a big incentive for the Army to ensure that we got demobbed on time, so 10 or a dozen lads at a time were taken to Idris airport to await any civilian flights that had space on them. I was lucky enough to be put on a Skymaster from South Africa. It was the first time I had been on a civilian aircraft, and to my delight I was given a window seat.

The stewardess came round with some fruit, and offered me a peach. I had no money on me apart from a few Egyptian coins, so I was a bit

hesitant because I didn't know if I was expected to pay for it. But she assured me the fruit was free, so I accepted it. A great memory.

And then...

Back home I was able to take up my old job at ICI, where I met my wife-to-be. We have been married now for 58 years, and have a son and a daughter enjoying successful careers.

I did not stay long at ICI but took a job as an auto-electrician. After a few years I became a sales rep for a large London company then went back to the engineering business with my father-in-law who ran a repair business selling all types of garden and general agricultural machinery.

After a few years there my son suggested that I used my engineering knowledge by joining British Airways at Heathrow, where he was already working. So I went to BA and worked for 20 years at Heathrow before retiring in 1991.

I moved to Wimborne in Dorset from Stoke Poges, Buckinghamshire seven years ago and wish I had moved a lot sooner. It is a wonderful county, and we have made a lot of good friends.

Oh, and I never did get that "staying on" money. And I have never heard of anyone who did!

— *Geoffrey Ellis©*

In Tripoli where I appear to have won a coconut

73

22326749 LCpl John Evans

We trained with live ammo, and one chance in 25 of being hit

THOUGH I was an apprentice carpenter and joiner when my call-up papers came, I asked go into the Army instead of finishing my apprenticeship. And I was sent for basic training to Warley Barracks, Brentwood, not much more than a couple miles from my home. Then I went to Aldershot on a physical training instructor's course with the Parachute Regiment, before going to Bury St Edmunds where I became a marksman on rifle and bren. At this point I was sent to join the Northamptonshire Regiment who were to take the place of the Glosters in Korea

We sailed from Southampton to Singapore on the Astorias, en route to Korea. But men were wanted for a battle training course in Japan so I stayed on and we were taken to village in the mountains called Haramura.

One day we were told three volunteers were required for a special duty. The sergeant stood us all in line. He looked at me and said: "What's your name?" Evans. "You'll do."

He picked another man. "What's your name? You'll do." The third "volunteer" was picked in the same way, and we were put on the gate as police to check the Japanese civilian staff coming into the camp to work. At night we had to go round in a jeep and check the brothels because only the permanent staff were allowed in them. Everyone on the course had to stay in camp.

A lot of the training involved live ammunition. We even had to crawl under a fixed line 18inches high while a Vickers machine gun was fired over us. It was expected that one man in 25 would be injured or killed. Finally there was a big battle with tanks and mortars and machine-guns.

When the time came to move to Korea we were marched back

In Korea shortly after I cut my arm on a piece of metal

25 miles to Kure and got on a ship which docked at Pusan. Then we were taken up to above the Imjin River.

Our camp was very primitive and we lived in tents full of holes and with the letters US on the canvas. That didn't mean United States, but unserviceable!

It was so cold that when we collected our fried eggs from the canteen they were frozen before we could eat them. Once a month we travelled 15 miles for a shower.

And I remember one terrible incident when a chap was helping out his friend in the arms store. But they were playing about with the ammunition, and the friend somehow got a stengun bullet in a pistol and shot him in the head and killed him.

I was in Korea for about eight months and was involved in several skirmishes when we went out on patrol.

I was then posted to Hong Kong and up to the new territories patrolling the Chinese border.

Before we moved from Korea we had been filling in monsoon ditches when someone threw a sandbag and hit me on the thigh. It felt like being struck by a lump of concrete. When we got to Hong Kong I was in a lot of pain and couldn't lie on my side. I went to hospital and they found a growth that had to be cut out.

Just before I left Hong Kong to be demobbed I was chosen to

Smartly turned-out members of B Company in Hong Kong. I am fourth from the left

74

Pictured recently at a military vehicle show

compete in the British Land Forces Far East shooting competition. Each team shot at their own base at different times, and before the scores were collated I had to catch the boat for home. So to this day I have no idea how I got on.

When I finally returned to the UK I was demobbed at Warley Barracks. My Army service ended where it had begun, in my home town.

And then...

I started work as an improver joiner with a building firm. My first job? Maintenance work at Warley Barracks!

It seemed I just couldn't escape the Army, because the barracks had also featured in my life just after the war when I was only 11. As I stood with my father at traffic lights in Brentwood a big car slowed down and the passenger looked out and shouted "Charles."

I had no idea who the man was, but my father went up to him and called him sir and said: "This is my little boy."

As they carried on chatting I could see the man was in an Army uniform, and as he drove away he said: "So nice to see you Charles, perhaps we may bump into one another again some day."

Then my father told me: "He was my CO all through the African Campaign when I was a sergeant during the war. He is just going up to Warley Barracks. His name is Field Marshal Montgomery."

After I started my own carpentry business in 1967 I was asked by an architect to take over a big building project, and I did this sort of work for six years.

But I changed careers after buying a large house with grounds big enough for my children to have horses. While I was teaching aerobics in a local sports hall I came to the conclusion that the town could do with a good sports and country club. And in 1987 that is what my home became, and I am still running it today.

— ***John Evans©***

These photographs from my album show that National Service left plenty of time to take things easy. Left, in Hong Kong, and above in Japan

23609631 Pte Richard Faulkner

Hornets were my frightening enemy in the Malayan jungle

AS I trudged along a steaming jungle track in Malaya, sweating my b---s off under the weight of a wireless set and all the paraphernalia that went with it, I turned to my mate and said: "It's my 21st birthday today."

"Oh, that's nice," he replied, "happy birthday," and we carried on through the undergrowth. Suddenly I saw a tree with a bunch of bananas. "Hey, look. My birthday treat," I said, and cut them off. But they were as hard as wood, and I had to throw them away.

But I did get one birthday present. That evening, when the rum ration was handed out our officer had been told it was my birthday and gave me what was left in the bottle.

Though I was just 21 and with only a few months of National Service under my belt, I had been involved with the Army since I joined the cadets in Romford when I was 11.

By the time I was called up I was in effect a fully-trained soldier. I knew fieldcraft, unarmed combat and bayonet fighting, and was proficient in rifle, sten and bren. And I held the rank of RSM.

So basic training at Warley Barracks in Essex — just a few miles from my home — was very easy.

Then I was trained to be a wireless operator, and learned Morse Code. And just a month after I married I was on a ship sailing to Malaya to help locate the few remaining Communist terrorists left in the jungle.

Though I didn't come across any CT, I did have not one, but three frightening encounters with nasties in the jungle — hornets

The first was when I climbed into a bush to retrieve a wireless aerial and was attacked by a nest of them. I fell out of the bush covered in the little stinging blighters. Hornets were up my nose, in my ears, and because I was screaming so much they were stinging the inside of my mouth. I rolled about the ground with this cloud of insects all over me.

My mates joined six-foot toggle ropes together, lassoed me and dragged me away from the bush. But I was in a right mess. I couldn't see or hear, and could hardly breathe because of the swelling in my nose and mouth.

I had four days living on soup and tea sucked through a vine. Fortunately I was still able to smoke, which was a relief.

The second occasion the hornets went for me was after an airmail drop. Unfortunately the mail was for a platoon farther in the jungle, and they had ours.

So it was decided to send out an officer, a sergeant, a wireless operator (me) and a Malay tracker to do a swap.

I was told there was no need to take a radio, and was given the mail pack. But just to make sure I didn't get away too lightly I also had to carry water bottles, a pouch with enough food for the 10 hours we would be away, a machete and a browning 9mm automatic with a spare mag of ammunition and some other bits of equipment.

We reached the other camp, swapped letters, had a brew and headed back. But I was getting slower and slower and dropping behind. After a couple of hours the others said they would march on.

I felt quite confident and ploughed on at my own pace, thinking about my wife Sheila so far away, and the little son I had never seen.

Suddenly as I brushed against a bush the noise I dreaded came screaming into my ears. A buzzing that made me run and run. I felt a pain behind my right knee, then another on my elbow. A third hornet got me in the neck.

I was still running, then...nothing. I woke up and found myself in long grass. And it was a lot darker. I lay there hurting in my arm, leg and neck. Is anything broken? No. Where the hell am I?

I had no idea the direction of the camp, so checked my gun and equipment and had a drink. At least they knew I was missing and would send an Aboe to find me. I hoped.

I realised that if I panicked and tried to find my way back alone I could well get lost. So I rested behind a fallen tree and waited. After a while there was a noise. A grunt and the snap of a twig. Was it an animal, a CT or the Malay? I cocked the Browning, heard another grunt and saw a grinning black face.

76

I told the Aboe what had happened, and he showed me how I had run about 75 yards from the hornets, and full-pelt between two monkey puzzle trees no more than two-feet apart. Six inches to one side or the other and I would have been impaled on the thorns. I had been lucky, but I still have scars from the hornet stings on my body today.

My third encounter with hornets came when we had to go along a pathway cut into the side of the mountain about 800ft up from the Perak river. It was very narrow and slippery in places with a sheer drop on one side into the river. A message came back that there were hornets near a tree on the track ahead.

I was petrified. "I'm not going along that track for anybody" I said, and an officer came along asking why we had stopped.

He threatened me with the book, but I refused to move. I explained why I was so afraid, and he agreed that I could climb into the jungle above the track and stay on the higher ground until I was past the problem tree.

My next spot of bother in Malaya was caused not by insects, but crystals.

We had to go into the jungle on the quick. A contact had been made. I rushed to the armoury and collected a 9mm Browning, went to the stores for four days' rations and checked that the fag situation was OK. Then I packed all the radio gear into the manpack and headed to the lorries in the MT park.

I was in the back of one of the lorries with the other men and a sergeant who was one of the most disliked NCOs around. I checked in my mind the things I needed, but could not remember signing for the crystals I needed for my radio to work.

We were getting farther and farther away from base as I frantically I searched in my pockets for the missing crystals. I knew I had to confess to this sergeant that I had forgotten the vital part of my radio. I began to make my way up the lorry to get to him. At once I was shouted at to "bloody well sit still." I stopped, but said: "I've left the crystals behind."

"You stupid f---r, what do you think we're going to do now?" I slunk back to my place and sat down. I felt sick, the officer had to be told yet. What would he say?

As it turned out, though he was annoyed he accepted that these things do happen and we set off into the jungle. As we made our way forward a few soldiers from an Australian unit

Cleaning my revolver in the jungle

appeared, and they had a radio. I was saved.

We made contact with my HQ and were given a map reference where we were told one of our signallers would meet us with the missing crystals. We got there early the next evening and made camp in what was practically a bog. Now I had to walk across this bog area, through some jungle and along a winding dirt track to a river, which I had to cross to meet the signaller with the crystals on the other side. Easy!

Off I set with a chap called Arthur for back-up, both of us armed with Sterling sub-machine guns.

We had just left the jungle area and were approaching the track when there was a loud crack. I went down and crawled into cover then

Now I use a firearm safely

looked round for my mate who was nowhere to be seen. "Arthur where are you?" No answer. Bloody hell, he's been shot. I waited a little while gathering my thoughts, then I heard a noise, and Arthur crawled into view.

We carried on along the track and the clouds that were hiding the moon slowly dispersed and the countryside lit up. It was a different world, the darkness had changed to the eerie appearance of a black and white negative. The shadows created a weird pattern on the ground.

Did I see something move up ahead? "Must be a bleeding ape," said Arthur. "Well, if it is, it's wearing a f---g hat," I said, and cocked my gun as we moved cautiously forward.

My heart was pounding and I tried to tell myself that it probably was a monkey or something harmless, and not a terrorist.

But then I saw not one but two men walking along the track towards us, and one was carrying a rifle. They must be terrorists because none of our chaps were around here.

They were about 40 yards away as Arthur hid down behind a boulder with his weapon pointing up the track. We were both ready to kill. It was them or us. I aimed and started to tighten on the trigger.

Stop. I had glimpsed a yellow colour very

faintly on the hat of one of the men. "Arthur, it's all right, they're our side."

I made my gun safe, and we met the two soldiers in the middle of the track. They had my crystals. "We came up here to save you walking all the way to the river," they said.

I pointed out that the rendezvous was the other side of the river, and anyone seen anywhere else was probably a terrorist. I added: "You were a second away from being shot."

One of the chaps went as white as a sheet, and I thought he was going to pass out. He now realised just how very foolish and very lucky he had been. Both of them had learned a very important lesson, do as you are told to the letter.

I collected the crystals from them, and we had a smoke and a friendly chat before Arthur and I made our way back to the camp in the bog.

I can recall another incident that illustrated the importance of obeying orders. On that occasion I almost shot one of my mates.

We had returned from the jungle and were in a rubber plantation waiting to picked up to return to camp.

I was on guard duty in an old bomb crater about four feet deep, and I was bored. So I took out my revolver, removed the six rounds and cleaned it.

Our orders were that whenever we were not on active duty we should load only five rounds so that if the revolver was fired accidentally the firing pin fell on the empty chamber. But I didn't like the idea of seeing a CT, drawing my gun and getting only a click. I wanted a real bang.

So I reloaded the gun and resumed watch when suddenly there was a thud behind me. I turned, and there was my mate, Robbo. After my heart had slowed down a bit I asked what the hell he thought he was doing, jumping into my hole and scaring the shit out of me. He laughed and said he was in the next hole and thought he would join me to pass the time away.

I told him I could have shot him, and then an argument started about who was fastest on the draw. He removed the magazine from his machine-gun and before his gun had got up to my chest I raised my revolver to his face and pulled the trigger.

He turned pale and slumped to the ground. I was trembling thinking of what had nearly happened. There were only five rounds in the cylinder so the revolver had not fired.

But I had proved one thing, the way the Army teaches things is instilled in your brain without your actually realising it. Why did I load only five rounds in the revolver even though I would have felt safer with a full cylinder? Because I had been taught to do it. I had not been in any danger of being confronted by a CT, and did what I had been taught without any further thought.

Some time later my mate asked what would have happened if I had killed him while we were playing. I reminded him that he had jumped into my bomb hole and I would say I had turned round in surprise and shot him as a reflex action.

But it didn't happen, and we both learned not to play games with guns. Even now, so many years later, I hate any child to point a water pistol or cap gun at me.

That was the end of my "close encounters" with hornets and other horrors in the jungle, but these extracts from the diary I kept in 1960 will give an idea of the routine in Malaya.

Monday September 12

Colombo Camp, had breakfast, left camp around 0800 and made our way to Aykaria by three tonners. Weather was warm, quite a nice journey, we arrived at around 1130hrs and waited until noon for the arrival of the boats to travel to Grik which never arrived. We then had a brew-up made by Harry Roberts, then a game of football on the airstrip, all this was at the nearby camp of the 1st RA Regt. After the game we all showered, went for tea. Wow, what a tea, how the other half lived. A film show at 2000hrs. The Square Peg.

Pictured, left, with Robbo, the chap I nearly shot

Wireless ops Christmas party in 1960. I am third from left

Afterwards we had a couple of beers, I bought some fags, went to bed 2200hrs.

Tuesday September 13

I was woken up at 0615 and we all had breakfast at 0630, packed our gear up, drew our weapons. I collected my .38 Smith & Wesson revolver and we waited for the lorries to take us to the boats which had eventually arrived during the night. Checked my fag ration, 50 dry smokes. We then travelled along tracks beside the Sungie Perak to where we enlighted onto the boats. In my boat was two Malays and a medic. It was the most nerve-wracking experience riding in this log boat, it lasted thank goodness for about 40 minutes and we reached our destination a little way from our proposed base camp area. I put my basha up and then commenced to contact HQ, had to get the wire aerial up a tree. I did but not good contact, tried again this time was a good 'un. Sent the usual sitreps and stuff, had a brew-up, a tin of something gooey, stood to, had my rum ration then listened to Radio Malaya (not really allowed, wasting the batteries so they said), then the heavens opened and it rained and stormed. Shit! I had to disconnect the aerial in case the lightning found it.

Wednesday September 14

Got woke up for stand-to at around 0530. I eventually got out of my pit at 0600 to report the Bn HQ sitreps and check on my wireless net of Support Coy. That done breakfast, my what a meal. Tin of beans and sausages with the lovely tea. During the night the river had risen about 12 inches and the water had nearly swamped the aboes' bashas. The rest of the men went to work clearing the roadway until 1400hrs. Nothing happened until stand-to in the evening, usual rum ration, tea, something

to eat, then bed at 2000hrs.

Thursday September 15

Usual stuff-up at stand-to, breakfast of rice, contacted HQ all is well. The lads went out to carry on the work at the road at 0730hrs. My time between making radio calls on the hour to HQ and to my sub-stations at 15 minutes after the hour, was spent fishing for food for the Malays (and for my own enjoyment of course) who really appreciated fresh food. Didn't catch a thing today. Had trouble getting to 52, they must have moved, had to move my wire to get them loud and clear. At about 1330hrs the rain started again, the men returned because of the rain and storm, they had had a bad day.

Erected a Ground Wave wire for better reception. All worked fine. Went fishing, a bloody disaster I lost the lot, must have been a very big catfish, with nobody to dive in and get it out. Returned to camp, stand-to, rum ration that was almost ruined by a bloody great insect that had decided to get drunk. I had a sip but there was a strange taste, the bloody thing must have pissed in it, anyway there was a big army of ants nearby so they got the lot over them, after a short time there was not a lot of ants left.

Friday September 16

Same old routine, stand-to, breakfast beans and maybe bacon (tinned of course) with the good old Rosie Lee and plenty of sugar. The fag situation was critical only two left. Had time for a spot of fishing (I always had extra line and hooks) caught two small fish. Before the 1000hrs airdrop at the DZ I erected the aerial tuned to the frequency for the Valletta Aircraft piloted by Aussies and waited for the sound of his engines, stoked the fire with green stuff to make plenty of smoke (wind direction).

Great, here he comes "Hello five one for Valletta aircraft, how do you hear me? Over."

"See the smoke mate I'll do a pass to check OK?" (Their voice procedure was non-existent). "51 Roger out."

"OK mate 'ere we come, hope you get 'em OK. See yer mate, cheers." And that was that.

Well it was a success, except one chute fell into the river and was lost much to the grief of the Aboes it was their fresh days' rations that was lost. I told HQ of the loss and they said that they would send another lot up to us by boat tomorrow. We all hoped so anyway. Got in touch with Dick Birch c/s 52, who had trouble with a double aerial he had put up. All in all it had been a fair day so the routine continues, time passing but the good news is it's another day nearer DEMOB.

Saturday September 17

Woke as usual stand-to, a nice cuppa, a fag (now fully stocked) made the calls to HQ and Coy net. We had to go and wait for a boat downstream to take our officer out as he was ill with a temperature and possible fever. The officer replacing him for a day (yes only a day) was a Mr King. Very nice chap. Tracking Team officer, he had just returned from the UK from leave and some courses he had taken there.

Sunday September 18

Woke up and realised it was Sheila's birthday tomorrow, had a fag, cup of tea made the calls as normal. Wished her a happy birthday for tomorrow. Mr King left us at 1100hrs together with Pte Harding (digger) went with him with a severely cut hand. Mr Taylor arrived to take over, he is on the ball.

I knew Mr Taylor from previous operations. I went fishing, was quite successful, altogether I caught seven catfish various sizes, but good enough for the Malays to supplement their diet.

Finished today's notes in the dark while listening to Voice of America then discovered that an army of red ants have decided to invade my bedroom.

I can hear a motor boat grinding its way up river, not very nice in the moonlight, bad enough in the daylight. Bedtime tonight at 2330hrs.

Sorry, forgot a vital bit of news. I had to contact HQ by land line (telephone) for the resup, seems the operators were drunk having a demob party for someone. Still that's life.

Monday September 19

Woke up at 0745. Stand-to, fag, tea, make the routine calls. Many Happy Returns of the Day my love xxx. Well my pet I'm thinking of you.

Moved my basha I'm now with Trick, we shifted the aerial and went fishing. Then we learnt with the next platoon net calls that the platoon officer Mr Barnet of c/s 52 was ill, with suspected leptosirosis or something

like that, he was in a poor shape anyway. And he was medivaced out. Nothing else happened the rest of the day, nite-nite.

Tuesday September 20

Got up as usual, done the same things I've been doing since this lot started. Caught four big fish in the morning, same old routine sorry but that's life as a wireless operator. Very boring, nite-nite.

Wednesday September 21

Had a late night, missed stand-to eventually got up at 0730hrs, Mr Taylor let me lie in, missed the Coy net calls made HQ at 0735. Mr Taylor and I talked and he reckoned that the Para Regt is 100per cent regular now since 1950. Why he said this I do not recall. Anyway the good news is that there's an airdrop today. We got the drop all OK no problems, returned to camp sorted out the rations, the mail which was welcome.

Repaired the axes and the boys returned to their road repairs. Cpl Double was casavaced out back to Grik, he had badly cut his leg. I told our HQ who made arrangements for medical people to be there for him. Otherwise it was a normal Resup Day. Went to bed at 2330hrs thinking my little baby boy is four months old today.

How strange I woke up at 0745hrs. I don't know why but I was feeling jarred off. As it turned out it was a sod of a day!

After the morning routine it happened that Cpl Weston cut his hand and needed to be casavaced out. I couldn't get through because of interference, after a two hour effort to contact HQ I eventually got through.

Then after all that the officer wanted to know how a bloody rugger match had fared at the camp. Adrian cooked some chips they were really good. When the guys at the road were working a bloody great tiger appeared and the guy on guard took a shot at it and missed (as usual?).

Apart from that a normal day. Went fishing at around 1700hrs, caught a really big fish it nearly broke my attap branch rod. Adrian caught one last night. Returned to camp where Mr Taylor and the boys were talking about the Army, seemed to be quite a good chap really, he is after all an old dog! Went to bed about 2100hrs said a prayer for Sheila and my Michael.

Friday September 23
Les woke me up with a beautiful cup of instant coffee, made the usual calls, went fishing lost the lot hook line and stone, well annoyed made a model wooden boat with outrigger instead. First time it capsized ha! ha! Made adjustments all OK, The second attempt, well the last time it was seen it was a good 200 yards away and still going strong round a bend in the river. Will make a little raft next time. Meanwhile Les has cooked some Ipswich rice it was really good. Sykes came and made a nuisance of himself but he is OK really. Weapon inspection at 1800hrs (guns). After the inspection I tuned into Radio Malaya and listened to nonstop pop records until about 2115hrs.

Saturday September 24
Mr Taylor woke me up at 0720hrs and said that the boys could have the day off. I made a cup of coffee, had a couple of fags and made my routine calls to the other units. I have not said but daily patrols were still being sent out as a matter of course and it appeared that men were exchanging weapons with each other for some reason or another, maybe a chap with a rifle wanted more firepower and borrowed a Sterling sub-machine gun. Anyway as it happened I had just finished cleaning my revolver and was in the process of inserting five rounds into the cylinder, which swung out to the left side of the frame, I closed the cylinder. At this point the officer who was watching me grabbed the revolver and told me I had loaded it wrongly, the empty space was on the wrong side of the hammer if it was fired. (My revolver turned clockwise the empty chamber was at 11 o'clock so if fired accidentally the hammer would fall on the empty chamber). He claimed that this was a classic example of incompetence and tried to wrench the gun from my hand intending to alter the position of the unloaded chamber to the one o'clock position. The sergeant seeing us struggle asked what was up, we parted and with great glee I showed the officer how my revolver worked. The fact that he had a Webley .38 revolver which rotated the other way round. It all sorted itself out and the matter was not brought up again. Turned in earlier at 2100hrs.

Sunday September 25
Woke up about 0700hrs made a cup of coffee for Mr Taylor who is going home to the UK to join the paras. Our Major Jackson is due in at 1230hrs to replace him.
The lads returned to the road blowing up trees that were in the way and some to make the bridges with. I'm lying in the sun soaking up the warmth and getting a tan. Mr Jackson arrived at 1300hrs and started to flap about as usual. Well the bloody band turned up with him with their instruments. A little while later they gathered on the river bank and played as a convoy of small boats floated by. Bleeding Waltzing Matilda they played.

Monday September 26
Woke up done the same things as usual, but two lads came in from the road party John and Ray they didn't like it being in camp it was boring for them. They had been on leave in Singapore and returned on the 20th to the jungle.
Later as the lads returned from the road works they played them in to the camp. The feelings were mixed regarding the presence of the band boys playing to an Australian officer in a boat. We are building a road and bridges blowing up trees and making a real din, but playing music to a bleeding boat beats everything! The rest of the day panned out alright. I felt a bit rough was cold and shivery, had a good rum ration and went to bed.

Tuesday September 27
Woke up feeling a bit better than last night, Les made me a drink of coffee had a couple of fags, felt better. The lads returned to their roadworks, the band lads returned to the riverbank around midday tuned their instruments up and then this rather bigger boat came into view very slowly it went past with our lads playing Waltzing Matilda and we could all see an Aussie brigadier saluting us as he went by. Later an old EA officer came into our camp who had been with the Sarawak Rangers who were about two miles away to see the spectacle of the brigadier, but he was really pissed off that he had missed it all. Tricker made us a meal of rice to eat later. Mr Veitch turned up to speak to c/s 52 but missed the call by two minutes, boy was he mad.

The diary ends here, and eventually my National Service also ended. But there is one other story worth telling. And it is a story that had an amazing sequel nearly half a century later.

81

We were on patrol walking in single file across a swamp. The only way we could cross it was to step on tussocks of grass that grew on more solid ground. But as each person stepped on to the grass it was pushed farther and farther into the water, which was very deep.

There was only one chap behind me as we made our way, and then for some reason I looked round and he had disappeared. All I could see was his hat floating on the water.

I immediately got down full-length on the tussock, and another soldier held out his bren-gun barrel so I could hold it with one hand for support. With the other hand I groped around in the water until I felt a head. I grabbed the hair and told Kenny, the bren-gunner to lean back and pull me upright while I kept hold of the chap's hair.

This worked fine, and he came out gasping. But we then dropped him back in again — making sure to hold on to him this time — to get his weapon! I did not know the chap's name because I went on operations with different platoons each time.

I didn't think much more about this incident until years later when we formed a veterans group for men who had served in Malaya with the 1st battalion of the East Anglian Regiment. One day one of the members, Mick Holder, showed me his album of photographs from Malaya, and mentioned that while he was there someone pulled him out of a swamp and saved his life. I was amazed.

"That was me," I said. "I was the bloke who pulled you out by your hair." After nearly half a century I now knew the chap's name.

Mick also told me about a monkey he brought back from Malaya, which died only recently and was given a funeral with military honours.

And then...

In 1963 I started work as a plumber with Romford Council. I joined the union, but when I went to a meeting I realised that the people on the top table were pro-Communist. I told them I had spent two years in Malaya fighting bastards like them, and walked out.

I was a bit fed up, and when I saw an advert for a home study course in private investigating I took it up. But on the third lesson I discovered the cost of the equipment I would need. Far beyond me. Then it was back to being a plumber and working for a variety of firms, and then setting up on my own. But in 1995 my wife Sheila died from cancer. The effect was devastating. I had to return every night to an empty home, except for our pet dog, Domino. The hobbies we had shared, the dinner that had always been ready for me, the welcome cup of tea, watching television together — all this was missing.

I was in a terrible state, and needed something to occupy my mind. For the second time I spotted an advert about becoming a private investigator. I sent away for the course, and this time stuck at it, helped by the fact that I had now met Sylvia, a lovely lady, and Domino and I moved in with her.

I was still doing plumbing while learning to be a private eye in the evenings. I sent away for the advanced course, and then came the day when I put an advert in the local paper: R S Faulkner, Private Investigation Services."

The phone rang. A voice asked for the private investigator. I was dumbstruck, I had got a client. But I was even more surprised when the man asked if I could find a man and a dog!

It turned out that a *Reunited. Richard (left) and the man he pulled from the swamp* German Shepherd had savaged my client's small pet dog in a park in Colchester. He wanted me to find out where the man lived to claim damages.

That evening I asked Sylvia if she would like a walk in the park. It was pouring with rain, but she joined me and we got soaked. But I saw my man with his dog and stopped to talk to him. I pretended I had lost a dog and asked if he had seen one.

When he said he was wet and was going home I watched where he went, made a note of the house and next day checked the electoral roll for a name. Job done. I got paid.

So I continued as a plumber during the day, and a detective equipped with binoculars, camera, tape-recorder and case-notes at night. A bit different from the radio, aerials, machete and revolver I used to carry around the Malayan jungle. And not a hornet in sight.

— *Richard Faulkner©*

22649111 LCpl Brian Fillery

The General gave me top marks for my 'Latin' translation

DAD WAS assistant manager of the Gas Works at Hindley near Wigan at the beginning of the war and head of the Fire Brigade. Even though he was in a protected job he joined the Army, and my mother, brother and I moved to Sandhurst, Kent where we lived in a converted single-decker bus. I won a scholarship to Cranbrook School, a small public school, where I excelled in the school cadet corps.

At the end of the war I become a boarder at Cranbrook when dad returned from India and the family moved back to Hindley.

When my call up papers arrived for National Service I had to have a medical and an interview to see which branch of the Army I was fit for.

They looked at my record and said that as I had been in the signals section in cadets and had built a crystal set I was obvious material for the Royal Corps of Signals. I was quite happy to have something to do with electronics and radio, so I did not point out that the Army no longer used crystal sets.

Mum said to me that as I had to do National Service I should adopt the attitude of doing the two years and have a great time while doing it. I followed her good advice.

On March 28 1952 I left home clutching my suitcase and travel documents and took a train to Catterick Camp in Yorkshire for training.

Even though I had been used to boarding school and cadets it was quite a culture shock in some ways. The barracks were pretty bare to say the least but the worst thing was that our washroom had a broken window pane and no hot water. It is very hard to get a good shave in cold water with an icy wind from the North Sea blowing on your face. I was lucky that I didn't have to shave every day as some did.

The food was not the best but we were young and somewhat hungry after all the training we did. We could not go out for the first few weeks but after we had passed basic training we were allowed into town in uniform. I joined a youth group at the local church and we redecorated the church hall.

We were given a lot of lectures and shown films on various aspects of Army life. One film that was quite memorable was the one on VD. The film had some pretty horrible graphic footage of what the disease could look like and it had the effect that was intended. Many were put off sex for at least two days.

After basic training I was put into a group of seven recruits for officer training, during which we were told we had to become blood donors. If we didn't, we would not pass the course. That really annoyed me and I have never given blood since.

Though I was not kicked off the course as some were, I did not pass the final test. So after another interview it was decided that as I had some technical skills, I should become a radio mechanic. I was shifted almost to the other end of Catterick and joined the radio mech school, where eventually I passed.

While I was doing the course all sorts of interesting things happened. One night one of the camp guards got the fright of his life when he spotted a body hanging by its neck from a rope on one of the water towers. It looked like a suicide.

He called out the guard and an extremely nervous sergeant climbed up to cut the body down — only to find it was just a stuffed dummy someone had put there as a prank.

I also joined the Army Theatre Group, which put on plays for the whole district in their own theatre. For Pygmalion, in which I had a small speaking part, I did

Seated front left, in my early NS days

the female make-up. Before one performance I was in the women's dressing room where they were in various stages of dress and undress when a man opened the door.

There was a mad rush to cover up before he could see anything and shouts of "get out." Not that there was anything to see except some underwear, but I thought it a very strange reaction because I was in the room and they weren't at all concerned.

We used to have a party after the last night of the play, gin and beer-drinking binges that went on for hours, but because we were the theatre group we got away with not being in bed at lights out.

The theatre caretaker was a soldier, paid by the Army, who had been in the job for ages and was quite a good actor. He lived in a set of rooms underneath the stage and had a great life, no parades and cooking his own rations. All he had to do was keep the place clean and in good repair.

One night in the props room he found a brigadier's hat, a swagger stick and the proper shoulder flashes which he fastened on to his greatcoat. Putting this lot on he marched up the road from the theatre towards our guardroom.

The man on duty saw him coming and turned out the guard who presented arms in approved fashion. The guard was duly inspected and given a great rollocking for being badly turned out and not smart enough in their drill. The bogus brigadier then left and walked back down the road and into the darkness.

After he had gone the guard sergeant became suspicious because brigadiers usually arrive and depart in cars, and this one had walked. He reported the incident and eventually the culprit was arrested and put on a charge.

As a result he had to attend parade each morning instead of lying in bed until noon.

I was on guard myself one night when a soldier walked in and gave himself up after being absent without leave. I had to lock him up in a cell, which was a bit embarrassing because I knew him quite well as he was in our hut.

He was given 28 days' jankers. But when asked if he had anything to say he cheekily told the CO that he was sorry he couldn't do it because he was due for demob in two weeks. So the CO gave him 14 days. He was the chap who had planted the body on the water tower.

About this time I decided to grow a moustache. I had to ask permission and have it entered in my paybook. The moustache started off as a thin line, but eventually grew into what I called my Laughing Cavalier. Actually it was more like the RAF type with its swept-up ends.

Two people I remember well from this time are Ken Simpson and "Polly" Perkins. We went around together and got up to all sorts of larks. In Richmond there was a brothel which we planned to raid pretending to be the police. But before we could do it the real police raided it and closed it down.

We devised a coat of arms which I painted and put over the classroom door. It was a shield with a selection of radio mechs' tools on it, and underneath a scroll with the motto Fixitor. One day we had a visit from an inspecting general, and as he was leaving he admired the shield and asked what the motto stood for.

I told him it was Latin for "We repair things." He was quite happy with that, so either he was not a Latin scholar or he liked my cheeky explanation. It actually was short for "Fix it or F--- it."

We also wrote a poem which was typed up and pinned on the lecture room wall. I do not know to this day if someone knew some words of the original or if we just started it between us from scratch. It was inspired in part by one of our class who although told in no uncertain terms not to do it, stuck the prods of his Avo Meter into the 240 Volt AC mains to see if he could get a reading. This blew the meter up.

THE RADIO MECHANIC'S THEME SONG

In the little town of Electon,
Way out beyond Anode Bend,
Is the grave of a radio mechanic,
Who lies earthed at his positive end.

Let us give him his due, in all fairness
He was good at his job and had brains,
But he was once a little too careless
When fitting a plug to the mains.

Into the hole went his finger
To test that the plug was alright,
He opened his mouth like a singer
And lit up like a blue neon light.

He shot off the floor like a rocket,
Shocked to his innermost core,
His finger remained in the socket,
And the switch was switched on by the door.

In a flash he was really a goner,
The shock made him cry out in pain,
He was buried with full milit'ry honour,
And told not to do it again.

There's a moral to this little story,
A moral that's quite plain to see,
If you don't want short circuits to glory,
Don't fiddle around with HT!

I had my own copy and typed up copies for Ken and Polly. Some years later, when I was in Australia, someone enquired in the Amateur Radio magazine if anyone knew the full poem. I was amazed that it had achieved such fame. And as the original was getting rather battered I typed up a copy for him.

In my TA days as a 2nd Lieut

The end of the radio mechs course came and most of us passed. Then we had to await our postings, living in fear that we could be sent to the Korean War.

Polly Perkins went to Korea, but Ken and I were posted to Germany, but first we were all sent off to a transit camp in Devon. When we got there they had nothing about us on their books, so after we were allocated a hut to sleep in we were on our own.

We went on parades the first few days but our names were not called so we decided it was a waste of time. We got up just in time for a late breakfast, missed parades and spent most of our time doing nothing or going into town.

This went on for a week and then we were hauled up in front of the CO for not being on parade. We told him what had happened when we arrived, but obviously the papers for us had now come through and we were in trouble. We were given seven days' cookhouse duty, which was not too bad because we got extra food if there was any going.

The first day it was all peeling potatoes and washing up but then someone told us about the garbage detail, so we rushed off to find the bloke in charge and applied.Each morning we would load the garbage bins on to the back of a truck, collect our cut lunch from the cook and head off into the country to the garbage tip.

The funny thing was that the truck would be slow on the outward journey — must have been the weight of the garbage! It might break down, or even overheat, and we would have to stop on the side of the road to boil a kettle and eat our rations in the sunshine until it recovered. This was usually about the time we finished our lunch.

Eventually we would get to the tip, empty the garbage and spend the rest of the day making our way back via various cafes and pubs to arrive just in time for the evening meal. It was a great life.

But all good things, including garbage detail, must come to an end. Ken and I went by train to Harwich, took a troopship to the Hook of Holland and joined 1 Corps Signal Regiment just outside Herford in Westfalia.

The camp itself was on the Bad Salzuflen road in a pine forest, and I was posted into H/N Troop, which was the signals troop that provided radio communications for the heavy guns of the Royal Artillery.

Germany was colder than England but the huts were all brick built, fairly new and well insulated. They had several rooms housing six or eight men, on either side of a central corridor with a shower/toilet block across the far end. During the winter we had central heating which was so hot that we could leave the windows open even though there was snow on the ground outside.

We had a number of characters in the troop. One was Jock who came from Glasgow and, when he was younger, had been involved with street gangs there. I learned a great deal from him which made me a lot more streetwise than I had been.

He was always playing tricks, and once I returned to camp after an evening in town and found that my bed looked extremely neat and tidy. Too tidy. So I carefully uncov-

Retired, and enjoying my hobbies

85

ered it, and lying in the middle like an enormous balloon was a condom filled with water.

I knew immediately who would do such a thing so I lifted it up carefully and carried it down to Jock's room. I told him he could either take it or I would throw it at him. He thought it was very funny but he did eventually take it. He was dancing around the room laughing, with the condom in his hands over his head, when it split and covered him with water. Then everyone got a laugh. He would often put one inside unlocked lockers so when you opened the door it fell on you.

There was a troop storeroom in the upper part of the camp which was half empty and we used part of it for working on the radios. It was possible to get out of other work by having a radio set "to repair" or one that needed checking — provided you didn't pull the stunt too often.

Once an hour a bus to town ran past the camp entrance, but most of us saved our money and walked the mile there and back or cadged a lift from an Army truck. In town there was a YMCA right beside the river with an excellent canteen, a library and lots of games facilities.

One day when I was in there I found they had a couple of darkrooms in the basement, and were starting photography classes, so I signed up. This gave me access to the darkrooms at any time and also to a locked cupboard to keep my stuff in. All I had to do was buy whatever paper and chemicals I needed from the many photography shops in town, and these were relatively cheap.

So I started doing my own developing and printing and spent a great deal of time in the darkroom at weekends.

There was also a little pub in the town which was more in the nature of a cafe. Some of us would often go there for a meal instead of going back to camp as the food was good and cheap.

Often I would wander about the town on my own looking in the shops. Once I saw some nice looking biscuits in a bakery and went in. Not being that familiar with metric measures I asked for two kilos and was astounded at the size of the bag handed to me. However they all got shared out and eaten when I got back to the camp and they had cost me next to nothing.

We did quite a few exercises with other units, and one day I was on one when our CO, Major Morgan, said he was short of a driver and radio operator for a jeep. I could drive, though I did not have a licence so I volunteered. They got

me to drive round the camp in the jeep and as I didn't kill anyone they gave me the job.

I was assigned to an Artillery colonel as his driver and operator, and off we went to the Hohne Ranges where they did the live artillery firing. We were camped in a farmyard for most of the time. On one of the few free days we had some of us were taken to the site of the Bergen-Belsen concentration camp which was only a short distance away.

When I got back to the farm I asked the farmer if they had known about the camp. When he told me that they had not I got angry. "Surely" I said, they must have known because it was only just on the other side of a wood not half a kilometre away, and they must have seen the smoke from the crematoriums. Why didn't they do something about it?

After a while the farmer's wife said quietly that of course they knew of it, but if they had even mentioned it they would have been put in there themselves and so they kept quiet.

Early one morning I was ordered to drive the colonel to a hilltop where there were a few other officers. They stood there for a while and then the shells started coming over our heads and dropping in the valley below.

Apart from the noise of the shells it seemed quite safe and nobody else was bothered so I just stood there. After a while the colonel said, quite calmly, that maybe we should all move as sometimes in the cool of the morning the shells could fall short. You've never seen so many people and vehicles leave an area in different directions in such a short time.

The only problem with the colonel was that he sometimes wanted to drive the jeep himself, and I had to sit in the back. But every time he drove it he did something to the gearbox and then it would not select some gears. So when he was finished I would drive it back to wherever we were camped and take the gearbox top off and put the selectors back in place.

He reckoned the jeep was useless but I reckoned it was him as it never did it with me or anybody else. Mind you I was not stupid enough to tell him that. He thought I was a genius to be able to fix it myself without having to take it to REME, who did all the big repairs.

We had two sergeants in our troop. One was Sgt Matthews who was an arrogant know-all type, and I always seemed to be in trouble with him. Once I had a fault in a 19 set out in the field. The 19 set had a special locking mechanism on the tuning system so you could flick from one frequency to another. This could get jammed with dust so when this one failed I took it apart, cleaned it and spread it out on a blanket.

I had to make sure that the many plates and screws were in the right order and the right way up so I could put it back together again. At midday Sgt Matthews told me to go to lunch, and I told the blokes not to touch the stuff I had laid out. But when I returned the whole lot had been bundled up and piled together. I was mad.

I was even madder when I found out it was Sgt Matthews who had done it, and not only that, but he had put me on a charge for wrecking military equipment.

So I had to go to Major Morgan's office, marched in by an escort of military police. I was asked to explain myself, and said that I had a similar set at home and knew how to repair and clean it provided the parts were left in sequence.

The question then asked was who had touched the stuff and Sgt Matthews had to own up that he had. So it ended with him getting into trouble instead of me. The set was sent to REME and it took them three weeks to sort it out.

On another occasion we were out in the field and Sgt Matthews told me to stay with a broken set all night and have it fixed by the next morning or he would have my radio mech's certificate taken off me.

Eventually, in the early hours of the morning, I discovered that the brazing on one of the antenna tuning coils had cracked. The set would have to be repaired by REME because we didn't carry those parts as spares.

In the morning Sgt Matthews turned up with the bloke from REME fully expecting that I would not have found the fault. When I explained what the trouble was and showed him the broken weld the REME bloke complimented me for finding it as it was extremely hard to find, and even they would have been hard-pressed. The look on Sgt Matthews's face was balm to my soul

On one exercise we had three weeks camped on an old wartime aerodrome near Venlo. While we were going there along the autobahn I was in the back of a truck with some others.

We were followed by a Russian Army vehicle and one of the idiots in our truck stood up and pretended to fire at the Russians.

I took the gun away from him and waved and smiled at the Russian driver hoping he would not complain. But they overtook us, and then our convoy pulled up on the side of the road. I thought the Russians had reported what had happened and we were going to be in trouble. However all we had stopped for was a brew-up. I was somewhat relieved.

I found the German people pretty easy to get on with and mainly very kind. I only recall one Nazi type, who was a worker on a farm. He would rant and rave at us, and so we goose-stepped about with our fingers under our noses giving him Hitler salutes and generally taking the mickey out of him.

In contrast we received a lot of kindness from some of the Germans. Three of us were once camped in a farmyard for a few days. During the day the whole family, including the grandmother and the children, worked in the fields hoeing and weeding. But in the evening they invited us into their home.

It was just as well because every night at 7pm, regular as clockwork, there would be a big storm with thunder and lightning and the rain would pour down for an hour or so. Then the next day would be bright and sunny. This went on the whole time we were there.

And each night when the storm was due we were invited inside. One night after the rain had finished the farmer asked if we would like some beer and then asked us for some money, which we thought was a bit peculiar although they were apparently pretty poor people.

We gave him the money and he went out and did not come back. We thought we had lost our money, but after an hour he returned with some bottles of beer. I found out that as they didn't have any beer in the house he had cycled into the nearest village to get some for us.

Then there was the time we were camped in the back of a bakery at the edge of a village. At night time I was getting ready to bed down in the hay shed, and one bloke was already asleep in a farm cart and two more in the truck.

The daughter came out and kept saying something about it not being allowed. "It is forbidden, no sleeping," and she beckoned us into the house.

I thought for a minute we were all being invited in to sleep with her, but then she showed us a room with a great big bed and two sofas and gave us blankets. And next morning we were treated to a breakfast of hot coffee and fresh bread rolls and given hot water for shaving.

We did not spend all our time out on exercises

and had to do guard duty while in camp. I did not mind it unless it was cold, as you felt quite important wandering around while everyone slept. It was a bit of a farce because we carried rifles but no ammunition although we did have those silly little bayonets.

I became friendly with a soldier who had married quarters in town and often went to his place for meals. It was nice being in a family atmosphere environment again and seeing small children having fun.

They had a nice house that backed on to the river and a live-in German maid whom I became very keen on. Anyway, one thing led to another and one night while we were baby-sitting it happened. I lost my virginity.

I walked back to camp wondering why God didn't strike me down with a lightning bolt for the dreadful sin I had committed. But I must have decided I was being slightly melodramatic, because I went back for more.

The affair lasted a couple of months or so. Then I got a warning from a friend of the girl, another German maid, saying I would be better off dropping her as she was running around with other blokes while I was away on exercises or on leave.

It was very kind of her to give me the warning and I can't imagine why she did it. Possibly she realised that I was so innocent that it would never have dawned on me that my girlfriend might do something like that.

Maybe just as well that I did drop her, because not long afterwards a soldier in our troop was accused of being the father of the child a German girl was carrying. She wanted him to marry her and he was in a right state. The Army investigated and after a medical examination it was found that though the soldier had been in Germany for only two months, the girl was at least six months pregnant.

One of the best postings I ever got in Germany was to the transmitter station. This was some way from our camp in another town, up on top of a hill and surrounded by barbed wire and trees. It was just like a small prison camp and was guarded by men from the Displaced Persons Organisation who patrolled the outside with dogs.

All radio mechs, and some operators, had to do two weeks there to maintain the radios.

The place had a staff of five and there were about seven temporary mechs and operators. This made 12, but the official ration strength for the place was 30. This meant there was far more food than was needed and so we ate very well, and the kettle was on the stove all day long.

There were no parades and little work to do as the sets were all in good order. Other than the first day when we were shown around I never so much as looked at a set, let alone touched one.

I sat around most of the day reading books from the extensive library. When I got bored with that I would make a cup of tea or go out and chat to the guards patrolling the wire and make friends with the dogs.

We never saw the officer in charge. He lived in town, and showed up only if there was a problem or some form needed signing.

Eventually March 1954 came round and I was demobbed. But I had still to serve part-time in the Territorial Army for about four years. I was posted to the signal unit in Atherton, which was not that far away from home.

After I had been with the TA for a while the CO, Major Robinson, suggested I should go on the officer course and see if I could get a commission. This time I passed with no problems and was made 2nd Lieut.

I remember little of that course except for ripping my hand open on a nail on the assault course and being drilled by the infamous RSM Brittain who was British Army bullshit personified. He would stand to attention and salute when talking to an officer on the phone. Not only that but he would also tell the officer he was saluting and standing to attention and wait to be told to stand easy.

I would wear dad's dress uniform and Sam Browne belt when I had to, but otherwise used my old Army uniform which had the pips sewn on.

I also carried dad's swagger stick, which had been made for him by someone out in India and was different from the normal ones. On large parades I was often asked why I did not carry the regulation baton, but my reply was that it had been my father's during the war, and so I got away with it.

One problem with the Territorial Army was that I had to do at least one parade a week which meant I had to go to Atherton and back. Dad could not run me in all the time so he bought a Coventry Climax 98cc autocycle for me, which I paid back at so much a week.

The machine was designed to be pedalled up to speed and then the clutch was dropped which started the motor and drove the back wheel. I could ride this without a driver's licence. One day Major Robinson asked me why I rode the autocycle. I told him that I had never passed the driving test, though he knew that I had driven Army vehicles and motorbikes.

He asked me to leave my autocycle in the drill hall and drive him in the Champ (a Rolls-Royce engined jeep) to our home as he wanted to see dad. I think this was just an excuse, because when we got there he had a cup of tea and then signed a form saying I had passed the Army driving test for cars, trucks and motorbikes. I sent the form in and got my driver's licence,

I bought a Panther 600 motorbike new and had a glassfibre windshield fitted which came out to cover the handlebars.

If we went on any convoys with the TA I acted as dispatch rider even though I was an officer. This caused some fun now and then when I rode up in uniform on the Panther and everyone assumed I was just a dispatch rider and not an officer. So some guard at a gate would tell me to move it or myself, then realise and snap into a salute and an apology.

Then along came the Suez do. Egypt under Nasser decided that it would nationalise the Suez Canal, and British troops were sent in.

I was put on a secret 24-hour standby. If I got a phone call with nothing else but a particular code word I had to walk out of where I was

without telling anyone, collect my uniform and gear, and report to the TA. But it never happened.

And then...

After my time in the Army with all its adventures I had not felt like going to university. So I joined Pilkington's, the big glass works that dominated St Helens, as a time and motion study engineer.

Then, four years later in 1958 I became assistant transport manager in a company where I supervised the transport of heavy duty cooking appliances

In 1962 I emigrated to Australia, working as a welder and general labourer and then an electrician. Five years after this I became film supervisor with a television station and then spent 12 years as a films officer with the Queensland government. This involved producing and directing films and teaching photography. In 1982 I was with a company installing solar panels, retiring in 1998.

I have written computer programs and contributed more than 100 movie articles to magazines, and also written a book on archaeological photography. I am particularly interested in aboriginal archaeology and have recorded the aborigine Gumbaingah language.

— Brian Fillery©

The afternoon that I had a close shave with an NCO's authority

SOME 26 different locations in two years. That's my estimation of the number of camps I stayed in after my National Service began at Catterick in Yorkshire on a very cold day in January 1956.

I remember the first few days when we learned what discipline was all about, and also what to do if you went out and had sex with a woman. Very important things that we were told we needed to know.

The discipline was tough. We were shouted at, told what idiots we were and, according to the NCOs, were the worst shower they had ever had the misfortune to have to train.

We were marched up and down for hours on end and sometimes made to stand in front of a mirror saying: "Mirror, mirror on the wall, who is the biggest idiot of them all."

The NCOs would inspect our bedding every morning and if it was not just so, with everything square and neat and tidy, they would throw it down the room and you had to start all over again.

During our marches along the roads we had to have a flagman or a lamp man (depending on whether it was day or night) walking along 100 yards in front and behind us. This was because several sea cadets had been killed when a bus ran into them in Portsmouth.

There were of course a few who could not learn to march, and these would be marched up and down the square on their own in an effort to teach them.

I remember doing a guard duty one night when we were given pickaxe handles and told not to let anyone through unless they could identify themselves, as there was a danger from the IRA. What good we would have been with pickaxe handles against the IRA I don't know.

Near the end of the basic training we were called before an officer to see what we wanted to do in the Army. I desperately wanted to be a dispatch rider and in typical Army fashion was sent to be a wireless operator. Not just any wireless operator but an OP Spec.

I reported to a little village in Leicester just outside Quorn, 10 WTS, where I was taught Morse code including several letters from foreign languages, direction finding which I enjoyed, and how to read teleprinter tape.

One of the jobs we had was to stand in groups round the square at the entrance whenever the Quorn hunt met because the station was fairly hush-hush and they didn't want the hunt riding through the camp.

I was always very bad at time-keeping, and on one occasion missed the morning parade. I was brought before the duty officer to whom I apologised. He dismissed me, but before I could leave the room I was told to about turn and he said I was to do an extra guard duty that night. In that way nothing went on my record but I still got punished. After that I never missed another parade.

Two of us were not up to the standard required —I could only do about 14 words a minute — so we were sent back to Catterick to be ordinary signalmen.

Of course when we started with the rookies we were streets ahead of them and used to spend our time talking while taking Morse at the same time. We were also taught how to operate a 19 set among others and all about wavelengths.

While we were there we were moved to another part of Catterick (my fourth move) where the NCO came to me one day he said that I had not shaved. I replied that I had, and had witnesses. I didn't, but knew I could get someone to back me up.

When he again claimed I hadn't shaved, I replied that in any case, it was now afternoon. At this he just turned and walked away. Though I did not know, but he did, after midday you cannot be charged for not having shaved.

While I was at Catterick all the vehicles were

During training. I am second from left middle row

90

being painted a sand colour with a big white H on the sides and top. We guessed that something was about to happen but didn't know that it was in preparation for the Suez invasion.

We later moved to a different part of Catterick (my move number five) and when it came to my passing-out parade the RSM accused me of shaving my battledress trousers to get a good crease in them. The RSM pointed me out to an officer who asked how long I had been in the Army. When I told him 10 months he said the trousers probably looked shaved because I had kept ironing them, and let me off.

My next move was to Deveral Barracks at Chester were I was given embarkation leave before my scheduled posting to Germany.

I returned to Chester and was getting ready to board the transport for Germany when an NCO came into the room and called out for myself and another lad who had also failed at 10 WTS to go with him.

We said we couldn't because we were going to Germany. "No, you're not," he said, and we were sent instead to Ogbourne St George to Number 2 Press communication signal squadron, which was made up mainly up of reservists who had been recalled due to the Suez crisis.

We were on a two-hour standby, but had an easy time there. I was put on telephone watch one night and told to "let someone know" if the phone rang. No-one told me whom I should tell.

Fortunately nothing happened and after my watch I went to the cookhouse to get some food. Everything had been cleared away and there was only one cook there.

When I explained where I had been he said all he could do was a piece of steak on top of the oven. It was the largest and best piece of steak I have ever had. It was about 12 inches by 9 inches and it took a big effort to finish it.

When the order to move came we went to Wellington Barracks in London and stayed on the top floor of an old stable block. The next day we went to Stansted airport to embark on a plane to Cyprus.

Stansted did not have any of the terminals that are there today, just old Nissen huts. We went out on a passenger flight and were asked what we would like to drink. I did not know what to ask for so said a gin and tonic. Then we landed at Malta and had to wait for 24 hours while a new part was brought out from England to mend the plane.

On Cyprus we were put into a makeshift camp where I remember the latrines consisted of a trench about 30 feet long and 6ft deep with a piece of wood to sit on. There was a sacking screen around the entire area but nothing in between, and a big smelly drop if you happened to fall backwards.

We were then posted to Port Said. The invasion had taken place a day or two earlier, and we went in a Dakota which was equipped for parachutists. The seats consisted of a long bar at the top and another at knee height. Between the two was a triangular canvas which was ideal for parachutists who sit on their parachutes but no good for us who did not have one to sit on.

At Port Said we were taken to a block of flats that had been used by canal pilots and was requisitioned by the Army.

My first impression of Port Said was of a little boy sitting at the roadside begging. He was deformed and his face was covered with flies which he did not bother to brush off.

I also remember seeing a large pile of rifles and ammunition that had been taken from the Egyptian soldiers when they surrendered. Alongside this was a lorry with a row of bullet holes across the windscreen. There was another row across the back of the cab where the bullets had left, but with a gap in the middle where the driver would have been.

We had two Golden Arrow articulated vehicles. One was a radio transmitter full of valves with the name of the person who had made them written on the inside. I was told that this was so they could be sent back to him if they needed repair. There was no room for any other equipment in this lorry.

The second one was a receiver where the teleprinter operators sat to send their messages. Inside the truck was a big board with a series of holes, and plugs and cords linking some of the holes together. When I asked what they were for I was told they were for the frequency. Instead of having dials like the 19 sets, if any enemy came the cords were just pulled out and no-one could work out the frequency.

The Golden Arrows had several giant generators which were a pig to start and very unreliable. Our job was to send back newspaper reporters' copy to Cyprus for onward transmission to newspapers around the world.

If conditions got so bad that the teleprinters could not get the messages through, I was supposed to send and receive them using Morse. This would have been very time consuming.

Of course, the lads had the answer. They got

Today I am involved in charity work

the ticker tape, fastened the ends together to form a loop and just kept sending it again and again until it was received in Cyprus.

While there I became rather disillusioned with reporters as one from a small regional paper gave a graphic description of the front line and even gave the names of soldiers who wanted to send messages home. But we knew he had never left the building we were in the whole time he had been there. So the report did not get sent.

We used to pass the time when we were not on duty by going on to the roof of a six-storey block of flats and throwing a handful of cigarettes over the edge. When the kids came to pick them up we would tip a bowl of water over them.

They did not seem to mind as they kept coming back for more and knew exactly what we would do. I think it was a game for them as well as us.

We were only allowed to buy so many cigarettes a day. I think this was because some of the lads would sell them to the Egyptians.

Of course it was not all fun. When we first went into the block of flats we saw, facing the door, a shattered full-length mirror. Apparently a soldier had gone into the room and seen his reflection. Thinking someone was aiming a stengun at him, he opened fire — and destroyed the mirror!

My most frightening time was when I was put on night guard duty. I was at the back of a very well lit entrance hall and could see only about six feet outside the open entrance. The rest was darkness. After a while I thought "I am a sitting duck here," so put a round in the breech and took off the safety catch.

As I stood there getting more and more nervous a cat dashed across the front of the building. Luckily I did not shoot, so it escaped with one of its nine lives intact.

Another unpleasant experience was the night it rained heavily and washed up the bodies of some Egyptian troops who had been buried in makeshift graves.

When the United Nations' peacekeeping force arrived we had to leave Port Said on a tank landing ship. We sailed to Malta then boarded another ship for the journey back to UK. The sea in the Bay of Biscay was very rough and it took 14 hours to do one nautical mile. At midnight on New Year's Eve I had the privilege — given to the youngest person aboard — of ringing 16 bells.

Back in England we were not allowed off the ship or any communication with the outside world until the next morning. Then our vehicles were thoroughly searched, which took about eight hours. The reason was that someone had found a Russian rifle and taken it on board.

We had used it to shoot at wooden boxes trailed behind the ship. But it finished up at the bottom of the Thames when we were approaching London because the person who had it knew there would be trouble if we were caught with it.

I was questioned by Customs for a good half-hour because I had a camera and a watch that I had bought in Malta. They wanted to know where I had got the money and I told them I had swapped some cigarettes for the watch, and my father had sent me the money to buy the camera.

The Customs officer tried to catch me out with his adding up. But I can read very well upside down and am very good at maths, so I corrected him. "OK, put the watch back on," he said, "you'll be paying enough for the camera."

What he didn't know was that an officer had given me a bottle of Drambuie to take through Customs for him. Unfortunately I did not see him again and when I got home I had to drink it to save it from going to waste!

If he reads this I would be happy to replace it for him.

We were driven to Catterick camp, arriving very late and told to leave our rifles and ammunition in a cell for the night. We threw our ammo bandoliers along the floor into a heap, and the guards, who were all new recruits, nearly had a fit because they thought they would go off.

After disembarkation leave I was sent to the signals depot at Ripon. But they did not want me and sent me across the road to number 35 CER Royal Engineers who were in the adjoining camp.

I was put into the cadre corps which was a mixture of different regiments, Royal Signals, REME, Royal Engineers, etc. We were all dressed in different uniforms and the officers used to get quite annoyed when they were inspecting us. "Why are you not in battledress?"

"Because I am on battery charging and cannot wear BD for battery charging."

In the end we were told to go around the back of the huts and hold our own parade.

We did a lot of wireless exercises while there and got some very good results. We got through from Nottingham to Ripon in voice frequency, which was supposed to have only a very short range of about 20 miles.

On another exercise I also transmitted on a piece of wet string just to see if it would work. I got a weekend leave pass for that.

After Ripon I went back to Chester again and then to Millom where I was taught mobile defence — what to do if the atomic bomb was dropped.

I was shown how to rescue people from collapsed buildings, practising on buildings that had been specially built. On some we had to jack up two or three floors to get people out from underneath. We had to get across a hole in the ground without going down into it to rescue people from a solitary wall that was standing beyond it.

We had to find our way through smoke-filled rooms and under water in sewers. We were taught first aid, how to find out if something was electrified without using instruments and how to get through a brick wall in a cube about three feet on all sides.

On one occasion I was strapped to a stretcher and lowered out of the window three floors up by soldiers who had never done anything like it before. That was quite scary.

To be demobbed I was sent back to Deveral Barracks at Chester which, including the camps where I had stayed on exercise, I reckoned was my 26th Army home.

All in all I really enjoyed my National Service. Many of the things the Army taught me I have never forgotten and they have come in very useful in the past 51 years.

And then...

I had trained in horticulture before call-up, and after demob started my own business as a retail nurseryman near Warrington in Cheshire. But I was not earning enough to get married and buy a house, so took what I thought would be a temporary job as a night telephone operator, while running the nursery during the day.

But the temporary job lasted for 26 years and I finished up as a supervisor with a staff of about 25.

During this time I managed to build up the nursery until it was what everyone now calls a garden centre.

In 2001 I became seriously ill when my heart stopped 32 times in two days. So I sold the nursery outbuildings and expanded a caravan storage area on the land, which I am still running. I am also heavily involved with Rotary and other charity work.

— *Peter Fillery*©

23046110 Cpl John Fitzpatrick

I was excused all parades for the price of a packet of Rinso

I CAME TO England from Ireland in 1949. I was aware of the possibility of being called up for National Service, and I could have returned to Ireland. But when the time came I decided to bite the bullet and do my service.

During my medical a comment was made about my flat feet, which didn't concern me too much as I never had any problems with them. But this would turn out to be of some benefit later on.

I was sent to Blenheim Barracks in Aldershot where we were told that our parade would be the annual inspection parade for the camp, which meant spending the next five weeks on the drill square.

Outside the Orderly Room with my pal

After this we moved to Willems Barracks for trade training, only to be told (yes, you guessed) we would be the annual parade. After a couple of days drilling I was thinking of some means of escape and decided that my flat feet might be the answer.

I bought a small packet of Rinso soap powder, using half to soak my feet in water as hot as I could bear, and repeated the process the following morning. I reported sick and saw the medical officer, carrying my boots and socks and thoughts of being charged with malingering.

I pushed my feet as flat as possible to the floor as the MO looked at them and asked: " Yes, what's the matter?" I said: "It's my feet sir. They hurt when I am on parade and doing drill, and I have been getting reprimanded for moving."

He asked where they hurt, and because I had no idea where flat feet were supposed to hurt, I just said: "All over, sir." He told me to take a seat while he filled in two forms. One for me to take to the QM stores with my boots to be issued with Navy-type shoes. The other I should carry with me at all times. It read: "Excused boots, marching, drill parades and prolonged standing." Not a bad result for the price of a packet of Rinso!

But, as it turned out, this did not cut much ice with the sergeant-major when I was posted to Topsham Barracks at Exeter. He insisted that there was definitely no exemption from parades there. So, on one cold and frosty morning we all lined up on the square with me wearing a pair of tan slip-on shoes because it just happened that both pairs of my Navy shoes were in for repair.

While the inspection was going on I started to lift one foot at a time until the company commander spotted me.

As I went through the foot-lifting routine he shouted: "Fitzpatrick, you look like you want a shit." After the parade CSM Rooke snapped: "You, in my office." There I pointed out that I was excused parades, but to no avail. However, at least that was my last parade on the square. In future I attended only morning muster parades.

By the time of my posting to Exeter I was married, and had the advantage of living in married quarters. Before that I had spent some time in Hut 18, which was beside the D Company office and housed all the odd-bods. We became something of a target for abuse when we were seen going to wash when everyone else was on parade.

I had an interesting career

I was the courts martial clerk in the Orderly Room, and remember one occasion when there was an IRA alert and the adjutant had to update the depot Standing Orders. I had to type them because no-one else with positive vetting was available. I thought it was ironic that John Fitzpatrick, the only Irishman in the camp, was typing out secret orders about how to deal with the IRA!

Once we went out on an exercise, and took our own Orderly Room truck with tables, chairs and blankets. At night, when the convoy halted, we were told we needed a sentry. A new recruit with a rifle was sent to guard us, and when we moved again we took him into our truck with us.

Much later, after most of us had had a kip, we stopped and I went outside and overheard the adjutant on the radio: "One oboe roger missing." He repeated this several times, and finally I realised that the oboe roger — phonetic alphabet for other rank — was our guard, now fast asleep in the Orderly Room truck.

Another incident I remember was the amusing case of the RSM's cap.

I am not sure if it was a high government official or one of the Army's top brass who was to visit the barracks. But anyway, there was to be a big parade with a six-gun rifle salute. The RSM had to pick suitable "volunteers" for this job. One of my Orderly Room friends, being tall, was earmarked.

I mentioned to the RSM that soldiering was not exactly the old-Etonian's strongpoint. But nevertheless he was selected.

The gunners needed a few practice sessions on the parade ground. And after one of these the RSM charged into our office waving his blackened cap and screaming: "Look what that so-and-so has done to me."

Apparently when my pal fired his blank round his rifle was rather close to the RSM's head. Well, I had warned him!

The RSM was all for charging the poor fellow with practically anything and everything up to attempted murder. But I believe when he cooled down it was all forgotten.

Instead of being demobbed after two years I made a decision one day to sign on after looking through a little book on the depot establishment. I discovered that my job carried the rank of full corporal. So I asked the adjutant what I had to do to get some promotion.

He pointed out that as National Servicemen were in for such a short time it was not worth promoting them. I asked what my chances would be if I signed on, and he finally agreed that although it was highly irregular, upon signing on I would get one stripe and after six months would get the second one. So I stayed in for another year.

And then...

Since demob I have had a mostly interesting life, supplying the labour, supervision and equipment involved in air-conditioning and paper-drying. I worked in a variety of places, including television studios, paper mills, ships and prisons. And I once made the front page of the London Evening News.

Working at Broadcasting House in London my job was to drill holes in large columns in the basement studio.

Each day we had to go to the control room who would check that no broadcasts were scheduled, and then give us a "knocking chitty" allowing us to get on with the work. On most Saturdays the broadcasts were from Manchester, and on one Saturday I just telephoned the control room and was told to carry on.

I was on the fourth hole when the door burst open, and several people charged in shouting "Stop, stop!" Apparently Uncle Mac was doing a Children's Hour programme and I had put him off air. When he was back on, he apologised to his young listeners. The Evening News headline was Uncle Mac Doesn't Know the Drill.

Later I became a section engineer working on the Channel Tunnel where I supervised the installation of the pressure relief dampers, crossover doors and pumping stations. It was a difficult, but also interesting job. Unfortunately none of my work is visible to the thousands of travellers who use the tunnel every day.

— John Fitzpatrick©

Ordered to catch flies and put them in a matchbox for counting

IN APRIL 1953 I had just finished a four-year apprenticeship as a baker-confectioner when National Service called me. We arrived at Aldershot station and climbed into an Army three-ton truck. A man with three stripes on his sleeve shouted: "Right, you horrible lot. You may have broken your mother's heart but you won't break mine."

At the barracks we lined up to be issued with a uniform and boots. The items were thrown at us, fit didn't seem to matter. And if we complained they were the wrong size we were just told "this isn't a fashion parade, move along."

There were 10 of us in one hut with a highly-polished wooden floor that was never walked on. You had to edge your way behind the beds that were lined up either side.

I never got used to sleeping with nine other men snoring and moaning, with creaky beds and the noise of flushing toilets.

When I left school at the age of 15 in 1949 my father had arranged for me to be apprenticed to a baker and confectioner for four years, and when this was completed I began my National Service and became 23032291, but most times, when I was not being called insulting names, I was just 291.

This number had to be on every item of equipment, and there was certainly plenty of that. Metal items — cutlery, mess-tins and waterbottle — needed a hammer and metal die to imprint the number.

If someone lost an item he just pinched someone else's. It didn't matter that his own number was not on it, until an officer noticed. And then there was trouble.

Our parade ground was the size of a football pitch and covered in a mixture of soil and gravel which was trawled by someone with a garden rake to make straight lines. If the sergeant didn't like the lines they had to be done again. A thankless and pointless job. One of many.

I remember one day when I had my hair cut three times. The sergeant sent me to get it cut and I told the barber to trim a bit off. When the sergeant saw the result he sent me there again. Then he said: "I thought I told you to get your hair cut," and to make sure he took me to the barber's himself.

Happy days in the Army

The attention given to detail was frustrating, especially when it came to ironing clothing. Everything had to be the same size, eight inches by eight inches square. This was not easy when football shorts were ironed. Socks were folded a certain way and underwear did not fold easily. Every day we were inspected by officers who looked at the equipment laid out on our beds which had to be a certain design. You were in trouble if it wasn't.

All the time you were pushed to the limit of endurance to see how far you would go before you snapped. There was deliberate taunting by a sergeant or corporal so you were treated like rubbish while they waited for you to rise to the bait.

One of the sergeants used to say: "When I shout shit, you jump on the shovel." And we had to shout: "Yes, sergeant."

In every squad or platoon there was some poor chap with two left feet. The sergeant would make his life hell. "We will all turn to the right in threes except Smith 377 who has other plans."

In the Army it paid to be thick-skinned. For example we were asked if there were any Irishmen in the platoon. If the answer was yes, the sergeant would then say: "We need people to clean the toilets at their own convenience." And we had to laugh or we would be running around the parade square.

When ordered to do guard duties we would crease our khaki trousers by turning the inside out, rub soap and a little water along the crease and then turn them back and iron the crease to

Pictured on the left with a pal in the bakery

hold it in position.

This meant it was difficult to walk far because the crease would break up, so we were lifted to where we would be inspected before going on guard. This also protected our highly-polished boots.

Seven men were picked for the six-man guard, and the smartest on parade would be allowed to return to the barrack room.

Our guardroom had a horse-chestnut tree and a small lawn. And when the conkers arrived they were tied up to stop them falling on the grass, which was cut with scissors. The lawn was lined with rocks that had to be white-washed.

Inside the guardroom was a small fireplace with a coal bucket which was polished like a mirror. The coal was painted white.

At the end of my training, because I had already completed an apprenticeship as a baker, I was selected to be a cook, and they sent me to learn how to do the job the Army way. I was transferred to the Army Catering Corps, where I was taught to a high level of cuisine and became a chef. But I never really got the opportunity to use this knowledge because I was posted overseas where all the food was already cooked in tins.

Catering there consisted of providing for large numbers, which was achieved with "composite rations" — a large box of already-cooked tinned food. These were to feed 10 men for 24 hours. And can you imagine rashers of bacon rolled up in the fat they were fried in? Ten of them!

None of the tins had labels, but they did have numbers and the man who had been there the longest somehow knew what was what.

Sometimes there were mistakes, and when a tin was opened it might turn out to be rice pudding instead of Irish stew. Not a happy situation.

The tins contained breakfast, dinner and tea. If there were 50 men to feed for 24 hours that's a lot of tins to open with a tin opener so small it would have fitted in a matchbox. It was torture.

Fifty people meant five boxes of rations to be opened and heated. While this was going on I thought of the training we had had in England to become cooks to hotel standard.

My dual role as a baker and cook kept me occupied as I moved from country to country, Egypt, Cyprus and Aden. And they were all at war.

When I was posted to the Canal Zone, the 120 degree heat really hit me in my thick khaki uniform. So soon I was wearing football shorts. Though anyone without a beret was in trouble. Flies were a constant nuisance, and everyone had to catch a certain number in a matchbox which were counted in company office.

But bigger flying nuisances were the birds. Imagine the scene of men leaving the cookhouse with their meal in two metal mess-tins and a mug of tea. It was a 1,000-yard walk to the tents, during which time attacking birds would be helping themselves from the tins.

The chefs at Aldershot

There was nothing you could do because your hands were full.

Living in tents was a sweaty experience and in an hour the bedsheets were like a towel after a bath.

Toilets were just holes in the *I can swear in* sand which would attract the *Arabic* "shitehawks" that swooped in on your very inconvenient convenience until you shovelled more sand into the holes.

And then...

When I eventually returned to the UK for demob I became patissier in a three-star hotel where I made the dishes for the sweet trolley.

The hotel provided live-in accommodation and all meals. I also helped myself to an assortment of waitresses and chambermaids!

Work for the day ended at about midnight, so then we usually went out to clubs until 3am, and then back at the hotel where we paired off to watch TV — or whatever!

I did not need to start work until 10 in the morning and was finished by 3pm and could then join the holidaymakers on the beach.

But I had to be back at the hotel for work at six in the evening. I should have had one day off a week, but quite often it was a seven-day a week job.

At the end of each summer season, by talking to chefs at other hotels I would often learn that a pastrycook was leaving and I would go for an interview. Asked why I wanted to move I would say the wage wasn't very good and I hoped they could offer more. Usually they did, and over the course of a few years my money went up from £100 a week to £200. I was therefore astonished to find out that when I got a job at London's Ritz they paid only £75 because of the prestige of working for such a high-class establishment.

But it worked wonders for my ego. We were just a stone's throw from Buckingham Palace and Royalty came for elevenses, lunch and high tea.

Sadly the Ritz closed down after an inspector of kitchens wrote a bad report, and all the staff were dismissed. After a few months the premises were bought by the Trafalgar shipping company and re-opened. But by then I had moved on. I had no difficulty getting employment because working at the Ritz was a recommendation on its own.

I retired at the age of 60, and though I didn't think it at the time, National Service was the best thing that ever happened to me. It turned me from boy to a man. I travelled to the Middle East by plane and ship and had my daily tot of rum with the sailors. And I can swear in fluent Arabic!

— **Dave Garyford©**

19196092 Pte Alan George

I challenged a drunk, and found it was the camp commandant

IT WAS A bit of a shock to the system when I enlisted in June 1947 and reported to Bodmin Barracks, home of the Duke of Cornwall's Light Infantry. First we were issued with a towel, marched to the shower block and told to go under the shower while a corporal stood by with a big scrubbing brush. And boy, did some of those lads need a good wash!

Next up was a haircut, then on to get our kit issued and a palliasse which we had to fill with straw. Blankets were provided, and then it was over to the canteen for tea. That night I heard quite a few lads crying, but being an orphan I was emotionally pretty tough.

I had been brought up by an aunt in Woolwich and it was not a very happy time. So I was quite able to cope with Army life. Even the squarebashing didn't worry me too much because I had been in the Boys Brigade and knew how to march.

Our initial training taught us various ways to kill an enemy, and then we faced intelligence tests. After these we had to say what sort of regiment we would like to serve in. Thinking that it was a London regiment, I plumped for the Royal Fusiliers. But when I looked at the noticeboard to see where I would be posted I saw I had to report to Barton Stacey, near Andover in Hampshire, home of the Kings Royal Rifle Corps. I had never heard of them.

When I arrived at the camp they were just

At Tahag with my three-ton Dodge

mounting the guard and I thought they were running. I didn't realise that this was their usual marching time.

I was there for six weeks getting used to trail arms and not slope and learning the regimental history. We were made to feel proud to wear that Maltese Cross and the black buttons. Then I was given two weeks' embarkation leave prior to posting to the 2nd battalion in Palestine.

We boarded the Arundel Castle, and when we passed through the Bay of Biscay the sea was like a millpond. But as soon as we hit the Mediterranean it became very rough and a lot of soldiers were hanging over the sides. We stopped at Malta to let some troops off, then went on to Port Said. After a night in a transit camp a train took us to Port Suez to await another train to Palestine.

Looking at company orders I found I had been selected for guard duties. The guard sergeant shouted: "Slope Arms" and none of the riflemen moved. Someone told him that rifle regiments don't slope arms. Then he gave the quick march order — which produced bedlam because we went off at the rifle regiments' fast 140 steps to the minute. In the end the sergeant gave up.

I was on guard duty on the main gate one night when at about 2.30am a man got out of a taxi, obviously drunk and staggered towards me. I shouted: "Halt, who goes there?" but he just lurched past me saying "goodnight, sentry." It was the camp commandant.

Soon we were issued with a rifle and 10 rounds of ammunition and put on a train to Palestine. It had wooden slats across the windows because at every village we passed through we were stoned. Eventually we arrived at Gaza and were driven to El Buriej, the main camp of the 2nd KRRC. I was told to report to Capt Slater who was in charge of 11 platoon C company. He told me I was to be the HQ section bren gunner.

The platoon consisted of one half-track and three white scout cars, a sort of armoured vehicle. The battalion was very short of men — it had about 600 instead of 1,000 — so that meant I had no number two on the bren and had to carry the gun as well as a box of ammunition.

One of the jobs we had was to escort the Palestine police into Arab villages to sort out various crimes. We also had to escort Jewish convoys to kibbutzes because the Arabs were always setting up ambushes. In fact, if they had been able to shoot straight I would not be here today to tell this story. I had been told to report to the main gate where I was to go with three sergeants because I was a bren gunner. We went in a 15cwt soft-top lorry to pick up spare parts for the mortar section. It was dusk when we left, and by rights we should not have travelled in a soft-top at night. But the sergeants were old Desert Rats and thought it was all a big hoot.

Several times we came under fire, with bullets zipping through the canopy. I was trying to dig a hole in the back of the truck, but one of the sergeants told me: "Fire back." I said I couldn't see anything. "Just fire," he shouted. Which I did.

When we escorted the Jewish convoys to kibbutzes we were always invited to break bread with them — goat's milk and bread — which was most welcome.

It was quite an eye-opener when we saw inside the camps, well laid out with lovely lawns. Little did we know that beneath the lawns were concrete bunkers in readiness for battles to come.

Life went on with patrols and road blocks 24/7 until the country's mandate was due to finish. Shortly before this I was on detachment in a former Palestine Police station perched on the top of a hill. On one side, in the distance, was an Arab village. On the other a Jewish kibbutz. We had a searchlight on top of the station, but soon learned not to put it on because one side or the other would be taking pot shots at us.

Sometimes we stood on the ramparts and watched the Egyptian army attacking the kibbutz where the Jews were giving as good as they got. It was like seeing a film.

Eventually we were ordered to abandon the station. We could still see the Jews on one side of the hill

I am on the right here with pals from 661 Company

I spent 12 years in the TA

and the Arabs on the other, and we knew there would be a battle to secure the station. So Capt Slater got us into the vehicles, flung open the double doors at the back of the building and we raced away as fast as we could. Looking back I could see the battle already raging. Reaching the main camp at El Buriej I found that we were to be the rearguard for the move out. The Army was pouring past the camp on the main road out of Palestine, and all morning the RAF were flying overhead. I suppose they then went for dinner, because suddenly we were strafed by a couple of Egyptian Spitfires, but there were no casualties.

We withdrew to Port Said where it was announced that the regular soldiers would be returned home and the conscripts left behind.

I was sent to an RASC company, Coy 661, as a platoon rifleman. When the major in charge said: "Step forward those who drive," only about half complied. So after a few threats, the rest of us who didn't know how to drive, were told we were drivers.

I was allocated my own three-ton Dodge, but the half-shaft was broken so I was towed to the workshop. When the repair was made it took me quite some time to get out of the garage. Everyone had a good laugh watching me.

But once I got out on the open road with desert on both sides I was all right — until smoke began swirling round the cab. I had left the handbrake on!

As soon as the company was up to strength off we went across the Sinai desert, back into Palestine to a place called Rafah where there was a huge Army dump.

We filled our lorries with stores and towed another full lorry back to camp on the west bank of the Suez Canal. Next day we would be off again for more stores. This went on for about four months, and then I was transferred to a heavy transport company with 10-ton Leylands.

I had only a few months' National Service left when one day we were all ordered on to the parade ground for an announcement. There were rumours that we were at war with Russia, and we knew that if that were true, as a motorised infantry we would be up at the sharp end. But no, with a smile the major announced that conscription had been increased from 18 months to two years. That went down like a lead balloon.

At this point I was transferred to an Arab company at Tel el Kabir, TEK for short, where I served the rest of my time before returning to Port Said to board the Empire Pride troopship and the voyage home. It was packed out and the conditions were terrible and I had to sleep on deck. But we didn't care. We were going home.

We docked in Liverpool, and it was finally 10pm when we arrived at Farnborough. We were told we would have to wait until next day to be demobbed. That caused a riot, and in the end they stayed and demobbed us that night.

And then...

When I was in Palestine I had received a letter from a brother I didn't know I had. Wow, I thought, I've got family.

I answered his letter, and then wrote again, but I never heard another word from him. I found that strange. He had taken the trouble to find out my Army number and where I was, written to me and then let it all go. But it didn't bother me. By that time I was hard. I didn't want to find out anything about where I came from, or who my mother was. I was going to have my own family.

I had been writing to four girls while I was in the forces, and one of them was Roz. She was in a group that used to hang around our Boys Brigade meeting hall — primarily to take the mickey!

But she and I hit it off immediately and I used to go round to her house where her mother would make me very welcome.

We were married, but divorced in 1961, though we still keep in touch. In 1963 I married Eileen and we had twin girls. At last I had a family. I was over the moon, and the girls got all the father's love I had missed out on as a child.

But in 1995 Eileen died. Then I married Judy, a retired grammar school senior maths teacher. We had 10 wonderful years together before she died in 2008.

Over all these post-National Service years until I retired in 1991 I worked as an HGV driver. I had been a junior bookkeeper at Woolwich Arsenal when I was called up, but after life in the Army I decided I couldn't go back to office work.

For a short while I was an officer in the Boys Brigade. I also joined the TA, serving with the Queen Victoria Rifles for 12 years and was among those lining the route at the Queen's Coronation in 1953.

— *Alan George*©

Posing in Palestine

With a pal when we were volunteer regimental policemen

A photograph taken when the QVR lined the Coronation route in 1953

Go home and wait for call-up, I was told. I am still waiting

WHEN MY National Service papers arrived in 1956 I went for a medical and an interview. But today I am still waiting to be called up. I think I am now a bit too old to be marching around a parade ground or trying to shoot straight.

All my friends had been called up at 18, but as an apprentice carpenter and joiner, I was deferred until I was 21. I lived in Torquay and was saving hard to get married, so I was not looking forward at all to National Service. But knowing that the evil day couldn't be put off I thought I had found a good way of getting an easy life in uniform when the time eventually came.

My brother-in-law, who had already been called-up in the RAF said: "If I were you Jim I would learn to play a musical instrument, then you can get in the band when you have to join up and you'll have a pretty cushy number.

So I learned the trombone with the sole idea of getting into a band. But as it happens, I needn't have bothered. I didn't get into the services, let alone a band!

When my brother-in-law suggested the "play an instrument" plan I had taken myself off to Paignton and bought a trombone. This was 12 months before I was due to be called up, and though it was a bit of a tall order I was determined that in that time I would learn how to be a trombonist.

First I had to find a tutor. Fortunately, my father — who was the piermaster in Torquay — knew Charles Perrin, the bandmaster of Torquay Brass Band which often

Hoping to hit the right notes for an easy time in the Marines

played on the pier. And he agreed to give me lessons.

I got stuck in, and gradually made progress until one day Mr Perrin, who had connections with the Dartmouth Brass Band, asked if I would like to join them. So I became a member of the Dartmouth band.

I'm too old now for the barrack square

A few Marine bandsman from the Dartmouth Royal Naval College used to come along and play, and give us a bit of instruction, and I got to know the bandmaster quite well. Near the time of my call-up he said he would give me a reference when I went for my National Service interview.

So I took this reference along, and it worked. When the interviewer saw it he suggested that I should join the Marines and try to get in the band. Which was just what I wanted.

I did the medical and other tests and then, at the final interview, the chap said that even though I had passed all my exams to go in the Marines I would have to take a test of my musical ability when I got there. And if I failed that I would be just an ordinary Marine.

Well, I didn't fancy climbing up and down cliffs on the end of a rope and doing things like that. So I said: "No thanks, I think I'll go for my second choice of service, the RAF," hoping that I might be able to get into their band.

At that I was told to go across to the RAF induction area. But it was nearly lunchtime and

This is me with my son Tom, members of Torbay Brass Band in 1979

102

the lads going into the RAF had already been seen. The interviewers there, who were packing up, said I would have to go to Exeter and report to the RAF recruiting office for an interview.

There I took another series of tests and was told to go home and wait to be called up, which would be in about six weeks. Six weeks came, then six months, then six years. And to this day I have never heard a word from anybody. Why I was not called-up I shall never know. I only know that I was the one that got away.

And then...
I carried on working as a carpenter and joiner, became a site agent and then a college lecturer in construction.

But I continued to play the trombone, and in 1976 helped form the new Torbay Brass Band. Both my son — who took up the instrument at the age of nine — and daughter played in the band.

So though I never made it as a Marine or RAF bandsman, my brother-in-law's scheme to get me an easy time in the services paid off by providing me and my children with an enjoyable hobby.

— Jim Gill©

The Army can offer you a great deal; and it asks a great deal from you in return. But your two years in the Army is not time wasted. National Service is a great opportunity. What do you get out of the Army? You will find your health improves. You will have good accommodation, good clothes and good food. Most National Servicemen increase in height, chest measurement and weight. You have a good medical service to look after you. Army education, if you make use of it, can help you to carry on your schooling up to matriculation standard or even higher. You will find plenty of sport. The Army is always on the lookout for good athletes and you will find every sport is catered for; if you go to Germany or Austria or Trieste you will have an opportunity of winter sports. The Army gives you the chance to travel. You will get about the world seeing places and seeing how other people live.

—From You and the Army, a booklet issued to every NS army conscript

23459605 Cfn Lionel Gooch

I was given seven days' CB for fighting in the NAAFI

WE LIVED in a small Leicestershire village during the Forties and Fifties, my parents having moved away from Brighton soon after the outbreak of war. Therefore most wartime events virtually passed us by without any real effect, except for the occasional excitement of a plane crash-landing during take off from nearby Bitteswell aerodrome.

Following an engineering apprenticeship at British Thomson-Houston in Rugby, with my 21st birthday drawing near, I viewed the prospect of National Service with some trepidation. I was not looking forward to two years' disruption from the fairly relaxed existence I was leading, let alone the drop in pay.

While playing rugby for Lutterworth RFC I had been having some knee trouble from a cartilage that occasionally popped out. So a spell in hospital began to look attractive, with the thought that by so doing I might avoid call-up.

Some hope! All it did was delay my initiation for nine months.

So on March 13 1958, now identified as 23459605 Pte GOOCH L, I reported to Blandford Camp for basic training.

Those six weeks will never be forgotten, especially as the IRA had raided the camp earlier in the year, breaking into the armoury and in the process, wounding a National Service recruit, though fortunately not seriously.

It can well be imagined our thoughts on nighttime guard duty armed only with a pickaxe handle! Not even an alsatian or two to keep us company.

Taking it easy (right) with fellow NS men

The initial hell of being introduced to drill instructors fortunately did not last long, as we quickly realised that following instructions and commands to the letter could keep one out of serious trouble. All except one of our intake who was more of a country yokel than me. He was

With a pal in the barrack room. I am on the right

such an unco-ordinated fellow that the instructors could not in any way get him to march, let alone keep, in step. Before the end of basic training he was dismissed as unsuitable. Maybe he was cleverer than anyone else! Inoculations against all diseases known to man (or so it seemed) took place on our first Saturday morning of internment. It was quite encouraging to see a big hulking fellow fainting at the sight of a hypodermic needle being stuck into his arm.

It is interesting to note that I was the only one not to suffer any real after-effects, due I believe, to being requested (ordered) to play rugger in the afternoon, therefore quickly dispersing the serum effectively.

Every other member of my intake virtually confined themselves to bed for 24 hours, with one poor fellow being unconscious for two days and ending up in hospital.

Our instructor was Cpl Black, one of the good guys, who made a point of giving us advice when off duty. The rest were viewed with total fear and apprehension, being quite capable of making anyone who would not conform cower with mere verbal abuse.

Before the end of our spell at Blandford, those who had satisfied the instructors that they were taking aboard the discipline being thrust on them were let out on the last Sunday — provided they looked and behaved something like soldiers. A visit to Bournemouth by train was on the agenda. Bournemouth on a wet Sunday in April 1958 was virtually dead, though after being so restricted for five weeks, I found it thoroughly enjoyable.

Having already served an engineering apprenticeship, I was posted for five months to Gosport Trade Training School to be initiated in the skills of a REME armourer. A glorious summer. Getting sunburned at the open air swimming baths, therefore causing damage to the Queen's property (a chargeable offence).

Finally I came out with the second highest marks, which entitled me to second choice of the postings available. My choice was Catterick Camp as I did not fancy Libya where the rest of my intake would be sent.

The following 18 months as unit armourer at the School of Signals were some the best times I have experienced. In fact I seriously considered signing on for extended service. Probably being cosseted as an armourer attached to another unit did not give me a real insight into the daily routine for most men doing National Service.

My workshop was in the armoury where I was left to my own devices for most of the time except for the occasional inspection by a senior armourer. I had a stove which became a meeting point for cups of tea with my mates. And I was well treated by senior ranks and officers, most of whom actually knew me by name.

The overriding memories during the 18 months are of great comradeship and all-night card games, which were usually brag, completely against regulations, on pay days when the less skilful (or unfortunate) were broke come the following dawn.

There was only one blot on my Army record of which I was, and still am, totally ashamed. Fighting in the NAAFI. The incident was created by a Londoner who purloined the chair I had been using when I went to the counter for a cup of tea. As a result I was given seven days confined to barracks and the cleaning tasks evenings and weekend that went with it.

A strange thing is that Jack Shepherd, my combatant, and I became the best of mates afterwards.

On second thoughts, there was another incident, though an event that was not recorded on my military record.

Having a driving licence and a car, I was expected to act as chauffeur during weekends off duty. Returning to camp early one Monday morning with four friends, after a weekend at

home, I fell asleep and drove into a ditch.

Relaxing in retirement

The exhaust became damaged and, in trying to get the car back on the road, I was overcome by carbon monoxide and ended up in the hospital at RAF Leeming for two days. Unfortunately, I had failed to renew the road tax on the car, so a visit to a friendly policeman was requested. But I guess they took pity on this poor National Serviceman, because that was the last I heard of it.

What also comes to mind is that when hitch-hiking, always in uniform, how helpful motorists and lorry drivers were in assisting servicemen on their journeys. Also the superb, cheap meals that could be obtained at transport cafes.

While at Catterick I qualified as a marksman, became one of the unit rifle team and represented them at Bisley in 1959, though my results at 600 yards were not anywhere near the best. As demob date came nearer a decision had to be reached concerning my future. If I could have spent all my time as the School of Signals armourer I would probably have signed on for at least another six years, the comradeship experienced alone being a sufficient reason.

Realising though, that new postings would be inevitable, resulting in unknown environments, I eventually decided against extending my service and was demobbed on April 3 1960.

And then...
Surprisingly, my Army experiences did not end there. On March 15 1969 I re-enlisted as a craftsman in a REME Territorial Para unit. I thoroughly enjoyed the experience. Six-day exercises on Salisbury Plain, being raided every night by regulars using Chinese/Korean/Vietnamese tactics of trying to undermine morale. Experiencing the absolutely hair-raising flying skills of Army helicopter pilots. Night-time treks across Derbyshire. Weekend training on assault courses, and two weeks at a REME workshop in Cyprus.

Unfortunately by then, being in my mid-Thirties, the final Para test was an eight-mile timed march across Salisbury Plain tank training ground, where I could not finish within the allotted time. Though I had the satisfaction of seeing several men 10 or 15 years younger finish behind me. So, never achieving the required fitness level expected of a Para, I did not experience actually jumping out of an aircraft. Therefore, with work commitments becoming a problem, I resigned in 1972.

Finishing National Service saw me settle at Hawker Siddeley in Coventry from 1960 to 1968, involved firstly in ship-borne guided missile manufacturing, then ground test equipment installation for the Blue Steel stand-off bomb carried by the Vulcan and Victor bombers. This entailed spending time at RAF stations Scampton and Wittering.

From 1969 to 1982 I worked for a subsidiary of Rolls-Royce in Leicester, producers of a major component for civil and military aircraft engines.

In 1982 I made a complete change to shopkeeping and moved to Poole, Dorset, purchasing, selling and setting up another grocery shop before selling out to a multiple convenience store chain in 1989.

The next 20 years involved a variety of activities including building two cars, obtaining a near-derelict 4,500 sq ft garage and resurrecting its customer base, forming and running a motor racing team in the British GT championship and supplying the specialist car market with the components to build their own cars.

— **Lionel Gooch©**

Conscription in the UK ended in 1960, and assuming 18 as the call-up age then the youngest of us must be about 68 and the oldest 83. But at 68 these days many of us still have a lot of mileage still to put on the clock, so the potential for so much Alliance achievement is out there. The other side of the coin relates to those who have been beavering away at dreaming up ideas for presentation stands, exhibits and supporting material, and putting it together and taking it to venues up and down the country. There are countless ways we can put across our case, and at the same time educate both young and the not so old what conscription was all about. I believe we have a duty to enlighten modern society the debt it owes to those who went before. So if you feel you are in any position to help in any way, please give us a shout.

—**From the National Service Veterans Alliance**

2378586 LAC Alick Grant

My National Service became a journey of 35,000-miles

MY NATIONAL Service began on the first day of the new year in 1948 when I caught a train from Euston to Warrington to report to RAF Padgate. After kit issue I was posted to RAF West Kirby for square-bashing. The weather there was very cold and wet, but after suffering foot trouble I was given an excused boots chitty and issued with shoes, which made life a little more comfortable.

I must have done well however, because at our passing-out parade I was awarded the certificate for being best all-round recruit.

After a week's leave I reported to the No 1 Radio School at RAF Cranwell to learn how to become a radio/telephony operator. Though we still had parades and a certain amount of bull, life was easier here with more free time, and I played in goal for the squadron football team.

I was one of five on the course who passed, and after promotion to AC1 I had a spell at RAF Tangmere, before being told I was to be posted to the Far East.

In September I was one of about 3,000 men who boarded the Staffordshire at Liverpool for the four-week voyage to Singapore. On the way I spent an evening ashore in Colombo — the first land we had seen for three weeks — and took a rickshaw ride.

A week later we disembarked in Singapore and were taken by lorry to Changi, the former PoW camp which was now an RAF station.

There I was issued with rifle, bayonet and ammunition for the rather uncomfortable 400-mile rail journey into Malaya. Some remnants of Japanese had stayed behind after the war to wage a terrorist war on the planters, so we had to be alert. The train did stop once because of a bandit scare, but eventually we reached RAF Butterworth, where I began my work in Air Traffic Control.

At this point I was feeling a bit sorry for myself. The weather was wet, I hurt my foot and had to go to hospital for an X-ray and I was being eaten alive by insects. Then we heard that bandits had blown up the main railway line. I felt quite homesick.

As my foot got better I had ferry trips across to Penang and visits to the Shanhai, a cinema

within walking distance of the camp, in my free time. I also played quite a lot of football.

In November I made my first air trip, 1,200 miles to the Car-Nicobar Islands where I had a very interesting tour in a jeep.

Life continued mainly with air traffic duties, the occasional inspections and parades plus film shows at the camp cinema and the local Shanhai — and quite a lot of football.

Early RAF days

But there was a lot of activity early in 1949 because we were near Siam and so involved in several actions to trap terrorists crossing the border. There was trouble in Burma, and aircraft from Butterworth were used to bring out evacuees from Rangoon and Mingladon. And in April the Royal Navy's Amethyst was attacked in the River Yangtze.

Soon we were ordered to carry arms at all times, and I took part in a 48-hour jungle rescue exercise.

It was pouring with rain and the terrain was very difficult, thick undergrowth then rocks. We had to climb up to 1,500 feet using ropes to negotiate one-in-one slopes. When we camped for the night I was cold and wet, and did not get much sleep. Then we ran out of water and drank off plants and rubber tree shoots.

But eventually my demob time drew near and I spent three days in Singapore before boarding the Orduna for the journey home. On the way we had short stops in Colombo, Aden, Port Said and Gibraltar.

The weather was very bad in the Med and I slipped and injured my leg. But when we reached Liverpool I was given a lift to the dispersal centre in a lorry because my bad leg wouldn't let me march with the rest. Kit was handed in, and at 11am on December 7 I was a civilian once more. I caught a train to Euston where I was met by mum and dad.

I was glad to be home. During my service I had travelled some 35,000 miles, including 16,000 by sea and 8,000 by air.

RAF service gave me confidence and discipline. As a member of Air Traffic Control pilots relied on my decisions. I saw parts of the world that normally I would never have visited.

I am sure my experiences made me more community minded and gave me a willingness to help out where I am able.

And then...

Before call-up I first worked in the plan printing department with the LNER at Kings Cross station before becoming a messenger for a City plan printers.

On demob I returned to this job, but in 1954 set up my own photo-copying and printing company in the City. This was taken over in 1984, but I remained with the new company until retirement in 1993.

During the whole of my working life I was involved with some aspect of RAF service.

In March 1950 I enlisted in the Royal Auxiliary Air Force, the start of more than 30 years of voluntary service as a part-time airman and officer.

In 1957 I enlisted as an air defence operator in the RAF Volunteer Reserve where I was awarded the Air Efficiency Award. In 1962, the unit disbanded, and I was transferred to the RAF Police, serving in Germany and Cyprus.

In 1969 I joined the 2393 (Billericay) Squadron ATC as an instructor and two years later I was commissioned as a pilot-officer in the RAFVR (Training branch).

Later I commanded 2476 (Hutton) Squadron ATC, and in 1978 moved to the East Essex Wing ATC headquarters staff. I was promoted to squadron-leader and eventually retired from uniformed service as a wing-commander on reaching the age of 55 in 1984.

While serving with the Billericay ATC I organised the excavation of a Messerschmitt 110 which had been shot down in 1940, traced the German pilot and arranged for him to visit the

Still serving, long after demob. And here pictured with my wife Trisha and daughter Susan

squadron and see an exhibition of the remains of his aircraft.

I hold the Air Efficiency Award, the Cadet Forces Medal and the local council's Civic Award for Service to Youth. And I still enjoy carrying out voluntary work in various spheres.

— Alick Grant©

We dug with bayonets and cut the grass with table knives

BROUGHT up in a mining village in the North East of England I attended Alderman Wraith Grammar School in Spennymoor, leaving in July 1954 with 7 O-level and 3 A passes. I wanted to be a teacher, and though I was offered a place at Bede College, Durham University I had to do my National Service first.

I reported for duty at Cardington on September 1 1954. Here we were supplied with all uniform and kit, initiated into the mysteries of looking after the same, and after a few days given our postings for basic training.

Mine was to RAF Hednesford somewhere in the Midlands, and as I was to find out later, near the town of Rugeley.

The peace and calm of Cardington seemed light years away as we alighted from our coaches. Half a dozen screaming drill instructors had us quaking in our (new) boots, marched us off for a programme of jabs for everything under the sun and introduced us to our billets.

I thought I would have a good haircut before I joined, but there was a compulsory one at Hednesford when we arrived, and a few days later it was "get yer 'air cut, airman." Three crops in 11 days.

The next eight weeks seemed like living hell — especially as I had been appointed deputy senior man in our hut — with never a minute to ourselves. We were instructed in bulling boots, cleaning brasses, keeping the hut immaculate for kit inspection and how to square off items like shirts and PT kit using pieces of card board.

Happy days at Pitreavie, 1955

For the first couple of weeks it was almost guaranteed that we would return to the billet at lunchtime to find heaps of kit strewn along the centre of the floor where it had been thrown by our DI.

One immortal phrase comes to mind. In the words of the DI when criticising the neatness of the arrangement of kit on top of the locker: "Did you put that together at the other side of the room and kick the f----r up?"

Then there was sliding round the billet floor on old pieces of blanket to maintain the shine, foot drill, rifle drill, gas drill, bayonet practice, assault course and "changing parades" — a way of picking "volunteers" for fatigues. We lined up outside the billet in one uniform, say working blue, then were sent in to change into perhaps PE kit, then something else.

Each time the last two out of the hut were chosen for fatigues until the DIs had the required number.

I remember guard duty, the mortal fear of being put on jankers, and on NAAFI break just getting up to the counter when the DI screamed at us to get outside. I do believe that the actual square-bashing was probably the most enjoyable part of it all.

To lighten things up in PT there were cross-country runs in PT kit and boots, while for gardening we cut grass with our table knives and dug the ground with bayonets.

The middle two weeks of square-bashing were for fatigues, and I spent the bulk of my time spreading nearby land with human fertiliser di-

The main gate at Hednesford

rect from the local sewage works. Alternatively there were the delights of the "tin" room, details of which I won't go into, but any ex-servicemen will know exactly what I mean.

The following quotes stick in my mind and now bring a smile to my face, though they definitely did not when I was on parade in October 1954.

DI (pulling imaginary hairs from my chin): "Have you had a shave this morning lad?"

AC2: "Yes corporal."

DI: "Did you use a mirror?"

AC2: "Yes corporal."

DI: "Next time use a f---g razor.

Then, DI to airman performing badly at foot drill: "I'll march you round the square till your legs are worn away to stumps. Then I'll charge you for arsing about on the square."

So, along with the guys who took weeks to get a uniform because they were too tall, too short or whatever, those with beards because they were excused shaving due to a skin condition and the tick-tock men who never learned how to march because their left arm always went forward with their left leg and vice versa, we eventually passed out.

I left Hednesford on a week's leave before heading off to No. 3 Radio School at RAF Compton Bassett to learn to be a wireless operator.

There I remember a Polish corporal whose favourite expression was "You giva me the creeping sheets."

Generally speaking the atmosphere at Compton Bassett was much more relaxed, though there was still a fair amount of bull. Wednesday nights were bull nights, but everything stopped while we listened to the "in" radio show of the day, Journey into Space.

There were visits to the Astra camp cinema every time the programme changed — and that was four times a week.

Wednesday afternoons were sports afternoon when we could do anything remotely connected with sport. We once went to Swindon's league football ground (transport provided) to support an RAF team play-

ing another service side.

The nearest small town was Calne, renowned then for Harris's sausages and a pub called The Green Dragon where I once got drunk for the princely sum of 3s 4d — four pints of scrumpy at 10d a pint.

Saturdays were much more civilised, with a visit to the NAAFI club at Chippenham, a game of snooker, a couple of drinks and taking in a film at the local cinema.

I spent some weekends in Pompey staying with my aunt and uncle, and remember getting a few funny looks when producing my 1250 to get into the NAAFI club there. They were obviously only used to matelots.

During trade training our Morse instructor was a laid-back, middle-aged Geordie civvy who never seemed to put any pressure on us. Nevertheless, we achieved our target of 18wpm.

Soon it was time to proceed to RAF Pitreavie Castle, or to give it its full title Allied Command Atlantic, North Atlantic Treaty Organisation.

I set off with two mates, Brian Taylor and Jim Best on what was to be a nightmare rail journey from Wiltshire. On arrival at Newcastle Central we were informed that due to a derailment on the main line our train would be diverted via Carlisle.

The outcome was arriving at Waverley station, Edinburgh at about 3am, tired and not a little bewildered. Fortunately a friendly aircrew sergeant, also on his way to Pitreavie, took us under his wing and finally we got there.

I found out that I was to work in an underground anti-nuclear communications centre fondly known by all signals personnel as The Pit.

But seemingly there was no immediate work for wireless ops until some were demobbed. So Jim was posted to Ballykelly in Northern Ire-

Pals together at RAF Hednesford. I am in the front row, fourth left

land, Brian was sent on detachment to Keflavik in Iceland and I was to go on a combat training course to RAF Kinloss in the far north.

After two weeks spent chiefly firing Lee Enfield .303s and brenguns it was back to Pitreavie, keenly anticipating at last becoming a "real" wireless op. But no. Still nothing for me, and this time I was sent off to RAF St Mawgan in Cornwall for a radio course.

This proved to be an absolute gem of a posting. My billet was a Nissen hut just outside the main gate, which meant no passing the guardroom when going out. We were on the course with aircrew who flew every afternoon. So this left us free to go into Newquay or wherever took our fancy any day after lunch.

It was at least a mile between billet and radio hut, but that didn't matter because we were able to borrow camp bikes. And Cornwall in May 1955 had wall-to-wall sunshine. So St Mawgan turned out to be a very pleasant experience.

We were allowed to fly in Shackletons, a derivative of the Lancaster, on two afternoons on anti-submarine exercises called a Sub-ex. Brilliant, we thought.

For the seven-hour flight the aircrew had their own rations including chocolate and other delicacies, and we collected cheese sandwiches from the airmen's mess. Definitely "us and them."

We sat at the back of the aircraft with no access to the intercom, unable to speak to each other because of the engine noise and were allowed to visit the wireless op's position once for a couple of minutes. I repeat, us and them.

The end of this detachment coincided with the start of a rail strike and though I was able to get home for the weekend I had to make a tortuous bus journey back to Pitreavie.

After a very nervous start as a wireless op proper I soon got into the swing of things and with promotions to LAC and SAC soon became a competent operator working Coastal Command aircraft north of 53 degrees and marine craft (air-sea rescue launches) from Blyth, Immingham, Bridlington and Drummore.

Things could get very hectic with a few aircraft on channel at the same time, but most stressful of all was when a search and rescue was taking place. When I had become one of the most experienced operators on the watch it was usually, from the NCO in charge: "Gregg, open up search and rescue."

The opening message was: "All stations search and rescue in operation, I am in control."

This was OK, except that almost all the other operators on the channel were civvies. They were the professionals and the likes of a young National Serviceman an absolute amateur. So they acknowledged in Morse like the clappers hoping to tie us in knots — which they sometimes did.

The height of humiliation for any self-respecting wireless operator is to have to ask someone to send more slowly. With a speed of 25wpm though, I coped most of the time.

Life at Pitreavie, a relatively small camp with both airmen and WAAFs, was very easy-going. As we worked watches we were often in bed till early afternoon if we had come off nights, and there was very little bull and few parades.

The main gripe was about accommodation. We lived in old huts with no sanitation, and the ablutions block was 50 yards away down a slope. No joke on winter mornings. Just before I was demobbed work began on a new state of the art barrack block, but I never saw it finished.

The NAAFI provided our main source of relaxation, but we had regular trips into Dunfermline for the cinema, to watch football at East End Park, shopping and haircuts. But usually, when not on watch, we went to the Saturday dance at the KB ballroom. This, of course, was at the height of the dance hall era.

I have many memories of Pitreavie, mostly good. I can recall the fabulous sea views and coastal scenery when travelling through Northumberland on the east main line for a weekend or going on leave. And the amazing Scottish Highlands on that journey to and from RAF Kinloss.

I remember the friendships made, listening to "Geordie" Nicholson's rock 'n roll and swing records in the NAAFI. And I enjoyed the job I was doing.

Early in 1956 I was sent on detachment to the Marine Craft Unit at RAF Drummore on the Mull of Galloway. To say I was excited is something of an understatement. Here was my chance to work on one of the boats I had only ever communicated with on the radio.

On the day of leaving my train schedule took me from the local station at Inverkeithing via Glasgow to Stranraer.

This leads me to one of the less pleasant experiences of my stay in Scotland. Imagine if you can, arriving in a desolate Stranraer at about 10pm on a wet and bitterly cold February evening to find the last bus to Drummore had gone, and feeling utterly lost. However survival instinct prevailed and I somehow managed to reach RAF West Freugh (Drummore's parent station) where I got a transit bed for the night and eventually got to Drummore next day.

This had to be the best RAF station ever. Everything was under one roof – sleeping quarters, mess, the lot, even the NAAFI. There were only about 20 or 30 airmen on site, and even the CO was just a warrant officer. This is where I first learned that there was actually a trade in the RAF, boat crew.

Three 'barrow boys' at Pitreavie Castle. Left to right, Brian Taylor, Charlie Brown, Fred Gregg

Among those who went to sea the only ones not volunteer seamen were the wireless ops, and after one was demobbed that left three of us to cover the two boats, 30ft seaplane tenders and the smallest launches in RAF Coastal Command.

The thought of having to go out into the Irish Sea in one of these filled me with more than a bit of trepidation. As it turned out the worst job was going out first thing to check the radio, not bad if the launch was at the quayside but fearsome if it was anchored out at the buoy.

On the bright side we were issued with seamen's sweaters, sea boots and duffle coats which made you feel 10ft tall when you went to the pub in the evening. And taller still after a test run across Luce Bay when the locals came out to see the smart launch tied up at the quay while we swaggered down to the local coffee shop.

Many hours were spent at the less glamorous task of sitting in the control tower amending Queen's Regulations, but on the other hand there was time for exploring the locality and playing football.

But all good things come to an end, and soon it was time to return to RAF Pitreavie Castle.

They say "never go back," and that is something I certainly found true. When I took my wife, Joan to Drummore about 20 years ago to show her this marvellous camp where I was stationed for a while, the tower was derelict, there were no sleek launches moored in the harbour and the billet had been taken over by potato packers, with sacks at the windows. Never go back!

Returning to base does not imply that there

was anything wrong with Pitreavie because I enjoyed my time there more than any other in the Royal Air Force.

One or two interesting incidents come to mind. Like the time I was practising the trumpet in an empty billet when without my noticing, the station warrant officer with a group of officers came in. I was mortified, but breathed again when the SWO asked if I would play the Last Post at some forthcoming parade. I was by no means good enough but referred him to an MT driver who was a really good trumpet player.

When we went on duty we left our mugs and irons on a shelf outside the w/t room and on one occasion, very busy with a lot of traffic on air, I glanced up to see the signals officer standing with a face like thunder, holding a rather grimy mug with my name on it. I kept my head down pretending to be very busy until he moved off somewhere else.

One day I was having great difficulty contacting an aircraft due to frequent very loud bursts of static. Tearing the headphones off I shouted: "F---g hell." Only as I turned round did I remember that the watch NCO was a delightful WAAF corporal, Greta Rooke. I apologised profusely, and that was that. Or so I thought.

Next day I had just finished telling the story to one of my mates in the w/t room when I saw Greta right behind me. The ground opening up took on a whole new meaning.

I enjoyed playing football, and even though I was no better than average, usually played for signals against other sections.

One Army team asked specifically to play a section side because they said the station team would have been much too good for them. But they thrashed us 6-0, and we asked why they thought they wouldn't have given the station team a good game. When they said they had seen them play we pointed out that it wasn't the station side they had been watching, but RAF Scotland!

In August 1956 an international situation was building concerning the Suez Canal which had been controversially nationalised by the Egyptian leader, Colonel Nasser.

With two weeks to demob, we were ordered to pack our kit ready to leave for Suez at short notice. Talk about sweating buckets! Leave — and demob — was cancelled. But wonder of wonders, everything was resolved in time. And on August 31 1956 I had my bags packed again, but this time to say goodbye to the

Holiday from school in the Lakes

RAF. All my clearances were signed, and a taxi was ordered to take me to Inverkeithing station and all I was waiting for was to be paid.

It had to happen. As he handed over money due to me, the station warrant officer barked: "Get your ruddy hair cut." I replied: "Yes sir." and moved smartly for the waiting taxi.

End of an era, and I have often wondered whether I could have made a good career in the Royal Air Force.

And then...

Anyway, in September 1956 I duly took my place at Bede College, Durham with a lot of other bods who had just completed National Service, and qualified as a teacher in June 1958.

During the long summer holiday I worked as a porter at the local hospital where I met my wife to be, Joan, then a student nurse.

I took up my first teaching post at a boys' school in the neighbouring pit village of Chilton. I stayed there until 1960 when Joan and I were married. We had decided to live in Billingham, and I obtained a transfer to a junior school in the town. There I remained until in 1969 I was appointed to a deputy headship in Stockton-on-Tees.

I later became head of St Edwin's Junior School in Barnsley, and taught in Barnsley until 1990 when I made the decision, at the age of 54 to take early retirement.

I laughingly believed that after a lifetime, apart from the RAF, in education I would try my hand at something different. It didn't happen, and I drifted into supply teaching until I secured a post teaching English at a high school in nearby Hemsworth.

This proved to be the change I had been looking for. I stayed at Hemsworth High School (now re-named Hemsworth Arts and Community College) until 2001 when I thought a forthcoming triple heart by-pass would end my teaching career. But by the beginning of 2002, well recovered, I was back at Hemsworth working part-time.

In 2005, with nigh on 47 years of teaching behind me I finally called it a day, or so I thought.

In December 2008 I had a phone call from a friend at school who was head of maths. One of his staff had decided unexpectedly to quit at Christmas, and would I like to come in part-time to teach maths till the end of the summer term.

I didn't really have to think about it. Three years almost vegetating at home was enough, and I figured it would do me no harm. So here I am, 73 and still teaching. I wonder if I'm in line for some kind of record.

Since September 2006 I have also worked one day a week as a volunteer steward at the Yorkshire Air Museum at Elvington near York, where we have the only fully-restored Halifax.

The museum was an RAF Bomber Command WW2 base flying Halifaxes, first by 77 Squadron, then two French squadrons, suffering a total loss of about 130 aircraft.

— *Fred Gregg*©

22885005 Cpl Tony Guest

My square-bashing ended with a home visit from the Redcaps

HOME ON leave after 10 weeks' basic training with the Devonshire Regiment at Exeter, I answered a knock on the door and was confronted by two Redcaps. "Are you Pte Guest?" I said that I was. "You are absent without leave. You should be on a clerk's course at Chichester."

I was escorted back to the depot, immediately put on a charge and marched in before an officer.

The usual question came. "Have you anything to say for yourself?" I produced my leave pass, which still had several days to run. Case dismissed.

The same two Redcaps then rushed me off at speed to Exeter Central Station to catch the next train to Chichester.

The Infantry Clerks Training Centre, which adjoined the main barracks of the Royal Sussex depot, was more relaxed regarding discipline.

There was a good cross-section of infantry regiments on the course — kilted Scots, Ulster Rifles, Guards, Welsh Fusiliers and a selection of county regiments.

Evenings were spent sampling the local ale at Chichester's watering holes, at least until the money ran out — which on pay of £1 a week, it very soon did. We played some sport, and got up a team to play the Sussex depot, winning 6-4.

The course consisted of learning to touch-type and memorising Army terms and abbreviations, and the numbers of Army forms. At the end we qualified as Grade BIII clerks.

On returning to Exeter I was told I was being posted to the 1st Devons in Kenya. So in a draft of about 20 I embarked on the Empire Ken and sailed on November 5 1953. Nearly all of us were 18 years old and going abroad for the first time.

The Empire Ken had been built in Hamburg in 1928, taken as a war prize in 1945 and converted into a troopship with a capacity of 800.

A large majority of the troops were destined for

Retired mobile librarian

Shortly before demob

the Canal Zone, but as we were going to the farthest destination, some of the Devons were selected to be ship's police. We were sent into the bowels of the vessel to take control of the brig, the ship's prison.

Two prisoners were delivered to us. They were a couple of hard cases whose time in the glasshouse meant they were now doing their fifth year of National Service. We were told they were being sent to the Canal Zone "for special treatment."

After an uneventful trip through the Bay of Biscay and passing the coast of Portugal we reached our first port of call on Nov 10 at Algiers where the ship stopped to take on supplies.

As ship's police we were to continue our duties on shore patrol with the French Foreign Legion in the casbah district. The two legionnaires who accompanied us were German, and in spite of the language difficulties our patrol was made somewhat easier because all the establishments we were checking on had red lights outside the door.

As this was then French Algeria all the employees of these places were civil servants! We returned to the ship after what had been a very educating day for us 18-year-old lads.

Cruising through the Med our next port of call was Tobruk, where the order came for the Canal Zone soldiers to change uniforms into khaki drill and ourselves into olive green for Kenya.

The Canal Zone troops — including our two prisoners — disembarked when we reached Port Said. Our police duties were now over.

We were allowed shore leave to go swimming in the Mediterranean, taken by Army truck with a one-man armed escort and told to put all our clothes together so the guard could keep watch while we went for a swim. All our kit would have gone missing otherwise.

Before the ship proceeded down the Suez Canal we took on a battalion of Seychelles troops returning home after completing their National Service.

We entered the Red Sea where temperatures were the hottest so far. The temperature cooled a little when we sailed into the Indian Ocean.

We docked at Victoria on the island of Mahe in the Seychelles where the crowds were preparing a big welcome home for their troops. Shore leave was granted and a truck provided to take a swimming party to a beautiful beach lined with palm trees.

Here we were, 18-year-old National Servicemen enjoying the sunshine and seas of a wonderful tropical island, all at Her Majesty's expense. A great contrast to grey old England we left behind three weeks earlier.

I believe that the senior officer on the ship, Major the Earl Wavell of the Black Watch had organised the shore leave for us. Sadly he was killed in action against the Mau Mau on Christmas Eve 1953.

We arrived at Kilindini docks, Mombasa and boarded an East African Railways train, arriving at Nairobi the next day.

Then the draft went by truck some 90 miles north to Karatina, headquarters of the 1st Bn The Devonshire Regiment.

Adjoining the camp was a police post, also a detachment of Kings African Rifles. The company lines were all tents, with a hedge and wire perimeter.

New drafts were taken on patrol around the area to get used to the altitude of 7,000 feet. On our second time out the NCO in charge questioned a Mau Mau suspect who suddenly ran off. The NCO fired a shot which wounded him in the arm. He was then escorted to hospital and to have further questioning.

After our first week most of the draft were posted to the rifle companies, but I was to remain at HQ Company. I reported to the Orderly Room where I became the battalion documents clerk under the watchful eye of ORQMS Jock Hunter.

My main job was entering the record of promotions and appointments, trade and education qualifications etc of all other ranks.

The job of duty clerk was taken in daily rotation and involved sleeping in the Orderly Room tent and hoping the phone didn't ring!

Another duty was guarding the camp, when three pairs of men did shifts of two hours on and four off throughout the night. The two guards patrolled the perimeter, nominally 10 yards apart, though this was usually closer so at least it was possible to talk to one another.

The immediate action platoon was another duty which meant that you slept in uniform with your rifle by your side.

With the police station being next door to the camp, bodies of dead Mau Mau were brought in and put on display for identification purposes. A rather gruesome sight, and the smell from decomposing bodies was very unpleasant, though after a while you got a little more used to it.

One day a captured Mau Mau called General China, who was second-in-command of all Mau Mau, was brought in. He had been wounded in the neck but recovered, and later collaborated with the authorities.

Entertainment in the camp revolved around the NAAFI. On Sunday mornings storeman Pete Browning would play on the NAAFI piano music ranging from Chopin to popular tunes. Jimpy White played a guitar, accompanied by a bass made from a upturned tea-chest, a pole and a thick cord. Occasionally Lt Blake entertained us playing the ukelele. Films were also shown in the open air.

I remember Tony Dobson, one of the Orderly Room staff who used to run around the camp with a huge butterfly net collecting as many species as he could. These were mounted in matchboxes and sent home. After demob he set up a large collection and became an authority on East African butterflies and moths.

RQMS Patmore raised a pig next to the stores, and also in his charge was a bull, sheep, rabbits and chickens. In the end they went the way of all livestock.

Leave was taken down on the coast at Nyali leave camp near Mombasa, where as well as swimming and sunbathing one could draw out kit and go snorkelling. A new experience for us all. And visits to Mombasa town by Army truck were organised.

Sport was played when possible. At Othaya I attended a rugby practice session and was selected to play for the battalion. But Q Hunter said I could not be spared from my duties so my rugby came to an abrupt end.

Later, when at Limuru, I took part in a company cricket match on a coconut matting pitch.

When we moved from our camp in the centre of the Kikuyu reserve with its view of snow-capped Mt Kenya, to our new camp at Naivasha we travelled along the escarpment overlooking the Rift Valley. A great sight.

There were a number of other moves before we finished at Thika, where all the companies were brought together prior to return to the UK.

It was there that I was detailed as guard commander at the White Sisters Convent, where there were about 60 orphaned children. Their only form of security was one old African armed with an elephant gun. Thankfully the night passed without incident.

With the battalion's imminent return to the UK in early 1955 I was chosen to go on the advance party. So we handed in our rifles and bandoliers of ammunition, changed our olive green uniform for battledress and flew from Nairobi on Britavia Airlines.

Our destination was Seaton Barracks, Plymouth where we prepared for the main body who were returning by troopship.

There was a great deal of work to be done, and it was here that I was promoted to corporal. Then I was posted to the depot for demob, and my last act was to march the remainder of our original training intake across the road to the 4th Devon TA headquarters for release on June 9 1955.

One year later we all attended our first annual TA camp at Penhale, Cornwall and were presented with our African General Service Medal with Kenya clasp.

And we remembered 11 of our comrades, some of them National Servicemen, who would not be getting their medal. They lay in soldiers' graves in Kenya.

And then...

After National Service I had a variety of jobs before I joined Devon Library Services in 1968, driving a mobile library. In 1977 I became East Devon Mobile Librarian, retiring in 2000.

— Tony Guest©

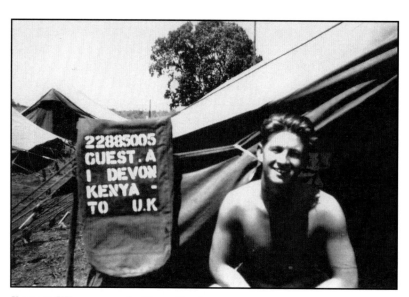

Kenya to UK — no wonder I'm smiling!

116

22739598 LCpl Sam Halliwell

I was discipline clerk, so had to write out my own chargesheet!

IN THE middle of 1952 I attended for National Service medical and selection. At the time I was waiting to go into hospital for a hernia operation and really didn't expect to pass my medical. But I did, and was graded A1. When we were asked to indicate our service preference I chose the RAF, followed by the Royal Navy and then the Army. Naturally I was selected for the Army!

I was sent to the RASC training battalion at Aldershot, and though my memories of that initial square-bashing period are dim I do remember vividly the cold, being woken at 5.30am to cries of "get your feet on the floor," the poor Army food slopped into our mess tins and being shouted at by inhuman NCOs.

But I learned how to kill people with rifle, sten and brengun, bayonet and hand-grenade. Which was the objective I suppose.

The subsequent clerical training at Blenheim Barracks was a little better. We learned to type to music, and a lot of Army jargon. Most of our intake of 120 was then posted to BAOR, Egypt, Hong Kong and other far-flung places.

I was sent to Topsham Barracks, Exeter as discipline and releases clerk in the Devonshire Regiment HQ Orderly Room. The warrant officer in charge there was ORQMS Dick Shorland, a friend to all and particularly helpful

After demob I lived in Australia

to we National Servicemen. He could only have been about 40 years old when I arrived at Topsham Barracks but had already seen active service in Malta, Ceylon, India and Burma and British West Africa.

I enjoyed my work, which soon became mundane, but there were a number of memorable events. One was when a deserter had been caught near Poole and was held at the police station there. I volunteered to be one of the escorts to bring him back to Exeter.

A senior NCO and I travelled there and back by Royal Blue coach. After signing for the prisoner I was handcuffed to him for the journey back. Fortunately he didn't need the toilet, and we had sandwiches with us for sustenance!

In the company lines at Exeter

In my early days in the job I completed a Discharge by Purchase of a regular soldier but mis-calculated the sum of money he had to pay. So he was discharged having paid only about half of the amount due.

The discrepancy came to light some weeks later, and the adjutant told me to write a suitable letter requesting the outstanding money.

The soldier (by now a civilian) replied, and basically told us to whistle for it. The adjutant was not at all pleased.

In charge of our billet was a corporal everybody in the hut came to dislike. He had a fondness for scrumpy and would often come staggering into the hut late at night, fall over everything, put on all the lights and wake everybody then pee out of the door and collapse on his bed and snore all night.

One day he put me on a charge. Well two actually, and very serious ones. I remember the wording distinctly because I had to type my own chargesheets. After all, I was the discipline clerk!

One charged me under Section 9(1) of the Army Act 1940 with disobeying a lawful command given by a superior officer. The other was for insubordination "in that he at Exeter on November 11 1953 when ordered to get out of bed at 0735 hours did refuse to do so, stating 'F--- off will you, and go sick'." I went in front of the CO, but received only a reprimand.

Some months later this corporal, who had become enamoured with a NAAFI girl, disappeared. And so did the NAAFI girl. I then followed procedure and notified both the civil and military police, and eventually they were found and he was arrested and brought back to camp under escort. And I had the perverse pleasure of preparing his chargesheet.

He was reduced to the ranks plus three months in Shepton Mallett Army prison.

Soon after this my hernia recurred and resulted in an operation at the Royal Naval Hospital at Plymouth.

Back at Topsham, apart from being on the roster as Orderly Room duty clerk, which meant laying fires in the open grates and buffing the lino-covered floors, I was put on only one camp duty. This was a fire picquet for which the guard commander was Cpl Les Crowley.

I was on the 12 till two "stag" and had to walk around the camp perimeter armed with a pick-axe handle to deal with any attack the IRA may have made on the gun store!

It was a cold night and several times I passed our hut where the pot-bellied stove was glowing enticingly. Things were very quiet so I decided to go in, sit on my bed and have a warm.

I soon fell asleep and the next thing I remember was Cpl Crowley, who had turned out the guard to search for me, shaking me awake at about 3am.

For some reason I wasn't charged, perhaps because I had only recently been in hospital, but I never did another camp duty. In fact I don't think I even attended a muster parade. The RSM used to say: "Fall out the sick, lame and lazy — and Cpl Halliwell." And I never wore boots. Because I had "a chitty."

It happened like this. On my return to Exeter I saw the medical officer, Major (Mrs) McKendrick, who examined me and gave me the magical chitty which excused me from wearing boots and said that I should do light duties only. That note lasted me for the rest of my time at Topsham Barracks.

My billet for attached personnel housed the "odd-bods" of the depot. And some were odder than others. I remember a batman called Lofty Williams, who had once been batman to the CIGS, Field Marshal Sir John Harding and had a signed photo of him prominently displayed in his locker.

Lofty wore highly-coloured pyjamas and a crimson dressing gown with a yellow cord. And on Sunday mornings would entertain us by dancing around the hut with an inverted broom as a dance partner.

Another character was Mick Old, who worked in our office. I remember Q once telling Mick he looked like "a bag of shit tied in the middle." Mick smiled and agreed, and Q walked away shaking his head.

Our office was on the first-floor of the Orderly Room, below which any soldier who was on CO's Orders had to stand bare-headed and without his belt to await his call to face the CO.

Mick's idea of fun was to raise the sash window and drop small stones from the window-box on to the prisoner's head.

Another interesting character at Topsham was Nichi Hooper. He was said to be one of the longest-serving soldiers in the British Army. As a lance-corporal he had only one stripe on his sleeve, but seven or eight upside-down service stripes.

He was a bit of a law unto himself and was more or less left to his own devices in the sports store where he was in charge of the equipment. He also had other odd duties, like being the camp rat-catcher.

Eventually the calendar on which I crossed off my days of enforced service had no more blank spaces, and I was demobbed in early December 1954.

But in October 1956 came the Suez war, and I was called up again. However, I got no farther than Bedford living under canvas before it was all over. The episode frightened me — I was almost a real soldier this time!

And then...

On demob I talked with my old company who had by law to hold open a National Service-man's job for six months. They offered me a post as a very junior clerk at £5 10s a week, which was about what I was earning in my last few months in the Army.

I turned it down and obtained a job in the fruit trade with a smallish company of importers in Liverpool at seven guineas a week. This was a princely sum to me and I started as a clerk/junior salesman in a trade which soon became my career.

After a couple of years I progressed to a wholesale company based in Liverpool with more than 100 retail greengrocery shops. I began as a trainee but soon became district manager, buying for and supervising a group of shops.

After nine years with them I was controlling the largest and most profitable group of shops, which extended as far as Preston and Blackpool.

In those days the district managers collected cash daily from the branches. And one day, as I was coming out of my shop in Ormskirk I was bundled into my car by two knife-wielding robbers who said: "Do as you're told if you want to see your family again." With a knife stuck in my ribs I decided to do just that! But then began a two-hour ride of terror which ended in Manchester where I was kicked out of my car.

The men were caught some five days later in Norfolk, minus the money. The ordeal of the court hearing, the press and photographers, was almost as traumatic for me as the robbery!

I then joined British Home Stores as their national produce buyer where I learned a great deal about the logistics of national distribution.

But I did not like living in London, and spent a couple of years in the Midlands before joining the CWS in Manchester where I later became national manager of their produce department. I had a staff of more than 300 and 13 depots, and there I remained until February 1971.

My marriage in 1956 had produced five wonderful sons. Sadly, in 1970, I divorced but was given custody of my boys and was allowed to take them to Australia where I was offered a job with the Woolworths supermarket company as a management trainee.

Within six months I was appointed state manager of produce for Queensland and had more than 100 supermarkets to look after, and distribution depots in Brisbane and Townsville.

The logistics were so different from the UK. For example, the stores in Darwin were serviced once a week from Brisbane — a two-day road journey. To get this into perspective, Brisbane to Darwin is 200 miles farther than London to Moscow.

I also had another store in Gove, Arnhemland, which had no road or rail link and could be reached only by air from Cairns.

After some years with Woolworths I joined a smaller supermarket company as national produce manager. I was based in Melbourne but travelled regularly all over Australia and Tasmania, and also to New Zealand, the United States, Canada and Britain.

In 1973 my family had the addition of a beautiful daughter who now lives in St Albans. But 10 years later I had a stroke and spent four months in hospital and seven months in rehab, learning again how to walk and say cat and mat.

In the mid-Eighties my wife wanted to return to the Midlands. So with our daughter, and me in a wheelchair, we left my sons in Melbourne with a large produce retail business which I had bought for them, and came back to the UK.

Unfortunately my marriage ended in divorce in 1993 and I returned to live with my mother in Liverpool, until her death in 2005.

I have continued to recover from the stroke and, although unable to command a commercial management position, as a consultant in the produce trade I have been instrumental in setting up business between Israel and Canada, America and Europe and Australia and the UK.

My sons meanwhile are still in Australia in senior management jobs in the wholesale/retail trade.

— *Sam Halliwell©*

23151466 Sgmn Geoff Harris

No hot water, so I washed and shaved in my mug of tea

MY MAIN memory of National Service is the occasion when I was on an exercise in Germany. The weather was freezing and I had to sleep in a haycart. In the morning there was no hot water, but I managed to scrounge a second mug of tea and washed and shaved in that.

I had been called up in 1955 and after getting off the train at Catterick station joined dozens of others who were herded on to a Bedford three-tonner. Then we had the experience of meeting the RSM, complete with peaked cap and beer belly. The Teddy Boys among us had a few answers for him until he let us all know who was in charge and what we were in for.

Interestingly though, the Teddy Boys were usually the smartest dressed when it came to parades, and very often got stick-man when the main gate guard was selected.

The first morning we were quite looking forward to our cooked breakfast. What a shock. The eggs were well fried and the streaky bacon was so over-cooked that it had to be stabbed rather than cut, resulting in one piece flying one way and one piece the other.

But our breakfast problems didn't last long because we were doubled back to our barrack rooms and told that our job for the day was to clean the washbasins and toilets. I remember one East End lad telling an NCO he had come to Catterick to be a soldier and not a housewife. So HIS card was marked!

My memories of the parade square — the sergeant-major's sacred ground — will never be forgotten. Marching with the rest of the squad we got the order "Left Turn," but I turned the wrong way and created a bit of a shambles.

The sergeant told me to report sick and tell the MO that I was deaf or daft.

I also remember the sergeant-major teaching us to refer to our .303s as rifles, and not

Getting dry after a wash in a mug of tea

guns. "Cowboys have guns, soldiers under my command have rifles," he would say. And reinforce the point by making anyone who used the incorrect word run round the square.

We had to clean the ablutions, but there was no Vim or rag, so it was just elbow grease and a bucket of water thrown over the floors.

If we were on fire picquet we had to wash all the pots and pans in the cookhouse. We had a handcart with a bucket of sand and a folded hose containing a few holes here and there.

We were taken on to the Yorkshire moors and told to survive for 24 hours the best way we could. We found an old hut that was used by the sheep, so you can guess what was plentiful. I decided to try to clean it away, and walked around until I found a length of wood to clear the floor. But as soon as I had finished it everybody rushed in for the best places, and I was left sleeping in the doorway.

I was posted to Soltau in Germany as a dispatch rider, which meant delivering paperwork to other barracks in a 100-mile radius. I also had to take information to units that were camouflaged in woods, and these were very hard to find because we were given only a map reference.

The Army's BSA bikes were not the best of transport, and neither was the riding gear, but

Taking it easy reading a letter from home

120

Now I repair mowers

we made the most of it. Most of the dispatch riders had a jeep or an Austin Champ, which was much better in the winter.

On one occasion we had an exercise that involved a 200-mile drive with about 60 vehicles. But I was on the bike, and though most of the drivers slept in the lorries, I had to try to find some sort of shelter from the cold weather, and slept in a haycart for three nights. That was the time I washed and shaved in my mug of tea. Being a dispatch rider meant I was out of the camp quite a lot and away from the discipline and routine. Sometimes I took some of the cooks with me to see a bit of the countryside, and that meant that whenever I was late back I would get a lovely meal.

Sometimes my duties included what was called Officers Disposal. That entailed either taking the officers' or sergeants' wives shopping in the Volkswagen, or taking the high-ranking people to visit their friends in the British Military Hospital at Hanover.

Sometimes I took the officers to the pictures in the evening, and was given five shillings to spend.

Occasionally some of the personnel were a bit the worse for wear, so when we knocked on the door of the married quarters we would get away pretty quickly.

And then...

After my service — which I can honestly say did me no harm — I became a bricklayer, and now my hobby is restoring old lawn mowers.

— Geoff Harris©

Trained as a baker, I ended up collecting the officer's rolls!

MY SPELL as a National Serviceman started on Nov 22 1948. I lived in the quiet village of Longham, Dorset and after leaving school at 14 worked in a garage for two years before taking a job at the JT Lowe horticultural engineering firm. I was ordered to report to the RASC at Aldershot, and I travelled from Bournemouth to Farnborough by train where we were met and taken by lorry to our destination.

We were met by a corporal who told us what we could and could not do, and then taken to our billet to sort out which bed to have. One chap was so tall there wasn't one long enough to fit, but eventually they found him one.

We were issued with our kit, given a vaccination and a couple of injections, and did a fortnight square-bashing. At the end of the training we were given three occupations we could apply for, driver, storeman or baker.

As I had been in engineering I opted to be a driver — and was told I was to be a baker.

About six of us were sent to the training bakery at Tidworth Barracks and spent three months learning how to make bread. It was a nice posting for me as we got most weekends off and I hitch-hiked home. My father always gave me the fare to go back on the bus on the Sunday night.

I palled-up with a Londoner named Albert from Shepherd's Bush and we stayed together most of our service. Our hardest job in that bakery was two of us having to mix two-and-a-half hundredweight of flour in a trough by hand, just to show that we could do it. Other times it was done by machinery.

Albert and I were posted to the bakery at Aldershot, where we supplied bread for most of the Army in the town. We worked from six in the evening until five in the

At Tidworth bakery, and pictured recently, below

morning for two weeks at a time, and two weeks on days cleaning up after the night shift.

While at Aldershot we were sent on a battle training course for a month at an ex-American hospital on Dartmoor, not far from Tavistock. We slept in Nissen huts and found it a bit hard having to do square-bashing and guards again. I don't remember too much of the time there, except having to go to Plymouth to get the bread and take it to a mobile supply depot with a grid reference given to us somewhere on Dartmoor so that other units could collect their rations.

We both put in for an overseas posting and Albert was sent to Nairobi. After 10 months at Aldershot, I was posted to the 15th Army Bakery at Rath, near Dusseldorf. It was like having a three-month holiday because the Germans did all the baking.

We lived in a billet which had been a hotel, and our meals were served at the table by two frauleins, Anne and Sophe. Far better than having to queue for our food.

My Army service ended in the captain's office filing papers and getting bread rolls from the bakery, and a tin of corned beef from the supply depot for our

I am third from the left, back row in this picture of some of the bakers at Dusseldorf

mid-morning lunch every day. Because I was in the office, another job I got lumbered with was acting as escort to anyone on a 252 charge and appearing in front of the captain.

On one occasion one of our mates had been absent without leave and got 28 days in the Army school of correction at Bielefeld. Two of us were given a stengun each, the first one I had ever handled, and with a corporal we had to escort him to Bielefeld by train which took all day there and back.

I often wondered what we would have done if he had made a run for it because we had no bullets and we wouldn't have shot one of our own even if we had.

I did 18 months in the Army and I am glad I went. I learned something new, made some new friends and had a good time. Though I lost touch with my friend Albert after we got demobbed, three years ago I was on the computer and found a program about finding lost friends,

I put in his name, and when one address and phone number came up I found it was Albert. So now we are in touch again after all those years.

And then...

When I completed my service I missed having mates around. I returned to my old job at Lowe's, but was a bit lost at evenings and weekends for a while.

After 30 years in the horticultural trade I took over a hardware business in Ringwood, which I ran with my wife until we retired in 1995.

— Charlie Hayter©

Anne and Sophe

Overlooking the bakery in Dusseldorf

5039154 SAC Mike Hillman

I'm glad now that I missed out on Christmas Island posting

PRIOR TO my National Service I lived with my parents in Hounslow, Middlesex and was working as a clerk in the cashiers office for BOAC at London Airport (now known as Heathrow). At the time BOAC employed the services of a certain Wing-Commander Jenks, presumably retired, whose job it was to interview those staff due to be enlisted into National Service. The purpose was to reassure and offer advice on preferred or recommended career paths during service. I had a keen interest in aircraft operations and discussed this with the wing-commander. Whether he had anything to do with the fact that I did indeed end up in Air Traffic Control I shall never know, but the fact was that I considered myself very lucky for I was given to understand that the job was listed among the top trades at the time.

I enlisted in January 1957 at RAF Cardington and after being kitted out did my square-bashing at West Kirby, then moved to RAF Shawbury for trade training as an operations clerk.

We all wanted an overseas posting, and at the time Christmas Island was seen as virtually a dream come true. We all imagined sunshine and beaches, and several of us applied to be posted there. In the event I was given what was considered a home posting to Germany.

As it now turns out with the stories of radioactive contamination being suffered by those who did get their dream, I was one of the lucky ones.

We were transported to Germany by ship from Harwich to the Hook of Holland. I remember we spent the whole journey on the deck.

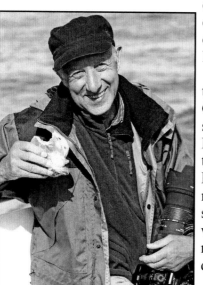
On a photographic trip in 2009

My posting in Germany was 2TAF working as an operations clerk in the control tower at RAF Gutersloh where I served the rest of my National Service time.

Beginning my National service

I have good memories of Gutersloh and can honestly say that I enjoyed the experience. I was with a great bunch of men, none of us got into any trouble and as a result we had very good relationships with our NCOs and officers.

The station commander was Group-captain MacFarlane, who was well respected by all his men. He lived in a lovely big house within the confines of the base, and there was a large pond in the grounds where we were allowed to go fishing for carp.

The area around the pond and the control tower was said to be haunted and one of our fishing trio, Olly, was particularly jittery about these rumours and so we decided to set him up.

Three of us used to go night fishing and one night in the pitch dark and eerie silence when Olly was standing at the water's edge I stood unseen way behind him and touched him on his shoulder with the tip of my fishing rod. How he did not suffer a heart attack, or at least fall into the water, we shall never know!

Two aircraft squadrons were based at Gutersloh — 59 Squadron Canberras, and 79 Squadron Swifts. We also had one Meteor and a Mosquito used for target towing.

I well remember the first time I walked upstairs to the operations room in the control tower. The corporal in charge had four telephones on the go, one in each hand, one under his arm and the other locked on to his shoulder with his chin. But it was not too long before we all accepted this type of scenario as a norm.

My job involved among other things monitoring aircraft movements, checking flight plans, obtaining weather forecasts, setting up the signals square in front of the control tower and driving the air traffic Land-Rover.

One other duty, which no-one liked — particularly with the stories of the tower being haunted — was to spend the night alone there to man the emergency telephone.

We also had to take it in turns to monitor the radio frequencies and listen out for aircraft calling Gutersloh on the different channels.

We also listened for emergency calls, and one day I received a call from a TR33 which had suffered an engine burn-out and was effectively gliding to our runway. Happily, the aircraft landed safely.

Another of our roles in Air Traffic was to light the gooseneck flares for night flying operations. The challenge was see which of the drivers could go up and down all the gears and be fastest between each of the flares while the passenger lit them with a flame or put them out with an extinguisher. This was usually combined with chasing the hares in the headlights of the Land-Rover.

A small Army unit with a couple of Auster aircraft was based on the station. On windy days one of our jobs was to position ourselves either side of the runway and run and grab the wingtips of the aircraft when it touched down so it wouldn't be blown over!

On one auspicious occasion Princess Margaret visited to the station when I was on duty and I took a few photographs through the control tower window.

Another notable day was when the first Beverley aircraft to land at Gutersloh flew in. The aircraft was the largest ever to land there, and we had to measure the taxiway width and holding area to ensure the airfield could accommodate it.

Each of our Air Traffic Control officers was an ex-operational pilot who occasionally flew the Chipmunk to top up their flying hours. I was fortunate on one occasion to be offered the passenger seat by Flt-lt Southwell. He took me over the Mohne Dam following the route of the Dambusters' raid. A very memorable experience. We then went on to perform some aerobatics, including looping the loop!

Other men managed to get a ride in the bomb bay of the Canberra bomber. Occasionally, if an aircraft was flying to the UK, some lucky airman due for leave was able to hitch a lift home. One caused a stir at Heathrow on his return journey when he checked in with his parachute on his back! Compulsory on the RAF aircraft of course, and he had to return it to the stores.

Besides fishing as a hobby I was, and still am, a keen photographer. We had a fully-equipped camera club on the station, which I used to run. I would sell my photographs to the men, and on one occasion I was asked to take "scene of crime" photographs for the RAF police following a robbery on the station.

I remember many times when we used to visit the local restaurant. The most popular meal ordered via "Herr Ober" was Kotelett mit Spiegelei und Bratkartoffeln accompanied, of course, with the essential Grosse Bier!

The one Christmas I spent in Germany was also very memorable. The station commander authorised a competition for the best bar in each billet, which we won. There were celebrations all round. The officers and their wives also kindly invited us to parties in their homes.

There was one very sad occasion when one of the airmen had a very serious car accident. The wreck of his car was placed outside the NAAFI as a stark reminder to others of the effects of

On exercise in North Wales during training. I am on the right, front row

125

dangerous driving. The driver suffered brain damage and I remember that I was one of a few who volunteered to sit by his bedside to assist the hospital nursing staff to care for him before he was returned to the UK. Sadly I never heard how he progressed.

I remember the Sunday visits of the Salvation Army van when we all queued for their speciality of mouth-watering malt bread and butter. Sunday was also special in the NAAFI for we had real butter at teatime as opposed to the margarine provided during the week.

We would take large chunks of the butter back to our billets where we had electric toasters, and for a few days enjoy the luxury of spreading our toast with the real thing.

My time in the RAF unfortunately ended rather abruptly when in September 1958 I was told that my father was seriously ill with tuberculosis and my mother had been diagnosed with the early stages of the disease.

I was granted compassionate leave, but never returned to Gutersloh because I was given a compassionate discharge in order to take over my father's retail fishing tackle business.

But I was later recalled to the RAF Reserve, and spent one very interesting period at the Royal Naval Barracks in Chatham in the vast underground operations control unit. There I performed various duties including plotting aircraft and shipping, and manning the old-fashioned plug-in switchboard. We slept in hammocks and received a daily tot of rum.

I often think what I might have done had circumstances not determined my premature departure from the RAF for I really enjoyed the life and may well have made the decision to sign on.

And then...

For the first four months after my discharge I continued to manage my father's business after which time, thankfully, he recovered sufficiently to resume working.

I then returned to BOAC as a clerk in the Post Office Mail department, before moving across to the air cargo side of BOAC operations and eventually becoming cargo duty officer.

I left BOAC, by then British Airways, in 1977, and joined Pandair, the air-freight forwarding arm of P&O Shipping, as operations manager. In the due course of time the company was bought and sold several times. It became Hat Express, Air Express International and Danzas, and is now known as DHL.

I survived all these takeovers and enjoyed my retirement in 2001 at the age of 63 years. Since that time I have become very much more involved in my camera club and am currently chairman.

My wife and I both have a keen interest in natural history and photography and we have travelled quite extensively in search of all things natural, but with birds probably topping the list.

— *Mike Hillman©*

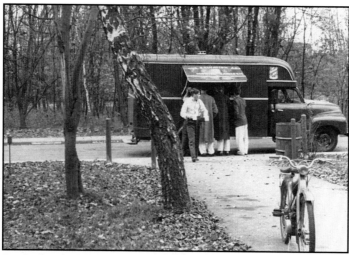

Just in time for breakfast from the Sally Army van at RAF Gutersloh

2409292 Cpl Raymond Howard

The Ace of Diamonds found out that I held the trump card

MONDAY morning arrived when I was to report for service, and I set off for Sheffield railway station en route to Padgate. The world seemed to be full of young lads like myself carrying brown paper bags and OHMS letters in their hands. The journey was an adventure for me, because only twice before had I been on a train.

When I changed at Derby I picked a carriage where there was just one other passenger, a man in his Thirties, immaculately dressed with highly polished shoes. But he looked like the type of fellow I could have a chat with.

In a space of a few minutes I had given him my life story and shown him the pair of RAF Regiment shoulder flashes that had been my father's. I told him I had been called-up, and my aim was to enter the RAF Regiment and to sew my father's badges on my arm. I also wanted to be a paratrooper.

He seemed to be listening, but the only information I gleaned from him was the fact that he was also travelling to Padgate. And he said he would make sure I didn't get lost.

When we arrived I was herded with other youngsters into a hut, and collected an armful of blankets and other items of kit like a knife, fork and spoon and a pint pot. Thirty of us were in this hut, each clad in a mixture of crumpled bits of uniform and civilian shirts and jackets.

There seemed to be two distinct groups in the room, those who were about to cry and the others, like myself, who were totally confused and wondering what might happen next.

Throughout the afternoon I had been repeatedly told that my number was 2409292, and I took the precaution of writing this on the back of my hand with a copying ink pencil that I thought might be useful to mark my clothing with my name.

At one end of the hut was a big loud-mouthed Scouser. In a matter of minutes he had reduced two of the quieter types to tears and followed up with obscene comments about their distress. Another was prompted to fight with him, but lost.

He was certainly of the opinion that he was king of the castle, and approached me and asked for a cigarette. I told him I was a non-

Early days in the RAF

smoker. Then he wanted to know if I had any money. I told him I had, but none for him, and added: "The best thing you can do is return to your part of the hut."

At that, he jumped on to my newly-issued boots at the foot of my bed, flattening the toe-caps, then laughed. I asked him: "What size boots do you take?" "Tens, why?"

"That's good." I said, "I'll have yours to replace mine," and walked towards his bedspace. He grabbed hold of me, and a fight started and there is no doubt that I was on the losing side.

So I grabbed a folding wooden chair by the two uprights and swung it on to his head and shoulders. The chair broke, leaving me with a weapon consisting of the two chair uprights and the metal spindle holding them together.

The rest of the billet were shouting me on, and by this time he was laid across the wooden table with blood dripping through his fingers which he held to his face.

Suddenly there was silence and I became aware that a uniformed figure had entered the room. He had the appearance of a three-dimensional recruiting poster, with the peaked cap half covering his eyes, a row of multi-coloured World War Two ribbons across his chest, a pair

On the Recruit Centre Training Instructors course at Hereford in 1949. I am in the back row, extreme left. Next to me is LAC Mountney, then LAC Cullum and LAC Hall. We were the only four to pass

of RAF Regiment labels on his shoulders and a paratrooper's badge on his sleeve.

But it was the corporal's boots that did it. I thought I had seen them before. And I had, on the train. He was the man to whom I had been revealing my ambitions to enter the RAF Regiment and to become a paratrooper.

He turned to the bully, Larry Carter, and told him: "Don't bleed on my table, go outside and bleed. I've been watching you through the window. If you feel like more exercise I can accommodate you in the gym."

Two fellow recruits escorted Carter outside to bleed in the ablutions as the corporal ordered: "Get this billet tidied up. I don't want to see blood on my nice clean floor. And I want a new chair in here in the next 10 minutes."

Next day was taken up by being fumbled by medical officers and queer orderlies and prodded with a series of blunt needles in our arms and backsides.

By this time we could recite our numbers without help, and just in case we forgot we were supplied with a length of string with two tags displaying the number around our necks, like a set of stray dogs without a permanent home.

After tea we congregated in the NAAFI. Even though we had known one another for only a little over 24 hours we clung together in adversity.

After eight weeks' training I appeared before a selection panel and was asked why I wanted to move into the RAF Regiment. I told them that in 1942 my father had been one of the first members. That clinched it, I was in.

Three months later I qualified, and sewed on father's old badges. But to achieve my ambition to progress to paratrooper entailed facing another selection panel, who decided that at nine stone nine pounds I was too light to join the elite group. Then as a result of a long chat and my exaggerating my skills as an athlete, one of the panel decided that I was just what he was looking for, a lightweight boxer. I was the correct weight for that purpose and the panel selected me for the Paratroop Training Flight.

In between getting soaking wet in the River Swale, blistering my tender feet and burning holes in my polishing fingers I managed to win the RAF Catterick lightweight boxing championship on points. Though I think the referee must have been in debt to the flight-lieutenant who "volunteered" me as a boxer.

A few weeks later I was again volunteered —

this time for the Technical Training Command championships. I lost on points, but as runner-up was presented with a glass butterdish to match the first one. And my nose had been moved for the first of several times to a new position on my face.

I had almost finished my paratrooper training when I was informed that not only was I too young but also seriously underweight.

I pointed out that most of the holders of the Victoria Cross were under 20 years old when it had been awarded to them. I made up the statement on the spur of the moment, and they obviously didn't know whether it was correct or not.

At this stage I had made my first seven jumps and had only one more to qualify for the rise in pay and the badge. I had made a good job of all the tasks I had been given, and also took second place in the RAF race-walking championships, equalling the record time that had been created in 1930. What more could they want?

Then they dropped the bombshell that the MO had decided I was suffering from varicose veins. So that was the end of my ambitions.

I was posted to the General Service Training School at Hereford, where there were two classes of "inmate." Those who were training to be drill instructors, and those who needed plenty of drill to remind them that they were in a disciplined organisation. The second category were from the sick, lame and lazy brigade, probably after being discharged from the glasshouse at Colchester.

Two weeks at Hereford and I had qualified, one of only four to pass out of 48. Three of us were posted as corporal drill instructors to RAF Bridgnorth in Shropshire. With me were Cpl Mountney, ex-Coldstream Guardsman and veteran of Arnhem and Cpl Cullum, who had taken part in D-Day.

The junior member (me) came under the total protection of the other two, for which, in return, it became my regular duty to escort them back to camp after a boozy night out and usher them past the guardroom window and into their respective bunks.

Our "finest hour" was the day that acting-sergeants Howard and Mountney were leading participants in the ceremonial parade to Bridgnorth Town Hall to accept the Freedom of the Borough which was conferred on the unit.

An officer (who was never seen) was in charge of a flight of 120 recruits in billets of 30 men, each under the command of a corporal, with a sergeant in general charge of the intake. And for a while there I was plagued by having the "Ace of Diamonds" as my sergeant.

No-one would have guessed he was a drill-instructor. Most DIs have creased trousers with weighted and neatly folded trousers over their gaiters. Not him. He screwed his trousers round his ankles and held them in place with the gaiters as though preparing for a cycle ride.

His webbing belt was stretched full-length in order to circumnavigate what many people described as "child-bearing hips" — his widest point. His torso crept past the normal place for shoulders where it merged with his neck and tapered into a head surmounted by a side-cap worn centrally as a crest from a point between his eyes to the back of his head.

Ankles to hips, and hips to cap ridge described a perfect Ace of Diamonds, hence the name by which he was universally known. And the Ace of Diamonds was also universally hated. At 5ft 6ins from his size six boots to the ridge of his cap he was short of height, temper and friends.

Knowing he was disliked did nothing to enhance his fits of temper and bad manners.

While we corporals were engaged in instructing our respective squads on the drill square, he would stroll round the ranks bawling offensive remarks into the ears of the frightened young kids just out of Civvy Street. Or spitting obscene and bullying comments into their faces as he stood within inches of their face.

His favourite threat was "to take you behind the drill-shed and beat some sense into you." Even though he never carried out his threat the recruits did not know that, and were scared to death of him.

I promised myself that if he ever offered the challenge to me, I would keep him to his word.

One day it happened, in front of a full flight of 120 recruits and my mates. There's no doubt that I did something wrong in the process of mis-interpreting his words of command, which were so battered with some sort of pseudo-Scottish dialect that often it was difficult to understand what his command had been.

He marched up and placed his face in front of mine, bawling out for all to hear: "I'll have you behind the drill shed... etc. etc."

Just what I wanted to hear, and my reaction was instant. "Too bloody true you're going behind the drill shed," I said, grabbing him by the back of his collar and arse of his trousers and propelling him across the drill square at full speed. He came to a sudden stop as his face hit

At attention as an RAF corporal in 1949, and pictured when I left the South Yorkshire Police as an inspector in 1982

the corrugated iron cladding of the shed, and fell to the ground feeling not very well.

Over my shoulder I could see my brother corporals marching the flight towards the scene, and they quickly formed a hollow square. Without exception they were cheering me on to "do the sod." There is no doubt they were being actively encouraged by the other corporals.

I picked the Ace of Diamonds off the floor and held him up against the drill shed and finished the job in a traditional Yorkshire fist fight. By this time he was even more crumpled than normal and lay on the ground screaming at the other NCOs to "fall in two corporals and escort this man to the guardroom."

They did as they were ordered, and three of us marched away. En route my escort promised that should they be needed they would support me in the charge that would no doubt result.

On arrival at the guardroom the RAF police sergeant laughed when he was told whom I was accused of assaulting. Next day I had to face the commanding officer, a group-captain by the name of Fuller-Good with a DFC to his name.

He was a regular rugby player and often I met him in the gymnasium when I was there for my race-walking training. Due to my success as a race-walker he knew me by my nickname of Johnny Walker.

I was asked to explain myself, and gave him the full history of the sergeant's habits and attitude to everyone about him and his daily threats to take people behind the drill-shed and bash some sense into them, as he had done to me on the previous day in front of a flight of 120 recruits.

I told the CO I had promised myself that if he ever offered the challenge to me I would take up his offer. The group-captain reached over his desk, shook me by the hand and said: "F--- off Johnny Walker, and don't cause any more trouble."

A few days later the Ace of Diamonds was spotted leaving the camp minus his stripes. He wasn't seen any more, but his name and his final act became part of the history of RAF Bridgnorth.

Every Friday morning at Bridgnorth there took place a continuous series of inspections of the billets, when the standard of bullshit displayed ascertained the type of weekend the recruits were likely to enjoy. Even the NCO's bunk was not exempt from inspection.

The more senior of the NCOs bravely displayed their campaign medals in a case on the wall, contrary to instructions. Sadly, I had but one lone medal — a Defence Medal earned as a boy Civil Defence messenger — and that was at home. But I considered I was entitled to my own unique display in my own place of residence, so had created a rather fine display of the group photographs of each of my recruit intakes. But on one station commander's inspection I was told: "Take that down."

Had he been a little more thorough he would have discovered a locker full of "contraband" under my bed. Three pairs of trousers creased ready for one of my daily changes of uniform, and a set of dirty webbing for weapon training purposes, thus preserving the issued set highly polished and in pristine condition.

There was also an extra pair of boots and a supply of rations for our nightly brew-up with the bacon sandwiches, fried up in a greasy mess-tin that was surplus to issue.

But I was more concerned that he had objected to my wall display, something of which I was very proud. So I had to devise a plan to keep the pictures of my old recruits.

Now the station commander's inspection always coincided with a Friday night dance at the nearby Women's Land Army hostel. The dances were held in a Nissen hut which would be decorated for the night with oddments of coloured paper and yards and yards of red, white and blue ribbon.

Centrepiece of the display was a large portrait of His Majesty King George VI, in the uniform of Marshal of the Royal Air Force. It appeared to me that this ought to become the centrepiece of my lowly display back at camp.

No-one noticed when I collected the portrait and a few yards of excellent coloured ribbon.

Quickly I rolled it up, thrust it under my jacket and nipped back to camp. I placed the picture in its new home and returned to make sure that I collected whatever other Land Army delights might came my way that evening.

Next day King George VI, surrounded by a neat red white and blue border of ribbon, made an excellent contribution to my display.

On his next visit the station commander, no doubt having been forewarned of my new decorations, quickly peered round the corner at the display, grunted, and walked out, forgetting to carry out his inspection of the billet proper.

Another day at Bridgnorth that I shall never forget was the day I was promoted to squadron leader — just for an evening.

The man responsible for my rapid elevation was a sergeant known as Curly, a typical ladies' man who was the NCO in charge of the NAAFI canteen, and obviously the NAAFI girls as well.

The sergeants on the camp were known generally as "drill pigs" and were feared by the young kids who had been coerced into the RAF. Curly was the exception, and was probably the most useful person to know on the camp.

His usefulness stretched from the newest recruit the group-captain. He was the hidden power and the controller of any fiddle that existed on the camp. Many owed their continued

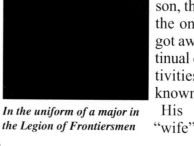

existence to his power of blackmail and ability to scrounge any item — from a new cap-badge or a bottle of cookhouse coffee, to a group-captain's uniform.

Curly was known to have a wife in Wolverhampton and one in Bridgnorth, a bevy of NAAFI girls and a couple of the girls from the Land Army camp down the road. All, for some silly reason, thought they were the only one. How he got away with his continual extra-marital activities will never be known.

In the uniform of a major in the Legion of Frontiersmen

His Bridgnorth "wife" lived in a typical chocolate box country cottage, with lupins, hollyhocks and ivy around the door, and capped with a picturesque thatched roof. Obviously ignorant of the other wife's existence she was well pregnant, and like any faithful wife awaited Curly's arrival from duty every night with a large cooked dinner.

One day Curly invited me to the cottage, and said he would collect me from my billet at 1700 hours for a slap-up dinner there."

Exactly on time he was banging on my bunk door with a large brown-paper parcel which he threw on to my bed saying: "Get that on. It will impress the missus." I saw that it was a squadron-leader's uniform with pilot's wings and a row of medal ribbons on the chest.

My many excuses like "how will I get past the guardroom?" and "lots of people know my face," were met with apparently reasoned arguments to suggest for instance, that "no-one ever looks at an officer's face." I was told he would call back for me in 20 minutes.

I got dressed in the uniform, which was a perfect fit, but the youthful face under the hat did not seem to be the same face that owned the pilot's wings and the medal ribbons.

I began to believe that I was heading for a court martial, and hurriedly covered the uniform with my greatcoat just before a Humber staff-car arrived outside. It was flying a squadron-leader's pennant on the bonnet, and I felt that there must be another court martial offence there.

Curly bawled out of the rear door for me to "get that bloody coat off and get in here quick," as the driver stood rigidly to attention, saluted and closed the car door behind me. I was in it, well and truly. "Squadron-leader" Curly reached out, shook hands and told me: "We're going to have a great night."

The staff car was driven out through the MT Section to a gate at the rear of the camp that until that day I never knew existed, and we travelled across the valley to the thatched cottage.

There was a welcoming smell of dinner, and the open fireplace promised a good evening ahead as I was introduced as "Squadron-leader Raymond Howard, a very good friend of mine from the mess."

I enjoyed a rather fine dinner and managed to reply to questions with what seemed to be the correct answers.

After we left the table to warm our feet at the wood fire the lady told me: "You'll laugh at this

Raymond, but I was beginning to think he wasn't even in the RAF. He always arrives home in mufti. I've often asked him to bring a friend home from the officers' mess, but you're the first."

Next day I reverted to my rank of corporal, which lasted until the last six weeks of my service when as a bribe to sign on I was given the temporary rank of sergeant and became the padre's sergeant. I think if the padre had been sober long enough he would have realised that I was not a good choice for the job. But at least it was a change from shouting at everybody all day long.

In another effort to get me to stay in the RAF I was offered the rank of warrant officer in the training establishment of the Pakistan Air Force. But I had made my mind up as a small boy that I intended to be a policeman.

And then...
I joined Sheffield City Police in 1950 and remained a policeman until I retired as inspector in 1991, having served with Sheffield City, Sheffield and Rotherham Constabulary, the South Yorkshire Police and the South Yorks Special Constabulary.

I had left school at 14 hardly able to spell. But since National Service I applied myself to study and gained a BA with Honours from the Open University. I am also a Fellow of the European Council at Strasbourg University, an Associate of the Institute of Administrative Management, an Associate of the Chartered Institute of Linguists and a qualified teacher in adult education. And I hold the rank of major in the Legion of Frontiersmen, which has only about 150 members in the UK.

Now, at the age of 80, I am learning Italian to add to the reasonable skills I have in Swedish, Danish, Norwegian and German which I learned while studying the police systems of these countries.

I own a collection of nearly 10,000 items of police memorabilia from around the world, but I am proud of my own medals and decorations, which include several awarded by police and service organisations around the world.

Among them are the Coronation Medal, the Golden Jubilee Medal, the police Long Service Medal and the Pakistan Independence Medal which I received after working in Lahore as an instructor with the Royal Pakistan Air Force.
— ***Raymond Howard©***

131

23631263 Pte John Howse

The 'deadly snake' that had me screaming and feeling a bit silly

BEING posted to Malaya with the 1/3 East Anglians in 1959 was not my idea of a fun way to spend my two years' National Service. Our task was to meet the threat posed by the Malayan Communist Party.

And I hadn't been there long when terrorists were spotted and we

Here I am, right, with my pals and ready for action

spent a week in the jungle in an ambush position. God, I was scared!

But on one patrol I was quite sure I was going to die. I had been given the job of shotgun, which meant that as the patrols were in Indian file I was always the bloke at the front to shoot or be shot at.

Leading the way through the jungle I suddenly felt a sharp pain in my neck. A snake bite.

I panicked, pulled at my uniform jacket and screamed loud enough to wake the dead — or certainly any terrorist within about 10 miles. "Snake bite, snake bite," I shrieked. "Where? Show me," said the officer as I screamed that I was going to die.

The officer examined my neck and told me I had been hit by a piece of broken twig. Did I feel a prat!

I had reached the jungles of Malaya via the East End of London where we had been bombed out twice during the war, and Debden in Essex where we were rehoused on a new estate.

At 15 I began work as an engineer, but suddenly I was called-up, and did my training at Warley Barracks in Brentwood, now the site of the Ford motor company headquarters.

We were told we would be going to Malaya on active service against the Communist terrorists.

Almost before I knew it I was on a boat half way round the world. We stopped at Gibraltar, Port Said, Aden, Ceylon and Singapore.

During the journey we were told what to expect when we arrived in Malaya — patrols in the jungle, ambushes and hardship. It sounded

horrific, and even worse when we spent six weeks in the jungle warfare training school at Kota Tingi learning how to survive, how to ambush and patrol and kill.

Then we moved up-country to our base at Ipoh from where our operations began. We spent up to three weeks at a time in the jungle.

On patrol we travelled through the dense jungle on a compass bearing for three hours and then returned to base. Patrols would be accompanied by Ibans from Borneo, who were quite remarkable trackers.

My patrol had a wonderful Iban called Sally. After the three hours we would stop and tell him to lead us back to base. Without the need of a compass, and with nothing to guide him except his knowledge of the jungle, he would retrace our route straight back to camp.

On one patrol I thought I deserved a medal for capturing the notorious terrorist leader, Chin Peng.

It happened when, as usual, I was leading the patrol and trying to be quiet and avoid being killed as we tramped through the undergrowth.

We were in a "black area" where no-one was allowed after a certain time, so I was pretty scared. All of a sudden I saw a uniform in front of me.

Using sign language I got the chaps behind me

At Ipoh (left) with three mates

132

Above (on the left) I don't seem too happy in the jungle. But pictured right it is obvious that I am definitely far more relaxed!

to fan out and advance in line abreast. When we were close to this fellow I shouted out in Malayan, and we grabbed him. He was obviously terrified. Ha! Chin Peng, I've got you!

We took him back to camp to Jimmy, the Special Investigations Branch interrogator. And I was dismayed to find out that "Chin Peng" was merely an illegal pig-trapper.

After about 15 ops we were given a new camp on the coast at Malacca. It was a great place for my last few months' service. A little bit of latrine cleaning and a lot of beach football. I really enjoyed myself there, and like all the National Servicemen near the end of their time took great delight each day calling out how many days I had left to do. It got on the others' nerves, but we "old soldiers" loved it.

But before I could get home there was one scare when our battalion was put on alert to go to Vietnam as part of a United Nations peacekeeping force. Oh hell, I thought, I survived the jungle and now I am going to get killed in Vietnam.

Then my release group, 59-13, was called to parade in front of the company commander. He told us that the Government had said that unless it was a major conflict, National Servicemen with less than six months to do would not be compelled to go.

But he added: "It's going to be a great show. so those who would like to volunteer, one step forward march." No-one moved. "Right, you bastards. I am going to work you until you drop." Finally the time came to leave, and after a three-week voyage, in the early hours one morning the shoreline of Britain came into view. I cried my eyes out.

From the docks at Southampton we were ordered to go to Bury St Edmunds in Essex for demob. But I had been met by my parents and sister, and I decided to have a meal and a drink with them before making my own way to Bury.

When I turned up the sergeant said: "Right, you'll be the last away from here."

"That's OK," I replied. "I have waited two years for this, a few more hours won't hurt."

And then...
When I left the Army I worked as a toolmaker, producing plastic injection moulds. I was there for 35 years, but when the business was about to close we did a co-operative buyout. I continued until I retired in 1999, when my partners returned my investment with interest, plus a golden handshake.

Now I spend my time with my grandchildren, and hobbies of fishing, walking and golf.
— ***John Howse***©

Most of my National Service was spent 100ft underground

AS A CHILD during the war I had watched troop movements through the streets of Bournemouth where I lived. When squads of soldiers were being trained on the clifftop, there would often be an instructor teaching them basic weapon training or fieldcraft. He stood in the middle of a ring of seated trainees with an outer ring of schoolboys hanging on to his every word. He would address his men: "Over there are six armed men camouflaged as bushes. When you are sure you can see one, raise your right hand — and you bloody kids sit still and shut up!"

When my own call-up papers arrived I was selected for training as a storekeeper in the Royal Army Ordnance Corps, whose responsibility was to supply the Army with all their requirements except the three Fs, food, fodder and fuel.

From the moment we jumped out of the back of a lorry that had taken us to the barracks in Aldershot, our lives seemed to consist of junior NCOs shouting five minutes to do this, or five minutes to do that.

For the next two weeks we led a whirlwind existence of medical treatments in the form of dental work, eye tests, injections etc, physical training, route marches and lectures and endless cleaning of personal equipment and clothing. And most importantly, learning how to live with a dozen or more strangers on a 24/7 basis.

At the end of two weeks we were issued with a 36-hour pass. Oh joy, oh bliss!

On our return we were mustered, issued with travel documents and posted to our various trade training units. I was sent to Hilsea Barracks in Portsmouth.

Now we were no longer rookies, we were soldiers in training. We went on five-mile route marches, spent regular periods in the gymnasium and on the sports field, had weapon training with rifle and bayonet and stengun and, once only, handled a Thomson sub-machine gun.

This was the weapon beloved of commandos and gangsters in the days of prohibition — as seen many times at our local cinema.

We had some lectures on our role in the Army, and on one occasion went to the local depot which held general stores. This was our only practical experience of storekeeping, our designated Army trade. We packed and crated three-piece suites for shipment to units overseas, and were told: "You are soldiers first and storekeepers second."

Posing for the camera at the end of training

We were also informed that if our depot was attacked, we would be the first line of defence. A sobering thought.

By now we were beginning to feel like soldiers, not civvies in uniform. We were not permitted to wear mufti, so sought permission to buy a side-hat and a red and blue lanyard to wear in our epaulet. We could wear civilian shoes, provided they were highly polished, and we were allowed to wear our own clothes at home during our weekend pass.

At last, after many rehearsals, we had our passing-out parade. Our reward for "a good show" was a 48-hour pass. For me this was very welcome. I packed my gear into my locker, queued for my pass and made my way into Portsmouth to catch the Royal Blue coach for the two-hour journey to Bournemouth.

On return our equipment was checked and we were posted to our units for serious soldiering. I finished up at the Central Ammunition Depot at Corsham, Wiltshire. The establishment consisted of a barrack block with a pocket-sized parade ground, compact fire station, a small power station and numerous hutments scattered around it.

It was rumoured that there was also a subterranean barrack block in case of hostilities, and there was also mile after mile of tunnels and storage areas protected by steel doors.

This whole complex was the old Bath stone quarries, now used to store three quarters of a million tons of munitions and high explosives. And we were there to take care of it. My job for the next 14 months was to spend the working day 100 feet beneath the ground as a member of the stocktaking team.

Before my life at Corsham became established I was destined to experience a taste of ceremonial soldiering. My first billet was with HQ Company and we paraded twice a day for roll-call and inspection, which was carried out by the duty officer.

However, one afternoon a very smart figure appeared on parade with us. He was tall, slim and immaculately attired in battledress bearing the insignia of a CSM in an infantry regiment.

This was Mr Finch, who was in charge of our military discipline as opposed to other warrant officers who supervised our technical life in the depot. He selected about three dozen of us and told us to go to our billet and return in double-quick time wearing our best uniforms, best boots and gaiters, and carrying our rifles.

Another inspection was carried out, this time Mr Finch was flanked by the unit tailor and armourer. Any part of our turnout that did not appear to be immaculate was changed for a brand new item, and we were issued with blue berets. These shortly became standard issue, but we were the first in our unit to possess one.

It transpired that the Defence Minister, Emanuel Shinwell was coming to inspect the depot and we were to be the Guard of Honour. For the next two weeks we were drilled and marched, and marched and drilled till we could have done it in our sleep. Uniforms were pressed daily, belts and gaiters Blancoed, brasses and cap badges polished.

The skill of bulling our boots was learned. This entailed the application of polish to the toecaps, melting it with candle flames and burnishing them until you could swear they were enamelled metal, and not polished leather.

On the morning before the great day we had our full dress rehearsal. We looked a picture. All the girls and office workers came outside to see. Whether it was the sight of so many pretty girls watching us, I don't know. What I do know is we were rubbish!

Our timing was completely hopeless, and the sergeant-major screamed and shouted at us but we could not get it right. Yet as so often happens, when rehearsals are rubbish the event

turns out to be flawless. The CO was so pleased that he gave us the rest of the day off.

We were shortly to be allotted to our working duties with the depot. I was detailed off to work under a junior NCO who had received special training as an ammunitions examiner.

Samples of the various crates of explosive or rounds of ammunition were removed by members of the Pioneer Corps from their holding bays to inspection bays by means of conveyor belts. One of these was reputed to be a quarter of a mile long. Once safely installed behind steel doors in areas where only rubber footwear was worn, we examined the ordnance for damage or deterioration. Then, depending on the report, it would either be returned to its storage bay or set aside for destruction.

This was achieved by taking it to the gunnery ranges on Salisbury Plain at the weekend where it would be placed in shellholes and blown up. Or in the case of large-calibre naval shells, holes were drilled in the casings and the shells were then dumped in the North Sea. Gun-cotton was fashioned into blocks, moistened and sealed in a tin box which was in turn packed into a slatted wooden crate fastened with nails.

If the nails were driven in carelessly and the tin box pierced, the explosive would dry out and become very dangerous. So periodically a quantity would be taken above ground and transported to a wooden building in the middle of a field, where each container was plunged into a tank of water. If bubbles rose to the surface this told its own story. It was separated from the main stock and removed for destruction.

There was a bonus to this hazardous task. The shed was situated in the middle of pasture land, which meant that in season we could gather the most beautiful mushrooms. These we took home at the weekend or bribed the cook back at the barracks to cook them in butter with bacon and fried bread.

In due time I was promoted to lance-corporal and appointed to the stocktaking team. Our chief task was to allot quantities of ammunition to be sent to active units serving abroad, and check deliveries of new stock from the ordnance factories.

As the weeks passed my fellow soldiers were posted abroad, mainly to the Far East. I dreaded the thought of serving in a steaming jungle and prayed that I wouldn't be selected.

My prayers were answered. I believe that as I had acquired a good knowledge of the labyrinth of tunnels it was felt better to retain me than to school a replacement.

Another bonus was that I never did another guard duty or fire picquet. If I was on duty at night or weekends I was orderly corporal with food brought to me at the company office, and my only task was answering the telephone, which seldom rang. So I spent the time reading library books, listening to the radio and pursuing my hobby of modelling miniature vehicles.

As we were confined to working underground, we made the most of our off-duty hours above ground by taking part in various sports. We had a football pitch, cricket pitch and even a putting green. Though I had no interest in team games I did like running, so in order to enjoy the lovely countryside on a summer evening, a few of us would go on a road run of several miles. This was after spending all day walking the tunnels, counting bombs and shells. We were certainly fit in those days.

One of the senior NCOs heard of our activities and asked us to form a team to represent the unit at the Regimental Cross Country Championships, hinting that there would be considerable advantages for us if we put our hobby on an official basis.

So Saturday morning drills and weapon training become a thing of the past, and instead of being roused at 6am by the orderly sergeant ringing a hand-bell and beating on the door with his fists, we were allowed to stay in bed until seven, and then assembled outside for a five-mile road run.

On our return we showered, shaved, made our beds, tidied our bedspace and went down to the breakfast which had been prepared for us. It sometimes consisted of porridge, bacon, eggs and toast. All on the same day!

After a while, murmurings of discontent spread among our mates. Many complained that they had never been asked to join the team, and claimed to be much better athletes than us.

So the recreation officer decided to put them to the test, and one Saturday morning all 200 of us reported in running kit to prove our worth. The first 12 men home would be recognised as the unit team. Some didn't get as far as the front gate before giving up. It is only fair to say that none of our selected team won the race, but we enjoyed the experience.

As my time as a National Serviceman began to draw to a close, I made the traditional demob chart for my locker door, and ticked off the days. I was interviewed by the CO, who assured

Enjoying a country life today

me that if I became a regular I would be promoted to full corporal, the first step on the ladder to a worthwhile career.

Meanwhile, the civilian superintendent offered me a position on his staff. But I declined both offers and elected to return to civilian life. Then I read on Company Orders that I was to attend a rifle course at Chickerell Ranges in Dorset on the weekend after my demobilisation date.

I went to the company office to point out their mistake, and was told that there was no mistake. My demob had been postponed for four days because several members of our unit due for demob were being released from military prison that week. Their kit would have to be checked into the stores and their documentation processed, and it was decided that as a junior NCO I had to accompany them to ensure that they completed the journey to the demob centre at Aldershot.

It was a day I shall never forget. We checked our bedding in the stores, had breakfast and reported to the company office where I collected our documents. Awaiting us was a three-ton lorry to take us to the station.

Demob transport always used the back entrance to avoid any disturbance to the company on morning rollcall. But to my horror the driver went past the parade ground, and all my companions hung over the tailboard whistling at their mates and shouting "get some service in" etc.

At the village station we found the gate locked because the porter did not come on duty until the first train was due. So I decided to buy a newspaper from the local shop.

When I returned, the padlock and chain were hanging loose on the gate and all the lads were on the platform sitting in the sun.

We had to make two changes before arriving at Aldershot, and on both occasions the soldiers dived off the train and disappeared along the platform. They returned, to my huge relief, only seconds before the next train steamed out of the station.

We reached the demob centre just as they were breaking for lunch, and I was instructed to leave our papers on the desk and return at 2pm.

At the given time we joined the crowd of eager young men waiting to be processed and sent home.

We were jostled and shoved in the confined space, and one of our group patted me in friendly fashion on the chest and said: "Oh well, just a little bit longer. I suppose National Service wasn't so bad."

As he spoke I looked down and discovered that my fountain pen was missing from my breast pocket. "I'll have my pen back Nick," I said to Pte Carter, who was called Nick not because his surname was Carter, but because he had spent so much time in the nick!

At that moment my name was called by the officiating officer. "Bring your party to the table Cpl Jeffery"

Because I had placed our papers on the top of the pile already waiting to be processed, we were the first to be dealt with after lunch. All thoughts of dealing with petty thieves left my mind. I was going home.

And then...

After a week's leave picking up the threads of life as a private individual, I returned to my job as a decorator with the builder I had worked for previously.

I quickly settled down to the task of honing my skills as a painter and decorator, and also learning new aspects of the work. Gradually, as my confidence grew and man-management skills learned in the forces asserted themselves, I became a charge-hand supervising a team on a particular job, and foreman with overall responsibility for the tradesmen on the firm.

I also became adept at estimating the cost of proposed work, a skill that served me in good stead when I became self-employed for the final 10 years prior to retirement.

Instead of joining the Territorial Army when I completed my service, I chose to sign on to the Z-Reserve, which involved a two-week refresher course with a regular unit.

Most of my pals who had already done their time claimed that this was virtually two weeks' holiday with pay. The units to which they had been posted found them at best a nuisance, and at worst a serious disturbance to their regular routine. There were tales of being sent on fruitless errands, removing daisies from football pitches with a clasp knife and sweeping the parade ground. So when I received my summons I wasn't worried. But I was in for a shock.

I decided to travel to camp on my motorcycle because it was quicker than taking the train, and I could use it to get home during the middle weekend. My back tyre punctured and tore when I was two miles short of my destination, but fortunately I was in a village, and the local garage agreed to repair it on the following Monday. Meanwhile, the garage proprietor gave me a lift to camp in his taxi.

During the evening I settled in and made new friends in the NAAFI. Tomorrow we would write home to our families and explore our surroundings. Wrong!

Sunday dawned to a muster parade at which it was explained that the unit was newly-formed and short of instructors. So temporary instructors were chosen from our number.

An NCO looked at me and demanded: "You laddie. Have you ever fired a rifle?" I replied that I had, and he said: "Right, you are a rifle instructor. Double over there and collect an instruction manual and study it."

The remaining men were marched to the armoury to draw their weapons, de-grease them and prepare them for inspection later that morning.

For the next two weeks we had weapon training, route marches, physical training, lectures and periods of marksmanship on the ranges. It came to a point when we even wondered if we were being trained to meet some threat by an unspecified enemy of the British Empire.

But I suspect they were honing their suitability as a training unit, rather than ours as combatants.

We finished our two weeks by negotiating the assault course, followed by a night exercise during which we had to defend a selected position against an attack mounted by the regular and National Service personnel who manned our host depot.

Selecting our strongpoint we posted perimeter guards. All we had to do was wait until the regulars found us and attempted to capture it, then we would demonstrate all we had learned during the past two weeks and repel the attack.

That was the theory. After a night of confusion and noise, sporadic rifle fire and the detonation of numerous thunderflashes, at 6am on the dot there was a series of blasts on whistles.

In the ensuing silence a cock crowed in a nearby farm, and it was over. We were marched back to our quarters where we handed in any blank ammunition in our possession, then cleaned and oiled our rifles and returned them to the armoury.

137

Until midday we rested and tried to catch up on some sleep. After lunch the officer in charge of our training, who had just returned from a tour of duty in Korea came to say farewell.

He thanked us for the hard work of the last two weeks and complimented us on our comradely attitude to one another.

He commented that though Z-Reservists were both veterans of WW2 and National Servicemen, we had all worked together with no jealousy or resentment. The attitude that prevailed was that it was for two weeks only, so let's make it an enjoyable experience.

I thought of this as I remembered explaining the basic components of a rifle to men who had taken part in the D-Day landings and had fought in the Western Desert.

Then the appointed umpires assessed the events of the previous night and told us that we had killed all our own patrols as they returned to our lines. Furthermore, we had expended 50per cent of our ammunition in doing so, not to mention betraying our position to the enemy.

The concluding remarks were: "If this performance is anything to go by, thank God we've got a Navy."

— Bill Jeffery©

Corsham as I remember it

How some may remember me

138

468596 Lieut Dale Johnson

If I had gone by the book I'd have started World War Three

IN EARLY 1962, as a National Service subaltern, I was almost responsible for starting World War Three. The tension created by the Cuban "Bay of Pigs" crisis meant that there was a very real threat that war would be triggered by a Soviet advance into West Germany. At the time I was serving in Germany as part of the 7th Artillery Brigade whose task, in the event of the Cold War warming up, was to provide low-level air defence to enable BAOR to hold a key bridge over the River Weser, so delaying the advance of Soviet troops.

Our regiment, together with 12 Regiment RA, was on Exercise Backlash to the north of Aachen, not far from the Dutch border. We were tactically deployed to test the capabilities of our equipment, with full air co-operation to enact our role as realistically as possible.

At 0215 hours on Thursday, May 24 the regiment was on stand-to, and as duty officer I was in the Regimental Command Post (a Bedford office truck with penthouse attachments) with the duty corporal.

The phone from Brigade HQ rang. I answered, acknowledged the single codeword and hung up. I looked through the Exercise Backlash code book to find what action was required. But the word I had been given was not there.

So using my key I opened the regimental safe and removed the Top Secret code book. And there was the word — first on the list — followed by the instruction:

TAKE IMMEDIATE ACTION. SOVIET FORCES INVADING. PROCEED TO PREPARED POSITIONS. AWAIT FURTHER ORDERS.

My next course of action should have been to relay this to our two battery command posts, who would then order guns, personnel and equipment to travel 200 miles back up the autobahn and occupy the prepared positions to defend the bridge across the Weser.

We would be on a war footing, and our ammunition supplies would be travelling in fast convoy to rendezvous with us at the bridge so we were ready to go into action. The cold war was now hot.

However, before starting hostilities I decided to check with the CO, who was sleeping in his tent a few yards away. Very wisely he decided to double check with Brigade before going into battle...and discovered that there had been a monumental mistake. The word I had been given had been taken from the wrong code book!

Panic over. The excitement had lasted 15 minutes, but it was a very long and extremely worrying adrenaline-charged 15 minutes.

My journey to Germany, and that longest quarter-hour of my life, had begun in September 1960 when I received my call-up papers and was ordered to report to Oswestry to join the 17th Training Regiment, Royal Artillery for basic training.

We were a typical intake of young men from every walk of life and every corner of the UK, all expecting — though National Service was now drawing to a close — to serve Queen and Country for the next two years.

We were issued with our uniforms, given numerous examinations, inoculations and injections and had almost all our hair shaved off. We were shown how to assemble our kit, sew on buttons and badges and how to conform to Army rules and regulations.

We burned and bulled boots and polished our brasses. And we were shown how to drill, and how to make our kit layout for the morning inspection. Our service numbers were stamped on everything.

There were some very interesting characters. One lad was most reluctant to have either a shower or bath, but after a few days he was placed in a cold bath and scrubbed with an assortment of brushes.

Like Marilyn Monroe, the chap in the bed next to me had six toes on one foot. He was "excused boots" and was doing his very best to ensure that he was excused two years' National Service as well.

But what he did not tell the MO was that the extra toe had not had any detrimental effect on his career as a professional footballer (Nottingham Forest, I seem to recall). What happened to him, and whether he was able to avoid his service I never found out.

After two weeks I was moved within the camp to 24 (The Irish) Battery RA where I was trained to be a TARA (Technical Assistant Royal Artillery). We were introduced to the delights of predictors, displacement calculators and all the equipment which would enable us to assist in firing 25-pounder field-guns.

Like most National Servicemen we had green denims for everyday wear. These were very ill-fitting, but we had to turn out smartly each morning and were expected to have creases in them.

We soon found that with an ordinary iron, brown paper and a wet shaving brush we could improvise a steam-iron to try to get the appropriate creases. One very cold morning I thought I had achieved a reasonable turnout, only to be told in no uncertain manner by the troop sergeant: "Johnson, you look like a bloody Sharpeville rioter."

One of our tasks was to line the parade ground at the passing-out of previous intakes, standing at five-pace intervals for what seemed like hours on end without moving.

On one parade the chap on my right fainted and fell forward, smashing his face on the ground. He was carried off with a broken nose and his jaw fractured in two places. He had also knocked out one tooth and driven four others through his lip.

On December 5, while most of the TARAs were taken to Welshpool to help rescue hundreds stranded by the heavily flooded River Severn, I went with two others to Barton Stacey for a War Office Selection Board. There we were to be carefully screened, interviewed and tested to assess if we would make suitable officer cadets.

It was bitterly cold and extremely wet, and we huddled around the small cast-iron stoves in the evenings to try to keep warm. The WOSB consisted of command tasks, the obstacle course, lectures, debates and interviews.

On exercise at Mons, above left, and right, now a fully-fledged officer

After four exhausting days we lined up to receive our results, and I was extremely pleased to learn that I had passed. So my next posting was to Mons Officer Cadet School at Aldershot.

At Mons we were intensively drilled and lectured, and instructed in "voice procedure" (correct speaking when on the wireless). We learned military history and military law, did numerous very muddy exercises day and night and competed in almost every type of sport known.

I teamed up with fellow gunner John Larder, and at Easter we completed the annual 125-mile Canoe Marathon from Devizes to Westminster. We were both very fit, but our 15ft touring canvas canoe was most unsuitable and we were very lucky to complete the course.

I competed again in 1964 with National Serviceman John Gmach in a glassfibre K2 canoe. And we were the first civilian crew (second overall) in just over 23 hours.

As gunner officer cadets at Mons we had a 10-day initiation into anti-aircraft artillery and guided weapons. Over two days we fired nearly 900 rounds on the Bofors L40/70 gun, which was probably responsible for my later tinnitus

Then finally, with the others who had passed-out, I marched proudly on to the parade ground in the pouring rain as the Royal Artillery band played Seventy Six Trombones. We were duly commissioned as officers and sent to all parts of the globe.

My posting was to 22 LAA Regiment Royal Artillery stationed at Llanion Barracks, Pembroke Dock in South Wales as part of 7 AGRA (Army Group Royal Artillery).

As a light anti-aircraft unit we had 16 Bofors L40/70 anti-aircraft guns, but were still using the slow but reliable wartime Matador gun-tractor to tow our equipment. Each gun crew actually required three Matadors, one to tow the gun, a second to pull the radar and a third to tow the generator.

While they were reliable, unfortunately they

Pictured (left) with fellow trainees

were also very slow, and in convoy were limited to 20 miles each hour. This allowed our slowest vehicles, the Matadors, to operate safely within their speed limitations while towing around seven or eight tons of gun, radar or trailer on 1960s roads without motorways and no Severn road crossing.

For this reason we moved at night whenever possible to avoid blocking the A40 between St Clears and Gloucester for hours on end.

Driving a Matador in convoy was not too bad, but driving a Champ, an Austin K9 or Bedford RL at this speed was a real pain. Not only was the vehicle likely to overheat on hot summer evenings, but it was all too easy for the driver to nod off for a few seconds.

That summer saw the regiment trundling off in convoy to various locations in southern England for exercises and training. These included Salisbury Plain, Stanford in Norfolk and southwest England — all of which involved the long drag along the A40 to Gloucester and then the long slog up the single-carriageway Birdlip Hill.

This was very steep and narrow, and extremely dangerous. Very different from today's sweeping dual carriageway with its gentle gradient.

On one return trip a Bedford RL and a Matador overturned while descending the dreaded hill in pouring rain.

During one night convoy I was in the lead Matador of six, towing two guns, two radars and two generators when I took a wrong turning. The narrow lane just got narrower and narrower until it ended with no exit.

Each Matador had to be unhitched, and all six pieces of heavy equipment manhandled to face the opposite direction. Then the Matadors were turned round and all the equipment re-hitched. Only then could we re-trace our tracks back up the lane. I was not the most popular of troop leaders that night. But as I said, at least it was not raining!

In the summer, as part of postwar NATO Europe, German troops brought their tanks to exercise and fire their guns at the nearby Castlemartin ranges. This was only 16 years after the end of the war, and the national press were very much up in arms, with headlines such as "Panzers in Wales."

We were visited by Army public relations officers and told to make the Germans feel very welcome but not to speak to any of the media.

When in recent years the Germans left Castlemartin the local population were extremely

sorry to see them go. They had provided many years of friendship, much goodwill and many liaisons with local girls that resulted in matrimony.

No-one messes with 2nd Lieut Johnson!

At Llanion the president of the mess committee was an old captain (well, so he seemed to us early-twenties subalterns) who said that tomato ketchup was an "un-officer-like food," and banned it from the officers' mess.

I also recall another rather elderly officer who went out on parade one morning and was very quietly admonished by his sergeant-major: "Excuse me sir, but you have your boots on the wrong feet."

The officer, glancing down to confirm this, replied: "Well, the damned batman must have left them out the wrong way round."

With the building of the Berlin Wall the Cold War intensified and 7 Artillery Brigade (re-formed from 7 AGRA) moved to BAOR. The re-designated 22 Regiment RA was despatched to Gutersloh in Nordrhein, Westphalia.

We left for Dover travelling at night at our stately pace, then crossed the Channel by chartered ferry and trundled our way on the autobahn network to Dortmund. There we stayed for some six weeks until Sundern Barracks at Gutersloh was ready for our occupation.

These had been a part of Goering's Luftwaffe headquarters, with full central heating for every building including all the garages and workshops. The CO's office, we were told, had been Goering's office. The adjutant's office, where I was to spend just over a year, had been his wine cellar with wine racks concealed in double wood-panelled walls.

In December 1961 I was fortunate to go with a party from our regiment and 12 RA to Norway to learn cross-country skiing. Unfortunately gale force winds and temperatures of minus 25C meant that I suffered second-degree frostbite and was extremely lucky not to lose the tops of my fingers and thumbs.

I returned early with others from our party driving my Morris 1000 Traveller on a round-trip of 2,720 miles. The MO and medical staff at RAF Gutersloh were very interested to see my hands when I called in for my monthly check-up for the following six months.

At the end of February 1962 I was appointed assistant adjutant, which was a very challenging but rewarding job — even though I nearly launched a war against the Russians!

The threat that they would invade West Germany was very real, so in our role of defending one of the bridges across the Weser every gun had a pre-selected position, which was changed on a regular basis.

One of my more unusual tasks was to take several sheets of blank paper and write boldly in block capitals TOP SECRET in red ink across the top and bottom of each sheet. I then listed the changed grid reference of each gun.

The next job was to recall all the previous sheets in exchange for the new ones, signing old copies in and new copies out. The final job was to destroy the old sheets, which was done with the combination of a metal paper bin, a box of matches and a long stick!

All the old papers were placed in the bin and carefully burned, then the remains were stirred round with the stick until there was only fine ash. This was flushed down the CO's toilet.

The "destruction certificate" was then signed and all the signatures were finally checked in the Top Secret ledger which was then locked back in the safe.

The Russian Intelligence operated a number of green-painted Volkswagen Beetle cars, each with a special sign and a number. These contained their intelligence officers who were watching everything that was going on in the West. And we were watching them watching us.

If anybody in the regiment saw one of these cars, we had to send in a form stating the number, location, time, direction of travel and the number of occupants. I imagine that somebody somewhere put these reports together like a jigsaw and tried to make out just what they were watching.

Regimental exercises were taken very seriously and included one working with the Canadians. Then the SAS joined in and started firing live rounds to make things even more realistic!

My remaining months in Germany were a mixture of hard work and lots of recreational activities which included sailing, squash, tennis,

rugby, canoeing over 500 miles, sailing on the Mohne See and lots of road and cross-country running.

I visited Belsen and the East German border, watched motor racing at the Nurburgring and drove to Holland for a week's camping. And I spent a two-week leave driving 2,580 miles

Still in uniform when we re-enact the war

through Switzerland, Austria and Northern Italy in my Minor 1000 Traveller.

In March, 1963 after thoroughly enjoying my time with the Royal Artillery, I left the Army. They tried very hard to get me to sign on as a regular, and I was very tempted but decided against. Even now, I sometimes wish I had agreed, but we cannot turn back the clock.

And then...

Before I joined up it was assumed I would follow my father and grandfather into the family furniture and furnishing business in Brighton. I studied for the National Furnishing Diploma and did a two-year apprenticeship in the furniture trade followed by two years as a junior salesman at Allders of Croydon.

But when I left the Army my father gave me a cheque for £500 and suggested I go on a working holiday to New Zealand.

I joined the Maple furnishing company in Auckland, but on my return found the family firm was not to my liking. So I returned to New Zealand as partner in a motel project. Then came back once more to the UK and in 1969 started a small furniture and furnishing business in Sevenoaks.

With my wife becoming involved, this grew and grew until we were the largest independent trader in the town.

We sold this company in 1985, bought a small farm at Wincanton, and for five years bred pedigree Romney Marsh sheep. Then I spent some 10 years working in the Bournemouth area as a healthcare assistant.

Since retiring in 2002 I have been involved as a volunteer on several preserved railway projects. And I now travel three days a week across to the nature reserve on Brownsea Island in Poole Harbour where I work as the volunteer "general factotum" with Dorset Wildlife Trust.

But I have maintained my interest in the Army,

and in 1980 realised an ambition and bought a Matador gun tractor, the same as we had used in the RA to tow our Bofors guns and equipment.

Since then I have been very fortunate to own, at various times, nine military vehicles, one Corgi motor-bike, a cycle and three assorted trailers.

For seven years I owned an Austin Champ, almost identical to the one I drove as troop leader almost 45 years ago, using this as my everyday transport and covering some 17,000 miles.

Also, for seven years, I owned a former British Army DUKW which I drove in the Lord Mayor's Show in London in 1983. In June 1984 we drove it to Arromanches and swam it in the sea as part of the 40th anniversary of the D-Day landings.

For some years I even owned a Sherman tank minus turret, having been given it if I could arrange to take it out of the huge vaulted barrel storage area beneath London Bridge station.

Today I am a member of The Real Dad's Army Home Guard Re-enactment group. When we pay tribute to the iconic BBC television series I remove my glasses, roll my eyes and take on the role of James "We'rrrraaalllldoomed" Frazer. When we re-enact what actually happened I am Lt D H Johnson, commander of 1 Platoon, A company of the 23rd (Hastings) Battalion, Home Guard.

I am a member of the National Service Veterans Alliance and have led our contingent at the Cenotaph for the past 11 years. And in November 2003 I had the honour to parade the NSVA Standard before the Queen at the Royal Albert Hall Festival of Remembrance.

— Dale Johnson©

I was a student at Brighton College and a member of the Combined Cadet Force

Not a police mugshot — just my first Army photograph!

I joined the Navy, saw the world (well, Scotland) & found a wife

WHEN I joined the Royal Navy for my National Service I was a lowly clerk in the vast (as it then was) Singer Sewing Machine empire, working at their head office in the City. I regarded myself as one of the lucky ones to get into the Navy. Mind you, I had four or five years in the sea cadets to try to ensure this.

I was instructed to report to HMS Pembroke, the barracks at Chatham, where I was issued with my number and kit and underwent basic training. I can't remember much about this apart from the fact that we did a certain amount of square-bashing and boot-cleaning but, from what I've heard, nothing like the Army entrants had to suffer.

After training most of us were drafted on to the aircraft carrier HMS Indefatigable and treated to a round-Britain cruise! All the high-spots, including the Isle of Skye and that dreary hole Scapa Flow. Returning from the training cruise the ship then took part in the Review of the Fleet at Spithead and very impressive it was too. I did not get to do the three cheers bit as Her Majesty passed us because I was below decks making innumerable bottles of soda water for the officers' jolly which followed the Review.

Once training was completed I returned to Chatham to await a further draft. Some of my classmates were sent to destroyers and cruisers in the Mediterranean. Lucky them. Warm weather and exotic ports of call.

Me? I got drafted, with several of my intake, to a fleet minesweeper based in Port Edgar, a small harbour near the southern end of the Forth rail bridge. We joined the Welfare, M356, on September 9 1953.

An Algerine class ocean-going minesweeper she was of a similar size to a corvette. The ship had a full wartime complement because after a few days we sailed to join in NATO exercises. We newcomers had to find hammock space wherever we could. My billet was outside the galley which was warm, but when turned in I could watch the cockroaches rushing about on the deckhead.

Our names were placed on the watch bill, a

complicated piece of documentation which told us where we should be depending on the state of readiness. My action station was as a supply number for the starboard-after Bofors anti-aircraft gun. As we only went to action stations once I didn't get much practice.

Returning from the exercise we National Servicemen were asked if any of us would volunteer to stay on the Welfare, and I thought well, I know the ship, not much spit and polish and the crew are OK, so why not? I then had the luxury of getting a hammock space on the messdeck.

Aboard the Welfare, and (top) the vessel in the Forth

Many of the crew were Royal Naval reservists who had retired after years of service and then been recalled when the Korean War broke out. Most of them were waiting for the day when they would be demobbed again. I remember the officers' steward started an ugly rumour that the reservists were to have their period of service further extended which called for a mass dripping (complaining) among them. But it was just a wind up.

It had come of something of a shock to me to be thrown into the world of not only washing my own clothes in a galvanised iron bucket, but also of preparing food.

Each mess appointed two cooks of the day who were on duty midday to midday. They were responsible for washing up after meals, making the tea for breakfast, stand easy and tea and preparing the food for the midday dinner.

Breakfast and tea were optional meals and for many of us the former was the time-honoured tea and a fag with perhaps a slice of bread or toast.

Dinner was the only cooked meal of the day and was often a roast (particularly pork) or a sort of casserole with vegetables. The more experienced would sometimes make dumplings for the casserole or a half-boiled/half-baked dumpling known as a boily-bake. Prepared food was taken to the galley where the leading cook or his helper would do the actual cooking.

For those with a good appetite weekends were a treat. The rations were issued on the basis of the number of hands on board in the morning. As some chose to go ashore later it meant that there would be an excess of food for those staying on board. Cries of "big eats" and "fill yer boots" at dishing up time!

One thing I didn't appreciate when opting for the RN was that I would suffer from seasickness. Not too badly, but enough to make life a bit unpleasant for the first 24 hours at sea. As a lot of our sea time was out in the morning and back at night this didn't help.

Most of our time was spent steaming up and down the Firth of Forth towing an anti-magnetic mine device known as the Loop. We did have a few longer trips mostly to ports in Scotland and one to the Faroe Islands where some of us went ashore. It poured with rain for most of the time but on the plus side the cream cakes sold in the cafe were delicious.

The other trip was to Bergen which took place in March. The weather was bad to start with and got worse and virtually all the crew were seasick. What a shambles on the messdeck. Broken crockery and sick on the deck and water sploshing about.

We reached the end of the fiord for Bergen early in the morning and weather conditions were unbelievable — the sun shone, the sea was dead calm and the wind had dropped. It was a real pleasure to be there.

The working day was quite easy. For the non-duty part of the watch this would involve tasks such as washing down paintwork, chipping off old paint and repainting, polishing brasswork and generally keeping the upper deck clean and tidy.

Once a month we had Captain's Rounds. This meant a good scrub of the table and decks, dusting off the overhead conduits, polishing all the metal utensils, having a general tidy up and laying out everything for inspection. The leading-

Pictured with my pen-pal wife

seaman would stay for the inspection while the rest of us made ourselves scarce.

Then the captain — wearing white gloves to check for dust — and a retinue of officers would inspect the mess. Fortunately we always passed, otherwise it would have meant repeating the cleaning procedure and having it checked again.

The duty part of the watch would be detailed off when at sea as lookouts, helmsmen and radar watchers for example. One thing I discovered on my first turn as helmsman was that unlike a car ships do not have instant response to turning the wheel.

On this particular occasion we were with two other ships in line ahead with us third. In the forward bulkhead of the wheelhouse was a scuttle through which I could see the ship ahead, and my instructions were quite simple — just follow.

The bow of our ship drifted off line a bit so I applied a bit of helm. Nothing happened so I applied a bit more, and then the rudder bit and the ship ahead was in the right position so I put the helm amidships and of course we continued to turn. So I applied opposite wheel and a similar thing happened.

Suffice it to say that we finished up swinging wildly from side to side, at which point the officer of the watch asked who was on the wheel and ordered the quartermaster to take over and restore stability.

I learned a lot from that episode and in time mastered the trick of keeping our head on a compass point with a fair degree of accuracy.

Sometimes the duty part of the watch would be detailed off as quartermasters, whose job in harbour was to guard the gangway and keep a log of comings and goings, messengers, etc.

It was when I was quartermaster that I got my only punishment, for being improperly dressed. I had not bothered to put on my jumper and collar, and as luck would have it I was called to Pipe the Still as a salute to another ship which was leaving harbour. The CO told me to take off my watch coat, and of course I was found out. I Piped the Still hidden out of sight and was put on the first-lieutenant's defaulters, getting seven days' No.11 punishment.

No.11 was quite easy, no leave and extra work sweeping the upper-deck before breakfast and when the rest had finished for the day. After that I made sure I was properly dressed at all times and this included boots on all watches.

Patrolling the upper deck during the night was part of the quartermaster's duties, and it just so happened that this meant walking overhead of the officers' cabins and alongside the CO's. So it was not long before an edict appeared on daily orders saying that quartermasters should wear PT shoes during the night watches.

The only two events of any importance during my service were being up-rated from ordinary to able-seaman, which was almost automatic after, I believe, six months. And reaching the age of 20, which enabled me to draw my tot.

As it happened we were at sea on my birthday, and as was the custom I was given "sippers" all round to celebrate. But I was on afternoon watch as helmsman, and I have to admit that our course was a little erratic!

When the officer of the watch asked what the problem was he was told it was my birthday. So he had me relieved and sent below to sleep it off.

Get any one to do you a small favour and the response was "I'll be round." There was a sort of unwritten exchange rate for favours ranging from sippers to gulpers.

On the subject of drinks, a very welcome one when at sea during the night was ki. This was made from solid chocolate melted in a pan with sugar and evaporated milk. It sounds really sickly but surprisingly it did settle queasy stomachs.

Two or three months before the end of my service the ship was going to be put into reserve. We were put in a dry dock in Rosyth and gave all the underwater parts of the hull a good chip and re-paint.

There were a couple more Algerines in at the same time and I know that chipping hammers went right through the hull!

I was eventually returned to Chatham and spent my time doing I don't know what until my discharge. I had one or two years' reserve service to do in the RNVR which simply meant attending HMS Chrysanthemum a few times during a year. As the Chrysanthemum was permanently tied up alongside the Embankment in London this was no hardship.

One good thing that came out of National Service was that it found me a wife. My mother asked someone she knew if her daughter would like to write to me. But the daughter already had several penpals so said she would give my name to one of her friends.

However, this friend didn't want to write so the daughter added me to her list of penpals, and I met her when I went home on leave. We got on well, and three years after my demob we were married. Recently we celebrated our golden wedding.

And then...
When I finished with the Navy I returned to Singers for a short while and then got a job in publishing, and remained in printing or publishing until I retired.

— **Chris Latreille©**

22348610 Pte Alf Lloyd

To get a beer meant a six-hour return journey over the Alps

BECAUSE I was on a five-year plumbing apprenticeship I did not get called up until 1950 when I had to report to Colchester Barracks with the Essex Regiment. At the end of basic training most of the intake were posted to join the Northamptonshire Regiment in Trieste, but with a few others I remained at Colchester on general duties.

This was at the height of the Cold War, and there was fighting in Korea. One day about 20 of us were ordered to report to the company office where we were told to draw rifles and ammunition and stand by in battle order at five minutes' notice. Apparently some limpet mines had been found on Navy ships along the south coast.

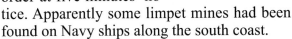
At the TA camp, where I am on the extreme left

At 5am next morning we had a meal and were taken by lorry to the US airbase at Lakenheath in Norfolk. Our job there was to guard the big B29 bombers because it was believed an attempt would be made to destroy them overnight.

We had four hours on and four hours off guarding each plane. We were armed with rifle and fixed bayonet and 10 rounds of ammunition. Our orders were if anyone approached to give three quick challenges and then shoot to kill.

During our time at Lakenheath we were able to use the Americans' PX store where we exchanged one English pound for three dollars to buy sweets and cigarettes. After two weeks we returned to Colchester. Then I was posted to Dovercourt in an old prisoner of war camp which we had to prepare for the Royal Signals to move in. We worked a 9-4 day with two hours for meals and a 36-hour pass at weekends. There were no parades, so it was a very

I am on the right here, with a couple of pals in Trieste

pleasant job. But soon I was told I would be joining the rest of my intake on advanced training in Trieste ready to go to Korea. This involved a lot of exercises, including a two-day march over the Alps. There were a thousand men on the trek plus the band, and we marched in single file with Alpine guides front and rear.

We were in a former SS camp from where it was just possible to see a wooden house on a distant peak. This contained a bar where it was possible to buy rolls and beer. But the journey took more than six hours there and back so we didn't have long before it would be time to return to camp.

Going there was not too difficult because we were able to see our objective, though often we were above the clouds and walking in rain or drizzle. But the return journey was not so easy on a slippery track across grassy slopes. If we got lost or darkness fell, we were told always to stay put for the night. The house had a visitors book which we signed, following the names of SS officers in the early pages.

I remember one day we were trying to destroy an old Alpine hut with two-inch mortars. About 10 of us took turns when one of the bombs misfired and popped out of the barrel about two feet in front of us. We hit the ground in a split second, but fortunately it did not explode. But after 18 months, instead of going to Korea I returned to the UK for demob. I then had a two-week Territorial Army camp plus three weekends and 30 evenings a year training on searchlights and anti-aircraft guns with the Royal Artillery.

A recent picture

And then...
I returned to plumbing and became a central heating engineer, working with one family firm for 34 years while it grew from about half-a-dozen workmen to around 70.

— *Alf Lloyd©*

Petty officer was a man of few words — most of them profane

ON DECEMBER 6 1954 I had my first sight of HMS Raleigh — the "brick battleship" in Torpoint, just a ferry ride from Plymouth. Along with a few dozen other young bucks I saw it from the back of the naval truck which had picked us up at the railway station and delivered us into National Service.

It had been weeks since I had received the invitation from Her Majesty that I might like to pop along to her Wanstead medical centre, get myself checked out and sit the exams that would determine the general direction of my life for the next couple of years.

Having coughed and then been grabbed and groped on a medical assembly line of nervous and self-conscious semi-naked teenagers, we were tested to see if we had any brains at all. Then, somewhat cynically, we were asked for our preferences, as if that made any difference to them.

Most of the lads had said they wanted to do their two years in the RAF, and were promptly shoved into the Army. But some of us had been deemed intelligent enough and/or had sufficient family connections (like a couple of uncles who had also served — including a distant one who hadn't reported back after Jutland) to be of interest to the Admiralty.

I was about to become Stoker Lynch C/K 946568, and spend a couple of years wearing what was then still considered to be the best bird-pulling gear on the dance-floor. And learning how to sink Russian warships at the same time.

Just to emphasise their keen and urgent need for my services they also sent a railway travel warrant. By the time the train reached Plymouth that day some of us had got to know each other in the station and train bars.

It was all pretty obvious, by our age and suitcases, where we were going even though not all of us were headed for the same uniform. Most were prospective khaki jobs getting off at various points along the line, but a few of us were headed for Plymouth, and HMS Raleigh.

Being quick on the uptake — having been proved intelligent and all that at Wanstead — we guessed that the blue truck waiting at the station with the big white letters RN emblazoned on its doors, probably had something to do with us.

Just in case we hadn't guessed, there was also a rather loud chap, wearing a peaked cap and dark suit with brass buttons to emphasise the point. Brandishing a clipboard he was soon inviting us, in some quite noisy and fairly intemperate language, to climb into the back of his truck rather quickly.

Chucking in our suitcases (which we had been told to bring so we could send our civvies home) we clambered aboard and, I suppose to add to the mystery of the tour, the end flap was closed behind us leaving us all cramped and hanging on for dear life.

We were all still making silly nervous jokes about "only two years to demob" etc, as our chauffeur hurled his truck through the back streets of Plymouth in the general direction of what was presumably Torpoint.

Eventually it stopped, the back flap was ripped open and there was Petty Officer Loudmouth again, still being very offensive. He shouted and hollered at us to get down and line up. Clearly it was best to humour him, and most of us almost fell out of the truck in our anxiety to please.

We found ourselves just inside the gates of HMS Raleigh, in front of a guardroom which had two rather attractive little cannons decoratively placed on each side, and a flagpole which was flying the White Ensign. We would soon learn to salute these guns whenever we passed them, either on our way into or out of Raleigh.

PO Loudmouth, having gained our attention and got us into some kind of straggly line, now noisily explained that he would be our mother and father for the next few months. In the course of his harangue he implied that he himself had not had such benefits, presumably having been born out of wedlock.

Clearly he was already having a bad hair day, and meeting us hadn't done much to improve his mood. He prowled up and down our ragged lines, stopping here and there to make some sarcastic remark at one or another of us. We were all dreading him stopping in front of us and, inevitably, he stopped in front of me. "Wherejew-comefrom?" he bawled in my face. I stammered that I was from London, and that seemed to make him even more uptight.

"Wot you doin' ere, then?" he snarled. "Wot do you know about ships and the sea dahn there in the Smoke?"

Now, in the course of the next few months, we would learn a great deal, and one of those things was to keep schtumm when faced with such questions. Me, I had to go and reply: "Been to Ramsgate on me 'olidays, sir."

I thought he was going to have a fit. "Sir? Sir?" he shrieked. "Listen, you lot. I am no bloody sir. I am your worst nightmare, a cow-son, a shit of the first order. I am a petty officer. You do not salute me, and you do not call me bloody sir, but you do whatever I bloody well tell yooz to do. Is that clear?"

He screamed the last few words, but at least he was screaming them to all of us, and no longer homing in on Yours Truly. In fact, he promptly found another victim when one of the poor sods he had at the end of his tongue asked about leave.

"Wot?" he shrieked. "Are you bored wiv us already? Do you fink we went to all the trouble to pay your fares here so we could send you 'ome again. You will not even leave this camp until you have your uniforms, and you ain't even been measured for them yet. So don't get your hopes up that you will be seeing mummy soon."

He was a man of few words, all of them bellowed and most of them profane.

It was true that most of HMS Raleigh would be closed for the Christmas fortnight, but apparently we would be too busy to worry about that. And he was dead right about the uniforms.

We were about to be issued with the best bird-pulling clobber at the Palais, but our intake had probably arrived too late to take advantage of it. It was a gloomy moment.

Next day we were issued with our kit. Work clothes, boots, bits of uniform like the big deep blue collars (that had to be scrubbed vigorously to get some of the blue out of them so the wearer would look like he'd got some sea time in) and our kitbags and hammocks.

They also measured us up for the bell-bottom trousers and jackets of navy blue, but it was doubtful they would arrive in time, let alone actually fit. Unlike the Army battledresses they had to be skin tight and pulled on over your head, which was a bit difficult once your jabs

had started working on your arms. Miserably we buckled down to basic training, slipping and sliding on the ice-covered parade ground with WW1 rifles rubbing our shoulders raw, polishing our new boots and being indoctrinated into Nelsonian traditions. Cornwall is a lovely county to visit — in the summer. But you try square-bashing there in December.

All the time Christmas was getting closer. Frankie Howerd came down to entertain us in the camp theatre, but we couldn't even get tickets for that. And there was no word on our uniforms. Our evenings were spent morosely drinking brown and mild and stuffing ourselves with pork pies in the teasingly decorated NAAFI.

The days ticked by. Loudmouth got louder and our arms got sorer from the rifle drill and inoculations. Our Civvy Street dosh was almost gone and all around us were other "students" of previous intakes, preparing to go home for a Christmas which for us was looking pretty bleak.

Then suddenly the uniforms turned up and Loudmouth told us that we could go home — provided we passed haircut muster and had all our badges etc. sewn on correctly. We sewed like mad and begged the barber to shear us.

Then, incredibly, we were back on the train, swapping our HMS Raleigh hatbands or HM Submarines hatbands (quietly acquired through black market naval sources), and back home with just days to spare. Then after mum's tears of welcoming joy, it was free booze in the Royal Oak and the New Year dance where my waltz suddenly developed a sailor's rolling gait.

It had been a close run thing though, and proved to be only a brief respite. For once we got back to Plymouth PO Loudmouth was true to his word, and worked hard to make our lives a total misery. He marched us in the snow from dawn to dusk, with battered old wartime rifles, teaching us the rudiments of drill in normal time, slow time and more often than not on the double.

Having supervised the issue of our kit he insisted on having it all laid out in proper order, according to the official diagram, every day. He had us swilling out the toilets (heads) before lights out, and sent us to the barbers so many times a week he must have been copping more backhanders than Andy Murray.

There were others also involved in making our stay in Torpoint memorable. One was the dentist. In those days I grew my own teeth al-

As a young sailor in my bird-pulling gear

though, having been turned off dentists by the experiences of opening wide for our school dentist, admittedly they were not in the best of condition,

The Navy, of course, insisted that we should have good teeth and thus we all had the usual inspections as soon as we arrived. Everything seemed well until one day PO Loudmouth called me out of parade and told me to report to the dentist who, having perused the results of my dental exploration, had expressed a desire to see me.

I was not best pleased at this. In fact, by the time I got to the surgery I was pretty wound up about the whole thing. I walked in and (me and my big mouth again) demanded to know why he wanted me. In hindsight I realise that I couched this request in the most inappropriate way, and he went spare!

He was, as he explained at length, an officer. And the likes of me did not speak to officers in the way I had. He shouted at me and ordered me to sit in his chair. The gist of his outburst was that it was my duty to just do as I was told and not to question officers' motives. I had a filling which needed doing and that is what I was going to get whether I liked it or not.

I have to admit he did a good job on the filling because it lasted for many years. My only regret at the time though was that, had I been a bit more respectful towards an officer, he might have given me something to deaden the pain instead of using cold steel to practise his arts on my dodgy molar.

Every ex-National Serviceman says it never did him any harm, but while he was doing it he wasn't usually in that frame of mind. Many of the lads my age saw active service in the Army and RAF in places they probably had never heard of a few years earlier. Some of them were killed or maimed in the jungles of Malaya or in places like Cyprus, Kenya and Korea.

But I got lucky. I fell into a job in the Navy that many would have given their eye-teeth for. I became part of an MTB "ferry crew."

When we got back from our Christmas leave we had all the delightful prospects of finishing our basic training by learning to be stokers at HMS Raleigh. But then they asked for volunteers for a special course on internal combustion engines.

The attraction was being drafted to an old Cunard liner (the Alaunia) which was moored up the river from Devonport, to do the course and leave Raleigh behind us.

We all volunteered, and three of us, Lenny "Swede" Broadhurst, Harry Willard, who was older than us because he'd first done his training as an architect, and me, were accepted.

The Alaunia was little more than a big empty shell containing living accommodation for those on the actual course. She was tied up alongside an old French destroyer called Dunquerque, and a flat-bottom gun monitor which housed the classrooms and the NAAFI bar.

For the first time we were living and working with real sailors, some of them with considerable sea time. We slept in hammocks, and learned by experience not to tie them with a convenient bow that could be pulled apart by some drunken reveller coming back inboard while we were asleep in them. We experienced real ship-

Now my seafaring days are over

board living and mess-deck catering. I also fell into a dream job without even asking. One of the crew of the captain's motorboat had failed to come back from leave because he was sick, and for some obscure reason I was allocated to it while we waited for the course to start. That meant lounging around the messdeck most of the day, waiting for the call for the captain's motorboat crew to man their boat.

When we did finish the course we National Servicemen came top of the class and were deemed fit to operate real diesel and petrol engines. That was when I found out that the ones who came lower down the list were drafted to aircraft carriers and the like, while we could be sent to either Coastal Forces (motor torpedo boats) or submarines.

Now, to be honest, the idea of being a submariner never really appealed, so I was quite relieved when Lenny, Harry and I all got drafted together to HMS Hornet in Gosport to serve in the MTB squadrons.

We were to be part of the Sixth Ferry Crew, a team which travelled to different shipbuilders throughout the UK to pick up new MTBs.

150

We would sail them back to Gosport, work them up by doing their trials and hand them over to the operating squadrons, while we went and picked up another boat.

It was a brilliant little number and no mistake, though there was one little drawback not obvious or too embarrassing at the time.

There was a class of MTB they called the gay boats because they had names like Gay Bombardier, Gay Charger and the like. These were in the days before the word was hijacked to mean something entirely other than happy of course, and for some time I walked around Portsmouth with the words Gay Cavalier emblazoned across my cap.

All in all, HMS Hornet proved to be a pretty good draft compared to what it could have been and although the only foreign place we ever visited in my Royal Navy time was Caen in France. But we did see British pubs from Cornwall to West Hartlepool.

The French thing is also worth mentioning because we were sent there on a courtesy visit to mark the tenth anniversary of the Normandy landings. We were assured we were popular in the town because it had been the British who had liberated Caen. What they neglected to tell us was that before D-Day the RAF flattened the place, so we were not all God's chosen people with everyone there.

Even worse, we went there with a submarine which was ordered home after three days because its drunken crew went berserk in the town. They had to be brought back almost en masse by the local French police one night.

Most of my service had been spent swanning up and down the coast in MTBs, such as the unforgettable Gay Cavalier. But it was cold sweats all round when the Suez war started in the autumn of 1956 because it was only weeks before I was due to be demobbed and we were held over pending what happened

However, it all blew over and Harry, Lenny and I arrived back in Chatham's HMS Pembroke to be demobbed within the fortnight. That was due on the day after my 21st birthday — a day which I spent in a coalhole and finished up as "Engineer Mechanic Harrison."

Some moments stick in your mind for ever, and when Dearly Beloved and I popped into the old Chatham dockyard one Easter some years ago, what came back to me with crystal clarity was that moment when I found myself staring up at an enraged naval officer pointing my own rifle at me.

In fact, had it not been for "Engineer Mechanic Harrison," instead of celebrating the end of my two years' National Service I could have served an extended version of it by spending an uncomfortable Christmas in a military prison.

Now anyone who did their bit in the Navy (and I suppose, the other services too) knows that on demob day you don't just walk out of the gates. You have to be booked out of a dozen different departments, so they issue you with a draft chit, which is a kind of skivers' licence that lets you spend days strolling round getting yourself rubber stamped out of service life.

While we waited for that magic piece of paper to be handed over however, we were press-ganged into Pembroke's workforce.

This was in November and I was due to be unleashed back on to the Palais circuit on my birthday on the twenty-second, and it was pretty nippy weather-wise.

So seeing my name listed for a boilerhouse working party did seem like a bit of a result. Certainly it would be warm in there.

But when we reported we were a bit surprised to be handed shovels before being marched off to the boilerhouse to shovel coke. And the coke we would be shovelling was outside in the very chilly fresh air, rather than inside a nice warm boiler-room. To this day I can hardly believe what happened.

Chatham Barracks was full of little boilerhouses, but not all of them had piles of coke to burn. In fact most were not even operational.

We were marched to one of those and ordered to bag the pile of coke that lay outside it. Naturally that took us most of the day. Well, little diversions like lunch and the rum issue took up some of the time, but we were in no hurry anyway.

We filled sacks with coke, put them on a barrow and were directed to lug this round to another boilerhouse at the other end of the barracks.

There we emptied out the coke into a pile again, and marched off for an evening's revelry in a Chatham boozer, content we had done a good day's work.

The next morning we were all marched back to the pile we had created the previous evening and ordered to bag it all up again and take it to another boilerhouse.

That was the pattern. Believe it or not, for 10 days we shifted the same pile of coke around Chatham, often to the same space we had emptied it from a couple of days before.

It seemed a bit pointless, but we were getting closer and closer to "the day" and that was the important thing.

Now my home at Dagenham was within easy reach of Chatham by train so I did have the opportunity to nip home for the weekend.

With the double celebration of my birthday and demob coming up as well, I was rather looking forward to my last weekend. Well, I was until I found out that, on my birthday and my last Sunday as a sailor, I was rostered for guard duty.

No-one would swap duties with me so I resigned myself to having a few birthday bevvies in the NAAFI before going on guard.

By the time we were due to go on watch at 10pm we had swallowed a fair amount of celebratory ale. We were not stoned out of our brains, but it would be fair to say we were gibbering a little as we put on the official guard-duty belt and gaiters before lining up to be issued with our unloaded rifles.

The officer of the watch went off to enjoy his bottle of wardroom gin, leaving the leading seaman in charge of the guard that night to organise us. One man on watch at a time. The rest could kip on the bare mattresses in an empty barrack room handily close by.

We drew lots for an hour apiece, and I drew the 1am to 2am slot and we all turned in, each of us having made a note of where the guy we had to wake up was sleeping. I was duly shaken awake at 12.55, and started my lonely vigil.

All we had to do was take a turn or two around the parade ground. It was very quiet in the early hours and nothing stirred but, bearing in mind the amount of birthday booze I had sunk a few hours before, I was not at my brightest. So I had to sit down and have a smoke on one of the benches around the parade ground.

Next thing I know, I am being jabbed ferociously in the shoulder. Through my befuddled consciousness I could hear shouting, some of it appearing to question the legitimacy of my parentage.

Blearily I became aware that the hollering was coming from a lieutenant-commander who was also poking me with my own rifle to emphasise his point.

Behind him lurked a smirking female of the civilian variety who was clearly enjoying her bloke's macho performance.

Thankfully this guy was not the officer of the watch. He was probably back from a heavy night in Chatham, bringing the girlfriend back

to show her his itchings. So he never had the list of overnight sentries with names. But he was going potty anyway, shrieking threats about Captain's Reports, and demanding to know my name and number. It was at this point that Engineer Mechanic Harrison rode to the rescue in my imagination,

I staggered to my feet, hauled myself up to attention, saluted and glibly reeled off his name and equally fictitious number. He wrote them down, read me my fortune, thrust my rifle back at me and ordered me to report to the Master-at-Arms by noon.

Then he swayed off, with giggling girlfriend clinging to his arm, towards the officers' quarters and presumably a night of lust.

I didn't have the heart to tell him I was actually planning to be in Dagenham by noon.

But then I realised I had another little problem. I saw it was 4.20am. I had not only done two other people's watches, I didn't know who to wake for the 4am slot, though I did know a mate who was on the 5am start.

So I stayed on guard, making sure to keep awake until then. The only way I managed that was by walking and walking and walking all around that bloody parade ground in the early hours of that morning.

Well, I had plenty to think about anyway, given that I had not only been caught sleeping on watch, I had lied to my back teeth about who I was as well. Eventually I staggered back to the dormitory and located the five-o'clock man, woke him and just fell on to my own bunk again.

Only a couple of hours later we were noisily woken, lined up for inspection and dismissed. No one questioned why they had slept through their watch, and not a word about reports was said by the officer of the watch. So far, so good.

We were due to leave the place by 10.30am, so for the next few hours I was sweating a little bit. The final touch of irony was when we went to collect our travel warrants and the Navy made its last despairing efforts to get us to stay.

"Have you thought about signing on?"
"Yes sir."
"You have? And what do you think about it?"
"No chance!"
"Right," His friendly tone changed, "here's your travel warrant, good-bye."

We could hardly get out of his office quickly enough, and I had my own special reasons. All morning, right up to the time we were handed that warrant and were walking out of the gate laden down with kitbags, I kept getting this nasty feeling I was about to hear an announcement over the public address system inviting Engineer Mechanic Harrison to report to the Master-at-Arms.

It never was, and I wasn't going to hang about waiting for it.

But I often wonder if a call was ever put out for Engineer Mechanic Harrison C/K...whatever his number was.

And then...

After demob I spent a couple of years in the Merchant Navy, then trained as an overseas telegraph operator before working variously as a Telex operator, a taxi driver and in childcare.

I then moved into journalism and worked as a reporter and later a local newspaper editor. I have also written a number of books, both biographies and autobiographical.

— Brian Lynch©

In the Army you stand on your own feet, you learn to keep your head and act quickly in an emergency, to look after yourself. You make friends, you are one of a big crowd entering into the comradeship of the Army. You get to know the other man by living with him, working with him and sharing adventures and perhaps dangers with him. In the Army a man is taken for what he is worth, neither more nor less. And, for the man who goes into the Army with the intention of giving his best, the Army will give its best also. Here's wishing you a pleasant and successful Army career and jolly good luck to you!

— from You and the Army, a booklet issued to all NS army conscripts

23011811 LCpl Brian Marks

Electrics in my office hideaway put the barracks lights out

AN EASY bus journey from Sidmouth to Exeter, followed by a five-minute stroll to Topsham Barracks and through the imposing gateway. Then it was life on the double. Double to the store for uniforms, double to the billets, double to the barber, then the mess hall and double back to the billet. Those first two days were a blur.

One chap wanted to know why he had two pairs of gaiters and was informed that one were for his ankles and the other for his wrists. And that is how he appeared on parade! He didn't stay long because he was transferred to officers' training. Well, he did have letters after his name.

During our basic training we were once on the parade ground doing rifle drill on a very cold and snowy morning. It seemed we were there longer than usual.

Later I found out that in the cold icicles were forming on the sergeant's waxed moustache, and he wanted to see how long they would grow before they broke off.

I remember a day on the assault course when Pete Hill slipped in the mud. Then he stood up, said something rude and drove the rifle into the ground barrel first. Oops.

On another occasion we went to the rifle range on Dartmoor, and on the return trip the convoy stopped to watch a film crew shooting one of those Knights of the Round Table films. On the hills in the background a steam train pottered along making lots of smoke. It showed up pretty well on the film!

One day we were at a range near Exmouth where a young National Service officer was in charge.

A line of us were waiting to fire while the chaps in the butts were still putting up targets. But we got the order to fire followed very rapidly, and in a different voice, by "cease fire."

The other voice belonged to a civvy driver. And when our officer demanded: "Who's in charge here?" he explained in no uncertain manner that it is not a good idea to fire bullets towards men standing in front of the targets.

After our passing-out parade we had a few days' leave and on return I was transferred from

At the TA camp (top, circled) and above, on the wide open spaces of Oz

the Devons to the Gloucesters ready to go to Korea. So I had to cut off my regimental flashes and sew on new ones. Then I was told they didn't want me after all, so I was given more leave and then returned to Topsham where I was re-badged once more into the Devons, who at that time were in Kenya fighting the Mau Mau.

But believe it or not, I was next informed that I wouldn't be getting the pleasure of meeting the Mau Mau. Instead, I could have another few days' leave. My girlfriend was beginning to wonder what National Service was all about.

When I returned to barracks this time my badge-sewing days were over. I was put on the permanent staff in the education centre. And because this implied that I had some degree of intelligence — well, I only just failed School Certificate — I was promoted to lance-corporal.

The boss, Capt RA McKitrick DFC RAEC, was a former RAF man and a great bloke to work for. Most mornings when he came in he would walk to my desk and watch me mark another day off my demob chart. I still don't know if he wanted to see the back of me or was upset that because he was a regular he couldn't get away.

Anyway, next he would reach for The Times and Telegraph while I took the Daily Mirror and Sketch. Then we did the crosswords. By that time it was NAAFI break, followed by coffee in the office. And soon it was time for lunch.

Occasionally our simple life was broken by an intake of new recruits when I had to set up a room with tables, trestle, soldiers for the use of. We old soldiers on one side asking the questions, and the nervous nignogs on the other giving answers which we wrote on a form. Sometimes replies could be quite amusing. I remember someone being asked: "How old are you?" "Eighteen."

"How old are your parents?" "Don't know? Well, they had you before they were married so we'll put down 19." "OK sir."

Among the recruits one day was my old school pal Dick Copp. He also joined the depot permanent staff a few weeks later, and on Monday and Wednesday evenings he would come into the education office library where I would always leave one table clear. Well, Dick had to iron his battledress somewhere! I don't remember that he ever borrowed a book.

Tuesday and Thursday evenings I spent at home at Sidmouth or with my girlfriend at Ottery.

At the back of one classroom in the education centre was an empty storeroom, about 10ft by 8ft which I decided would make me an ideal hideaway home. I moved in, and to make the place more comfortable connected a radio to the dangling light flex with a double-adapter. This was followed by an electric kettle. And when it started to get cold an electric fire was added to what had now become a whole series of linked adapters from the one light flex.

I was very comfortable in my new home, and everything ran well, except that about once a month there would be a bang and a fuse would blow. Being an ex-Boy Scout I got fuse wire and a spare fuse, so every time it happened I was ready — out with the old and in with the new.

The only problem was that when it blew large parts of the barracks were also plunged into darkness, and I could look out of the window and see people dashing about trying to find the fault and what had caused it.

I remember the day the Americans came to the barracks prior to their memorial service at Slap-ton Sands. As they rehearsed on our parade ground, I had never seen so many people in the education centre.

Our windows overlooked the parade ground and they were filled with everyone from the adjutant and RSM to corporals and umpteen others — all of them expressing the opinion that the Americans' drill was crap. Even the mild-mannered adjutant was swearing. And as for the RSM and company sergeant-majors, well I won't repeat their comments.

To get extra money some of us took a typing and general knowledge test. No names no pack drill, but I have to admit that we did know the answers.

When we got to the speed test one chap set the tab on his typewriter and was off like a rocket reading what he had to type and watching the keys. As the bell went on his machine at the end of each line, he still kept his head down as his hand shoved the roller along for the next line.

When the 10 minutes were up he looked at his work and found he had five minutes on paper and five minutes on the roller. The rest of us had learned that both tabs had to be set. Anyway we all passed.

Then came a mortar course with lots of fun bouncing high-explosive and smoke bombs off the basalt outcrops on Dartmoor. They were very heavy and noisy, but once again we all passed. More money.

There must be an easier way to play soldiers, I thought. Yes, there was, a wireless course. Whoopee, a lot quieter — and still more money and ear-muffs to keep out the cold.

One day we had an important barracks inspection carried out by very senior officers. They even tried to get into my little cave, now decorated with centrefolds from un-soldierlike magazines.

But the party went outside to the MT section where there was a Fowler Challenger bulldozer The chap with the baton wanted to see it work. So a poor little private hopped on to the seat, hit the starter and away it went — and didn't stop until it had pushed four trucks sideways into each other.

Eventually there were no more spaces on my demob chart. I collected my travel warrant home to Sidmouth via London where I stayed in the Union Jack Club with my fellow Topsham Barracks demob-happy mate, Brian Davis. We had a great time in the big city, then returned to Civvy Street before meeting up again at our TA camp at Totteridge later in the year. On the way home I got to Waterloo, hopped on to the Underground and got into a nearly empty carriage. Well, I was at one end and a London bobby at the other.

I lit up a cigarette, and two stations later PC Plod walked down to get off and inform me that this was a non-smoker. Why should he expect a Devon Dumpling to know the difference between a No Smoking sign and the Underground logo!

And then...

After National Service I decided to be a "£10 Pom" which meant a month of holiday on the Strathnaver via Suez, Columbo, Fremantle and Adelaide before reaching Melbourne.

Spent Sunday night in the city, then it was off to the migrant hostel in an outer suburb the next day. Tuesday I went job-hunting, and a compressed-air company called Holman Bros asked if I would start the following day.

I thought that was a bit quick, but agreed to join them at the beginning of the next week. I became the Australasian drilling demonstrator with an area from Japan to the Antarctic.

After 12 years of seeing this area from above, on and under I worked for Padley & Venables, with the same area and products, for three years.

Then I moved — with wife number two — to an earth-moving and forestry equipment company in South Australia.

This lasted for a few years until I became a rep for an industrial supply company, then their purchasing officer for about eight years.

After divorcing wife number two I moved to Adelaide with wife number three where we moved around quite a bit due to a recession.

I did maintenance work on a sheep/wheat farm then moved to the Riverland where I looked after nine centre pivots watering potatoes, with Rosie (Wife No. 3) on the harvester picking the things. We did this for nine years and then decided it was time to have our own place. Today we live a great life on our own 200 acres.

— Brian Marks©

While I was at Topsham I took part in a concert that was put on entertain troops at the barracks. In this dressing room photograph I am fourth from the right. Also pictured are two other contributors to this book, second left Gordon Bess, and fourth left Brian Davis

156

2488357 AC2 Graham Merry

I had a good time driving about with the weekend airmen

In 1950 I lived in South Shields and worked with my parents who ran two general stores and post office businesses. In May I had just passed my eighteenth birthday when my calling-up papers arrived. After talking with others I decided to apply to do my service in the RAF and was accepted and went to Newcastle and passed A1. On September 13 I received a rail warrant to travel to RAF Padgate to be kitted out, and during that week we received our postings for square-bashing. My destination was West Kirby.

During that time the services tried hard to persuade National Servicemen to sign on for three years or more as we would have a better chance to learn a trade, and also more pay. However two years was enough for me as I had a job to return to.

At the end of six weeks most of us who did not sign on were graded as admin orderlies, cookhouse orderlies and medical orderlies. I was fortunate to become AC2 2488357 GJ Merry and posted to RAF Box near Chippenham, Wiltshire as an admin orderly.

When I arrived at Chippenham station the transport officer did not know where RAF Box was as the site had just re-opened as a Fighter Command underground plotter station.

After much discussion I was informed that there were three sites at Hawthorn in Wiltshire. These were RAF Hawthorn, the accommodation block, RAF Rudlow Manor, the administration offices and RAF Box which was the

Horsing about (second from left) at Great Yarmouth during a two-week camp with 3507 FCU

radar plotting station.

Eventually, with three others, I reported to Flt-lt Swinthenbank for our duties. But there appeared to be little for us to do, and our tasks consisted mainly of upgrading Kings Regulations, cleaning up the offices and polishing corridors. Our hours of work were 8am to 5pm most days and a maximum of five days a week, so the four of us spent a fair amount of time in the NAAFI.

We did not have to do guard duty or have any kit inspections. It was a great time and the only problem was the journey to get home. But when my parents moved to Denham in Buckinghamshire to run a roadside cafe the journey was easier.

I had passed my driving test, and in January 1952 I was called to the CO's office to be informed that a posting had come through for me to join the MT section of 3507 FCU, the RAF

Square-bashing at West Kirby. I am on the extreme left front row

157

auxiliary unit based on the same camp site. The auxiliaries were weekend airmen, like the Territorial Army, who came in on Saturdays and Sundays. We worked the weekends with them and I was their driver when they had summer camps or had to go away to other RAF bases for extra training. I visited RAF Sandwich in Kent and RAF Coltishall in Norfolk as well as local sites, and had a very good last eight months' service.

My RAF days are now long gone

And then...

I was demobbed in September 1952 and returned to work in my parents' roadside cafe business on the A40 at Tatling End in Buckinghamshire. In 1953 we moved back to Bournemouth where we had lived when I was a child during the war. We bought a general store, and in 1957 I joined a company selling automotive products to the garage trade, as depot sales manager.

In 1972 my wife and I bought a run-down petrol site and cafe known as The Ace of Clubs at Lewdown in Devon. With hard work and long hours we built up the business which was leased to Little Chef. Five years later we moved to Ferndown, near Bournemouth where I had a part-time job running three petrol sites.

After starting a business selling BMX bikes we attended a bike show with our two sons in Las Vegas, which led to our being appointed importers and distributors of cycle products, skateboards and roller-skates to the sports and cycle trade. And I still work a few hours each week.

— Graham Merry©

Guys and gals from 3507 FCU get together for a meal

Boys-only night out at a pub in Box

A billet at RAF Hawthorn, still there when I visited recently

Happy days are here again. Demob squad, September 1952

Why I didn't get a medal for arresting General Grivas

MY NATIONAL Service career did not get off to a particularly auspicious start. In fact, I had twice made enemies with authority before I even arrived at the training depot. Being a junior reporter on the Daily Mail in Newcastle, I thought that as I could type and use a teleprinter I would ask to be put in a signals regiment. I told this to the interviewer when I had my medical, but when my call-up papers arrived I was ordered to report to the Royal Army Pay Corps at Devizes.

I was so annoyed that I telephoned the recruiting office to complain. And I was told in no uncertain manner: "Young man, you are going to the Pay Corps. The Army does not make mistakes."

I arrived at Devizes railway station at 7am with five other lost souls. We were met by a tiny lance-corporal who began hollering orders. The size of his mouth made up for his lack of stature as he screamed at us to get fell in, get lined up, get in the truck.

Politely I asked: "When are we actually IN the Army?" He said: "At 12 noon."

"Right," I said, "we've got five hours yet, so don't bloody well shout at us, mate."

That was a mistake, which was soon brought to my attention when I got to the depot and discovered that he was the lance-corporal who was to be in charge of me for the next 10 weeks of basic training.

At 12 noon on the dot he was waiting for me, and I was doubled round the camp for the rest of the day.

But I survived, and in a way actually enjoyed the bull. It was quite satisfying seeing mirror-bright boots. I also enjoyed drill. I thought I was pretty good at it, and if you are good at something you enjoy it. It was the thrill of achievement.

But I still couldn't avoid clashes with authority. You might accuse me of being a bit

Then and now

of a barrack room lawyer, but I don't like injustice. So when a corporal tried to stop us going to the NAAFI because he said our brasses weren't clean enough I told him: "We've worked our socks off today. So please go to the CO and tell him we have disobeyed you and gone to the NAAFI. Or you can come with us and have a beer." Surprisingly, he chose to join us.

After training I was posted with the Wiltshire Regiment to Cyprus, which in 1955 could be a pretty dangerous place. When mum saw me off I couldn't understand why she was crying. It never crossed my mind that I could be killed.

On the island I was promoted to corporal, and one day thought I would get a medal for arresting General Grivas. "Oh no," said the duty officer when I got the man back to camp. "Not him again." It turned out that the chap I had brought in was a shepherd called Grivas who was being arrested on an almost daily basis.

As well as working in the pay office I had to do guard duties and act as an escort for the medical officer.

One day I had to help him get six men into an ambulance after they had been in a truck blown up by terrorists. I carried one chap, but he died on the long drive to hospital in to Nicosia. Like me, he was a National Servicemen, and had

In Cyprus, and no longer bothering to look for Grivas

only a month to do before demob. What made it worse was that his wife was expecting their first child.

And then...

A few weeks after demob, when my meagre savings were dwindling I got a job, as "the world's worst insurance agent!" If it rained I didn't go out, which didn't do the insurance company much good. And as I was on commission, it didn't help me much either.

But during this time I had been invited to take part in a couple of plays at the original Newcastle Playhouse — another reason I didn't go out collecting insurance premiums — and later I was asked to join the repertory company full-time.

This was in 1957, just after my 21st birthday. And I remained an actor, playing theatres all over the country until, at the beginning of 1962

I heard that Tyne Tees Television were looking for an announcer/newsreader.

I auditioned, and was surprised to get the job. A couple of years later I was made presenter of the new nightly magazine programme, Newsview.

After a month or so I was approached by the BBC and offered the presenter's job on Look North.

That lasted for 32 years, until in 1996 I accepted an offer to return to Tyne Tees to head a specially-designed hour-long news magazine, North East Tonight with Mike Neville.

In 1990 I became an MBE for services to broadcasting. Following a pulmonary embolism in 2005 I decided to retire. Since then I have been awarded an honorary degree of Doctor of Civil Law by Northumbria University and made a Freeman of the Borough of Gateshead.
— ***Mike Neville©***

You will have to work hard, but you will also find life in a unit very pleasant. In Germany and Austria for example there are excellent leave centres where you may go when your turn for leave comes. You may be sent to the Middle East or the Far East, which will give an excellent opportunity to see other countries and other ways of life.

— From You and the Army, a booklet issued to every NS army conscript

I was in a war zone, but never thought about getting killed

I LEFT school at 15 with no formal qualifications and started work with a firm of general engineers. During this time I trained to be what was known as a plater/welder which covered most of the work the firm was involved in. During this period I joined the Army Cadet Force which was housed alongside a Territorial Army unit who took us under their wing.

At the age of 18 my enlistment papers arrived and I went through the ritual of medicals, tests and interviews. I was passed Al and chose to serve in the Army. My grandfather and one of my uncles had been in the Royal Artillery and I decided to follow them. Eventually the day arrived when I was to leave home and with my railway warrant make my way to Oswestry in Shropshire on the Welsh border.

This was the initial training camp for the Royal Artillery where we were fitted out and taught the rudiments of soldiering. The real stuff was to follow.

I opted to be trained as a signaller and moved on to Rhyl in North Wales. The TA unit that was linked to my army cadet unit was an Artillery

Still proud to wear the Red Beret

Airborne Regiment, and while at Rhyl I decided that was what I wanted to be, an Airborne gunner.

After passing out at Rhyl, next stop was Aldershot for the Airborne selection course, which was three weeks of intensive physical and mental challenges. Having completed and passed the course I went on to RAF. Abingdon to be trained as an Army Parachutist, as they were called in those days.

This was an exiting three weeks culminating in gaining my Parachute wings. I was destined to join the 33rd Airborne Light Regiment RA in the Canal Zone. A two-week voyage on a troopship found me on January 29 1952 at Port Said. Shortly before I arrived, after a few weeks of mayhem in a town called Ismalia orders were given to disarm the Egyptian police, and a fierce action took place to achieve this.

This heralded the start of trouble that was to last until 1954. My regiment was part of the 16th Independent Parachute Brigade who were in the forefront of operations. As an 18-year-old these were exciting times. None of us gave a thought about getting injured or even killed, as happened to my friend Chris.

I was involved in many security operations, searching villages and vehicles for hidden arms and explosives, and guarding the water filtration plants and hospitals that were becoming targets for the underground movement. Eventually it was time to leave Egypt and head for home.

And then...

My two years' National Service certainly changed my outlook on life, having met people from many walks of life and various occupations. But it was difficult to settle down, and one thing was for sure I did not want to carry on doing the same job that I had left behind. Ambition kicked in and I decided that I would like to become an engineering draughtsman. At 20 it was a bit late for formal training so I attended night school. Then I got a post as an improver-draughtsman with a firm named Roneo who manufactured duplicators and office equipment, and never looked back.

As the years rolled by I met my wife-to-be, married and settled down. Roneo closed, so I made a change of direction and took a job with a firm involved in mechanical handling, staying in that industry and working my way through management posts until my retirement.

I remember thinking at the time I was called-up that this was a great opportunity to travel. I had an exciting two years and made some good friends.

— John Norman©

22074136 Cpl Michael Owen

A soft life on the Rock, and a post as the Cathedral organist

MY FATHER was the vicar of All Saints Walton-le-Soken, the ecclesiastical name for the town and surrounding area of Walton-on-the-Naze in Essex. In the large vicarage I lived a sheltered life, shielded from the worst excesses around me. My daily routine was to catch the 8.06am train to Colchester's Royal Grammar School, a very elitist establishment, returning home at about 6pm. The routine continued with an evening meal, then an hour's piano practice followed by homework.

The weekend was pretty full too. For as well as being in the 1st rugby XV with matches played on Saturday (including bruising encounters with the Infantry training units stationed at the Colchester Garrison), I played the organ in church on Sundays.

My parents were both pacifists, and I suppose they expected me to refuse the instruction to report for National Service duty.

However, I was 19, and the prospects of escaping the vicarage routines, and the opportunity to see something of the world at the taxpayer's expense persuaded me to throw in my lot with the Army.

So bravely I struck out into the wide world and reported to the RASC at Aldershot.

Unlike some recruits, I looked upon the next stage of my life with some enthusiasm, as living in a vicarage did cramp my style. It was not quite a monastic existence, but my circle of friends and school mates was limited.

Like many National Servicemen, my introduction to Army life was a total shock to the system, living as I had been in the rarefied and refined atmosphere at home. It was a devastating experience which the Army calculated would break the resistance of the most stubborn of individuals within a fortnight.

Oudenaarde Barracks, situated in the middle of Aldershot and named after Marlborough's victory over the French in 1708, seemed to be in a state of permanent decay.

Though apparently due for demolition at the turn of the twentieth century, they were considered suitable for habitation by National Servicemen. For any other group they would have been condemned as unfit for humans to live in.

I discovered two major facts about the situation confronting me. One, I was not alone in my predicament. And two, the whole structure of the Army was apparently corrupt from the top to bottom. These two factors helped me survive the 15-day initial training course and to get to know my fellow-sufferers.

At the end of the fortnight we were allowed out on a 48-hour pass and I travelled home to present to my parents a shorn hairstyle and an ill-fitting battledress.

The corruptive influence of the Army led me to the discovery that by purchasing a three-monthly return Underground ticket from Waterloo to Stratford one could effectively avoid paying for a return ticket back to London.

That was all right when the train to Liverpool Street stopped at Stratford, but the system broke down when it did not. And I well remember the occasion that ticket inspectors visited the train and the whole compartment was caught red-handed.

From this lapse from the high moral plateau, degradation followed. The only justification seemed to be that it saved money from our meagre pay.

I could survive most things during our training period except for the abrupt method of being woken in the morning. This consisted of the barrack-room corporal raising and lowering the end of the bed and shouting very loudly: "Hands off cocks, feet in socks."

I learned very quickly how to avoid this horrendous awakening. I would get up just before the visitation, which gave me the additional benefit of what hot water was available before the rest of my fellow-sufferers.

Life continued in a routine manner through fatigues, square-bashing and bulling — the whole exercise designed to break the spirit of the individual.

Then the day dawned when we bade farewell to Oudenaarde Barracks, and I found myself en route to Blackdown, and a totally different atmosphere.

We were grouped on a pre-OCTU training course, preparatory to going before a War Office Selection Board as suitable officer material. There was a camaraderie which bound us together against the common enemy.

I met a fellow pianist, and we played duets in the NAAFI, where we were surprisingly tolerated by other customers.

From my earliest days I had studied the military mind, and at Blackdown I put the theory into practice. I discovered that I was not challenged about anything provided I had a piece of paper in my hand and was marching purposefully in a specific direction. This approach stood me in good stead until I left Blackdown for WOSB at Lingfield in Surrey.

I tried to bluff my way through the various exercises there, but the final bluff came at the end of the three days when confronted by the brigadier asking whether I would be interested in becoming a regular soldier.

When I declined the invitation I was returned to Blackdown to start a clerk's course. I looked on the bright side by reflecting on the civilised comforts at WOSB and the fact that the time spent there had "used" another three days of my service.

We all aspired to the good life that went with a commission, but there was one among us who felt that as a member of the aristocracy, it was his God-given right to pass the selection board.

He was Valentine Bagheot Rudolf Haliet Walker Ramsey, son of Guy Ramsey the international bridge player. But he failed the board like the rest of us and was, in the words of P G Wodehouse "if not actually disgruntled, he was not exactly gruntled."

However, his aristocratic breeding came into its own when he was deputed to sort out the end of course dinner. He spent a happy afternoon selecting choice wines from the cellars of the local hostelry and putting the maitre d'hotel and the sommelier right on a number of points of etiquette.

Prior to our festivities we had enjoyed the various tasks set as part of an initiative course, one of which was particularly memorable.

Deposited in the middle of nowhere with no money, we were given a list of items to collect before returning to camp by 1700 hours. Our greatest achievement was to thumb a lift from a car being driven by a brigadier who was indignant, to put it mildly, until it was explained that we were "using our initiative."

The clerk's course was a walkover, particularly as our sergeant was determined that as the creme de la creme platoon we would all pass

out with 100per cent marks at the end of eight weeks.

In that time we were expected to touch-type at 30 words a minute. And the instructor had a splendid way of ensuring the desired standard was achieved by stating that "you will f---g stay at the keyboard all night" until you pass the test.

Then we awaited our postings. I had expressed a desire to use the free travel facilities proffered by the RASC to get as far as possible, preferably the Far East. My thinking was that the time spent reaching the destination would mean only about a month in post before I would be on the way home to return to civilian life.

But the nearest I came to the Far East was Gibraltar, which was, I suppose, in roughly the right direction. And even this nearly turned into a disaster.

The RASC holding battalion was, horror of horrors, based at Colchester, where the two parts of the camp site were divided into "waiting" and "embarking."

On the waiting side you were given mindless chores to fill out the days and nights until you were moved to the embarking side, dished out with appropriate kit for the warmer climes and given your instructions on departure dates.

Life was easy on the Rock

Display boards on the wall showed the state of play of each draft, and I saw that a staff-sergeant and three privates were chalked up for Gibraltar. But the board showed that so far only the staff-sergeant and two privates had arrived. It seemed that I was in the unenviable position of being stuck in Colchester for the rest of my service, which was not part of the plan at all.

What had happened to my dream of seeing parts of the world which I could not otherwise afford to visit at my own expense?

I had the temerity to explain the discrepancy to the movements officer, and the sergeant was not best pleased with my direct action of pointing out to the officer the error of his ways.

He obviously got a rollicking, and took it out on me by declaring: "If I decide you will stay in Colchester for the rest of your time, hard luck." However, I took this to be bravado on his part, for I found myself in the embarkation group and by using my plan of being somewhere else when it mattered, I did only one guard duty and three cookhouse fatigues.

There was a one narrow squeak when we were lined up on the parade ground for various duties to be allocated, and I heard my name called out for guard. But before I could respond another soldier with the same surname stepped out. So I stayed back in line.

Eventually embarkation day dawned, and that night we stayed in a deep shelter under Goodge Street Underground station. It was a colossal place 150 feet below ground with about 250 steps to go up and down each time we wanted to go out. Needless to say, I did not bother.

Next morning we got up at five-o'clock and marched to Euston to catch a troop train to Liverpool via a very circuitous route to board the Empress of Australia.

On the voyage I played the hymns for the C of E service in the main lounge and hobnobbed with the captain and officer in charge of the troops.

The only bit of work I did was a 24-hour guard duty, but I slept my time during the night so it was not so inconvenient. I am still puzzling over the need to have a guard at all, since it was most unlikely that anybody would pinch a ship bristling with the finest selection of fighting men that the British Army could muster.

We arrived in Gibraltar early on a rainy Sunday morning with the Rock shrouded in mist. Not a very favourable impression. The Garrison Employment Company, which was the accommodation for all the Fortress Headquarter staff, would be my home for my time defending the outposts of the Empire.

I found that being a clerk on the Rock was the best job because there was practically nothing to do. Clerks dispensed with all webbing and gaiters, and were allowed to wear civilian shoes and tunics with open lapels and a tie.

Reveille was supposed to be at 0630 hours, but about 0730 there was usually a sudden awakening because breakfast finished at 0745.

Sometimes the duty NCO would bring round a cup of tea to everybody and announce what was on the breakfast menu. At 0830 we toddled up for working parade.

Most of the clerks wore brothel creepers, so there was no smart sound of boots coming down on the ground as we went through the basic drill — rather a soft-shoe shuffle as we

dispersed to our various duties at 0900.

There followed a break for a snack at 1030 and a meal break from 1245 to 1415 before work finished about 1615. I did not think I should become a complete physical wreck at this rate.

A seat in the sun as demob day approaches

And an illustration of the life of the clerk to the Garrison adjutant is given in this letter I sent to my mother:

"Having just fallen asleep in the office and been woken up and told to do something I shall take the opportunity to start a letter to you. One has to give the impression of work if nothing else. After all, we must fool the taxpayer into thinking that he is getting something for his money and that the great British dominions and colonies are being defended to the last man.

Whilst I am in the office, I may as well take the environment into consideration and tell you a little more of what does not go on there. Some of our specialities are known technically as "clangs" which are dropped in considerable numbers almost every day.

These "clangs" take the form of mistakes, some intentional (thrown in to send Fortress Headquarters more haywire than it is already.)

However, in most cases, repercussions are felt at a much greater distance, notably at the War Office where I believe there is a special office to sort out all the mistakes that are issued from the Garrison Adjutant's Department Gibraltar. After all, we must keep the red tape churning out. A notice will probably be posted up to the effect that "clangs will not be dropped but will be wrapped in cotton wool and lowered gently to the floor."

One day in the NAAFI I saw a worried-looking parson. He introduced himself as the Precentor of the Anglican Cathedral, and said the organist, who was a serviceman, had just left the Rock on his way home.

I told him that the ways of the Almighty were indeed wonderful. Here am I, send me.

Now retired after a varied career

It was therefore not long before I was installed as resident organist for the time I was on the Rock. And further good news transpired. The big fish in the cathedral was also Clerk to the Magistrates' Court, and I was practically adopted into their family, the Norton-Amors, from that time. Thus I was among people who were involved in both music and Church and was able to pursue my musical studies. I gave a recital on the piano in the cathedral and later on, an organ recital.

My routine on Sundays was occupied at the cathedral and going up to the Norton-Amors for lunch and tea.

The garrison adjutant, a major in the Royal West Kents, seemed to have established his modus operandi from the Bluffers Manual.

He would spend a little time in his office, then poke his cheery head round the corner of the door to say he was going up to the Garrison employment company office.

Meanwhile, the CSM rings me enquiring the whereabouts of the major, and I reply: "He is with you."

The CSM's response? "The crafty b---. He's given me the slip again".

The GQMS, an ancient member of the Inniskilling Fusiliers, had a desk in the office but was seldom seen.

When he made one of his rare appearances it was to catch up with the handover documents for officers' married quarters. He had a remarkable memory and could recall details going back weeks.

To maintain this phenomenal feat of memory he pulled out a bottle of whiskey from his trousers pocket saying: " I shall be after going to have my breakfast now." With that he would disappear for another few weeks.

I managed three-day "Army welfare" trips to Seville and Granada and a visit to Cadiz with the Norton-Amors.

One remarkable fact about travelling with them was that whenever the car was seen approaching the frontier gates, all the officers and men turned out and saluted as it sped through. There was no question of being stopped either going out or returning, which explained the supply of sherry and wines in the boot of the car. This was another example of knowing the right people both in the civilian sphere of influence and also in the Army.

An instance of this occurred when I was picked to play rugby for the garrison team. As Gibraltar does not possess a blade of grass or an area of ground flat enough to accommodate a rugby pitch the teams went just over the border into Spain. When asked what position I played I replied: "Right wing threequarter."

Sorry, came the reply, the Medical Officer of Health is already booked for that particular position.

So I said I would play inside centre, which proved to be an astute move on my part, as after the match the MO said if I needed any time off on spurious medical grounds this could be arranged.

One day I discovered that the adjutant had submitted my name for a trade test. I protested vehemently that I could not remember my clerk's training or my typing skills. Nevertheless, I was promptly put through the test and found myself at the end of it promoted to corporal. This was financially rewarding, and on the basis of my sudden new-found wealth I booked a fortnight's holiday in Tangier before I was due for demobilisation.

One of my modest responsibilities was to be custodian of St. Michael's Cave, situated high up on the Rock. The cave was formed after the geological upheaval that had formed the Rock in the first place, with many fine stalagmites and stalactites displayed along with lakes.

The Royal Engineers had discovered the cave after tunnelling in the area — a habit Engineers had during the war.

In fact there is probably more space inside the Rock than outside, with a fully maintained hospital, adequate air-raid shelters for all the population and ammunition and food stores connected by a two-lane road running the length of the Rock itself.

When it was particularly hot and oppressive, sitting in St Michael's Cave was a blessed relief as the temperature did not vary by more than one or two degrees around 65 Fahrenheit, and it was far from the madding crowd.

When my life in Gibraltar came to a close the Empress of Australia duly appeared on time and I was despatched back to Liverpool well within my release date.

And then...

After demob my life took on a somewhat confused direction. Previously I had studied physics, chemistry and music. But as I had continued to play the organ and had written some compositions for various combinations of instrument, and at the same time neglected the science side it seemed to me that music was after all my most important subject. And that was how I came to be accepted for the Honours School in Music at the University of Durham.

Asked what subjects I should take in Years 1 and 2 I offered organic chemistry and physics. This reply was greeted first with a stony silence, and then the remark that music came into the arts faculty while chemistry and physics were part of the science faculty, and ne'er the twain shall meet.

I never did get a satisfactory reply when I pointed out that in the Second Year of the Honours School of Music there was a paper on acoustics. But I finished up by taking English Language and Literature and Arabic as my two subsidiary subjects.

When I came down from Durham, aged 25 and without a degree I had no prospects of a job.

However, though I was too old to apply for the Civil Service Executive Grade, I found that the London County Council had a very similar structure where I could sit a "major establishment examination" to advance into the administrative grades. And this is what I did.

When the LCC was disbanded in 1965 and replaced by the Greater London Council I took my chances with the newly-created London boroughs.

I served in Islington planning, Southwark architects and finally Tower Hamlets community services departments where I advanced up the grades.

But a new director called me soon after his appointment to ask whether I had ever thought of early retirement. Quick as a flash I replied: "Yes from the day I started work."

So after 30 years devoted to the cause of local government I made my escape to the delightful town of Wimborne Minster in the heart of Dorset.

While I was with Southwark Council I was encouraged by a neighbour who was a professional singer working at the BBC, to resume studies and complete my degree course. And after three years I finished with a B MUS (Lond).

While all this was going on, I held a local post of organist and choirmaster on Sundays in Beckenham and a further post in a reform synagogue in Edgware on Friday night and Saturday mornings. It was fortunate that the two religions did not operate on the same days!

Then the post of Town Clerk became vacant in Ferndown, the next town from Wimborne, where for the next eight years I manipulated the council in the way I felt it should go. I finally shook off employment in local government in 1985, with the intention to travel more.

But I am still pursuing academic studies through the Open University, and I have collected a Diploma in Music.

— *Michael Owen©*

166

My days of fun roaring around in a monster Centurion

IN MARCH 1950 I left Kings Cross station on the longest journey of my life. First stop was Catterick in Yorkshire, but that was just a beginning. By the time I returned home two years later I had seen some of Somerset, a fair bit of Dorset and quite a lot of Germany.

Yes, this was my rail ride into National Service. The train was met at the station by a convoy of Army lorries to take us to Catterick camp where we were kitted out and marched — in a fashion — to our billets.

Next day began very early with a wash and shave in lukewarm water. Then down to the cookhouse in those ghastly uniforms to sample Army cuisine. Yuk!

The next five weeks was basic training, or basically learning to do what you were told without question. Physical training, square-bashing and route marches were all part of this learning process. Of course, there were always lighter moments. I remember when we lined up for inoculations seeing a couple of lads in our unit who were built like tanks keel over in a dead faint as soon as the needle went in — not into *their* arms, but into the arms of the blokes in front of them!

Many evenings were spent shining our boots. The pimples on the toecaps had to be removed by ironing them flat with a heated spoon and polishing them for hours on end with shoe-blacking, spit and elbow grease.

Once this had been done it was easy to keep the mirror finish. Unless some clot who still didn't know his left foot from his right marched on them on the parade ground.

One of our squad, a real strong-as-an-ox farmer's boy, was a bit slow on the uptake. One morning, discovering that he had no polish left,

From Trooper to Craftsman...and now MR Paffey

he decided to use the blacklead used to clean the billet stove. As soon as he got outside in the sunlight his boots turned silver. This made the staff-sergeant's day. "You with the silver boots, what do you think this is, some sort of a bloody pantomime?"

This was the same NCO who had a habit, if he saw anyone slouching around camp, of shouting: "That man, over here, double." Then followed a dressing-down as you stood to attention in front of him.

One morning, as the staff-sergeant came into camp one of our squad looked out of the window and called out: "That man, over here, double."

We spent the next half-hour running round the square with rifles over our heads.

At the end of basic training a number of us were given a tank corps' badge to replace the mailed fist insignia of the Royal Armoured Corps. Now in the 2nd Royal Tank Regiment, we were posted to Norton Manor in Somerset for a four-month motor mechanics' course.

We were taught to drive lorries, and learned a lot about the internal combustion engine, though I doubt that many of us would have made it as motor mechanics in Civvy Street. But the bonus was that at least we came away with a "certificate of competence to drive" which meant that when eventually we were demobbed we could claim a civilian driving licence without taking a test.

After Somerset I was posted to Bovington in Dorset for a two-month course on tanks. This was probably my best time in the Army. We were usually dressed in overalls instead of those itchy uniforms, and learning to drive a tank was great fun. I roared around Salisbury Plain in a monster 52-ton Centurion driven by a V12 Rolls-Royce Merlin engine that also powered the Spitfire.

Before I went into the Army I had been a keen boxer, and one year did quite well in the ABA championships. So at Bovington I joined the camp boxing team. This had a few advantages like a special breakfast and escaping a lot of guard duties. On the other hand I had to spend a lot of time out running on the moors to keep fit

Actual bouts were few and far between and I can remember having only three fights, winning two and drawing the other.

The heavyweight on our team was the guard-house sergeant, who was from a Scottish regiment. He always wore a kilt, and was a very imposing sight standing outside the guardroom with his German Shepherd awaiting the arrival of the last bus from town. Everyone had to get off the bus and wait while he inspected it for any signs of damage or miss-use.

I returned to Catterick at the end of my Bovington course and was then posted to Germany to join the 2nd Dragoon Guards at Fallingbostle on Luneberg Heath.

The Dragoons, also known as The Queen's Bays, were originally a cavalry regiment and served in North Africa during the war, which entitled them to wear an arm-badge showing a gerboa — a desert rat — which was very useful for chatting up the girls.

"What's that on your arm?" "A desert rat."

"Wow, are you a desert rat?"

Home and dry!

At Fallingbostle I spent most of my time in the workshops and was usually excused parades. But I still had to do guard duties, mainly on the petrol dump which consisted of thousands of gallons of petrol, all in five-gallon jerry-cans.

On my first duty I was walking around this mountain of cans in the dead of night when... pssst. I nearly jumped out of my boots.

What I didn't know was that because gas builds up in the jerry-cans they are fitted with a device that allows it to escape — hence the psssing noise! No matter how many guard duties I did the sound always frightened the life out of me.

I remember another scary incident which happened when we had to take our tanks into a wood and camouflage them. Fighters from the 2nd Tactical Airforce were sent up to see if they could find us.

The corporal wanted me to help him do a plug change on one of the Centurions, and we set off across a clearing towards the tank. Suddenly he shouted "Get Down" and threw himself to the ground. I flung myself down beside him, wondering what on earth was happening.

I soon found out. Roaring out of the clouds came a jet fighter whose pilot had obviously spotted us. The ground vibrated like an earthquake as it screamed towards us, then pulled out of its dive and screamed back into the clouds. It was a terrifying moment, and I was thankful I was only *playing* soldiers.

Just before I returned to the UK for demob, the top brass decided that tradesmen should be in the REME, so I lost my rank of Trooper and became Craftsman Paffey.

And then...

Trooper, then Craftsman — now it was *Mr* Paffey, as I returned to Civvy Street to begin a new life. But I was rather disillusioned, and wished I had signed on as a regular. Three square meals a day, a roof over your head, a bed to sleep in, clothes provided and lots of mates.

Instead, I got a job in Ilford working for a firm making cables and conveyors, where I became a toolroom machinist.

One day one of my friends there, who played in goal for a Sunday football team in Basildon, asked me to take some photographs at his next game. So I went along, and then offered the pictures to the local newspaper, the Basildon Recorder, who asked if I would go to matches for them every weekend.

But this stopped when two men from the cable company set up their own business in Liverpool, and offered me a job.

So I moved there, and eventually became works manager. But when the firm was taken over I decided to look round for something different. I asked the Basildon Recorder to let me know if there were any photographic jobs going. And when a vacancy came up, I returned to Essex, working for the Recorder and other local newspapers until I retired.

— Arthur Paffey©

168

Japanese papa offered 'a lower caste girl to satisfy our urges'

THE YEAR 1947 was a year of post-war austerity and uncertainty when a nerdy 18-year-old trainee chemist with the Ilford Ltd photographic firm received a letter from His Majesty's government inviting him to serve in the Royal Air Force. He reported to West Kirby, south of Liverpool for a few weeks of state-sanctioned abuse, degradation, humiliation and exhausting exercise. The experience however installed in this youth a sense of discipline, power structure and pride. Luckily my sense of self-justice and commonsense remained intact.

My dream was to become a pilot, but the service was overburdened with trained aircrew back from commonwealth flight schools without planes to fly and wars to fight.

They were mess-hall servers, cooks, clerks and general dogsbodies waiting for demob. So no dream role for me, but I was lucky to be assigned to Air Traffic Control and despatched to Cranwell for training.

At the end of this radio and procedure course my allocation was to Watchet, a small camp in Somerset where the soldiers of the RAF — the Royal Air Force Regiment — were trained. No runway, no radio (except in the NAAFI), or control tower in the vicinity. With no flying-related tasks I was given title "assistant instructor" and the job of moving model tanks and men on a moulded terrain table map used to instruct infantry.

After three weeks I submitted a request to see the Commanding Officer, unprecedented for an aircraftsman. I told him I had been trained in Air Traffic Control, radio and direction-finding at some expense to the taxpayer, and was now wasted in the menial task of moving toys.

After he called me a cheeky young pup we had an intelligent conversation about what I could and would wish to do. Learning I was a chemist at a film company, Eureka! I was made camp photographer.

The armaments section held an excellent professional camera and well-equipped darkroom and was managed by a charismatic, enthusiastic flight-lieutenant. We hit it off immediately. I took photographs of camp activities and special occasions, not an onerous day-to-day employment. Then we discovered a gold mine.

Young recruits to the RAF Regiment were arduously trained as specialised infantry, and on passing-out were granted their equivalent of wings, their blue beret and cap badge.

Working on the first colour film emulsion at Ilford Ltd

What was their next wish? A glossy head and shoulders photograph to send home as evidence of their valued achievement.

For a very modest fee and the armament officer's complicity (we shared the proceeds) they could prove their new status.

Once a week the flight-lieutenant and I left the camp separately and enjoyed a few drinks and meal together on the "company profits." All went well until after an excess of alcohol and over-confidence we returned together under the influence. At my next interview with the CO I was castigated for fraternisation with an officer, and told I was being posted off camp.

The CO asked where would I like to go. My answer, "overseas, and as far possible" brought my transfer to the occupation of Japan.

Two weeks later, with 19 others, I embarked on a troopship in Liverpool en route as potential members of the RAF token force in BCOF (British Commonwealth Occupation Force) Japan. A wonderful journey through the Mediterranean and Suez Canal, lazing, sunbathing and eating well. No specific incidents until mid-Indian Ocean when a practice emergency drill was activated and off to boat stations we went.

A routine roll-call revealed that we, the 20 National Servicemen, were not on the manifest. Had the ship gone down there would have been no search for us!

We continued to Singapore where the confusion about our posting, our true destination and role led to our disembarkation and a three-week stay in Changi while the wheels of bureaucracy whirled in Asia and London. Each day we

169

At last I achieved my ambition to become a pilot

cadged flights to Malaya, Indonesia and Thailand. At last word arrived, Japan it was. Now of course there was no transport, so we were issued with civilian clothes and booked on a Chinese tramp steamer to Kobe via Hong Kong and a couple of Chinese ports.

At these stopovers the captain's launch was put at our disposal to go ashore and return as we wished. Three weeks of travel and into Kobe, Japan.

A long train journey took us to RAAF Iwakuni, a large military airfield close to Hiroshima, run by the ANZACS (Australian and New Zealand Commonwealth Services).

First act, an address by the CO, a New Zealander, who told us the two-month delay had led him to replace us with Australians. So nothing for us to do. "Just enjoy yourselves mates, go and see what you wish, and ask for any help you want."

So began a millionaire's package tour. We commandeered a Japanese destroyer for a two day "cruise," took a jeep loaded with food for two or three-day trips across southern Japan visiting obscure, out of the way villages that had never before seen a Westerner ("Roundeyes," as we were known).

Here the head-man — who kept records of farm output, details of births, deaths and marriages and information about the hydro-electric power the village used — would surrender to us. They wanted us to say that everything was in order, and indicated that we should sign their papers accordingly.

Of course everything was written in Japanese, so today if anyone consults any of these documents they will see they are signed: "Looks OK to me, Cliff Passmore."

We broke the non-fraternisation rule by getting to know a local middle-class family with two very attractive daughters. Twice a week we sat with them in their bedroom listening to records and drinking weak sake.

On about the third visit papa-san bowed and asked via an interpreter that we did not violate his girls. But he added that "should the urge and need occur" a lower caste cousin could be drafted in!

We were shown a photograph of the much older cousin — and never took up the offer.

On the beautiful slopes of Mount Fuji was a luxurious holiday-leave hotel, about seven-star by today's standards, where two-week breaks could be enjoyed. Swimming in hot pools, massage, all sports including horse-riding, Sumo wrestling, good food, Asian cuisine plus European drinks. A couple of stays here developed my tastes for future years.

After a few months of this hedonistic life, bureaucracy caught up with us again, and we were put aboard a troopship going west to Singapore.

The anti-British communist uprising had begun and reinforcements were required. So back to Changi camp with a job to do. My task was to sit in the jungle in a DF (direction finder) hut identifying radio signals from aircraft approaching the airfield, calculating their bearing and giving corrections to locate the base.

Because of the threat of attack by guerrillas, each man was armed. But the only time I pointed my weapon in anger was when a five-foot long salamander dragon reptile came into the hut and walked around while three of us sat on a table! To our relief, it left without the need for a shot to be fired.

All too soon our two years was up and a troopship took me home and back to the lab. Did I gain anything? Yes indeed. Self-confidence, knowledge of other lands, cultures and peoples, willingness to try anything plus a little humility.

And then...

If National Service had not intervened, my days would have ended mixing chemicals, smelling awful and looking forward to my annual rise. Instead I became an international businessman and entrepreneur, chairman of a public company in the medical instrumentation business and involved in developing the first ultrasound camera that produced a picture instead of a graph. Later I joined the Baring Bank where I was in charge of various venture capital activities.

Oh, and I did gain my licence to become a pilot, flying throughout Africa and Europe, and even crossing the Russian border. I became a gliding instructor, and today still fly microlight aircraft.

— Cliff Passmore©

22612083 LCpl John Pearson

What happened to recruit who Blancoed his drawers cellular?

I JOINED His Majesty's Service at Crown Hill Barracks, Plymouth in September 1951 where I have memories of marching to the barber's for the regulation haircut, then to the quartermaster's store to be given more kit than I could carry. And finally staggering to a wooden hut that was to be home for the next six to eight weeks.

One incident that still makes me smile, was after having been told to Blanco our kit, one member of our intake came back with every piece of his kit covered in Blanco. And I mean everything — including his "drawers, cellular, green."

As he was not with us later when we joined our regiment maybe he was not so daft after all.

At the end of training I was sent to join the 1st battalion Dorset Regiment stationed in Vienna. Having passed as a marksman on the brengun, I joined B company, and wanting to see a bit more of Vienna and Austria, I managed to transfer to the MT section.

As I already had a driving licence I was soon driving Army lorries in very wintry conditions with lots of snow and ice.

Then followed a return to the UK for six weeks to train as a driving instructor at the Army MT school in Bordon, Hampshire. Then back to Vienna, there to do guard duties in buildings like the Palace of Justice.

Vienna, being a divided city, still shared international guards between the British, American, French and Russian armies. I was also on duty as part of a guard at the military service commemorating the death of King George VI. I managed to see more of Austria, as our support company was based in Klagenfurt, about 300 miles through the Russian zone.

After I had been about eight months in Austria, the regiment returned to the UK to re-form for deployment in the Far East. We sailed from Southampton on the Empire Fowey and eventually arrived in Hong Kong. Our camp was about 40 miles north on the Chinese border at a place called Fan-Ling. The camp was called

Trigger happy! And (right), still happy in retirement

San Wai, and I spent some time there but was then posted to the 27th Brigade HQ at Volunteers Slopes camp as an MT lance-corporal.

I was lucky when my time for demob came up, because the regiment was about to go to Korea. But for me it was a journey on the New Australia sailing via Singapore and Colombo back to Southampton and Dorchester Barracks. Thus my time ended in *Her* Majesty's service. Two years serving two monarchs.

Then there was three years' TA and eventually many years later the letter that said "you will not be called for military service."

And then...

Before being called up I lived in Ferndown, Dorset, and was working as a locksmith for a company in Bournemouth. I had attended Ferndown School and then Bournemouth School of Art.

Back in Civvy Street I spent two years working for a jobbing builder before joining a major oil company in the aviation department, retiring as a shift manager in 1983 after 34 years' service.

— John Pearson©

171

3106728 Cpl Geoff Perrior

Spyhole in the German brothel was a real eye-opener for me!

YOU HAVE the right build for the RAF police, I was told at the end of my basic training. And it was made quite clear that if I refused to join the police I would most likely have to become a cook. Policeman or cook? Probably two of the most unpopular people in the services. The choice was mine. And that is how, with my white cap and white webbing, I became a "Snowdrop."

After leaving school in 1943 I had been a Post Office messenger boy and then joined Ilford Selo at Brentwood in Essex. I worked in the laundry room until I had a chance to move to one of the production departments.

I was a member of the local air cadets, and when my call-up papers arrived I saw I had been selected for RAF training and was to report to Padgate on June 27 1947, my birthday.

From Padgate I was posted to RAF Wilmslow in Cheshire for six weeks' initial training. I was in the first batch of 200 conscripts to enter the camp, which was the training camp for the WAAF. But we were segregated, and not even allowed into their NAAFI canteen.

I was one of 30 recruits allocated to Hut B12, and as soon as we got there through the door came a well-built sergeant with a pace-stick under his arm. "Stand by your beds. Move." Then: "Step forward one pace any Air Training Corps cadets." Several of us moved towards him. Looking at one chap, he said: "You are hut leader." Then he looked at me. "You are deputy hut leader."

Next we were all told what he expected from us. How to fold blankets and sheets. How our kit was to be laid out for inspection. How to spit and polish our boots and clean the studs on the soles.

Demonstrating how the hut floor was to be dusted and cleaned, our sergeant produced a heavy block on a thick broom-handle. "This is a bumper for cleaning the floor, and I want to see my face in the floor on the day of the officer's inspection."

Some bright spark asked where we would get the polish and materials for cleaning. "That's your problem airman, don't ask silly questions."

The hut leader and I set up a roster for the week, giving four airmen the job of cleaning the centre gangway of the hut with the bumper. We had no idea where to get the polish so went down three blocks and asked the recruits whose floor was already polished.

"We can sell you a couple of tins," we were informed. It cost us three times the NAAFI price, and we were also sold half an old blanket to be cut up. Then the bumper went into action.

By the fourth week of training, after bags of bumping, loads of drill and dozens of kit inspections, we were getting closer to the standard the RAF expected.

We had learned how to march and do rifle drill, and to accept the drill instructors' parade ground taunts, like: "Were you born, airman or scraped off the roadway?" and: "Am I treading on your hair laddie, it's long enough." We were very nearly real airmen.

On payday the sergeants would have a raffle with a box of chocolates and 50 cigarettes as the prize, and no airman dare refuse a ticket. It was against King's Regulations to operate a raffle, and the sergeants knew it, but with 30 men to a hut, and 10 huts, that was good profit for their Saturday night beers. So we had a raffle.

Then came the time for our trade tests, and when we were informed of our results I was offered flight mechanic, engines, airframes or armourer. I said that none of these interested me, and that was when I was given the "police or cookhouse" options.

I was sent to the RAF Police School at Staverton in Gloucester where I quickly discovered I had left one hard-discipline camp and arrived where it was even worse.

The dreaded drill instructors, all senior NCOs more than six feet tall, were hand-picked ex-Guardsmen. Every march for meals to the cookhouse, which was about a mile on the other side of the airfield, was like a passing-out parade.

During classwork and study sessions all aspects of RAF law, King's Regulations, powers of arrest and civilian common law had to be learned. It was hard work, but I made friends with another trainee, grammar school educated Paul Christopherson, who was to play an important part in my future RAF service. Only the top four airmen on the course would go to the sought-after police headquarters (Provost Marshal) wings. The others would end up as guardroom police at RAF stations, or in some unpopular overseas posting like Palestine or the Suez Canal.

Paul said to me: "We are going to pass this course in first and second place so we get the best postings." His plan was that every day we would skip the evening meal and also opt out of going to the NAAFI with the rest of the lads.

Instead, we would use this quiet couple of hours when everyone was out of the hut to ask each other questions on what we had been taught in class that day.

The course became harder and harder but my friend Paul kept me to this nightly study. And when our exam results were read out, it was: "First, Airman Christopherson. Second, Airman Perrior."

All our hard work had paid off, and we were posted as acting corporals to the RAF Police headquarters at Princes Gate Court in Kensington.

This large block of flats which had been requisitioned by the Government, was a palace compared with the two training camps. With four other airmen I shared a room with underfloor heating. And we had our own bathroom.

My first duty was a 12-hour night shift in the cells on the ground floor. The cell unit had originally been a flat occupied by Ribbentrop, the German ambassador.

Most of the prisoners were "one nighters," airmen picked up for being absent without leave, or long-term deserters, who had to be supervised because of the likelihood they would try to escape.

The cells were not punishment units, but used only as detainee quarters before the prisoners were handed over to escorts and returned to their units.

My next duty was a seven-hour patrol in Piccadilly Circus. Every two hours I had to report in from the Metropolitan Police phone box outside the Swan &

I spent 37 years with WH Smith

I am here, right, with Cpl Mantkelow, a fellow RAF policeman on patrol in London. A couple of hours later I was put on a charge because my shirt collar was not properly ironed

Edgar department store. The job was to check that airmen were correctly dressed and carried leave passes, and were not loitering in the Soho red light district.

As corporals our powers of arrest were up to RAF warrant officer, Royal Navy chief petty officer and Army RSM.

Officers who were incorrectly dressed had to be approached, saluted and offered the compliments of the provost marshal and requested to adjust their dress correctly.

Of course RAF policemen also had to be immaculately turned out. It was a serious offence to be seen on duty with a soft collar, so ours were starched at the Chinese laundry in Kensington. Starching six collars cost 2s 6d, quite expensive, and each collar would last about three days.

Patrols were carried out at all the London main line railway stations throughout the day, and at weekends three or four pairs of patrols were on duty.

The volume of servicemen using the railway stations was very high. Liverpool Street — a place that was to feature prominently in my after-service career — had three troop trains every night leaving for the Hook of Holland.

Sometimes four patrols on a railway station were expected to bring back not fewer than 200 cautions. All airmen without leave passes or absent without leave would be placed in the cells overnight to await an escort to their unit.

The next day you would be sent on a mobile patrol in an open jeep, backing up all the patrols in certain areas, and stopping RAF vans and lorries to ensure they were not carrying stolen property.

Many airmen on leave visiting London would be accommodated at the Union Jack Club in

Waterloo, or London's two deep air-raid shelters at Tottenham Court Road and Clapham North. These places would be checked out about once a month in the search for long-term deserters or absentees. Airmen did not take too kindly to being woken up in the middle of the night to have their leave passes checked.

Because many letters of complaint were received from retired service officers regarding the bad dress and deportment of junior ranks, we also had to report airmen for things like dirty boots, untidy dress and long hair. A report would then be sent to their station commander who would be expected to take action.

One of our other duties was escorting prisoners to correction establishments such as those at Colchester and Shepton Mallett, run by the Corps of Military Police prison staff.

I shall never forget my first visit to Shepton Mallett. I thought I had encountered all the strictest systems of discipline, until I got there.

I was one of four escorts and two prisoners. We rang the bell, and a door flap opened. "Escorts and prisoners will march in and face the wall standing to attention." We were all frisked, then the order: "Escort about turn, march forward, halt, about face, stand at ease."

We faced the prison warders. Another voice shouted: "Escort stand still," and we realised that, just like the prisoners, we were under strict Army discipline.

A huge gate into the prison yard was opened and we were ordered to double to the reception area. "Left right, left right, hold your head up high. Move! Move! Move!"

Up an iron staircase we were met by the RSM. The escorts were then fallen out to stand easy. Documents were handed over, and the prisoners were stripped and ordered to the shower room.

All their clothes were searched and lapels were pulled down and brushed out. All pockets were turned out and all tobacco fluff removed. After signing over the prisoners, escorts were marched at the double to the main gate.

Once this closed again behind me I had an immense feeling of relief, and hoped never to be chosen again to escort prisoners to Shepton Mallett.

One day I was told to report to the main room at our headquarters. On the floor was a huge gym mattress, and I was told I was to be the victim of an unarmed combat demonstration for one of the London newspapers. They were writing an article on how women in the RAF police were trained.

I had to pretend to attack a female flight-sergeant with a knife. She would then use her unarmed combat training to throw and disarm me. We did this three times, but on the last occasion I landed rather heavily and dislocated my shoulder. As a result I had my arm in a sling and 14 days excused duties. Returning to duty, I was transferred to the Absentees and Deserters investigation section.

Our object was to bring back as many short-term absentees as possible and to carry out deeper investigations into long-term deserters from the Second World War.

I was now involved in plain-clothes operations, which in the main was a dull routine and did not often produce good results. For every absentee you caught another probably went absent. But I did get meal and clothes allowances.

In 1948 the Berlin Airlift had begun, which meant more RAF personnel were required in Germany. At the airfields, airmen were working longer shifts and more hours so the movement of RAF personnel coming home on leave increased. And there were more absentees and forged leave passes.

I had to appear several times at courts martial in Germany to give evidence. On my first trip to Germany I boarded a Douglas Dakota at RAF Northolt on a flight to Buckeburg, West Germany. The route was manned by an RAF crew, but our lunch was served in BEA logo boxes.

On board were a number of civilians, including the King's Messenger to Moscow and Government Control Commission officers.

On another of my trips, I was taken to Cologne and was quite shocked that more than three years after the surrender of Germany, rebuilding had not begun. All the rubble had still to be cleared, and only the roads and tramways were clear. The scene looked as if a bulldozer had gone straight down the middle of the road and pushed everything to one side

People were living in the basements of destroyed houses, and you would see them open a trap door in the ground and go to the water pipe and tap protruding from the ground.

Once I accompanied the vice-squad who were checking the papers of the brothel owners. I shouldn't have been there because only married men were allowed in the vice squad, but the sergeant said I could go along.

We arrived at a huge house where two queues of men stretched each side of the yard. The sergeant produced his warrant card to the madam of the house and requested to see her official documents. He asked if any RAF men — who were forbidden to use the "facilities" — were in the building. A corporal took me into the reception rooms where about a dozen scantily-dressed women were sitting around waiting to be selected by their clients.

We passed along a corridor of small bedrooms and the corporal told me to take a peep through the spyhole on one of the doors. "Don't look too long, you might spoil it!"

I was just 19, and I realised there was a lot about life that I didn't know!

On the way back to HQ the sergeant leaned over to me and said: "Don't tell anyone where you have been today."

My first quarters in Germany were an ex-SS barracks with tiled walls and huge coke fires which also controlled the heating and hot water systems.

There six RAF policemen had their own cook and two German room maids, who also did all the washing and ironing. They even pressed my uniform every day and washed my dirty shirts and socks.

I noticed that the uniforms of RAF men where we were stationed were very much smarter than mine. The secret was that theirs had been tailored, and the battledress jackets pleated and the trouser creases stitched all the way down the seam, American-style.

One of the corporals said he could get my uniform altered for a packet of cigarettes. Considering that we received five free packets of 20 every week in Germany, it was a bargain.

But on returning to London I stood out like a sore thumb on my first commanding officer's parade The inspecting officer, Group Captain Champion, was very strict on RAF tradition and dress standard. He looked at the station warrant officer and said: "Put him in the book, defacing the King's uniform."

That afternoon I was ordered to destroy my American-style uniform and pay for a new one. It cost me all my allocated uniform allowance for the first 18 months of service.

I visited Germany once more to give evidence in a big forgery case and was away for 10 days before settling back in the Absentees and Deserters section.

The pending file was always full of new cases and some were marked priority. So the periods of surveillance began again.

One day I was summoned for an interview with a Daily Mirror reporter who was writing a series of articles on the duties of various servicemen stationed in London.

My section officer told me what questions I could answer and what I should not answer. As "Corporal Seed of Absentees and Deserters Section, RAF Police HQ" I had to describe the daily routine of an investigation.

When the article appeared it included quite a bit of journalistic licence. The story claimed that I used a bicycle to make myself mobile. Completely untrue. And according to the newspaper my final quote was: "We bring 'em in, but as fast as we knock 'em off, another slips away." A complete fabrication.

The report concluded with the comment: "His opinion does not matter in Whitehall, so many more bike rides lie ahead for nine-shillings a day Cpl Seed."

A new CO who believed in changing sections around arrived at headquarters, and I was posted to a small police unit with only a dozen airmen at Biggin Hill.

But it was not long before I was on the move again, this time to Titchfield, near Fareham in Hampshire. We covered the whole of the county including Southampton docks, Portsmouth and the Isle of Wight.

Southampton was very important for servicemen embarking and disembarking for places like Singapore, Hong Kong and Aden and many other areas in the Far East.

The docks were also the BOAC flying boat terminal, which brought in many overseas government officials and heads of state visiting Britain. We had to provide the security escort at the docks until their official security parties took over from us.

One morning after we had carried out one of the escort duties, we marched along the quay and halted near a ship that was being painted red. The painter was in a cradle on the funnel, and I saw him deliberately flicking his brush into the wind, producing little red dots on the top of our white caps. Obviously he did not like RAF policemen. We marched back for a clean-up before our next duty.

One weekend our flight at Titchfield had to report with full kit for a major exercise at RAF Odiham. My CO, Squadron-leader Allard, sent me to the briefing because of my previous experience in the Absentee and Deserter section.

But the officer in charge of the exercise was Wing Commander Sheppard, the CO at London HQ who apparently had taken a dislike to me and posted me to Biggin Hill.

When he spotted me he ordered me to leave the briefing room. I reported what had happened to the CO and he went into the room. He returned and told me to go in but make sure I sat at the back. It was the first time an officer had stood up for me.

On the exercise six RAF pilots had "landed behind enemy lines" and were attempting to make their way back to their base at RAF Odiham. The job of the RAF Police was to capture them before they could get there.

The pilots were dispersed all over Hampshire and given orders that they could change into civilian clothes by begging or borrowing and hide their uniforms. But we had to keep our RAF blue uniforms, and our vehicles would still be marked RAF Police.

We set road blocks and drew up a plan to encircle the airfield over a five mile radius, keeping off the roads and looking at fields leading directly to the outer perimeter fence,

We covered our jeeps with hedgerow stumps and hid in ditches with binoculars, looking out for the advancing pilots. And much to everyone's satisfaction they were all captured within five hours.

Soon afterwards I was called for my demob interview and asked if I was willing to sign on for regular RAF Service.

This was something I had been considering for some time, but I just couldn't make up my mind. In the end I decided to return to civilian life and the complete freedom that went with it.

So I handed in my RAF equipment, stuffed the rest into my kitbag and walked through the main gate. I had enjoyed every minute of my time as an RAF policeman, and wondered what the future would hold.

And then...

Readjusting to civilian life was not easy. The strong bond of friendship and duty and all the laughs that went with it, had now gone. It was like being in a void, and took some getting used to.

Years later I reflected that maybe I should have remained in the RAF. I know I would have enjoyed it, and after 21 years could have retired on a pension.

Instead, I returned to my old job at the Ilford Selo works in Brentwood, and then a few months later took a job with WH Smith, which was to last until I retired after 37 years.

For 31 of those years I worked on the WHS bookstall at Liverpool Street station — my old RAF police stamping ground — where I started as an assistant then became area manager in London and East Anglia, ending up as news manager for the whole network of WH Smith bookstalls on Liverpool Street station.

One day I was having breakfast in the staff room there when I suddenly realised that I was in the old RTO office where service personnel would book in, and where I had carried out many of my RAF police duties.

— *Geoff Perrior©*

176

22177156 Cpl Bill Phipps

So I was a driver who couldn't drive and a typist unable to type

I HAD been in the Army for only a few weeks when I was told to get into a Bedford truck which was to be moved into a parking place at Tilbury docks. My protestations that I couldn't drive cut no ice. The Army had told me I was a driver, therefore I had to drive.

My National Service had begun at Aldershot and I found it all quite frightening, having never been away from home before. The situation wasn't helped when I got to know that some of the guys in our squad had come direct from Borstal, complete with stabbing knives.

After various inoculations, vaccinations and body examinations it seemed everyone was deemed fit and healthy. Wrong. On the first five-mile half-march, half-run, one of our team failed to return. He was subsequently found dead, apparently of an undiagnosed heart condition.

But I found that all the exercise, drills, marching, learning how to use brenguns, stens, grenades and other methods of killing people was really quite uplifting. And at the end of basic training I felt as fit as a fiddle.

In due course we were paraded to be told where we would be posted for the remainder of our Army career.

As we stood at ease an officer told one of the sergeants in front of us that four men were needed to go to Purfleet. Asked if the men needed to have any special abilities, the officer replied: "Yes sergeant, they are to be as tall as possible."

The sergeant looked us over. "Right, you, you, you and you." The last you was me. And the four of us were told: "You are all drivers."

I looked at the chap next to me and said: "He doesn't mean us does he?" "No," said Tom, "the blokes behind us." Then the officer shouted: "The rest of you into the lorries for shipment elsewhere," and the sergeant gave the order "Dismiss," which we obeyed.

The officer shouted: "What are you four doing?" Tom said: "Sir, we are not drivers, we thought you meant the four behind us."

"Then you weren't paying attention, were you?"

"But sir, we can't drive."

"And you didn't listen either, did you? I'll say it again, you four are all drivers."

Two days later we arrived at Purfleet, settled in, had a chat to the lads in the billet about what we would do next day and were told "just do as we do."

Next morning we were told to wear our worst uniform. "What, on parade?" I said. "Parade," said Harry, "what's that?"

By 8.30am we were in the back of a truck on our way to Tilbury docks. The police at the gate had a quick look inside to check the number of bodies and see if we were in possession of any illegal contraband.

We got out and lined up for the sergeant to inspect us, and waited for our SQMS George Wright, whom we had to address as Q. The sergeant, I noticed, called him George.

Having taken stock of us new bods Q asked our names and informed us that our driving licences would be available in due course, and explained what we had to do.

It appeared that a vessel called an LST, carrying vehicles like Bedford three-ton lorries, tanks, motorcycles and a few Austin 10s, was in dock being unloaded by the dockers.

But the dockers would not allow us on the ship, so we had to wait until each vehicle was pulled from the ship to the bow section, which opened up like a pair of garage doors allowing it to be towed out.

I watched this operation, and when there were five or six Bedfords on the dockside a Scammell being driven by a "proper" driver hooked on to the first truck, which in turn hooked on to the second and so on until there was a chain of vehicles.

Then it was the turn of us, the "special drivers."

We were all ordered to get into the cab of a truck and release the handbrake. I asked the sergeant where the handbrake was. He looked at me as if I had flipped. "You are Phipps, aren't you?"

"Yes sergeant."

"You are a driver, aren't you?"

"No sergeant, the four of us have only just joined and we were told we were drivers. But we can't drive." He stood for a while looking at me, then said: "Get in the cab. That is the handbrake. You don't actually have to drive the vehicle. Just follow the truck in front, OK? When I give the word to the Scammell driver, release the handbrake and you will all move off."

It was my bad luck to be in the middle of the train and I noticed a brick wall about seven feet high. As we were passing it I realised that the Scammell driver at the front had made his turn a little bit too early and my truck was heading into the brick wall. I quickly turned the steering wheel the other way and was horrified to see that this made no difference. Bang! I hit the wall and knocked it over.

Everything came to a stop. Except the sergeant, who appeared at my open window and shouted: "What are you doing, Phipps?"

"I couldn't help it, sergeant. I tried to turn away but it didn't make any difference."

He walked to the front of the lorry and examined the dent in the bonnet. "Well, don't do it again."

By this time the Scammell driver came round and admitted the accident was his fault. He said: "I've only been driving this thing a few days and I am not quite used to it."

All the lorries were unhooked and eventually nudged in line together with the rest of the shipment of Bedfords. The Scammell then proceeded to drive behind the last lorry and push them all closer. As we watched, bonnets began to bend and crush. "Blimey Tom," I said to my pal. "I just got told off for putting a little dent in a bonnet, and now look at that lot."

The tanks, armoured cars and lorries were loaded on to a trailer and taken to a railway spur line in the dock, winched on to low-loaders and taken away to I know not where.

After a month or two we four alleged drivers were called into the office and given our driving licences.

My only driving lesson had been being shown the location of a handbrake, but now, according to the Army I was a "driver." If the Army wants to call me a driver, so be it!

Now, as each ship was unloaded it was reloaded with brand new Centurion tanks with Rolls-Royce engines. Of course, only highly-qualified drivers were allowed to drive them to the ship where specialist dockers took over to get them inside the hull.

Our self-appointed "specialist" was SQMS Wright. But when he climbed into a Centurion

we would be warned by those who had witnessed this show before not to get too close to the exhausts. Great clouds of smoke poured from them. The engine howled its head off as the tank began moving slowly. Then I could smell burning. "He does it every time," I was told. But George knew it all, and was awarded the BEM for services rendered!

One day the sergeant came across a field to where I was working. "You are wanted in the office." I wiped as much mud, grease and oil off my hands as I could and nervously made my way to the office. I knocked on the door. "Come in."

Q was sitting at his desk and next to him was Cpl Davis. I stood rigidly to attention and Q told me to relax. "What is your first name?" I wondered what this was all about, and replied: "William, but I'm usually called Bill."

"Right Bill," said Q, and I couldn't work out what was going on until Cpl Davis piped up: "You are taking over from me as typist and general office wallah, do shorthand and manage your own filing system."

I looked at Q and thought it must be a big joke. But he said: "That's right, Mike here is demobbed in a couple of days and you will take over."

"But Q," I said, "I can't type."

"Maybe not," he replied, "but you'll learn. Mike did. Just use two fingers, and you'll soon find out where the keys are."

So, from a driver who couldn't drive, i was now a typist who couldn't type.

But Q was right, quickly I was able to type satisfactorily, and was made up to lance-corporal, then full corporal.

Shortly after this Q said he had some good news. "Bill, four men will be coming in today to join the crew. But wait for it, one of them is a highly-skilled typist."

"That's good news," I said. "What are the other three, drivers?"

Q looked at me quizzically for a moment. "How did you know?"

"Oh," I said, "just a lucky guess. Do you arrange the licences or do I?"

"Ee, not sure. I'll let you know," and off he went, back to his tanks.

That afternoon there was a knock on the door and when it opened four smartly-dressed soldiers came in and stood in front of me like four pokers, eyes fixed firmly over my head into the distance. One stepped forward and announced: "Cpl Phipps, we have been ordered by the sergeant to report to you"

"Relax guys, you're not on parade now," I said. " This is the 20th AFV office, not the parade ground. By the way, which of you is the typist?"

The driver who couldn't drive. And (right) at the Dorset Steam Fair in 2008

The spokesman again snapped to attention. "I am, Pte Stegle." As it turned out Pte Stegle was a hopeless typist, so I still did the letters and he did the filing.

The other three men, the "drivers" were never issued with driving licences.

And then...

After demob I returned to Moss's, the building firm where I had been employed before call-up. I used to help in the carpenter's shop, then in plumbing and the blacksmith's shop where I learned a great deal about metals, gas welding and general engineering.

Back there after my National Service the boss asked if I could drive. "Here is my licence," I replied. "I can drive anything, all groups including track-laying vehicles."

"National Service seems to have done you a bit of good," he replied.

In no time I was driving men to various building sites, repairing any machine that may have broken down and also welding fractures in cement-mixer drums. About this time a new secretary was employed in the office and I fell in love with her. She became my first and only girlfriend and three years later we married and are still together after 54 tears.

At the same time my workload increased dramatically and I was not getting home until after midnight. So my wife said her father would try to get me a job where he worked, a small firm called Hoover. He told his boss I was good with engines and could drive, and they took me on even though they did not require any more men.

I went to the Hoover training college in Nottingham and was instructed in the complexities of the Hoover products. After seven weeks I returned to Perivale and joined my father-in-law in the contracts department. We were specialists trained to repair and service machines for banks, hotels, airlines, shops, the P and O shipping line and the Royal Household.

All went well for seven years and I enjoyed my work until Hoovers received a directive from the parent company in America that all service men must be sacked.

It appeared that Hoover in Great Britain was about to shut up shop. But they offered the contracts department men finance, spare parts and toolkits if they formed individual companies to service and support the important clients still using Hoover products.

The London district was split between the men taking up the offer. And my pa-in-law and I ran one of the areas until he retired after 10 years on reaching the age of 65.

My wife then took over the other half of the partnership and we continued for 30 years, our main customers being shops, hotels, banks, local authorities, Pan-Am Airways and hospital groups. Also on our books was the Queen Mother, whose steam irons were sent to me for repair.

Eighteen years ago we moved to Verwood in Dorset and I spent my leisure time building steam engines until this work became too heavy for me. Now my hobby is making wooden toys for my great-grandchildren.

— Bill Phipps©

23000428 Cpl Roy Pickard

My boxing debut became quite literally a bloody disaster

HAVING passed the Civil Service Clerical Officers Exam, I was working for the Ministry of Pensions and National Insurance when I was called up in 1953. When I went for assessment and medical I was one of the first to arrive at 8am and among the last to leave at 5.30pm. The reason was that as my father had been in the Navy, I had requested entry into the Navy as my first choice.

I filled in various forms before the official interview where I was offered a minimum of seven years as a stoker. No way!

My second choice was for the RAF, and I went through the same procedures again, ending in an offer of five years, which I did not accept.

So I had to go through everything once more for the Army. After the IQ test, yet another form to fill in, but this time there were choices of where in the Army I would like to serve.

I forget the order of my three choices, but included the Pay Corps, the Signals and the RASC. I ended up in the infantry, but I was pleased that it was in the Devons, my home county regiment.

I had to report to Topsham Barracks, Exeter where we were issued with uniform and kit at the quartermaster stores and given Devon shoulder flashes. Then we had a medical with a vaccination and various jabs.

A few days later we went to the gym and I was put into a boxing ring for the first time in my life. I was dreading it. The first punch thrown at me knocked off my vaccination scab and there was blood everywhere.

I was taken to the medical centre and never put in a boxing ring again. That was divine providence, so far as I was concerned.

Because I was slow getting ready for parades and was invariably last, I worked out that the only way I could get more time to prepare was to eat my meals quicker. Thus today I am still a fast eater.

There was a lot of square-bashing, most of it with snow or ice on the ground. One of our recruits, called Hansford, was a farm labourer from Dorset who couldn't march. He strolled along with a slouched posture, albeit seemingly in time. Cpl Porch was often heard shouting: "Hansford, you are walking behind that bloody

One punch, and my boxing career was over!

plough again!" The company sergeant major used to watch us drill from an upstairs window in the brick billets. One week he decided he didn't like our efforts, so cancelled the weekend leave passes and gave us extra square-bashing on the Saturday morning.

In one part of the drill he gave the order Fix Bayonets. Not the easiest of drill movements. I happened to be in the middle of the front rank and, for no sane reason, got mixed up and did half of Fix and half of Unfix Bayonets. Don't ask me how. But I was obviously noticed as I tried to correct my error.

A regimental policeman was standing on the edge of the square for just such an incident. The CSM yelled out: "That man with eye-glasses, step forward." Which I did. He then ordered the policeman to escort me to the glasshouse.

I hated trying to tackle the assault course. I was sure I would be the first to fall from the plank over the water. Thankfully, I made it to the other side without getting wet.

But the worst part of training was bayonet practice. I felt sick every time I plunged the bayonet into the straw sack that represented an enemy soldier's stomach.

We also learned about the three weapons we had to master, rifle, sten and bren. Hold butt tight into the shoulder, aim and pull the trigger gently but be prepared for the kickback. But how tight is tight for goodness sake!

The barracks range was equipped with 6ft targets only 25 yards from the firing position. No-one could possibly miss. Then the order came: Prepare to fire and fire when ready.

I pulled the butt into my shoulder, held the rifle firmly, aimed for the bullseye, pulled the trigger and...missed the target completely.

The rifle exploded with a tremendous bang, jumped out of my hands and fell on to the ground beside me. I went deaf.

There were a few choice words from the sergeant, which I would not repeat to my family. And I remember thinking that my father would have been very disappointed with me as he had

180

been a crack shot. He was a member of the Devonport Naval Shooting Team, and at Bisley in 1937 won the coveted McQueen (Entente Cordiale) Cup.

One day we were taken on to Dartmoor to fire a brengun. I was convinced I had my helmet on as tight as possible, but the vibration of rapid fire made it fall over my eyes, so I had no idea where the bullets went. Another disaster for my dad to witness from above!

However, by the end of training I passed as a marksman on the sten and also gained second class on both rifle and brengun.

Nevertheless, I still have a lot of whistling in my left ear, which is very sensitive to noise, and I require a hearing aid in my right ear. Back in the 1980s the ENT consultant said my hearing difficulties were typical of problems caused by firing guns. So having worked on war pension matters I made a claim for my disability and was awarded a lump sum gratuity.

On one three-day exercise we were taken to a spot on a hill and had to dig trenches in pairs. Fortunately, I was paired with a chap who had been a fireman on the railway and was used to using a shovel. He suggested that he dig the trench and that I could hide the earth and camouflage the trench top. So it worked out well.

Our enemy was the potential officers cadre who raided us during the night while we were asleep in the trench. We had both lost hold of our alarm rope and slept through the raid. The "enemy" went over our trench without taking us prisoner, so the camouflage must have been good. We woke up when the raid was over.

It was February and the weather was very cold and we had our first experience of shaving with icy cold water. We even had to break the ice to get to it and all shared the same bucket.

While we were on the exercise I was bitten by an insect, and the bite turned septic. The MO gave me antibiotics to take over the weekend and I went home to Plymouth.

The bite was so bad on Saturday morning that I went to the chemist who advised me to go to hospital outpatients where the wound was lanced and my arm put into a sling. I still have a scar on my right wrist which my grandchildren call my war wound.

After passing-out parade we had three weeks" leave which was over the Easter period, after which I was destined for an infantry clerks course at Chichester.

I passed third on the course so was quite pleased. I had never used a typewriter before but managed to reach the required standard of 25 words a minute.

On return to Topsham Barracks I was put on fatigues peeling potatoes in the sergeants mess kitchen, washing up and scrubbing the floor.

Then we were all issued with tropical kit in preparation for posting to Kenya and given jabs against such things as malaria and yellow fever.

Two days before embarkation I was told I was required at Wessex Brigade headquarters, a small unit in the corner of the barrack square. I was offered a job there because their corporal clerk was about to be demobbed. My duties involved speaking to the depot commanders of the six regiments on drafting programmes and personnel matters.

Thus I spent the rest of my service on office work punctuated from time to time with physical education for HQ staff, which took the form of following the beagle hunt arranged by the brigade captain near his home on Exmoor.

And then...

In March 1956 I returned to my old job at the Ministry of Pensions and National Insurance in London and later became a supervisor and part-time instructor on specialist courses, including teaching overseas students about the British Social Security system at Headquarters Staff Training Department. I also helped set up and teach at a New Entrant Training Centre in Billingham.

Later I moved to Birmingham for training to become a welfare officer for the war disabled, and took up a post at Bristol in December 1973. Five years later I was transferred on promotion to Overseas Development Administration in London as manager of the Colonial Officer Pensions Computer Input Section.

When the ODA Colonial Officer Recruitment and Pensions Sections were relocated to East Kilbride I set up the computer input section there and became Registrar with a staff of 50. After hours I became a counsellor with Glasgow Council on Alcoholism and helped set up a new counselling service in East Kilbride.

Finally I was manager of Pay and Allowances for the Ordnance Survey Department in Southampton, before being given medical retirement in 1988.

Looking for a new interest I joined Southampton hospital radio in 1999, and now present several jazz and swingtime programmes and a Sunday morning programme of sacred music.
— **Roy Pickard©**

2342197 AC1 John Pope

I didn't seek a cushy number — it just happened that way

REPORTING for duty should be a doddle, all my plans had been made. Get to Euston station and the rest will just happen. That's how it turned out. I remember the LMS steam express pulling out of the dreary old terminus, then nothing but a fog, as if there had been no in-between, as we crept gently into Bank Quay station at Warrington. Was I the *only* rookie ploughing a lonely furrow to RAF Padgate on that January day in 1947? Looking around the grimy compartmentalised carriage, I could see elderly ladies and gentlemen, a middle-aged man with his thinning hair brushed tidily down, a uniformed train official...but not a sign of anyone likely to be responding to the National Service Act.

It needed just a few paces on the platform to find the "gang" — tall ones, short ones, long-haired ones. Surely these guys were not heading for a life in the air force?

Amid the chaos on the station, a couple of corporals emerged from the mayhem and told us to follow them out of the station (goodbye freedom!) and into a couple of wagons. So far so good. Fifteen minutes later, we came to a stop. We were inside the camp, alongside a large hut, and a fair-haired corporal — the name Jephson rings a bell — began pouring cups of tea. After one sip one became aware of a "presence." Even if you couldn't see the man, whose stature was swallowed up by the crop of quite a few rather tall recruits, you could feel that the Lord was about to speak. If he had been as meek and mild as the corporal, we might have had a chance to gulp a second mouthful of tea.

After demob I edited an Army magazine

The welcoming flight-sergeant, a Scotsman, must have struck us all, perhaps 50 to 100 fellows, like the detonation of a 500lb bomb. No more time even to take a backwards glance at our abandoned cups of tea. It was march — yes, left-right, left-right, that sort of march.

Then, formalities over, it was off to the huts, all those metal and wire-framed beds, 30 to each room. Set up your biscuits (mattresses),

I was given some cushy numbers

unfold your blankets, run your slip over the awful bolster and think, for just a few seconds, that you might now get comfortable. Cockneys, Taffies, Jocks, Geordies, Scousers, you name it, your hut companions had come to serve the nation from all quarters of Britain. And we were all in the same boat, there wasn't a soul who actually *wanted* to be there.

In three weeks, I was fortunate, they were sending me back to Euston on indefinite leave because the severe winter had caused all water on camp to freeze and there was no fuel to keep us warm. That emergency leave, allowing me to go back to work, lasted into a fifth week.

Just days back into my square-bashing with Five Flight I was sent to a service hospital at RAF Wilmslow, for "investigation." Could that mean I may be re-graded to Three, a discharge? Was I going to be released?

No, I was to remain graded One and return to Padgate. But I would not resume training at the beginning as a new recruit, but instead be passed out, since my group had already been posted. So no more drills on the square. Maybe this National Service isn't so bad after all.

I wasn't looking for some little number in which you could tuck myself up for hours and skive. I had never intended to do that sort of thing — it just happened.

My first dot on the two-year trail was at a small-sized maintenance unit with the huge concrete runways and perimeters where in wartime giant RAF and United States bombers might have been lining-up for an attack in the Ruhr.

Far from the normal billet huts, I was put in charge of a linen and furnishing store, so isolated it was quite heavenly. I was able to wear civvies some of the time, and my accommodation was in the store — a bed and all mod cons, you might say.

I had my own little radio, no-one to quarrel with, no interference from anyone, and after duty I could simply lock up and go out on my bike to the hillside home of Barbara, my girl-friend. It was idyllic, but did not last.

My next assignment was to report to the fire section, again a largely trouble-free task, no colour-hoisting parades or inspections. And no queueing for your meal in the mess. You were driven there, a mile and back.

You went everywhere with the appliance and were given priority everywhere you went. What a life! Except, that is, on the night a huge hangar caught fire and, sleeping like logs, no-one heard the alarm at 2.40am. Anyway, our Karrier Bantam did not have enough hosereels to reach the nearest water source.

Then they moved me (as well as every single member of the section), and my next task was as clerk at MT. Cars, Dodge trucks, Bedford troop carriers, most used as "liberty wagons," and, my great coming of age, the ability to drive 10-ton Leyland Hippo lorries.

The worst moment there was being ordered on a public holiday, the Queen's wedding day in 1947, to mount a four-hour guard on the section with an empty and bent stengun!

My stay at this great little RAF station, 12 miles south of Oxford, ended suddenly one day in 1948. "You are going to Cambridge," and it wasn't the university!

There were a few cold sweats, that's for sure as, wearing special soft clothing and all-rubber wellington boots, I joined a small team whose daily task was to despatch for destruction the remainders of high-explosive bombs not used up in the 1939-45 war.

Very large and extremely heavy, they rested on trestles in shallow trenches, and our labours ensured that one-by-one each bomb was wrapped in a sling, hoisted by crane and swung through 90 degrees to be lowered gently into open railway trucks.

It does not sound like a tough job, but there were huge risks and every move brought beads of sweat. One day a bomb slipped from its hoist and crashed to the floorboards of the railway wagon with a great thud.

I can tell you this now only because it did not blow out the windows of half of Cambridge and tear us into tiny shreds. And thanks to that, we were never rostered again for that particular duty at RAF Lord's Bridge.

Many of my tasks were given to a really comfortable little slot — being responsible for the cleanliness of the NAAFI throughout the day. This gave me ample chance, and undisturbed, to hear George Elrick or an associate with radio's daily Housewives' Choice.

All too soon, despite my pending demobilisation, they posted me again, just up the road to RAF Great Ashfield near Bury St Edmunds. I was not required to parade and there did not seem to be any duties for me and a handful of others.

So most mornings it was out to a nearby hamlet where a good lady who kept a small cafe would satisfy our appetites for an English breakfast in the Suffolk countryside.

The others got their discharges and set off for Lancashire to become civilians again. My service book had been written up between blue covers and I would need to wait for a yellow one, but over a week had gone by and my demob seemed to have been forgotten.

My parents did not appreciate this and Mrs Pope senior popped in to see our MP, Dr Edith Summerskill (Lab, Fulham West) who in turn had a word with her Fulham East counterpart, Michael Stewart, who happened to be War Minister.

Mr Stewart had a word with his Under Secretary of State at the Air Ministry, Geoffrey de Freitas who sent on a word or two in the form of a signal, to the unfortunate commanding officer. Within an hour, I was on the train to Preston to become a free man.

And then...

I actually returned to the forces in 1968, but not to the RAF. Instead I became editor and publisher of Fanfare magazine for the Royal Military School of Music (later Corps of Army Music) at Kneller Hall. I also joined the editorial staff of the Daily Telegraph. Then, from 1973 to 1983, I was an impresario, presenting military band and jazz concerts on London's South Bank and in Westminster.

— John Pope©

2741577 LAC Geoffrey Price
We kept guard in the armoury, but couldn't use the arms

HAVING passed the tests for medical and selection for the RAF, I was sent my call-up papers to attend RAF Cardington — the station with the WW2 balloon hangars. This meant getting a lift from my father to the railway station at St. Albans. Mother was too upset to come with us. On arrival at Cardington station those nice men with white tops to their hats herded us on to buses and lorries. We were allocated the old-fashioned billets in Nissen huts and then marched off to get our bedding and overalls.

As this was taking place in the first week of December 1954, we also had to pick up the hut's allocation of fuel for the duration of our stay. This was to light two large coke burners spaced out at one third intervals down the middle of the hut.

During that first week we were issued with uniforms, shirts, shoes and boots as well as underwear, as near as possible to a reasonable fit. Some miss-shapen individuals had to wait until the square-bashing station before they could get tailor-made uniforms. The rest of us had our uniforms altered to fit, as necessary.

We were also required to parcel up the civvy clothes we had arrived in and send them home, and to write a postcard telling our parents that we were happy in our new situation!

Next stop as a National Service flight was RAF Padgate near Warrington where we were handed over to the loving care of the drill instructors. I never understood why we had to scratch off the painted label on our blacking tins and polish it with Brasso, which was also used for cleaning the windows.

After three weeks we were sent home for Christmas leave wearing our fresh uniforms complete with greatcoat and best blue uniform. On our return to camp, a lot of time was spent delivering coal to the married quarters as the square was unsuitable for marching on.

Drill and PT sessions were conducted in hangars. I remember the PT instructor kept shouting at us to stop talking in the ranks, and when we carried on he sent us outside in the cold to continue our exercises. Unfortunately for him, the exercises kept us warm while he

became colder and colder in his singlet until in the end he ordered us back inside so that he could get warm himself.

Any punishment drill was always after the evening meal which meant the drill corporals missed out on their leisure time. But we had nowhere to go so it didn't bother us. Wednesday afternoons were sports

A picture taken in 1954, and a recent one of me in uniform during a re-enactment

afternoons and if you had a sport you could get out of square- bashing. "Who likes long-distance running?" asked the billet corporal. I was a cross-country runner, so I said I did. "Right, run across to the other side of camp and post my letter in time for the collection." That was the last time I volunteered for anything.

As a National Service flight the DIs were constantly trying to get us into competition with the regular flight. This had the opposite effect and we were declared a lot of useless b---s. However, at the passing-out parade, in front of those relatives that could make it, we were declared the best and a credit to the instructors.

My next posting was to RAF Yatesbury where I was trained as a Radar Operator PPI (Plan Position Indicator) and sent to RAF Sopley as an AC2. There we lived in bungalows built from breeze-blocks with an integral corporal's room, lounge with open fire and two baths, washbasins and WCs.

Our work stations were down the "Hole," an underground bunker beneath the radar aerials. We plotted the aircraft that came into our air space. These were always given a hostile number until they could be identified as friendly. However if they could not be identified from their logged flight routes and therefore remained hostile, two fighters were scrambled to intercept, guided by us under the command of a pilot-officer.

At other times the pilot-officers in our cabins designated one fighter as "enemy" and vectored the other on to the enemy in a mock attack. On one occasion the pilot-officer kept the aircraft too long away from base and one crashed having run out of fuel.

The pilot escaped by parachute using his ejector seat, but it was us ordinary airman who had to guard the crash site from souvenir hunters, armed with pickaxe handles.

Other duties included guarding against the IRA by sleeping in the armoury armed only with a panic button. Though we were surrounded by guns and ammunition it was locked away. You were let out of the armoury in the morning so you could give the cooks on breakfast duty a wake-up call.

On one occasion, the standing orders were altered so that billet orderlies now had to go on parade with the rest of the flight and not wait for the orderly officer's inspection.

I had failed to see the change and was put on a charge for not being on parade. I got seven days' jankers, but the billet corporal, who also had not seen the change was not disciplined.

Kit inspection could be a nightmare as anyone who had lost an item was liable to recover it from an easy target. I had the misfortune to lose my cap but was saved by the flight-sergeant who sold me a spare.

I mustered out as a leading-aircraftman, although I now say that my rank as AC should have stood for air commodore.

And then...
At the end of National Service I rejoined the Ministry of Health. I did voluntary work as a Civil Defence volunteer and switched to full time employment with the Home Office at its Civil Defence staff college at Sunningdale. Then I took a post as Civil Defence instructor with the London Borough of Harrow.

Following the shutdown of the Civil Defence I trained as a legal assistant and continued in various posts as a conveyancer in local government and then in private practice. I moved to Bournemouth in 1972 and retired as a licensed conveyancer in 2001.

— Geoffrey Price©

You will find your days are pretty full; you will be working from 8.30am to 5-o-clock, with occasional breaks and an interval for dinner. You may find some of your muscles aching at first but after a while you will feel yourself getting tougher and stronger and more active.

— From You and the Army, a booklet issued to all NS army conscripts

22468368 L/Bdr Ernie Robinson

I landed an easy two-hour a day job on the Isle of Wight

I LEFT school in 1947 aged 14 and had a variety of jobs ranging from working for Southend Water to a couple of jobs in sawmills. But one day early in 1951 I received my call-up papers ordering me to report to the barracks of the 47th Coast Regiment, Royal Artillery at Oswestry. This was quite a coincidence because my father had served in the RA in the first world war, and my elder brother in WW2.

So on a very cold March day I got myself to the appointed place, and with a whole bunch of other rookies was greeted by some very stern-looking Army personnel. We lined up to present ourselves to the quartermaster who made a cursory assessment of each of us and tossed over a bundle of gear which he thought would fit.

We were marched to our billet, a large room with beds each side and a stove in the middle, and then told to parade outside for our march to the messroom to eat.

It was far from four-star catering. Just some luke-warm concoction thrown into our mess-tins which we were told to eat as quickly as possible so we could return to our barrack room and learn how to treat our new home. This entailed instruction on bed-making, polishing the floor and window cleaning.

We were woken next morning at 5am when the barrack doors burst open and a fierce-looking soldier with a snarling alsatian in tow stamped into the room bellowing: "Hands off cocks, on with socks."

It was snowing outside, and the next order was to get out there to wash and shave in a row of metal washbasins with only cold water.

After six weeks' square-bashing I was sent to Plymouth, based in what was known as The Citadel. There we were subjected to another six weeks of drill under a sergeant I am sure no parents would claim as their own! We were taught how to fire a rifle, throw grenades and survive a gas attack — and how to kill someone with a bayonet.

We were then regarded as trained soldiers and enjoyed a somewhat more comfortable existence. I was directed to work in the company pay office which was interesting work and enabled the three of us in the office to carry out

My job is at a fun park

pay parades at other locations.

This entailed taking a pickup truck and visiting the bank with an armed guard to collect the cash to pay everyone.

The pay parades were very tedious, often made even slower by the sergeant-major who would march in the rookies and remonstrate with anyone who put a foot wrong. After a lot of cursing and swearing eventually the work would be complete and we had to get back to camp and make sure the books balanced. These were then authorised by Capt Dodds, "old Doddy."

After about a year in Plymouth I was posted to Newport and then Tenby in South Wales. At Tenby I was running the battery office, responsible for all sorts of events at the camp. This was quite satisfying and laid the foundations for my later life when I went into office management.

We were also required to look after the Territorial Army bods who were called up after National Service for two weeks each year to be sure everyone was ready for the next call to arms, if required. So for two weeks every now and then I had to pack up my office and transport it to the Isle of Wight. I worked for about two hours a day while the TA lads were out training. An enjoyable time.

One thing we learned from National Service was to look out for ourselves and for others. There was a lad in my billet who could neither read nor write, so I would write his letters home to his mum in Sheffield.

And then...

Demobbed in 1953 I returned home to get on with my life. Most of my career was office work, but now I am retired and have a little job at a fun park in Southend. I began in the cashier's office but now work in the art and design department where we make the signs and posters and banners.

— *Ernie Robinson©*

22950637 Cpl Ian Rogers

I picked the plum — a posting to a Japanese holiday island

I MADE UP my mind what I wanted to do during my National Service when I was still at Wimborne Grammar School in Dorset, where I was a sergeant-major in the Combined Cadet Force. One day a former pupil came to talk to the seniors. He wore a corporal's stripes and I asked him what he did in the Army. He told me he worked in munitions. He was in Southern Command and travelled to Army units to check that their ammunition was safe. He reckoned it was a good job because he also got to do a lot of rifle shooting. And, living locally, could get home regularly.

This sounded great to me, so when it came time for my call-up I signed on for an extra year knowing I could choose the regiment in which I wanted to serve and the trade. I was determined to get that highly-desirable munitions job that I had set my mind on.

First however, I had to do my square-bashing, where I found that because I had been a senior NCO in the school cadet corps I knew more than most of the instructors. They nicknamed me Sergeant-major, and if a recruit was having difficulties they would say: "Take him behind the billets Sergeant-major and show him how to do it."

But then I was told I was potential officer material and would be put on a unit selection board with the idea of getting a commission. I kept telling them that my aim was to get into munitions and I had no desire to be an officer. But they insisted, which meant even more square-bashing.

After that I had to go before the War Office Selection Board, but of course my heart wasn't in it, so I didn't pass.

So then they said OK, ammunition college, it's a 10-month course. But I had to wait for a place, so now, after basic training and officer training I was stuck in a general office marking exams for military tests.

Even then, it seemed, people were trying to thwart my ambition to get into munitions. "You're doing well here," said the staff-sergeant, who was in the Intelligence Corps. "Why don't you apply for Intelligence ?" I said: "No, I want to be an ammo man."

Eventually I did get on the course, during which I did everything from learning about the various types of fuses to blowing things up.

After 10 months I gave my first choice for posting as Germany. And as a second choice I chose Southern Command, which was where the chap at school who told me about the ammo job had been based. If I got this I would be well placed for getting home from time to time.

What did I get? The Middle East. That didn't sound very interesting, so I was not too keen. Then I found out that someone else on the course had been given the Far East, which sounded a lot more interesting. And he was National Serviceman.

I guessed that he must have been in for more than a year already, so wouldn't have too long to go. So I said to my sergeant that it seemed silly to send a National Serviceman to the Far East. By the time he got there after a six-week journey it would be practically time to turn round and come back.

That, I pointed out, was a waste of money and human resources. I was in for three years and still had a long time to do, so how about a swap?

The sergeant told me I could put the suggestion to the OC. First I spoke to the other soldier, who said he didn't care where he went and was quite happy to change postings with me.

So I went to the OC and suggested that maybe they had made a bit of a faux pas. "OK," he said, "swap over." And that was it. Soon I was aboard the Devonshire en route for the Far East.

There were various jobs to do on the voyage, and mine was Man Overboard duty. I was put in charge of eight soldiers and had to make sure there was always someone on both port and starboard looking over the side in case anyone was taking an accidental swim.

Though I was ostensibly on duty all the time, I had little to do except to take the men tea during the day and cocoa at night.

When we reached the Indian Ocean we hit a terrific electrical storm. The ship was bouncing about like a cork, water was hurled over the decks, the props came out of the sea and the whole thing was vibrating. My lookout men

Larking about in the paddy fields above Kirigushi

had to be tied to the rails, and at night, by the time I got to them with their cocoa I was saturated and the mugs of cocoa more than a little bit salty "Thanks corporal, we've been dying for this," they said as they gulped down what was about 10per cent cocoa and 90per cent seawater.

Eventually we reached the transit camp at Kure in Japan where we had to parade and go up one at a time to collect our transfer papers for wherever we were being posted.

Most of the chaps were sent to Korea, but when the officer came to me he said: "Rogers, you've got the plum. Kirigushi, on the holiday island." I assumed he was being sarcastic, and wondered what I had been landed with.

Next day I was told to take two men and go to the ferry terminal where there was a military launch. I asked if it was going to Kirigushi and they said yes, they came over daily to get mail. "Get in."

We got across the bay to the island of Itajima, and I started to march the two soldiers with me towards some buildings I could see. Coming towards us was an "elderly" chap — probably at least 40 — in shorts, big belly, hat awry. Seeing that he was a sergeant-major, I shouted: "Detail, halt."

The sergeant-major looked at me and said: "Cut all that out. We're one happy family here, and I'm daddy."

My job there was to check the munitions brought in by ship and make sure it was safe, or write it off if necessary to be dumped or blown up.

Though the whole atmosphere was very laid back sometimes there was a lot of work to do and we could be working 72 hours on the trot with minimal breaks.

I worked in a lab in a huge building which was mainly timber surrounded by blast walls. Then it was decided a clerk was needed, and I was detailed. I planned all the work programmes for

hiring tugs and lighters and booking all the ships for sea-dumping of dangerous munitions. I had my own office and a typing pool of Japanese girls.

This was a pretty good number because it was reasonably interesting work and I was earning good money. I got danger money and an overseas allowance. And because we were part of the United Nations there was an additional payment that went into a pool to be used for whatever the major thought appropriate. He usually considered that weekend parties were the most suitable use for this money!

Because there were only about a dozen of us we used the officers mess where we were served by Japanese girls. Girls also cleaned our billets, and we were allowed to travel about in the Army launch. We were completely spoiled. Now I understood why I had been told I had the plum posting.

One Japanese girl in the lab spoke reasonable English, and now and again I would say to her I thought it about time we had a suki-yaki party.

We would hire a hall in the village with the traditional low tables and Japanese food cooked over charcoal burners. Each chap had a girl to instruct him in suki-yaki and feed him.

Officers didn't know about these parties, and when the OC heard about them he was upset that he had never been invited. Of course, we eventually put this right.

After some months I was posted to Hong Kong where I was spoiled again. I was given two Chinese staff and went round to units checking their ammunition reserves and safety precautions etc.

I also had to go to Korea for a couple of months to clear mines and booby traps. We had a 15cwt truck to go up to a huge stark area of nomansland almost in North Korea. It was completely bereft of life, no birds, no animals, nothing. It was a horrible place, and one could tell that death had occurred there.

Finally demob time arrived, and I didn't know what to do. I was enjoying Army life, and debated whether stay on. In the end I opted to quit.

And then...

I wasn't really sure what I wanted to do in Civvy Street. I had returned home to Dorset where my girlfriend — later, my wife — lived next door. One day her father asked what I was thinking of doing. I told him I wasn't really sure, but was considering something like cinema management.

Still enjoying life, 50 years on

He said what about Woolworths? He knew the manager of Woolworths at Poole, and they were looking for someone.

So I went along and saw him, and by Monday I was "an assistant." That meant sweeping floors, clearing rubbish, working in the stockroom, unbaling deliveries, all the menial tasks.

Occasionally I was visited by the area manager, and one day he said he was putting me down as a "recognised man."

"What's that?" I asked. He replied that I would be considered as a potential manager — and to start with would get more money.

That sounded pretty good to me, and soon I was put on floor as a trainee manager and had to wear suit and collar. I had to do absolutely everything, office work, wages, ordering, tax returns, stocktaking, the lot.

Gradually I got promotion, but after seven years with Woolworths I decided to come out and had a series of jobs in the retail business.

My wife and I returned to Dorset and took a VG shop in Corfe Mullen. We also had a couple off-licences and sweet shop, and even a couple years as publicans.

Next I did seven years in a print works before going to college to train as a teacher and taught for 10 years at a secondary school in Poole.

— Ian Rogers©

You have probably heard a great deal about the restrictions of Army discipline. There is nothing to be afraid of in this. Whenever you have a number of young and high-spirited men living and working together, you have got to have control. Discipline is a quality which distinguishes an Army from a mob. It is a quality produced by training according to certain approved rules, which develops in men the habit of working together, and following one leader. You will find also that the "bullying sergeant-major" that some people talk about, doesn't exist in the Army today. Non-commissioned officers are chosen because they are men who can lead.

— From You and the Army, a booklet issued to all NS army conscripts

Learning to use a sten, I nearly killed my training sergeant

I BEGAN my National Service at Topsham Barracks, Exeter straight from the sixth-form at grammar school and was immediately confronted with a whole new vocabulary of words and phrases. The holy trinity of Bullshine, Blanco and Brasso, something euphemistically called Barrack Room Damages and that most dreaded word of all, "jankers."

My bullet nearly hit the sergeant

Within this new lexicon my particular favourite was "drawers, cellular, green" — a very fetching garment!

Additionally, it also appeared to be necessary to preface every word with one beginning with the letter B, C or F. These could be used in any combination, either as an adjective, adverb, noun or verb. Some of our more imaginative sergeants were highly skilled in being able to use all four in the same sentence.

I was selected for potential officer training, during which I was first instructed in the method of burning the pimples out of the toecaps of my boots. This involved a hot spoon heated by a candle, then endless hours of spit and polish.

Knife-like creases in our battledresses were achieved by lining the inside of the crease with soft soap and then pressing with a very hot iron. Any scorch marks created on the uniform were removed by rubbing with a half-crown.

Perhaps the most futile piece of bullshine involved a pair of bootlaces that were never worn. Instead they were polished and coiled around in the fashion of a catherine wheel. The laces were then mounted on pieces of white card about two-inches square and held in place by black thread.

These useless items were then used as star attractions when our kit was laid out for inspection on our beds.

One enterprising conscript actually sent a replica of this fine piece of bull to the Daily Mirror. The newspaper duly published a picture of the offending item, adding a very derogatory comment about the waste of time involved in producing such a useless object.

I remember that the RSM was not at all pleased with the article, and vainly hoped that he could lay his hands on the perpetrator of the perceived crime.

Our training NCOs doubted our parentage and hinted that we resembled "sacks of ordure tied up in the middle with string." One colour-sergeant even appeared to have an unhealthy interest in doing unmentionable things to one's anatomy with a rough pineapple.

The nightmare of inspection of our kit and appearance was always with us. This of course, often gave the CSM the chance to trot out the time-honoured rhetorical question: "Am I hurting you?" followed by: "I should be, I'm standing on your hair. Get it cut."

During our training I was astonished to find that the weapons we were given were so antiquated. American Lee Enfield rifles — relics of WWI — all-but obsolete light machine-guns and the ubiquitous stengun which cost 7s. 6d to manufacture and was worth even less.

I worked in Canada after demob

Once, while I was learning to fire the sten, a round became jammed, and in accordance with procedure in such circumstances I pointed it towards the ground and gave a sharp bang on its side.

This had the desired effect. In a nano-second the weapon fired, the bullet ricocheted off the concrete and winged just a couple of inches past the ear of my pug-nosed training instructor.

He didn't flinch, but merely exclaimed, with the addition of colourful expletives: "You won't shoot me, Roulstone, cos' I'll shoot you first."

As he was a hardened soldier who had been captured by the Chinese while fighting with the Glorious Glosters in Korea, I felt this was a distinct possibility.

We all experienced the pleasures of trips to the firing ranges at Ripon Tor and Broadhembury, throwing hand grenades and digging foxholes on Woodbury Common where we later slept as the rain poured down and the water level rose.

At the conclusion of one exercise when we were all feeling dejected, thoroughly fed up and just wanted to get some rest, the rather effete training officer finished his address to those gathered in front of him by saying: "On your way back to the barracks I want you to laugh and sing, and let there be no limit to your enjoyment."

At the end of potential officer training my inherent subversive and rather cynical nature must have shone through as I didn't progress any farther along the officer trail. Service with the Devonshire Regiment 1st Battalion in Kenya now beckoned.

But at this point Dick Shorland — who was the depot's chief clerk and carried the title of Orderly Room Quartermaster Sergeant (ORQMS) — entered my life. For some long-forgotten reason I had to go to his office, and while I was there he asked if I would like a permanent position "and join the other educated bastards here in the Orderly Room."

Faced with the options of going on night-patrols in the jungle tracking down Mau Mau rebels in darkest Africa or remaining in Exeter, 23 miles from my home town did not present me with too difficult a decision.

So I became a clerk in the Orderly Room where I recall that ORQMS Shorland was a kindly man, and to us an almost father-like figure with a good sense of humour and fair-play.

Apart from the other National Service clerks, the Orderly Room also employed two civilians.

One seemed to have an obsession with washing his hands. Much to our amusement, he told us one day that he bought a hedgehog from a gipsy and was quite upset that it disappeared when he put it in his garden. The other civilian would often return, red-faced and lubricated after a lunchtime beverage, and quietly whisper bets down the phone to his bookmaker.

On intake day the Orderly Room clerks sat at trestle tables in the Education Centre and documented the recruits as they arrived. On one occasion a titled member of the Devonshire gentry was scheduled to appear, and as the newcomers arrived we each tried to guess and identify him as he entered the room. But no-one spotted him. He turned out to be quite an undistinguished personality.

But we did have one old-Etonian with an aristocratic background in the Orderly Room. He was highly intelligent and urbane, but completely impractical. This naturally made him a target for much mickey-taking.

When his turn came to be duty clerk, a job that involved cleaning six offices, he was completely bewildered and at a loss to know what to do.

During the winter months one of the tasks involved clearing out the coalfire grates and lighting them in the morning before the CO, adjutant and the Orderly Room staff arrived. Never having lit a fire in his life, he sought advice from his fellow clerks who advised him to put the coal in the bottom of the grate, sticks above that and the paper on top.

After following these instructions he obviously encountered a few difficulties in getting the fires started! Subsequently, whenever it was his turn as duty clerk, he went into a hardware store in Exeter and bought a packet of fire-lighters.

At the end of the Orderly Room corridor was the office of the adjutant, Captain Donald Stone, an ex-Indian Army officer and like me, a former Torquay Grammar pupil. He was very fair and approachable.

On one occasion the Orderly Room staff felt they were being ordered to do an undue amount of guard duty. We considered that as we had to perform as duty clerk as well, we were being unfairly treated.

It was decided that we would protest at this perceived injustice, and write a letter of protest. As the senior NCO among the protesters, I was called to present the signed document to the adjutant, who later summoned me into his office.

Holding our signed letter in front of him he looked over it at me and said with a wry smile: "I suppose you realise that could be construed as mutiny?"

Then, after a brief and amiable discussion he said he would see what he could do. We were never bothered in quite the same onerous way again.

Working in the Orderly Room was sometimes regarded with a degree of contempt and disdain by other members of the depot permanent staff. The company sergeant-major had a particular dislike of the Orderly Room minions and at the time I was promoted to corporal he came into our office and looked at me contemptuously. "I hate you," he said. And turning to the others in the office said: "I hate you all."

All-ranks dances were held from time-to-time in the barracks gym. They were invariably advertised on Company Orders in a very patronising manner. Invited to attend were "officers and their ladies, other ranks and their women."

191

The dances were usually good fun and provided golden opportunities for us squaddies to encounter the local beauties. On one particular occasion I had a couple of dances with a young lady when she surprised me by asking: "What would you say if I told you I was married?"

As this was obviously a loaded question, I backed off. Not through any self-righteousness, more through naivety and suspecting a whiff of danger.

My concerns were justified when another of the Orderly Room clerks began an association with her. He met her one evening when another clerk and I were with him, and the four of us went to the local swimming pool.

Afterwards we all adjourned to a cafe opposite the baths. As we sat enjoying our coffee a large man appeared in the doorway. In the same instant, the young lady jumped from her seat and bolted past the figure standing by the door. It was her husband, a Royal Marine sergeant.

He immediately confronted my pal and asked him to step outside. This he did, but he had the presence of mind to quickly pick up his cup of coffee and saucer and take it with him, figuring that the sergeant wouldn't hit him while he held something in his hand.

While he resisted the demands of the husband to "put down your cup and come round the corner with me," a heated exchange of words followed.

Eventually he was able to wriggle free from a potentially explosive situation, and we all walked back to barracks giggling and re-living the incident.

Standing Orders required anyone encountering any sign of fire within the barracks to run to the guardroom shouting "Fire, Fire, Fire." The alarm would then be sounded, the fire brigade called and everyone would have to turn out and assemble as quickly as possible on the parade ground.

From time to time, practice fire drills were initiated. and on one such occasion a smoke-bomb was deliberately set off in one of the wooden huts used as a washroom. The smoke-bomb started to emit acrid fumes as the adjutant, the RSM and various NCOs stood by to await developments.

Very soon a soldier called Trooper Cooper, who had been seconded to the depot from the SAS, entered the hut to wash. Seeing an officer present he saluted smartly, and while smoke billowed from the bomb in the corner nonchalantly began his ablutions.

The RSM shouted at him: "What do you think that is?"

"That's a Mark IV Smoke-Bomb, sir" replied Trooper Cooper.

"Well, what are you going to do about it?" barked the RSM.

Trooper Cooper casually went to a nearby bucket of sand and poured it over the smoking bomb and rapidly extinguished it.

Following a very swift interchange with the now apoplectic RSM, Trooper Cooper's feet hardly touched the ground as he doubled frantically to the guardroom screaming "Fire, Fire, Fire!"

In December 1956, on my final day in the Army I made my way to the bus station to catch the bus home for the last time. Somehow, it seemed very odd. An event that we all had been looking forward to had finally arrived for me, but the reality had not yet sunk in.

As I waited for the bus, I was approached by a fellow soldier whom I had vaguely known at the barracks. Someone who had a reputation for scrounging and borrowing money from other comrades. So I wasn't surprised when he asked: "Can you lend me ten bob till pay day?"

I took a certain delight in replying: "Sorry mate, I'm not coming back."

And then...

After Army service I went to train and work in London as a ladies' hairdresser. In 1958 I married Frances, a girl I had known since school-

Topsham Barracks, Exeter in the mid-Fifties

192

days. A couple of years later I was offered a position with Elizabeth Arden in Toronto. So, being adventurous, off we went to Canada.

We returned 10 years later and I opened my own hairdressing business in Devon which I ran until I received an offer I couldn't refuse, and sold out.

At this stage of my life I had had enough of hairdressing and needed a change of direction. I was fortunate in obtaining an interesting position with Royal Mail, and spent the last 20 years of my working life happily in the Exeter and South Devon postal areas. I am now retired but seem to be busier then ever. I have always had an interest in history and have been researching family history as a member of the Devon Family History Society for more than 30 years. Currently I am leader of the South Devon Group.

I am also involved with our local history group, and tutor evening classes in family history at the local grammar school.

My other interests include photography, walking, bird-watching and exploring the backwaters of Devon.

— *Colin Roulstone*©

My views of Topsham Barracks from the Orderly Room. Above, looking towards the main gate from the front office window. Right, rear aspect overlooking the bathhouse (the gabled building on the right) and past the MT garages to the playing fields

I drummed my way through an Army career on two continents

BEFORE call-up I was working at Littlewoods near Liverpool and playing drums six nights a week in a dance band. Pretty tiring for a 16-year-old. At one time during a period of teenage depression I told my father I was going to end it all. His response? "Can I have your ration book?" That was parental sympathy in 1946. I made sure I used every coupon, and snaffled his chocolate bars as well.

Arriving at RAF Cardington in 1948, I was apprehensive about the three months' basic training to come. However, the rebellious mode had started to insert itself into my personality. I was developing as a musician and being flattered for my ability as a drummer. So I felt just a little bit special, and was not looking forward to being just one of the young sprogs in an ill-fitting uniform, being shouted at and treated with contempt by any other sprog with two weeks' longer service than myself.

On arrival, as we all filled in our personal history and indoctrination forms, a pleasant looking flight-sergeant strode into the room. "Attention!" he shouted. We all stood.

"Not that type of attention. Please sit and just listen. Fill out this form concerning any special interests you may have, such as playing football, rugby, hockey, swimming, cricket or even musical skills."

I pricked up my ears. "We have a marching band and a dance band on the station. If you are accepted in any of these sports or musical activities, you will be excused guard duty and fire picquet, but you still have to attend all classes to complete your basic training."

I filled in the form and it was securely clamped on to his clipboard. "Scott?" Nervously I stood up. "Report to the band room at 1700 hours."

The band room was not hard to find. I had already noticed the squeaks, wails and thumps that are the indication of this hive of musical industry anywhere in the world. I hesitated in the open door and the flight-sergeant waved me in. "Can you read this?"

He held a march card up and pointed at a drum on a stand in the corner. "Just do two three-beat rolls, and I'll thump the piano." As I played the

introductory rolls he strode to the piano, and began playing The Thin Red Line. I drummed along with him.

"Good, that's fine. I'll give you the chits for your corporal. You'll only be missing physical training." As I turned to leave he asked: "Have you done any dance band work?"

"Yes, I played in a big band for two years," I replied hopefully. He nodded. "Good, we have dancing five nights a week here and our drummer is posted at the end of the week. Come to the dance Tuesday night and sit in for a few numbers. If you do OK, you'll have the job for the next three months.

Music man. At Catterick Camp in 1948

I arrived back at the green hut, my new home, and noticed my compatriots were all busy folding blankets and placing stuff into their foot lockers under the direction of an immaculately groomed corporal. "What's happening?" I asked the nearest fellow sprog. The corporal swung in my direction. "No talking. And where have you been?"

I pulled the two chits from my pocket. "I don't need to see your last will and testament, just watch what we're doing because by tomorrow morning you will be expected to do the same."

He turned to the airman who was actually performing the tasks required to complete the making of a perfect bed and arranging a perfect foot locker. He gestured to the airman. "Thank you, Olckers. They are just two of the tasks you will perform on a daily basis. Do them as well as Olckers just demonstrated and all will be well, if not — repetition is the best teacher." His eyes swept the room, and as he turned to leave he gestured for me to follow.

Outside the hut he relaxed and sighed. "Chits please," he said pulling a pen from his battledress pocket. He glanced at the pieces of paper, initialled them both and handed them back.

"So, no fire picquet or guard duty. That will make life easier for you, but remember you still have to have everything else up to snuff or I can have your band duties revoked.

"Being in the band does not make you special

194

or give you a position of prestige. To me, you are just another sprog that has difficulty folding a blanket, making a bed, standing erect, shaving, marching and knowing left from right. Understood?"

Feeling quite deflated I slunk back into the confusion of bed-making and locker sorting.

"That's Corporal Truscott," my bedmate informed me. "He comes from Cornwall and I can't understand a word he says when he gets excited."

I laughed. "I had trouble when he wasn't excited." My pal flopped on to his half-made bed, and went on: "Seems a nice bloke though, looks like a movie star, jet black hair, beautiful teeth and brown eyes. Nice body shape and a tailored uniform." I looked surprised at his quick assessment of our corporal.

"I'm a hairdresser, it's very important to read people in my job. My friends call me Flash," and he extended his hand.

"Allan," I replied. "That's no good. You're from Liverpool so I'll call you Scouser."

"Scouser, it is," I grinned and returned to my blanket folding.

The following Tuesday evening found me scrubbed and polished, and with Flash for moral support heading for my audition. I played three arrangements with the band, one of them being Hawaiian War Chant which features a drum solo. I knew it well, and was given the thumbs up.

The dances were Tuesday to Saturday and the pay was 12 shillings a night, which tripled my weekly pay!

"Buddy Rich couldn't have done any better." Flash commended. "You look a bit square though, you need to look a bit more with-it." I frowned at him, my Liverpudlian sensitivities being exposed. "You have to look like Buddy Rich. What you need is a crewcut."

Flash's power of persuasion soon had me seated in the ablutions on an upturned red fire bucket with a towel round my shoulders as Flash, clippers and scissors in hand, slowly circled round me.

"Right," and he began the operation. My head was tilted to the left and to the right, and lastly I was ordered to look up and straight ahead. All I was aware of was the quantity of hair amassing at my feet.

"That's it, what do you think?" He rotated me to face the mirror.

"It looks like an upside-down toothbrush." I gasped. Flash stood back admiring his handi-

work. "Think what you'll save on Brylcreem."

My new hairstyle was admired by all. Within a few days Flash had built a thriving business and performed his skills on nearly all 110 members of B Flight at the modest sum of sixpence a head. Plus he had a sweeper-upper and a shampooer complete with hand-held dryer.

Cpl Truscott huffed and puffed the first time he wandered in to find this thriving business flourishing in Hut 22. Flash used his Cockney charm as he explained that it was done in our own time and everything was cleaned up each evening.

"You have great hair corporal, I could give you the latest style from London. Like this," and Flash produced a glossy photograph from among his equipment. "Plus it's free for first-time customers."

"OK, but if you muck it up there's three sacks of potatoes waiting to be peeled in the cookhouse."

"Good, a shampoo first corporal, get that greasy stuff out of your hair." He placed him in a chair by the sink. Flash winked at us as he rubbed the soap into our corporal's hair. The hair was dried and the cutting began.

"Lots off the top, but little off the sides, moisten, dry, comb and brush, and voilá, the latest London style." He turned his victim to the mirror. "Really hip, corporal. Nothing to fall over your eyes, and great for dancing."

Our corporal looked impressed. "Good work Flash. I like that, and I only came in to get two volunteers for the cookhouse. You and you!" and he pointed at two sprogs lurking and smirking in the background.

Mornings started at 0600 with our corporal pushing open the door and chanting: "Wakey, wakey this wasn't how the British Empire was built, lying abed all hours of the day." This raucous awakening was followed by him banging on our metal bedsteads with his pacestick, and out he would go.

I never heard him swear or yell. He knew just the right words to encourage, shame or berate us, the future saviours of King and Country.

Three months later we graduated. We took up a collection for our corporal and having heard he liked to write, bought the biggest dictionary we could find. And with 110 signatures inscribed, it was my privilege to present it.

Later in the mess after a few beers, I asked our mentor, why he, unlike the other NCOs never swore, screamed or belittled the slower members of our flight.

At home in Victoria

"Well," he said. "If you have to stoop to bullying, threatening and profanity I think you lack one of the basic qualities of a real Englishman, a good vocabulary."

"Plus a good haircut," Flash concluded.

I signed on to stay in the RAF, and played with the RAF Regiment Band at Catterick and then the RAF Central Band. This was a wonderful job, lots of variety and playing in many different locations and situations.

I left the RAF Band when my 10 years were up, and toyed with the idea of joining the Royal Canadian Air Force who were recruiting for their three bands in Canada. The pay was good, plus promotion to sergeant and lots of travel, and I already had friends in the band.

But at the time I wanted to see what musical life as a civilian would be like in the UK. I played as extra percussion with the BBC Concert and Symphony Orchestra, and worked six nights a week at Slough Palais. I did three months in France and Germany, then I had a beautiful summer season in Jersey and a musical at the Saville Theatre. So I was busy.

But one night, after a concert at the Royal Albert Hall I came out into a thick, cold London fog. I walked past Canada House with big posters in the windows showing beautiful snow-clad mountains, blue skies, people on skis and in kayaks. And next to them a notice saying: "Required. Musicians for the Royal Canadian Air Force music service."

Next morning I was knocking on their door, and six months later I was flown to Dorval in Quebec. "You'll be there for a few weeks," I was told. But when I arrived they knew nothing about me, and I was not allowed to leave the base until my documents arrived. So they suggested that I start basic training until the information arrived. Me, aged 29, and 150 18-year-olds. My nickname was Prof, because they thought I knew everything.

There was no compulsory military service in Canada, and only about 100 of the 150 volunteers in our flight were needed. That meant the training was rigorous with recruits being discharged on a daily basis

After a couple of months I was called into the CO's office and told that my documentation had arrived and a band somewhere out west wanted to know what had happened to me!

But by now I was almost a father figure among the recruits, and a lot of the young guys relied on me. So I said I would stay another month until the training was complete.

At the passing-out parade I met a lot of proud parents and was amazed how many of them had heard about me through their offspring. One mum said her boy was amazed when I showed him how to make a bed.

After this we all went our separate ways, and I was posted to the RCAF Edmonton Training Command Band for five years, with lots of travel and new experiences.

And then...

When I left the air force I joined the Edmonton Orchestra, after which, to escape the winters, I moved to Victoria and bought a picture-framing shop. When I sold this I enjoyed myself travelling to South Africa, Rio de Janeiro, Kenya and the Cook Islands

Now I live in Victoria and spend my retirement enjoying the gym and inline and ice skating.

— *Allan Scott©*

22990549 Pte Jim Shaddick

We gave demonstrations for VIPs at the School of Infantry

I WAS BORN, the third of six children, in Budleigh Salterton in Devon. Times were hard, with very little money and hand-me-down clothes. When war came in 1939 things got worse, we couldn't even afford toothpaste and cleaned our teeth with salt. My father, who was too old for active service, was an air-raid warden. Like most people, we had a Morrison shelter in the house, and during the worst of the raids we would all crouch in the shelter.

Budleigh had its share of bombing, and across the street where we lived five houses were demolished and several people killed. The main street was machine-gunned and shows the scars to this day. A lot of incendiary bombs were also dropped in the area

I left school in December 1950, and being very fond of the country I would have loved to have been a farmer. But my family could not afford the agricultural college fees, so I got a job on a small pig farm where they also grew vegetables and apples, and stayed there until call-up.

My papers arrived in 1953 and I had to attend for a medical and assessment in Exeter, where I was passed A1. I applied for the RASC, but was sent to Topsham Barracks in Exeter to join an infantry regiment, the Devons.

We were issued with uniforms and kit the same day and shown to our billet which, much to my surprise was in a brick building. Others were in wooden billets. Our NCO, Cpl Spencer, was respected and well-liked because he was always willing to discuss any problems.

After a further medical and jabs, training began with square-bashing, gym workouts and bar work, climbing ropes and other exercises. This was followed by training stints on Woodbury Common and later a three-day exercise marching there from the depot and back again. We must have looked a sorry sight, still wearing camouflage make-up.

On Salisbury Plain, April 1955

Prior to the exercise we were shown how to strip and clean the .303 rifle. Shooting was not new to me as I had used a shotgun for several years prior to call-up and was a member of Budleigh Salterton Rifle Club. So I enjoyed the rifle shooting on Dartmoor, even though the weather was very bad, with deep snow and biting winds. But I managed to become a marksman on sten, and first-class on rifle and bren. When I returned to battalion HQ in 1955 I shot .22 for either the brigade headquarters or the depot, I can't remember which.

After our passing-out parade we were sent on very welcome leave and at that time I was as fit as anyone. On return from leave we were informed that we were being rebadged Wiltshire Regiment, or we could sign on in the Devons and go to Kenya. I chose not to sign on.

Shortly afterwards we moved to Knook Camp just outside Warminster where the Wiltshire Regiment 1st battalion were stationed as the demonstration battalion for the School of Infantry.

Once we settled in I was put in the S Company machine-gun section as a driver. All drivers and vehicles were kept at Knook with the MT section, and

On parade, third left, at the School of Infantry

Now a collector for the Royal British Legion

the whole of S Company was stationed at the school.

I enjoyed my time at Knook and we spent many days on Salisbury Plain and Imber village either being involved in or watching the demonstrations. These were for the benefit of visiting officers and VIPs of all services. It could be very noisy — the tanks were the worst — and my hearing has been affected since those days. I should have claimed for the damage but was never advised to do so either then or since.

There were bull demos where drivers paraded in best BD, with vehicles cleaned and polished. The tanks, brengun carriers, TCVs, three-ton lorries and various others were then driven up on to the plain in the mud. This continued until mid-1955 when I was posted back to battalion HQ at Exeter as driver to Col Chandler, the brigade colonel.

On days when he did not require the car I drove the depot medical officer, Major (Mrs) McKendrick, and remained at Exeter until my demob in February 1956.

I found National Service to be a thoroughly interesting two years, but on reflection wish I had signed on and gone to Kenya with the Devons.

And then...

Following demob I returned home to Budleigh and pondered my future. I eventually found the firm of J W Palmer — the largest firm in the town — which did everything, house furnishers and removers, building contractors, estate agents, auctioneers, electricals and funeral directors.

I started in the furnishing side, but being tall and strong also helped on the funeral part of the business. This work steadily increased and eventually on the retirement of the funeral director I was offered his job.

Two years later I qualified with a diploma in funeral directing. I represented Devon at the inauguration of the British Institute of Funeral Directors to which I was admitted following my qualifications.

I remained a funeral director for nearly 30 years before retiring in 1999.

After demob I became a member of the Royal British Legion and still collect for the annual Poppy appeal.

— Jim Shaddick©

Few people under the age of 50 seem to be aware that it was predominately National Servicemen who maintained the peace so dearly won by our older brothers. The freedom fought for in war, and won by them for the benefit of all was placed in our hands for safe keeping.

For two whole years of our lives this freedom was taken away from us while we were compelled to take the reins and to guard it for everyone else! But it didn't end there. Our two years with the colours were followed by compulsory evening parades, weekend camps and two whole glorious weeks in summer...and all on service pay!

—From a leaflet by the National Service Veterans Alliance

A hoopla stall scam that earned me my railway fare home

AFTER two weeks' basic training with 185 Battery, Royal Artillery at Oswestry — which included three haircuts in a week — we were transferred to Kinmel Park Camp in Rhyl to train as regimental signallers. During this time we were allowed a pass at weekends, but I couldn't afford the train fare to Southend. Until one day when I went to the fairground in Rhyl.

The man on the hoopla stall asked if I would like to like to earn some money. He said all I had to do was give him sixpence to have a go, and he would give me a shilling change and a cuddly toy to hold up for everyone to see, pretending I had won it. I did four days of this, which gave me my rail fare home.

Before call-up I attended Wentworth High School for Boys in Southend, leaving when I was 15 to work at the Corona soft drinks company. Then I received the dreaded National Service call-up letter.

When I was posted to Kinmel Park I had to do most of my guard duties at the main gate from 4am to 6am. Once I was asleep when someone asked me to let him into the camp. Clearing my eyes I asked who he was, to which he replied he was the boilerman. I asked him not to say anything about my being asleep, and lucky for me he kept his word.

On one occasion a small contingent of us was sent to a place called Transfynnd. Not only was this the bleakest place you could imagine, 300 feet up a mountain, but we had been told to guard it. To this day, I can't imagine why anyone would want to go up there and steal from an Army camp.

The only good thing to come out of it was when I had to do guard duty for

In Cyprus (left) with a pal, and apparently finding something interesting in Reveille

two hours. I had been told that when I passed the kitchen there was always an urn full of rum and cocoa. By the time my shift had finished, I was just about able to get back to my bed.

I was then transferred to Woolwich Barracks for a few weeks which included home leave before being posted to Cyprus. I could not believe the difference when our first meal at Woolwich was all laid out with silver cutlery. I wondered if it was the last meal for the condemned man. We were told to assemble at the airport at Southend, my home town.

It was a dark evening and I all I could see was this massive Dakota aircraft waiting on the runway. I didn't believe it would be able to get off the ground with all of us on it.

We were ordered to remove our boots before we boarded, and I could only think that it was to do with the studs causing a spark. As I had never flown before I started thinking of what could happen if the plane hit trouble, but I was now a soldier and not allowed to show fear.

We touched down in Malta and I wondered why we had to sit on the runway for two hours. Later we were told there had been engine trouble but that it would be fixed. That cheered us up for the final leg to Cyprus where we all arrived safe and sound at Nicosia airport.

We were then coached the short distance to our new home, a tented camp in a village called

Now we're real soldiers. I am fifth from right, front row

Ayios Dhometios. I was now serving with the 188 Radar and Searchlight Battery RA, which had seven radar sites around the island and one troop in the Troodos mountains.

I was assigned to the communications room — a tent — alongside Gunners Griffiths

At Oswestry, with me on the right, front row

and Snow and a trooper from the Royal Horse Guards. This had to be manned day and night.

We were able to get out and view the island, which was a beautiful place especially around Kyrenia when the hills were strewn with poppies. We would stroll down steps which led to the waterfront where we could have a beer or coffee, after which we returned to camp in the back of the truck.

I was on duty one day when the alarm went up and we all had to go to the armoury to collect our weapons, but after a while we were told to stand down. Not long after this we were all confined to camp for about seven months.

We didn't have much entertainment but we did have a Hibbert House Café which did really good English food. And the unit also had a very good band, though I only saw them perform once.

We had to do the occasional guard duty and were told that if anyone suspicious approached we had to shout the English halt, stamata (Greek) and dur (Turkish) three times. I doubt that a terrorist would have given us time to shout the second and third order! Luckily, I never had to face this situation.

Due to being confined to camp, we used to volunteer for patrols or escort duty (mad fools!) but it did help to break the monotony.

Break for a smoke and a cuppa with my Sunny Southend mug

I remember one patrol in a village called Kythrea, a well-known spot for terrorists. When we set off in late afternoon there was a curfew on every village for the residents to be off the streets by 7pm. One at a time we were taken to our dif-

ferent parts of the village armed with our trusty .303s.

As darkness fell my surroundings became surreal, all low roofs, moonlight and a deathly hush except for the sound of my hobnail boots.

The night drew on, and things started playing tricks on my eyes. Passing a church hall I could swear I saw something move in the doorway. Not wanting to take any chances, I stabbed it with my fixed bayonet believing that it was either him or me.

But when nothing moved and my eyes had a chance to focus, I realised that it was actually a big sack.

Then I saw a house that had a large hedge with a dry ditch below it, so I hopped in, relieved to be hidden out of the way. While I was waiting for my patrol time to be up, I heard footsteps. My heart started racing and I saw a figure coming into view. It was the officer, and I just managed to scramble out of the hedge in time.

"Everything OK Smeeton?" he asked. Bravely, I managed to say "no problem, sir" and to my relief that was the end of my patrol duty.

I also patrolled Ledra Street where an officer would deliver early-morning drinks to us on a trade bike

Ledra Street was another hotspot for killings, and one day I saw a suspected terrorist passing us in a Land-Rover. I assume he was being taken to be interrogated. A while later he passed us on the way back with his head bandaged. He must have had a very bad accident!

Our bombardier in charge actually got married in Cyprus. His bride worked in the main telephone exchange at a place called Kykko, along with Jenny and Jasmine with whom we had regular contact. Needless to say they made life a little easier for us. The wedding was absolutely marvellous and was a new experience for me. The downside was that as we were confined to camp we had to be back at 6.30pm, so missed the reception.

When hostilities relaxed, it was a joy to be able now to go out in groups of four, though you can imagine the sight of us in the bars with our Lee Enfields propped against the wall while we were drinking.

There was an unfortunate incident one evening when three of us had our rifles and the other lad had a stengun. We bought kebabs, and all was going well until suddenly the chap with the sten began waving it in the air, causing the magazine to fall out and scatter bullets all over the place. The Military Police were immediately on the scene and asked what had upset him. He replied that he had been short-changed.

The MPs told us to find every bullet, which we did, and get him back to camp as quickly as possible. What a let-off that was. One lost bullet equalled 28 days' detention.

Eventually, we were allowed out in pairs without arms, but we were still apprehensive. One day my mate and I were asked by Rainus, who ran the camp store, if we would like a lift into Nicosia. We got into the car and there were two other lads in it.

As we drove along Rainus asked if we had ever met them before. We said no, and he told us that one of them was the person who handed the gun to the terrorist who had shot a sergeant in Ledra Street. We couldn't get out of the car quickly enough.

We would have to go the ranges for gun training with the .303s, bren and sten. The first problem I had was that I am left-handed, and the bolt action on the .303 is right handed. So it wasn't easy for me.

We were expected to do 10 rounds of rapid fire, and fortunately I was able to do this in the allotted time. After a while we would have to go into the butts to do the scoring while other soldiers fired. Lead was flying everywhere. If someone scored a bullseye we would put up a miss, and vice-versa, which nobody queried!

British Legion standard bearer

I think my proudest moment was marching up to the officer's table to receive my medal. I felt 10-feet tall.

My mother used to send me the week's copies of the Daily Sketch, which would come in a complete set. We also had a wireless rigged up in the communications tent so we could listen to the programmes.

We couldn't get enough of the Goon Show, which was absolutely wonderful.

During this time I had two penfriends, Kathy and Cindy, who corresponded with me throughout my whole service in Cyprus. I even managed to visit Kathy when I had finished in the Army and her parents made my friend and me really welcome.

We left Cyprus, sailing from Limassol on the TS Devonshire. The Royal Horse Guards were at the front and the rest of us to the rear.

We had to march up the gangplank behind the RHGs, but what they hadn't prepared us for was that their marching time was faster than ours, and as we were trying to keep up with them some of us nearly went over the edge.

Each soldier had to do some sort of job for the journey home. We all had to form a queue, and I was behind my mate Griff. He went up to the desk with his chest puffed out and without hesitation said "cookhouse." I told him he must be mad but he replied: "Think of all the food you can have."

When it was my turn I asked what was available and was told deck-cleaning, which meant that after breakfast going round our end of the ship and sweeping it. I said that would do nicely.

Next morning I duly swept the deck and was finished for the day at 9am. When I went down to dinner, I asked Griff how it was going. The poor man was sweating profusely. I told him I would see him later as I was going to rest for the remainder of the day.

We arrived at Southampton and had to go through the dreaded Customs. I was a bit worried because I was carrying about 900 cigarettes, but Griff told me to follow him, and this time he got it spot on. They just asked where we were from and after telling them Cyprus they let us through. Other poor souls weren't so lucky and were made to turn out everything.

We had to report to Connaught Barrracks, Woolwich where we unloaded our kitbags and left them with someone to look after before going to Griff's house in Stepney for the evening.

The following morning I had to report to QM stores for demob. When I got there the queue was massive. But luck was on my side as one of the men noticed me and asked where I had served.

When I told him I had been to Cyprus he asked if I had any cigarettes and said if I gave him a couple of packets he would let me go through. So I went straight up to the front of the queue.

Then he had the cheek to charge me 7s 6d for a missing gasmask, which I had ditched on the way home to lighten my load.

However, soon I was home at last, though it was strange in the sense that I hadn't seemed to have been away. Now I had to adapt with working for a living.

And then...

I had a number of jobs in the building trade, working mainly in concreting gangs, or barrowing and hodding.

But work was not always easy to get, and on one occasion my pal and I walked about 30 miles in deep snow trying to find a job. Then in 1970 I packed it all in to take my two-year-old daughter to Germany for treatment for a cancerous tumour on her jaw, which fortunately was a success.

After this I decided to learn a trade and became a plumber working for Southend Council for 24 years, including three years in management.

I am now enjoying my retirement to the full. My wife and I are members of the Royal British Legion, and I am the standard bearer.

— **Brian Smeeton©**

593133 LAC Derek Threadgall

Memorable times as I helped project the RAF's good name

SOME years ago, I paid a nostalgic visit to the RAF Museum at Hendon. Why nostalgic? Because the museum is based in the hangars of RAF Hendon where I spent my National Service in 1958-59 working with the Air Ministry's promotional/recruiting arm, the James Bond sounding Inf. 1b.

The hangars housed our promotional exhibits including a mock-up aircraft (Provost jet trainer), a portable 16mm cinema in a mock-up fuselage, exhibition stands and equipment, a guided missile (Fairy Firestreak, or was it Fireflash?) and Queen Mary low-loaders to ferry everything to all points of the UK while we travelled by train.

The waves of nostalgia increased when beyond the car park perimeter fence one small building remained intact after evidence of habitation by we RAF sprogs. This undistinguished building was where I and two other LAC projectionists tormented the small team of signwriters with whom we shared this workplace.

Tormentor-in-chief was Glaswegian Eric Graham, ably assisted by Huddersfield ladies' man, Brian Quarmby, sadly no longer with us.

Eric and Brian were firmly established as the unit troublemakers when I joined them, and I quickly learned their art. Unfortunately our projection room, where we checked, edited and serviced films from the RAF library, was at the far end of the hut. Most mornings we ran the gauntlet of irate signwriters inevitably smarting from the pranks played on them the previous day. Yet we were all in the same boat and good friends.

The concrete forecourt in front of the hangars was our football pitch, Projectionists versus Signwriters. We always lost because they had two more players than us.

Hendon was my second stint in the RAF because in 1956 I had been an administrative apprentice based at RAF Credenhill before working as a projectionist at the South Bank Telekinema.

So when I was called up in 1958 basic training at RAF Bridgnorth came quite easy to me.

Then I was posted to Hendon as a projectionist and became part of a small team travelling the country promoting the RAF at public shows.

At the time RAF Hendon was a cosmopolitan camp, which is what made it so interesting. The commanding officer was a wing-commander, which reflected its inevitable downsizing in the RAF's larger scheme of things.

Hendon was also a transit camp. Servicemen from all branches passed through it on their way to and from world trouble spots, the most notorious at that time being Cyprus.

Our NAAFI was always full with these men either returning from a tour of duty, or about to leave on one. Tragically, many of those National Servicemen returned to Hendon a shadow of themselves. Some did not return at all. EOKA terrorists had left their mark.

We never quite knew from day-to-day what was happening in the camp. The defunct airfield was used by film companies, the London Fire Brigade and sundry other organisations to shoot films, test equipment and rehearse doomsday scenarios, etc.

A narrow road separated RAF Hendon from the Hendon Police Training College. And as my cousin was in the latter when I was in the former, we took turns to sample each other's canteen delights.

Inf. 1b was run from the Air Ministry. A government civil servant, Victor Kirby, was assigned to the unit as the Ministry's representative to ensure everything worked as it should. The day-to-day operation of the unit was run by Flight-sergeant Duffield assisted by a small group of NCOs.

One of these was an Irish corporal, who, when we were exhibiting at an Ulster agricultural show, disgraced himself in a Belfast restaurant by asking a young waitress if she would like to be "blasted into maternity by a guided muscle."

Agricultural shows, many Ideal Homes exhibitions, the Royal Tournament and Battle of Britain anniversary shows were among the events we attended to publicise the pleasures of life in the RAF.

For much of the time we lived out of suitcases, spending more time away from camp than we did in it. On arrival in yet another town, our first port of call was the local RAF recruiting office. They had prior notice of our arrival and were requested by Air Ministry to look after us and, as we were all young men, to "keep an eye on us."

With their help we found digs, for which we were paid subsistence money. Theoretically, the money was enough to find good-quality accommodation. In practice, we found the cheapest digs and kept the balance. This did not always work to our advantage as proved by an experience in Derby.

At RAF Hendon (left) with three other projectionists

Having found the cheapest digs we could, we were shown a large room containing six beds positioned on a sloping floor. We quickly laid claim to three beds, mine being at the bottom of the slope. Eric and Brian took two beds opposite mine. We were told that we would be sharing the room with two Irish labourers, which caused some consternation in our ranks.

I placed my slippers on the floor by my bed ready for the morning. The two labourers arrived in the room in paralytic mode after lights out. One started undressing by the bed next to mine and then, in the dark, I heard the dreaded sound of water gently cascading from his person on to the floor. I forgot that the floor sloped. Suffice to say that next morning my slippers had disintegrated and were no more.

But this was just one of my many memorable experiences while serving Queen and Country. Here are some of the others.

Schoolboys Own Exhibition at Earls Court.
The morning countdown over the PA system prior to opening the doors was: "Three, two, one — let the little bastards in."

As the hordes swarmed in, the RAF stand was the first they saw. In no time a group had picked up our eight-feet long missile and run away with it, hotly pursued by the recruiting officer.

We also made the mistake of not disabling the rudder controls in our Provost jet, which the kiddies were allowed to sit in for a few seconds. One day one urchin waited until he saw the recruiting officer in the cockpit mirror sauntering past the aircraft tail. Then he hit the rudder controls. Exit one unconscious recruiting officer en route to hospital. Also, exit one urchin from cockpit twice as fast as he entered it.

Derby Ideal Homes.
A rather staid show was enlivened when we stuck a page torn from a Health and Efficiency nudist magazine on to the end of the barrel of a fieldgun on the Army stand. It took them three hours to work out why their exhibit was so popular!

We also enjoyed the delights of Derby's public baths. For 6d. (2.5p) one was given soap and towel and shown to a vacant bath surrounded by dozens of others, most of which contained male bodies scrubbing and singing. This huge echoing room reminded me of the sheep pens at an agricultural show.

A young man ran the hot water and tested it with his highly-tuned heat-sensitive elbow for the right temperature before allowing one into the bath. No health and safety in those days!

Lewis's store, Manchester.
We had two 16mm projectors, a Bell and Howell and a French Debrie. For this show we took the Bell and Howell machine. In the confined space of our projection room at the rear of our aircraft fuselage cinema, the heat from the projector's 1000-watt lamp was ideal for making toast. This was achieved by placing a slice of bread across the grille protecting the lamp housing. In no time we had a slice of toast with three rather burnt lines across it. Add butter and jam and this snack helped allay the monotony of continually showing a film of low-level flight to the audience sitting inside the fuselage.

Battle of Britain Anniversary, Brighton.
When the cinema was not required at a show, we projectionists were recruited to help man the stand. This was the case at the Brighton show shortly after the Russians had sent a monkey into space.

I was looking after an Armstrong-Siddeley Sapphire jet engine, a cutaway model with Perspex over the open section in which one could see the innards of the engine. A little old lady slowly wandered up to the engine, looked around it, then came over to me. "Young man. Where do they put the monkey?"

Yorkshire Ideal Homes, Bradford.
The show organisers paid us to clean up the site each day after it closed. This took us around four hours each night. A bonus was the pressure cooker demonstrator leaving us the food cooked that day. Other food and drink exhibitors fol-

lowed his admirable gesture. So long as we were ready on the stand when the show opened to the public no-one minded our unofficial arrangement.

RAF recruiting promotion, Jersey.

Highlight of this show was an invitation to attend a party given by a very rich Yorkshireman to celebrate his daughter's engagement to a young RAF officer. The retired father owned a brewery and enjoyed an income of some £9,000 a week (in 1958).

His Jersey mansion was straight out of Hollywood, and included a huge garage with six top-of-the-range luxury cars, including a Rolls-Royce. None of us had seen such riches and opulence, yet he, his wife and daughter were charm personified. A great evening.

It was not unusual for us to arrive back in camp in the early hours of a morning. As our billets were opposite the cookhouse, we were given food and drink before retiring to bed.

In many respects, Inf.1b was a law unto itself at Hendon. We were tucked away on the far side of the airfield well away from the camp headquarters building. The only times we saw our wing-commander was when he called a snap inspection parade to keep us on our toes (which was not very often) or one or more of us was hauled before him and his adjutant to answer a charge made by a girl's parents concerning her recent pregnancy.

Unfortunately, on one embarrassing occasion I had that rather dubious honour. I denied the charge — twice, because the adjutant wanted everything at least in duplicate. But in any case, the charge was untrue.

Admittedly that kind of accusation was one of the occupational hazards of our job, considering that the quality pecking order for the many girls in the UK looking for dates with a British uniform was first RAF, second Navy and third Army.

At the time a leading-aircrafts-man was the equivalent of a c i v i l i a n

Now I talk and write about cinema history

roadsweeper in terms of promo-tional prospects. Projectionists — a very late edition to the RAF trade ladder — were both misunderstood and considered far too thick to be given any real responsibility. Therefore our promotion prospects began and finished with LAC.

So we languished in our projection room annoying the signwriters and showing occasional naughty films to ourselves.

Hardly surprising then, that with no promotion from which to be demoted, our activities bordered on the anarchic. My *piece de resistance* in this respect, which received grudging admiration from Eric and Brian (but not from Flt-sgt Duffield), was to get the undivided attention of a Brighton nymphomaniac when manning our stand in Hove.

Her mother sussed me out first, before launching her daughter on a pre-emptive strike.

Back at Hendon after the show, Mr Duffield paid a rare visit to our hidey-hole, and handed me a letter. A perfumed envelope covered in red lipstick kisses. It had a Brighton postmark. No prizes for guessing who sent that. Even the signwriters were impressed.

And then...

After my RAF service I worked on commercial film distribution with the Rank Organisation before spending five years in studio management at Shepperton Studios. I was responsible for transportation when location shooting was required on such films as Lawrence of Arabia, Dr Strangelove, Day of the Triffids and many others.

Later I was third assistant director on Stanley Baker's The Sands of the Kalahari, after which I formed a company producing documentaries.

I have also run a public relations company and written for a number of magazines and other publications. I have organised charity events, and before retiring in 2003 was chief executive (UK/Ireland) for an international property company based in Spain. Now I give talks and write about cinema history.

I have visited RAF Hendon on one or two occasions over the last 40-odd years. Each time I have smiled at the memories of the camp, the shows and my personal nympho from Brighton whose perfumed and lipstick-covered envelope I still have. Perhaps one day I may have an opportunity to re-unite the envelope with its sender.

— Derek Threadgall©

My drop on Suez with a camera opened the way to a new career

STAND UP. Prepare for action. That command by the RAF dispatcher, shouted above the roar of the four Bristol Hercules engines of Transport Command's Handley Hastings aircraft would have at the best of times disturbed the butterflies in my stomach. But this time it was different. This time it was not a practice jump. This time it was for real. The 3rd battalion The Parachute Regiment were about to be launched into harm's way on the behest of Prime Minister Anthony Eden to capture the airfield at El Gamil, Port Said.

I was taking part in Operation Musketeer, which needed the element of total surprise to succeed. All 660 men had to be on the ground and ready for action within four and a half minutes.

At 0415 hours on November 5 1956, we parachuted in. The drop was conducted under fire and cost us four killed and three officers and 29 men wounded.

But what was an East End kid doing there in the first place? After leaving school I had been working in a tailoring sweatshop training as a tailor's cutter and following in a family tradition.

My great-grandfather, David Lieb Halevi Wasserman arrived from Poland in 1890 and was a master tailor. His son Samuel was also a master tailor, and my father David was a skilled tailor's cutter. But I had other plans and was about to break the mould.

I was just 17 and knew that within a year I could be serving in any of the armed forces around the globe from Germany, Aden or even Hong Kong. That seemed exciting. But then, of course, it could be two years in Catterick as a cook. Not so romantic.

So I decided to buck the system. In April 1954 I walked into the Army recruiting office in Wanstead and volunteered to join the Parachute Regiment.

Why the Parachute Regiment? Well, for two reasons, both of which look ridiculous 50 years on.

One, my Uncle Harry had served in 9 Para and taken part in the D-Day landings. They had to capture the German Battery at Merville, which they did with only a quarter of the battalion, the rest having been dropped miles away from their objective. A truly heroic feat, which made a great impression on me.

Two, in 1953 I saw the film The Red Beret starring Alan Ladd, and I fancied myself in that distinctive headgear.

Thus, in June 1954 I found myself on a train journeying to Aldershot with orders to report to the Airborne Forces Depot at Maida Barracks.

I was directed with other recruits to a barrack room and ordered to await instructions. We all sat around on the beds for half an hour before we were alerted by the sound of hobnails on flagstones. Then somebody marched into the room.

That "Somebody" was about five foot five, and ramrod straight. He wore a red sash across his battledress, which was adorned with a row of medal ribbons and three stripes. He carried a pace-stick under his arm and held a clip-board in his hand. Sergeant Nick Carter MM.

"Right you lot. I am your platoon sergeant. When I call your name, stand up and shout "Yes sergeant."

Those who have done time in the services will know that lists are always called out in alphabetical order, and always starting with A, never Z.

So if you are a Zimmerman or even Waterman, you sometimes have a long wait.

Eventually the sergeant had nearly run out of names, and reached Waterman, who was in full Teddy Boy regalia with fashionable DA/Tony Curtis haircut. I jumped to my feet and shouted "Yes Sergeant" as loud as I could, anxious to make a good first impression.

Sgt Carter MM looked up, his face turning a shade of scarlet that matched his red beret. "Get those f---g silly clothes off and get into something proper."

Two hours later I was dressed in Army denims two sizes too big, and sported a short back and sides that made me look like an oven-ready turkey.

This was my introduction to three life-changing years in the Parachute Regiment.

The next 10 weeks was a very steep learning

curve. As a teenager I thought I was fit, being a keen cyclist, but I quickly found out just how unfit I was. Daily road walk-and-runs of about five miles and visits to the assault course soon changed that.

How to strip down a brengun and put it back together blindfolded. Shooting practice on Ash Ranges where I became a marksman and was allowed to wear a crossed rifle badge on my uniform. The rules of camouflage — shape, shine, shadow and silhouette. All this seemed to me what soldiering should be all about.

But the "bull' side of training was a pain in the backside. Having to make up your bed blankets into a box shape and lay out your kit every day was a bore.

Spit and polish on your so-called "best boots" so that you could see your face in them, seemed an unnecessary chore. We even had to shine the top of our tin of Cherry Blossom boot polish. And with no mother there to do it for us, we learned how to iron our clothes properly.

The argument for it was of course, it gave you pride in your appearance.

And by the time we had finished basic training and had our passing out parade, we truly believed that by wearing the coveted Red Beret we were invincible.

But. And a big but…we still had to prove ourselves by passing the dreaded P Company selection and then the parachute course at RAF Abingdon before being accepted into the regiment as fully trained airborne soldiers.

In P Company volunteers from other units joined us, including marines, the medical corps, engineers and drivers. All hoping to make it into the 16 Para Brigade.

We were formed into 10-man squads and each given a number which was painted on our helmets. These we had to wear at all times so our instructors — all hand-picked from the

I am here front row right with my Para mates

Army Physical Training Corps — could keep tabs on us. Ranks were mixed. NCOs and officers all had to perform as well as us "Toms."

The next two weeks were the hardest I was ever going to experience in my life before or since. The course was designed to weed out those who could not make the grade or did not have the will to succeed.

From the start it was impressed on us that our squad was the most important single item in our lives.

Everything we did we did as a squad and we had to finish the tasks with the squad intact, leaving no man behind. This included all our road-runs, assault courses and the most trying of all tests, the dreaded log race.

Imagine a telegraph pole, pulled by 10 men attached to it by individual ropes, and a two-mile cross-country run up and down a steep hill in ankle-deep mud. That was the log race. And we had to finish with all our team.

My squad included a major and CSM both from the Royal Army Medical Corps and both quite a bit older than the average Airborne recruit. So they were not the fittest among us.

They gave it their best shot but couldn't keep up without help. In consequence after the first mile we had two bodies to help over the terrain as well as the heavy pole.

I honestly can't remember much about the last half mile except a red haze and lungs that seemed about to burst. I was counting one, two, three, four, one, two, three, four over and over again in my head and trying to make my legs keep up with the count. We made it with the squad intact.

This story has an interesting sequel because the RAMC major was a surgeon, and two years later he was to accompany us to Port Said where he did sterling work operating on our wounded in a makeshift operating theatre on the airfield. So I was glad to have played some small part in helping him to pass into 16 Para Brigade.

The two weeks of P Company came to an end. We were paraded into the cinema to be told who had made the grade. There were three possibilities, a pass, a fail, or for those who had what it takes but perhaps could be fitter, a re-course.

I had already made up my mind that if offered a re-course I would not accept it. I just couldn't face those two horrendous weeks again.

The wait was agony. But as my helmet number was two, I was soon put out of my misery. Pass.

The next step was what it was all about. Parachuting. After a short leave we were off to the RAF Parachute School at Abingdon.

The parachute course lasted a month, during which, to earn our coveted "wings," we had to complete eight jumps.

For the first two weeks we jumped off ramps, swung from swings and leaped

Circled here with my fellow Paratroop recruits

from a platform about five metres high with only a fan to break our fall. Some considered this more frightening than making an actual jump.

It was about then that I faced the 64,000 dollar question, one I always hoped I would not be asked. Cpl Bevin, one of the parachute jump instructors said: "You are not seventeen and a half, are you?"

Now is the time for a confession. The minimum age one could volunteer for Army service was then 17 and six months. In my eagerness to get my time over as soon as possible I gave my date of birth as December 10 1936, though my correct birthday was May 20 1937. My heart sank at the question. I had gone through too much to be found out just before I had finished my parachute training.

Ducking the answer with a reply to the effect: "Of course I am. How else could I have got this far?" I walked away, and that was the last I heard about it. Consequently I have Cpl Bevin to thank for my being able to write this account of life in the Paras.

However, the day came for our first balloon jump. A cage suspended under the balloon took four parachutists and the dispatcher. When the

anchor cable reached about 800ft the balloon came to an abrupt halt and the dispatcher took the bar away from the door. One thing immediately struck you. How quiet it was. No engine noise, just the breathing of your fellow trainees

"Number one stand in the door." That broke the silence. I shuffled forward not daring to look down. "Go."

One and a half seconds later I looked up and there was the beautiful 28ft of nylon which was the X- type parachute.

What I didn't know at the time was that this was to be my first parachute jump of over 2,000, and I would still be parachuting into the 1980s.

Before our eighth and final jump at the parachute school, our jump-master made a formal announcement: "This is the last jump which you will be able to refuse. Once qualified and been given your wings, to refuse will be a court martial offence."

Once we were presented with our wings — a very proud moment — we were told where we would be deployed within 16 Para Brigade.

Most of us from 20 platoon at AFD were posted to 3 Para, and with half a dozen others I was allocated to the signal platoon.

The year 1955 was a year of exercises, guard duties and a major review of 16 Para Brigade by the Duke of Edinburgh. Luckily I was on other duties so missed all the bull and rehearsals such an event entails.

But 1956 was very different. Jordon's King Hussein had sacked the commander of the Arab Legion, Glubb Pasha (Sir John Bagot Glubb KCB, CMG, DSO, OBE, MC). This, according to the Government put British lives and property in jeopardy.

So 1 Para and 3 Para were flown to Cyprus in case they were needed in Jordan to protect the "British lives and property."

The Jordon crisis dissi-

This was our para passing out group. I am on the left, back row (circled)

pated, but in Cyprus there was a more serious problem, EOKA. So 1 and 3 Para remained there to combat the "terrorists" who wanted union with Greece, spending many weeks yomping over the Troodos Mountains searching for them and their elusive leader, General Grivas. As the military in Cyprus were not expecting us, we were not allocated a barracks and had to make do with four-man tents. These were erected on a piece of virgin scrubland near Nicosia airfield and were our home for nearly a year.

There were no toilets, ablutions, cookhouse or canteen. So all these had to be built, mainly by our own pioneer section.

In the pioneer section was Cpl Joe Groot, an expert at digging deep trench latrines. These were 12-seaters built over a trench about two metres deep, normally down-wind from the main camp. To keep them clean and sterile quicklime was used, but sometimes petrol was poured down and set alight to do the same job.

On one occasion Joe had poured in the petrol but had run out of matches, so he popped off to get some. In the meantime somebody had been taken short and settled down to do the necessary. Joe returned and threw a lighted match into the trench. You can well imagine the result!

While in Cyprus I was part of a party that surrounded the Palace of Archbishop Makarios, arrested him and took him to Nicosia airport to be put on a plane to be exiled in the Seychelles.

Then in the summer events took an interesting turn. Col Gamal Abdul Nasser, the Egyptian president, nationalised (seized) the Suez Canal.

This hit British economic and military interests in the region and the Government decided on military intervention to avoid the complete collapse of British prestige there, and to regain control of the Canal. And 3 Para were to play a major part in the action.

But there was a problem. We hadn't parachuted for nearly a year. So very quickly we were airlifted back to the UK and did a couple of exercises as a battalion on Salisbury Plain. And there was a surprise waiting for us in Aldershot.

Fellow battalion members who had finished their service and to whom we had said our goodbyes weeks before, were back to boost our ranks. They were not looking too pleased. Among the many former National Servicemen was one of my fellow squad members from P Company and Parachute School, Cpl John Wood. He had enlisted to the Paras via The

Sherwood Foresters and was to die as a result of the Suez action.

A couple of weeks later we were back in Cyprus and once again looking for EOKA in the mountains. But an attack aimed at regaining control of the Suez Canal was imminent.

And this brings me to Father Casey, 3 Para's Roman Catholic padre, a worldly-wise Irishman who was "one of the bhoys." Indeed, he had to pass P Company and the Parachute School to serve with us. While we were in the Troodos he came round to administer to the Catholics among us.

I must tell you here that although on my paternal side my grandparents were Polish Jews, on my mother's side they were Irish Catholics. The maternal side won. I was brought up a Catholic.

So Fr Casey arrived to where we were sleeping under the stars and got all the Catholics together saying: "Well boys, in the next few days we might being going into harm's way. So wouldn't it be a good idea to make peace with your Maker and go to confession?"

Though I had been taught by nuns and had even done a stint as an altar boy, I had long given up my faith. But it would be a good idea to take out insurance. Just in case.

I found myself kneeling on one side of an olive tree with Fr Casey on the other — very biblical.

"Bless me father for I have sinned."

"How long since your last confession my son?"

There's a conundrum, I thought. Just how long was it?

"About seven years."

"Well, everything except rape and murder?" said he.

"That's about it."

"Three Hail Fathers and two Hail Mary's and a good act of contrition. God bless you my son."

With that I went on my way absolved.

We were recalled to our camp in Nicosia, and it was sealed. No unauthorised entry or exit. The battalion was gathered on the parade square for a briefing before our drop into Egypt.

The CO, Col Paul Crook, said that casualties on the drop zone were expected to be as high as 25per cent.

That figure worried me. There were four in our tent. That meant there was a good chance one of us would become a casualty. And what did casualty mean anyway? Anything from a flesh

Kitted out (right) for the Suez drop with Joe Groot

wound to a fatality?

News came that the attack on the airfield at El Gamil, Operation Musketeer, would be on Monday, November 5. Two days' time. What a hive of activity that stirred up.

Training on how to exit a Hastings with 30 parachutists, all with heavy weapon containers, within 20 seconds. Packing the weapon containers with all we needed to make us a fighting force immediately on landing.

My weapons container weighed in the region of 100lbs and contained a 38-Set, the standard inter-company battalion wireless set, spare batteries for same, several 36 grenades, extra 2inch mortar ammunition, 9mm ammunition for my Browning pistol, a lightweight blanket and some field dressings.

I was to be number three from the starboard door, which meant I didn't have to drag my heavy load far before exiting the aircraft. In front of me was Major Geoff Norton and Colour-sergeant "Dusky" Graves. Geoff Norton was Support Company OC, and I was his signaller.

On Monday morning, November 5 we had breakfast at 1am and made the short drive to Nicosia airfield. Parking close to our Hastings aircraft, we lined up in stick order with number 15 ready to emplane first.

As I reached the steps up to the Hastings, a voice above me said: "Let me give you a hand with that son." It was the RAF aircrew signaller who on this occasion was doubling as a dispatcher because not enough fully-trained PJIs were available.

He looked just like my grandfather, silver hair, round ruddy face and a

friendly smile. Bending down he took hold of my weapon container and attempted to lift into the aircraft. "F---g hell! What have you got in there? The kitchen sink?"

"No just some presents for Nasser," I replied and took my seat three places from the starboard door. I was going to be dispatched into battle by my grandad?

"Stand up and prepare for action." That brought us all to our feet. There go those butterflies again.

The doors were taken off both sides of the aircraft and the roar of engine noise flooded into the fuselage. We hooked the weapon containers to parachute harnesses.

"Tell off for equipment check" We had practised this a dozen times. Fifteen OK! Fourteen OK! Thirteen OK! You shouted loud enough to be heard by the dispatchers near the door, at the same time slapping the man in front on the shoulder. "Three OK!" I shouted when it got to me, and hit Dusky Graves. "Two OK!" he replied and slapped Geoff Norton. "One OK! Starboard stick OK!"

We were ready. All we needed now was the red "stand by" and then the green "go" light. The engines throttled back. Any moment now. Red on!

Suddenly the aircraft bucked and side-slipped. We had run into anti-aircraft fire from guns positioned at the end of the runway. Dusky Graves fell backwards over the static line cables and was struggling to get up, helped by the dispatcher. I was still holding his static line strop. You are responsible for the strop of the man in front and have to make sure it runs clear as he goes through the door.

Green on. Go. But the dispatcher was still helping Dusky up, and hadn't seen the green.

Aircraft lined up ready for take-off and the drop into Suez

210

Bloody Hell, come on let's go, was going through my head.

Geoff Norton went through the door followed by Dusky, who was still trying to get upright. I threw his strop clear and moved to the door as fast as I could, right foot leading.

Hand on door, a push and I was into the slipstream. Phew! That for a moment was very hairy.

Now I was out and under an open canopy. But hell. I had twists. Kick out of them fast! At the same time pull the leg strap pin that's holding down my container and then the two quick releases, which let the container fall free to the end of the rope.

All done. Good. Now, where am I? And what's that noise?

It was the sound of war, and I was still a couple of hundred feet above the ground being shot at not just by rifles but the anti-aircraft guns that almost caused havoc in our aircraft. Geoff Norton, just in front of me had several of his rigging lines severed.

Our MO, Sandy Cavenagh was injured in the eye. Gillespie from C Company was shot in the groin. One sapper had so much of his canopy shot away that he broke both legs on landing. All this before we had even landed.

Thank God our jump altitude was brought down to 600feet and not the usual thousand. Less time in the air to be shot at.

Hardly any wind drift, and my landing was so light I almost did a stand-up. This sometimes happens when you jump with a weapons container. It hits the ground first and the canopy then has less weight and slows a little.

I took stock of where I was and looked for my objective. I was almost opposite the control tower and in the middle of the DZ.

Right, first thing open my container and get my wireless working. It was wrapped in my lightweight blanket (the only bedding I had) which I removed and put in the sand next to me. Straight into some donkey shit. Great! What a good start.

I took my 9mm out of my smock, cocked it and put it in the holster on my belt with safety catch on. Can't see anybody to shoot at anyway. All the incoming fire is from at least 200 yards away, and the rifle companies will deal with that. It's their job and they're getting down to it already, judging from the brengun fire I can hear.

My job was to establish communication. But first I

My photographs which were published around the world. The helicopter in the picture below is hovering just above the airfield control tower

took out my camera — which I should not have had with me — for some quick exposures of the parachutes, still landing around me, and the heavy drop with their large parachutes blossoming out as they left the aircraft.

A figure I recognise comes towards me. It's George Tawse, a Scot and fellow signal platoon buddy. He's holding his arm. "I think I've been shot" he exclaimed. I take a look. Just a small hole in his sleeve and not much blood and little pain but he can't move his arm.

"Better go over to the Regimental Aid Post," I suggested, which I knew was being set up near the control tower.

"Good luck," I said as he made his way there. Unfortunately, though I didn't think it was a bad wound, the bullet, which had entered at the elbow, was deflected up his arm severing muscle, arteries and nerve tissue on the way. Despite great work under less than ideal conditions at the RAP, George was to lose his arm later.

As I was crossing the DZ there were sounds of explosions behind me. Rockets!

Everybody dived for cover, which was virtually nil on such a flat open airfield. A heavy-drop weapons container was lying near me waiting to be opened by the DZ clearance party. I dived behind it and held my hands over my ears waiting for the next salvo to land. Fifty yards the other side of me the earth erupted as the rockets landed, and I was horrified to find I had taken shelter behind a container of mortar ammunition.

Arriving at the east side of the DZ I found Dusky Graves who was already organising our defence. "Dig in there" he commanded. We needed no second telling. Now I was beginning to appreciate the many exercises on Salisbury plain when, whenever we stopped were told to dig in.

Here, there was no hesitation. We were digging like demented gophers only to find that two feet down we struck water. Unable to go deeper we built ramparts to give cover.

Soon the radio net was up and running and I could hear the traffic from B Company to control. They were getting the worst of the Egyptian resistance having landed on the Port Said side of the DZ and taking most of the casualties, including the company commander, Major Dick Stevens.

Taffy Williams, with whom I shared a tent, should have been their wireless operator, but I didn't recognise the voice on the B Company set. The prophetic 25 per cent casualty figure

had proved to be correct.

The Regiment Aid Post medics, anaesthetist and surgeon soon had an operating theatre up and running in a garage behind the control tower and were getting their first clients. Within the hour they were running out of stretchers as more and more wounded were brought in.

This photograph of me, taken by Joe Waldorf, was given to my mother

Later in the day a French Dakota landed, though the odd mortar was still falling on the airfield. I went over to the Command Centre for spare batteries just in time to help load some of our wounded into the Dak.

There on stretchers were two of my mates, National Service recalled reservist, Cpl John Wood and tent-mate Taffy Williams. John had a chest wound but seemed quite alert, but Taffy had extensive shrapnel wounds in the back and looked the worse of the two.

In the event Taffy's wounds were superficial but John later suffered from severe shock and died the next day in Cyprus. My other wounded signal platoon buddy, George Tawes walked into the Dak unaided.

By mid-afternoon most resistance around the airfield had ceased and we then did what we had all been waiting for — and probably would have done sooner but had been ordered not to. We put on our distinctive red berets. Now we were true Red Devils. By nightfall word got around that the commander of Port Said had made approaches for a surrender.

Next day several members of the media arrived by air. One was photographer Joe Waldorf from Illustrated Magazine. He came over to our positions and took photographs. Seeing that I was carrying a camera he inquired if I had taken any images the day before. When I answered in the affirmative he offered to take my films back to the UK for development.

I handed him my rolls of film with no idea that this would start a chain of events that was to affect my whole life.

I thought no more of the incident, as I had other more important things on my mind.

Cut to 33 Montgomery Crescent, Romford — my home address — a few days later.

My mother answered a knock on the door to

212

Battle over. My shooting is now with a camera

find a young lady who introduced herself as the assistant to the editor of Illustrated magazine. She handed over a letter from the editor.

In it he explained how Waldorf had met me and had taken the films back to London. He wanted permission to publish the photographs in the next issue of the magazine. He assured my mother that when the photographer left me I was safe, well and in good spirits. And he sent my mother two copies of a photograph Waldorf had taken of me on the DZ.

My mother gave her consent for the images to be published and the result was four pages of photographs in the November 17 issue of Illustrated.

The pictures were the first photographs of mine to be published and syndicated worldwide. Of course, I should never have taken a camera into action, and I had to answer for this later. I was put on orders but no action was taken because I think that secretly the high-ups were rather pleased with the publicity.

Two weeks later, after the UN had stepped in and stopped hostilities we found ourselves aboard the New Australia on our way back to Cyprus.

And then...

That chance meeting with Waldorf and the publication of my photographs changed the direction of my life. After demob, when I was still only 19, instead of resuming a career as a tailor's cutter I worked for a photographic agency. By the early Sixties I was a freelance, contributing pictures almost exclusively to the Daily Sketch during the week and the Sunday Mirror on Sunday. I was British Sports Photographer of the Year in 1974. I also won the sports section of the British National Press Awards in 1971, and the features award in the World Press Photographic Competition in 1972.

Many of my successful pictures were taken on a helmet-mounted camera after I took up skydiving in 1964.

By the time I packed up my parachute for the last time in the mid-Eighties I had made more than 2,500 skydives and represented Great Britain four times in world championships, twice as team leader

In 1992, after selling a corporate video production company I had established I moved to Spain and started a holiday company catering exclusively for photographers. I am now based in permanently in Spain.

My medals, the General Service Medal and Bar for Cyprus and Suez are now in the Airborne Forces Museum next to VCs and MMs earned during two world wars and the Falklands. They were requested by Geoff Norton, the officer with me on the Suez drop, who became curator of the museum.

— David Waterman©

Unloading an anti-tank gun

The signal platoon in Cyprus. I am on the extreme right

23011837 Cpl Eric Watts

I drew the sergeant-major's pay and became his money-lender

WHAT the hell has happened? That was my first reaction on arrival at the Devonshire Regiment headquarters in Exeter on the first day of my National Service. But of course we were not expected to think, or indeed to do anything other than follow orders. I remember going on the first day to the CQMS store for my kit After that came The Haircut. Then the horrors of square-bashing.

Within days I was opted out of Salamanca platoon to join the potential officers' squad, and the daily programme of drill, weapon training, exercises, assault courses and more drill became even more horrific.

Like the majority of our squad I failed to get a National Service commission and there was no way I was going to sign on for three years there and then in order to have another go.

Eventually, after 10 weeks of square-bashing, I was taken on to the permanent staff at the barracks to work in the company office as potential officers clerk and company clerk under CSM Brooks.

As each intake arrived I had to take all the potential officers and do their form-filling and then their reports leading up to the interview at Brigade HQ before they went off to the War Office Selection Board.

My memories of company office are of so much waste of time, having to type company orders *Retired, and a* every day, supervise the cleaning *keen Rotarian* of the building by those unfortunate enough to be on fatigues and attending to all the demands of the company commander.

The sergeant-major had a deserved reputation as a hard man on the barrack square. But there was a good side to him as well.

He was a hopeless manager of money and I used to draw his pay for him every fortnight, pay back to myself what he had borrowed during that time, and then give him the balance.

At times there was little to give back, which led to him borrowing from me yet again. But when I was demobbed I made sure he did not owe me anything.

Now and again we were asked to undertake specific duties and training. I landed the job of

representing the barracks NAAFI at national level and used to attend conferences in London. Being a mere corporal among many commissioned representatives was a quite daunting experience.

I was also selected to train as a cinema projectionist — something which came eventually to have a very special significance in my life.

The course at Bulford Camp was taken by a civilian who was the brother of actress Flora Robson. Once I had qualified I had the job of showing all the training films at the barracks, and also at Home Guard meetings throughout East Devon. One day in January 1955 I had to put on a film for the Home Guard at Budleigh Salterton, and was driven there in a three-ton Army truck by Ron Juniper from the MT section. When the equipment was unloaded Ron asked if he could go off for a couple of hours while I showed the film.

Early days in uniform

When he returned he said: "Hey corp, can we go back to this youth club I press-ganged my way into? Stacks of maids there."

And so we did, and when the youth club ended that evening several student nurses who had been there asked if they could have a lift back to the hospital because it was raining.

Naturally I agreed, but as I did not know where the hospital was, I said one of them would need to sit with me to show the way. As we turned the truck in the hospital gateway I told her that we would come down to the club again the following week — so long as she promised to be there too.

Next morning the nurses were on the carpet because there had been a lot of noise and they had woken all the patients when we took them back to the hospital.

The following Wednesday I asked I colleague from the Orderly Room to join me, and we cycled down to Budleigh. There we were greeted

214

by the young trainee nurses — including Marion, the girl who had sat with me on the journey to the hospital. Three years later we married.

Marion was with me just a week before my demob day when I began the evening with her at the pictures in Exmouth and ended it in Exeter Hospital having my appendix out.

I had been getting pains during the film, so went to Exmouth Hospital. But because I was a soldier they would not look at me, and I was taken by ambulance back to the barracks. The regimental policeman on duty contacted the MO.

At one o'clock in the morning the MO, Major (Mrs) McKendrick, was not at all happy about being called out. She stormed into the guardroom where I was lying on a bed, demanding: "Have you been drinking, corporal?"

"No ma'am," I said. "In which case I will look at you." After she had examined me she called the ambulance again, and later that night out came my appendix. As a result I was not demobbed with the rest of our intake because I could not get my uniform on. I was sent on sick leave and had to return the following month to be demobbed separately.

And then...

After National Service I returned to Barclays Bank, where I had been a trainee, and worked in various branches before becoming assistant manager at Torquay in 1972. I was manager of two branches in Exeter and worked at local head office for a time before ending my career as manager at Sidmouth before taking early retirement in 1989.

Always interested in social work, I was at one time involved with 19 different organisations. During the Sixties and Seventies Round Table was uppermost in my social life, and I was area chairman for Devon in 1972.

At the age of 40 I went into Rotary, and I am still an active member of Exmouth Rotary Club. I am rather proud that I am the only person in the West Country who has served both as area chairman of Round Table and district governor of Rotary.

— Eric Watts©

Training Company staff at Topsham Barracks. Left to right: Tony Herring, Eric Watts, John Greening and John Kerslake

2578399 SAC Michael Wells

The scary moment when a man tried to put us in the picture

SOME of my RAF National Service was spent in Egypt, and though we were able to get out of camp we were still warned to be careful and alert. So when, outside the Cairo Museum, four or five of us spotted a large man wearing a fez and long white robes approaching, we were more than a little concerned. "What do you think he wants?" asked one of my mates. We became even more jittery when someone else said: "He's got his hand hidden, maybe a knife or a gun. Now he's just a couple of yards away, watch him!"

The man withdrew his hand from his clothes. "Afendi, you want see dirty postcards?"

I was born and brought up in Ferndown — then just a small village — in east Dorset, and attended the local school and then Wimborne Grammar School where I spent an undistinguished five years.

I suppose I didn't really appreciate its educational value at the time, but left with an Oxford School Certificate which proved very useful in the years ahead.

At weekends and during school holidays I had really enjoyed working on a local farm, so when I left school at 16 I went to Exmoor to live-in and work on a farm.

After a year I moved to a large pedigree Friesian herd at Fordingbridge where the owner asked if I would like him to apply for exemption from National Service for me due to my essential job. This seemed a great idea as I was not looking forward to two years in the services.

Then I had the chance to run a farm in Gloucestershire for a few weeks while the owner was on holiday. But by so doing I broke the exemption and after a few weeks my call-up arrived. And on December 5 1952 I took a railway journey to RAF Padgate, followed by a posting to Hednesford for square-bashing.

I don't recall very much about Hednesford but I do remember the drill instructor saying to someone: "If you don't keep your bloody arm still I will tear it off and beat you to death with the soggy end."

The unit I was on was a POM (Potential Officer Material) unit, I suppose because of the grammar school education and my Oxford School Certificate. This meant I didn't have to take education tests and enabled me to apply for aircrew. But I failed the first medical when it was discovered that one of my big toes was not working properly. This was because some years earlier a very large cow decided to stand on it!

The downside of the School Certificate was that I was told I would almost certainly get an admin job. And being shut in an office for the remainder of two years was not my cup of tea.

A photograph taken at the end of my training

Then I discovered that if I signed on for an extra year I could choose a trade. So I asked for mechanical transport training, which I felt would be useful on farms later, and was sent to RAF Weeton in Lancashire.

Close to Weeton was a well-known pedigree Friesian herd. And I met a very nice girl from a local village. In my free time I would either pay the Friesians a visit, or take the girl dancing at the Winter Gardens in Blackpool.

At the end of the MT course, while awaiting a posting, I was picked out by the station WO from a crowd lined up for fatigues. His clerk had left and he instructed me in the art of general dogsbody, answering the telephone and basically accompanying him to fetch and carry. He was very smart, and I can see him now, drilling the station parade and marching beside the leading WAAF saying: "Come along now, stomach in, chest out."

A weekend pass was no problem, and those very enjoyable weeks flew by. I thought what's wrong with an admin job? But too late now. The posting arrived for No 9 Mechanical Transport Base Depot, El Firdan MEAF 10. Where the hell is that? The Canal Zone. Oh great! I've got more than two years still to do!

So off to a transit camp in the dark somewhere in Wiltshire where we had to bash up a door to get the round stove working because there was no coke or coal.

Then early morning to RAF Lyneham and on to an aircraft with canvas seats and uncovered

216

metal all round and extremely cold. The pilot was a very laid-back flight-lieutenant who said we could go up front to see what went on if we wished "but not all at once or I won't be able to keep the bloody nose up."

We had refuelled in the south of France, and when I went up to the cabin some time afterwards the pilot appeared to be asleep and the co-pilot was reading. I coughed and said: " Excuse me sir, is that the North African coast?" He stirred, looked at his watch and said: "Bloody hell, we're making good time."

At RAF Fayid the aircraft seemed to be dropping at times, but we made a perfect landing with sand flying all around. The pilot got out wearing his hat on the back of his head. I had never seen an officer like that before.

Then it was off to El Firdan, a huge camp with hangars full of engineering equipment, hundreds of vehicles and acres and acres of sand. We had tented accommodation and a large NAAFI and cinema surrounded by barbed wire and huge searchlights on towers.

The usual routine was full-guard duty on the first night — two hours on and four off, swinging searchlights on the towers or lying behind a brengun at the main gate and being eaten by mosquitoes.

The second night was sleeping on rifle in a large tent beside main gate. Third night, sleeping on rifle in own tent. Fourth night off. Next night back on full guard. And all while still working all day. Well, up to about 1pm because it was too hot after that.

I was sent to the testing unit, which was a great job testing vehicles which had been completely rebuilt in the camp, or checking new vehicles delivered from the UK.

I remember one day banging my head on a propshaft when checking a vehicle over a pit because a scorpion crawled out of the sand. I

Off duty (right) with a couple of pals

gave it the heat treatment — a squirt of petrol and a match.

I managed an occasional trip for a swim in the Blue Lagoon, which sounds good but was actually part of the Suez Canal.

During my stay at El Firdan I had the inevitable Dear John letter from the girl in Lancashire who had been writing to me regularly. I was too long away and she had met someone else. The Lancashire Friesians seem to have forgotten me completely!

I was lucky to be moved into a tent with a guy who did evening work in the Astra cinema as a projectionist. He said that when there was a similar vacancy he would get me in, which he duly did.

No more guard duties and we were paid, but it was incredibly hot because the cinema had a corrugated tin roof and the projection room contained two huge UK cinema projectors lit by carbon arc rods.

We showed all the usual UK films, and I remember showing the Glenn Miller Story many times.

Later I got on a moral leadership course trip to Jerusalem, flying from Fayid to Amman, then from Amman to Jerusalem by bus. On the way the front wheel fell off the bus and rolled down a hill, but the bus seemed to work quite well on the brake drum for a while till it stopped. Then two officers held up a car, went off in it and returned a little later with another bus.

Almost the whole of Jerusalem was controlled by Jordan, so we were able to see all the historic parts and mingle with an incredible mix of religions, C of E,

Our camp in the desert

Now happily retired

Roman Catholic, Franciscan, Armenian, Greek Orthodox and Jews.

Some time later I moved to the unit in Port Said for a while, checking and supervising the loading of vehicles on to large ships.

About this time a treaty was signed with the Egyptians, and we were able to get out and about in Egypt. And that is when we were accosted by the dirty postcard man!

Work by this time was slowing down at No 9 MTBD El Firdan, and because I had been on the testing unit and had a full RAF driving licence up to and over 10 tons I volunteered to transfer to 51MT Kasfreet and spent the last weeks of my time in the Canal Zone driving vehicles like 10-wheel Leyland Hippos to various RAF locations for loading and then to Port Said for shipment out.

Driving a lorry that size with no power-steering and a crash gearbox in the Canal Zone heat was rather hot work.

I did several trips with 51MT by boat from Port Said to Famagusta in Cyprus. What a lovely island with beautiful water to swim and lovely orange squash. They were very enjoyable trips, and it was much cooler in Cyprus.

My time in the Canal Zone was at times very boring but Port Said duty and 51MT was very enjoyable, and the projection room work was great.

All of a sudden it was all over and I returned to the UK in December 1955. I had learned a great deal about mechanical engineering, met some great people and some not so great people and experienced being with other nationalities But it was time to get back to my civilian occupation, which was described on my Certificate of Service as "cowman."

And then...

I spent a year on a farm in Eynsham near Oxford and then a year each on two farms in Dorset. About this time came the realisation that I would never have sufficient funds to farm on my own. So I searched for work that would keep me within the farming community.

I applied for two reps jobs with agricultural merchants and also replied to public appointment ads for the Ministry of Agriculture. Just as I was offered an interview with one of the agricultural merchants there came an invitation for an interview with the Civil Service Commission in London.

In the end I chose the Civil Service and spent the rest of my working life in the Ministry of Agriculture working in England, Scotland and Wales, mostly with the farming community for whom I have the greatest respect. When my wife and I retired we returned to our native Dorset.

Some time early in 2003 I was told that anyone who served in the Canal Zone between 1951 and 1955 might be entitled to a medal. I was persuaded to apply and weeks later the General Service Medal (1918) Canal Zone arrived, very shiny and duly engraved.

I really can't think what I did to deserve it, but have put it in a box that contains the Maundy Coins presented by the Queen to my father at Salisbury Cathedral many years ago.

— *Michael Wells©*

<u>23459693 Cpl David Williams</u>

No regimental blues? What a tight lot, said Prince Philip

MOST PEOPLE would agree that as one gets older it is far easier to remember things which happened decades ago as opposed to those which occurred yesterday. This is certainly true so far as my time spent doing National Service is concerned, with those early days in the Army still fresh in my mind. At the time the very thought of serving two years was frightening, but on reflection the time went fairly quickly and it wasn't as bad as those early days indicated.

I was born in Southampton at the beginning of February 1939. Later I used to think that if my parents had been more considerate and delayed my arrival by some two years then I would have missed being called up for National Service. However this opinion was to change in time, though not enough for me to sign on as a regular.

During the summer of 1940, with my mother and older sister I was evacuated to Tenby in South Wales to stay with my father's parents. My father had to remain in Southampton as he was a Professor of Music lecturing at Southampton University.

My grandfather was of the same profession, and I very much regret that I did not inherit their musical talents. One of my earliest recollections of Tenby, apart from playing on a superb beach, was being run over by an Army motorcycle despatch rider shortly after my fourth birthday. The exhaust pipe caused a nasty burn to my left thigh which resulted in eight weeks in hospital.

Skin grafting was not very advanced in those days and I was left with a large scar as a permanent reminder.

I felt a bit guilty because although the accident was entirely my fault, I was awarded £50 compensation to be paid when I reached 21. Ironically when the compensation money (£60 by then) was received I put it towards a motorcycle.

I did not see much of my father until after the war when the family returned to Southampton, though he did visit whenever possible subject to obtaining petrol coupons.

I used to enjoy sports, and when I was about 10 occasionally watched Southampton play football at The Dell. I was allowed to go by bus on my own, and the supporters would always let me through to the front.

I managed to pass the 11-plus exam, which gave me a place at the local grammar school. I still enjoyed sports but of course homework started to become a priority. On leaving school I joined a local firm of shipping agents until the dreaded day arrived.

For several years it was accepted that National Service would have to be served. Opting out was not an option, so when my time arrived I had made up my mind to make the best of it. Anyway it was only for two years, not a lifetime. Though at times it felt like it.

Before joining up it was necessary to have a medical but basically so long as you were breathing and did not have flat feet you were passed A1.

I remember standing stark naked in a freezing cold room being examined by a medical orderly. Not one of the most memorable occasions in my life. Once the medical had been completed I was interviewed by a sergeant who said: "You are just the type of person the Army is looking for," and invited me to sign on as a regular soldier.

With great willpower, after a couple of seconds, I managed to decline his request. Did they honestly expect people to commit themselves at that stage? Anyway he obviously got his own back, because only nine days later I was instructed to report to the Royal Army Pay Corps training centre at Devizes.

That fateful day arrived when as a raw 19-year-old I caught the 9.16 train from Southampton, and after changing twice arrived at Devizes. While I was the youngest member of our gang in Southampton, most of my colleagues had already begun National Service so I had a reasonable idea what to expect. But nothing could quite prepare one for what was to follow.

Three of us stood on the platform when an Army NCO enquired "Pay Corps?" which, as we must have looked lost and bewildered, should have been pretty obvious.

Nervously nodding we climbed aboard a three-ton truck which took us to the camp, thereby ending freedom for the next two years.

The first few days in the Army you didn't know what hit you, and probably thought them the worst days in your life.

adopt the squat position the sergeant bellowed: "Williams, you look like a Hindu having a shit."

I heard a chuckle from the row behind. I was

Same spot, different times. Photographs taken at Hohne/Bergen 30 years apart

You were doubled everywhere and continually shouted at.

One of my earliest recollections, apart from receiving a short haircut, was to be kitted out at the quartermaster's stores where they seemed to guess your height and uniform size.

We were divided into A and B companies. I was fortunate, although not aware of it at the time, to be allocated to A Company where I would be trained as a company pay clerk to be attached to a regiment, as opposed to being sent to a command pay office.

There were 24 of us in our platoon, all from different backgrounds and from all over the UK. Lieutenant Sumner, Sgt Fowler, Cpl Scarisbrick and L/Cpl Maddocks were given the almost impossible task of trying to turn us into something resembling an Army unit. But they succeeded.

Upon hearing our first reveille at 6am there was a mad rush to the washroom. Shaving was compulsory even if one had not started shaving at home. The first few weeks were spent learning to march during the day and bulling our kit in the evening. One of the first tasks was to cut the buttons off our greatcoats and then sew new ones back on!

Yes, it was tough, and all for £1 5s 6d a week initially. But we were all in the same boat and a bond quickly developed where everyone mucked in and helped one another.

I remember Jock, who would switch on to automatic pilot on hearing reveille, fumble for his cigarettes and lighter, inhale deeply and then cough and splutter. If reveille didn't wake us then Jock would.

After a couple of weeks the Army psychology came into force. One morning we were actually praised for our drill, the NCO saying: "This is a far better squad." Basically we were awful, but by the afternoon we had improved no end.

Rifle drill was introduced, and one day while practising grounding arms where you have to

probably no worse than anybody else, just my turn to be picked on.

A variation to constant drilling were visits to the rifle range where we practised firing our .303s. It was noticeable that here the instructors seemed to adopt a more humane approach, no doubt because we were using live ammunition.

Army language was colourful to say the least and I am sure the NCOs had a phrasebook of various pleasantries to refer to, eg. our platoon collectively reminded the drill instructor of resembling "a bucket of stewed a---s."

After six weeks the technical training began, to prepare us for our future role as company pay clerks. Drilling of course continued in preparation for our passing-out parade, which fortunately went well.

Our first leave came after three weeks when we were allowed home for Easter. This is when I first tried hitchhiking. Fortunately, in those days if you were in uniform most people would stop.

We were not allowed leave again until after we had passed-out.

However we did enjoy a trip to Aldershot in April to see the Army Cup Final between the RAPC Training Centre and a REME Training Centre. The Queen presented the cup, but unfortunately not to the Pay Corps.

During training we got caught for only one guard duty and somehow I managed to be selected as "stick man." I well remember a voice from behind muttering "you jammy a---.

Eagerly we awaited our postings. I had decided to volunteer to go overseas. During training I had got on well with Roger Mason who came from London, and we managed to get a joint posting to Germany. We didn't know where, apart from it being BFPO 30.

There were comments that being in the RAPC you had it cushy. In some cases this was true once you had been posted, but our basic training was as tough as that of any other regiment.

On returning from our last leave in June Roger and I travelled to Harwich via Liverpool Street station to catch the troopship to the Hook of Holland. There were three trains, and fortunately we caught the correct one, which took us to Soltau in North Germany.

We then proceeded to Luneburg and joined the 8th Kings Royal Irish Hussars as company pay clerks. The regiment was one of the founder members of the 7th Armoured Brigade, the Desert Rats, whose emblem we were entitled to wear on our uniforms. The camp was only about a mile from the centre of Luneburg, and considered to be a good posting. There were four pay clerks, a sergeant and a major, and Roger and I quickly settled into our new role.

I well remember one incident when a leaving party for our officer was held in a local hostelry. The drinks flowed, and being a raw 19-year-old I felt it my duty to sample everything going.

Two of us had to be taken back to camp early by Sgt Borley, who got us safely to our rooms. I was always in his debt, but I did suffer the following day.

A lesson was learned, because although I have always enjoyed a pint I have not mixed drinks since that day.

Unfortunately our stay in Luneburg was to last only three months as the regiment was being moved to Hohne/Bergen in preparation for the amalgamation with the 4th King's Own Hussars. Prior to this move I was awarded my first stripe, and the second came about a year later.

The amalgamation took place on Balaclava Day, October 24 1958 when the two regiments became the Queen's Royal Irish Hussars.

The Duke of Edinburgh took the salute and later in the day visited the corporals' mess. We Pay Corps lot were the only ones not in regimental blues, and on reaching us the Duke jokingly remarked that we must belong to a very tight regiment!

Hohne/Bergen was a very large camp, quite isolated and just down the road from Belsen. Several regiments were based there because the camp was close to the Hohne tank ranges.

Roger and me leaving camp on demob day

I shared a room with Roger and we used to moan about the camp, but on reflection the facilities were not too bad.

The tank ranges were also used by the US Army several weeks of the year and it was interesting to meet them, usually in the mess. They were quite embarrassed when they compared their pay to ours.

We used two types of currency, deutschmarks and a form of sterling paper money known as British Armed Forces Special Vouchers. These could only be used on camp in the mess or NAAFI.

I was the pay clerk for C Squadron, the Army Catering Corps and also the camp's Military Police section, which of course had its advantages.

I once managed to persuade the crew to let me have a go at driving a Centurion tank. On another occasion an exchange of troops was arranged with a Royal Navy ship which was visiting Hamburg. A very enjoyable evening was taking place in the corporals' mess when the Navy lads persuaded one of theirs to perform the Dance of The Flaming A---s, which culminated in the "volunteer" dropping his pants and inserting a copy of the regimental Part Two orders into

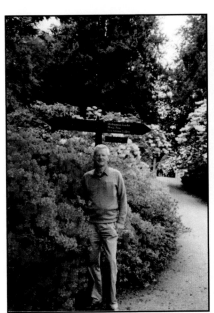

Army days are over, so now it's "at ease" on holiday

Off duty in Germany

a certain orifice.

A match was then applied and the resulting fire was extinguished by spraying the contents of a bottle of Carlsberg on to the flames. Demob day finally arrived on March 11 1960 when Roger and I set off for home. We had a farewell beer at a pub near Liverpool Street station, shook hands and off we went. We did keep in touch for a number of years but unfortunately contact was lost.

One member with whom I have kept in touch to this day is Eric Austen and we became our respective best man. We both moved a few times but now live about an hour's journey apart.

"If I never see this place again it will be too soon," is a common saying when you leave camp for the last time, but what did I do when touring Germany some 30 years' later?

The guard commander allowed us to enter the camp and take photographs outside the same building that had been there during my National Service days. But now cars were parked where we used to have parades.

We chatted about the camp and I asked if a certain infamous watering hole was still there. "Yes" he replied, "but it is out of bounds at the moment." We had a good laugh when I told him that it was also out of bounds when I left.

And then...

On returning to civilian life I joined the offices of Cunard in Southampton. They were great days when most of the world's greatest liners would visit the port. The early Sixties was also a brilliant time to be around, with the music scene really starting off.

In 1965 I married Maureen and we are still together. Just after getting married I had a change of occupation when I joined a bank. In the early 1990s I was offered early retirement which I accepted. Since then and until recently I have kept occupied by having several part-time jobs which I enjoyed doing, probably because I didn't have to.

Of course you sense a feeling of euphoria on being demobbed but it was only some years later that I appreciated how much benefit was gained from National Service. It was a great leveller, and one experienced comradeship that could never be found in Civvy Street.

You lived, worked and socialised with other people from all walks of life. It helped to make you independent, and taught discipline.

Okay, some of the things you were ordered to do were unnecessary and probably pointless, but because of your training you just accepted it.

In recent years I have become a member of the RAPC and QRIH regimental associations, but unfortunately have not been able to make contact with any former colleagues.

— *David Williams©*

23040267 LCpl Norman Wright
Shoot first, said the officer, and he was killed in our ambush

AFTER MY square-bashing I did an engineering course on tanks, where we kept being told how much this intensive training was costing the country. So I was rather surprised when at the end of the course I was sent to Kenya — where there was not a single tank!

Since then I have spoken to several chaps who did a course on lorries and were then posted to Germany to work on tanks. That's the Army for you!

I had been called up in June 1954 when I was 22, having been deferred to complete my studies for an HNC in mechanical engineering. Basic training in the REME at Honiton was not a pleasant six weeks. For the first five of them we were not even allowed in the NAAFI. But I do remember the comradeship in the billet, which was something I have never come across since.

Our corporals all thought they were gods, and we had to treat them as such. So it was amusing one day when I saw a tank transporter pull up at the main gate. A soldier in dirty overalls, with his beret stuck on the back of his head got out and shouted at the guard corporal: "Hey mate, where's the pisshouse?" That boosted our morale, because we realised that life after basic training could be normal.

One very hot Saturday at Honiton we had to line the square to watch a passing-out parade. The sergeant had said that anyone who felt faint could fall out. But one poor chap collapsed and fell forwards, still at attention, and broke his jaw.

I was posted to Taunton for trade training as a vehicle mechanic on lorries, and after passing with a good mark went to Bordon for the tank course.

Then I spent some time at Aldershot waiting for the Kenya posting, and my fiancee and I decided to get married. She managed to organise a white wedding in the local church hall, all

Training over, now life can be "normal"

within a week with a special licence.

Before I went to Kenya I had a lot of injections, and remember as I queued up seeing a Parachute Regiment sergeant who had a broken nose and looked a real hard nut. When he came out he was actually crying! I thought if that's what it does to him, how will I feel?

While I was at Aldershot a big general inspection was held. The whole camp was cleared with the exception of our draft, and we had to change our kit and bull the camp to put on the parade. We were getting up at 4am to get everything done.

Then we went to Liverpool to board the troopship, where the REME men had to do all the chores. The food was poor, and served on aluminium trays with shallow depressions, which meant that often by the time you got to a table the gravy and custard had become mixed together.

I finished up working in the officers' and sergeants' kitchen, which was run by civilian chefs. They gave us a very good meal before they served the officers but then left and we had to clear-up

I did 32 years with Ford

and throw away all the unused food. I would take as much as I could back for the lads, but a lot was wasted.

In Kenya I was stationed in three different workshops which had between 12 and 50 men. There was plenty of vehicle repair work, and apart from a roll-call in the morning and having to do guard duties life was organised just like any civilian workshop.

All the camps were friendly, and we were on first name terms with many senior soldiers. One CO even took four of us on a fishing trip.

One of my postings was at Nyeri where Baden

223

Powell is buried, and another at Nanyki on the Equator. Both townships were in the foothills of Mount Kenya, a magnificent sight in the moonlight.

My first shock on arriving in Kenya was the speed at which the sun set. It was full daylight at 6.45 and completely dark by seven. And if there was no moonlight you could not see your hand in front of your face. The African guards were dressed in black, and the first you knew of their presence was a call: "Halt, who goes there?"

One day an officer set a series of ambushes to catch the Mau Mau and ordered his men to fire first and ask questions afterwards. Then he tested the ambush and was killed.

Because of the Mau Mau problem we were limited in what we could do in our free time. But there was a film show once a week and it was possible to get a 72-hour pass and hitch-hike to Nairobi, about 100 miles away. We would stay at the YMCA and get a hot bath, which was very welcome because the ablution facilities at the camp were very basic and without hot water.

At Nanyki we could walk to a river and supplement our rations with trout.

I made two trips to see something of the country. The first was a five-day climb up Kilimanjaro and the other a trip around Lake Victoria on a cargo boat. This entailed a long train journey first. We were the only Europeans on the train and at dinner time they stopped the train and took us to a hotel for a meal.

On my return to the UK I had my only brush with the military police. It was June when I came in to Waterloo station, but I felt the cold and was wearing my greatcoat, though I did not do up the buttons. I saw two MPs at the far side of the station and somehow I knew they were coming for me.

I quickly did up the buttons and waited. I let them have their say, and then told them I was demobbed. They asked for my paybook to prove it and then said that as I was still wearing the Queen's uniform, I should make sure I was properly dressed.

I went straight to the Territorial Army centre and was told I had to do two-week camp. I could go the following week or in a year's time. So I said I would go the next week, and was sent to Salisbury Plain to live under canvas.

There was very little to do and the only thing I remember was when the orderly officer came round at one mealtime and asked if there were any complaints.

I said the food was awful, and he replied that as I had been out of the Army for some time I was no longer used to Army food. When I told him I only left a week earlier, he just walked away.

So that was the end of my Army career. I gave my capbadge and medal to my grandson when he was four, and he loved them.

And then...

I joined Ford Motor Company in their research and engineering division on the design and development of engines and worked there for 32 years.

— *Norman Wright©*

224